ASSASSINATION IN VICHY

Marx Dormoy and the Struggle for the Soul of France

Assassination in Vichy

Marx Dormoy and the Struggle for the Soul of France

GAYLE K. BRUNELLE AND
ANNETTE FINLEY-CROSWHITE

University of Toronto Press

Toronto Buffalo London

© University of Toronto Press 2020
Toronto Buffalo London
utorontopress.com

ISBN 978-1-4875-8837-3 (cl.) ISBN 978-1-4875-8838-0 (ePUB)
ISBN 978-1-4875-8836-6 (pbk.) ISBN 978-1-4875-8839-7 (PDF)

All rights reserved. The use of any part of this publication reproduced, transmitted in any form or by any means, electronic, mechanical, photocopying, recording, or otherwise, or stored in a retrieval system, without prior written consent of the publisher – or in the case of photocopying, a license from Access Copyright (the Canadian Copyright Licensing Agency) – is an infringement of the copyright law.

Library and Archives Canada Cataloguing in Publication

Title: Assassination in Vichy : Marx Dormoy and the struggle for the soul of France / Gayle K. Brunelle and Annette Finley-Croswhite.
Names: Brunelle, Gayle K., 1959– author. | Finley-Croswhite, S. Annette, author.
Description: Includes bibliographical references and index.
Identifiers: Canadiana (print) 20200212192 | Canadiana (ebook) 20200212257 | ISBN 9781487588373 (cloth) | ISBN 9781487588366 (softcover) | ISBN 9781487588380 (EPUB) | ISBN 9781487588397 (PDF)
Subjects: LCSH: Dormoy, Marx, 1888–1941 – Assassination. | LCSH: Assassination – Investigation – France – Vichy.
Classification: LCC DC373.D59 B78 2020 | DDC 944.081/5092–dc23

We welcome comments and suggestions regarding any aspect of our publications – please feel free to contact us at news@utorontopress.com or visit us at utorontopress.com.

Every effort has been made to contact copyright holders; in the event of an error or omission, please notify the publisher.

University of Toronto Press acknowledges the financial assistance to its publishing program of the Canada Council for the Arts and the Ontario Arts Council, an agency of the Government of Ontario.

 Canada Council   Conseil des Arts
for the Arts   du Canada

 ONTARIO ARTS COUNCIL
CONSEIL DES ARTS DE L'ONTARIO
an Ontario government agency
un organisme du gouvernement de l'Ontario

Funded by the   Financé par le
Government   gouvernement
of Canada   du Canada

For Marx and Jeanne

Contents

Acknowledgments ix

Note on Sources xiii

INTRODUCTION	26 July 1941: Explosion	1
CHAPTER 1	1888–1941: Marx Dormoy and the Fall of France	14
CHAPTER 2	1941: A Long, Hot Summer	38
CHAPTER 3	26–30 July 1941: Anatomy of a Crime Scene	50
CHAPTER 4	14 August 1941: A Bombing in Nice	69
CHAPTER 5	Summer 1941: Recruiting the Assassins	86
CHAPTER 6	August–October 1941: The Net Widens	108
CHAPTER 7	October 1941–March 1942: The Waiting Game	129
CHAPTER 8	18 April 1942: The Return of Pierre Laval	149
CHAPTER 9	23 January 1943: German Intervention	168
CHAPTER 10	26 August 1944: Liberation	189
CONCLUSION	Today: The Legacy of Marx Dormoy	203

Glossary of Names 223

Organizations 227

Timeline 229

Notes 233

Suggested Reading in English for Students and General Readers 277

Bibliography 283

Index 297

Acknowledgments

Historians spend long hours poring over documents that are often nearly illegible. Even so, the pursuit of the past is thrilling whether that results from an unexpected archival find or, in our case, a wintertime adventure over the frosty and foggy mountains of the Ardèche to unravel the mystery of an assassination.

    We have been friends for a long time. And that friendship has not only produced some extraordinary journeys across the byways of France but also a goodly amount of published material. It's a friendship enmeshed in old pieces of paper, stacks of books, maps and GIS technology, and innumerable rental cars that took us to the far corners of the country. Along the way we experienced the culinary delights of each region including their delicious smells and tastes, for this story took place, in no small part, near the lavender fields of southern France and the nougat factories of Montélimar. Together we pursue the darkest of stories, but our friendship fills the scholarly process and deep conversations necessary for co-authorship with adventures steeped in laughter and fun. There's nothing quite like writing a book with your best friend, and we've done it twice.

    Every historian owes a debt to the archivists who work with them. In our case, we are extremely grateful to Denis Tranchard who took great interest in our project and facilitated access to documents that were soon to be declassified at the Archives départementales de l'Allier where he is the director. His efforts to expedite our request to see Jeanne Dormoy's sealed file on her brother's murder were greatly appreciated. Tranchard's willingness to send us documents via airmail when we were in the United States deserves special mention. Among all the archivists we have met over the years, his support and assistance were exceptional. Vincent Tuchais at the Archives de Paris also went out of his way for us, even providing comic strips to entertain Annette's then-eleven-year-old son who was trapped in the archives while his mother verified citation information. Mathilde Pintault and Boris Dubouis also aided our searches at the Archives de Paris. Local archivist Laurence Debowski helped us identify sources in Montluçon. Special mention goes to Michaël Nicolas, a journalist with *La Montagne*, who shared with us early photographs of Marx Dormoy's statue from his journal's archive.

One of our most delightful experiences was a day spent with then mayor of Montluçon Daniel Dugléry who invited us to a marvelous lunch at the Hôtel de Ville and then took us on a tour of Marx Dormoy's former office. Dugléry has also written a book on Dormoy, and his insight was extremely helpful, especially with anecdotes about Dormoy that never made it into print. We understand why Marx Dormoy so loved Montluçon because our experience of its hospitality seven decades later was extraordinary. The personnel at the Montluçon public library and the Archives municipales were enthusiastic about our pursuits and even the wait staff at the bar *Le Moderne* could not have been more welcoming.

In all projects there are many colleagues behind the scenes who offer advice and encouragement along the way. We have always had Bertram Gordon in our corner, which is important because we were trained as early modernists, but Bert went out of his way to welcome us to the field of modern French history. He shared archives and unpublished interviews with us and was always encouraging. Chris Millington, Kevin Passmore, and Caroline Campbell have also generously offered us their insights, and we especially thank Millington and Passmore for inviting us to a conference in Wales that allowed us to explore our ideas on far right-wing violence in early twentieth-century France. Scholars Moritz Florin and Johannes Dafinger welcomed us to an international conference in Germany to share our knowledge of right-wing terrorism. Historians J.P. Perrin, Eric Panthou, and Joel Blatt also shared citations, thoughts, and sources, and Marc Masurovsky directed us to documents in the United States.

Several people have shown great interest in our work. Nigel Jones in England has been enthusiastic about every project we take on. Jacques Cohen sent us archival leads, and Michel Rateau shared with us his research on the military aspects of the Cagoule. Michèle Halligan deserves special recognition. A grandniece of Annie Mourraille, one of the assassins of Marx Dormoy, Halligan offered us the private journal of her great-grandmother (Annie Mourraille's mother). Mme. Liliane Latry grew up in the Relais de l'Empereur and spent a lovely afternoon with us in Montélimar sharing stories of the hotel she so loved that had been sold and boarded up a few months before we arrived for our site visit. She also gave us mementos from the Relais. Local photographer Pierre Morand shared pictures of the Relais with us as well.

Many friends in France consistently come to our rescue. We have known Hélène Teisseire since she was nine years old. Today she is an accomplished archivist and archaeologist, and she has facilitated solving many an archival quandary. Her parents, Bernard and Christel Teisseire, have always supported our work with enthusiasm and remain our great friends. Philippe Andrau is another dear friend who offered us the use of his Montmartre apartment on occasion and often translated obscure document verbiage for us. Anne-Marie Chevais accompanied us on our first journey to Montélimar and has always been fascinated by our work. Sylvette Lemagnen has also been a loyal friend for decades and generously shared her mother's memories of the struggles of ordinary French people in the Occupied Zone during World War II.

In addition, we would like to thank our editor at the University of Toronto Press, Natalie Fingerhut, for her advice and support as we wrote and revised the manuscript for this book, and we thank the anonymous reviewers as well. Our managing editor Barbara Porter and copy editor Tania Therien made the editing process efficient and smooth. We also thank California State University, Fullerton and Old Dominion University for promoting our research and granting us research funding and leave to work on this book. Annette especially thanks her former and current supervisors, Chandra de Silva and Katherine Hawkins, geographer Thomas Chapman, librarian Karen Vaughan, and technical writer David Simpson. Lifelong friends from the University of Richmond helped to vet possible book titles.

In every research project family pay the dearest price. Gayle wishes to thank her parents, Robert (Wally) and Joan Brunelle, brothers Robert and Michael Brunelle and their families, and her husband, Bernard Allaire, for listening while she bounced ideas off them and encouraging her to stay the course as she pursued the monumental task of researching and writing this book. Annette thanks her parents, Eula Finley and the late Clyde L. Finley, and her brother, C. Stephen Finley, for positive reinforcement as well as her husband, Chip Croswhite, and sons, Alex and Matthew Croswhite, for enduring her absence whether she was home or not. We appreciate the devotion and patience of our families who have shaped and formed us and without whom we could not succeed.

We dedicate our book to the memory of Marx and Jeanne Dormoy. Their devotion to France was exceeded only by their love for each other. The authors well understand the love sisters have for their brothers, and in this sense, Jeanne Dormoy merits a special commendation for collecting and preserving her brother's archives, which contributed in no small part to the documentary foundation of this book.

Note on Sources

Many of the documents used to write this book are housed in the *Archives de Paris* and were compiled after the war under the heading PEROTIN, 212/79/3/47–51. Boxes 49–51 in particular concern the Marx Dormoy affair. PEROTIN contains the bulk of the documents in the Archives de Paris related both to the history of the *Cagoule* and *Cagoulard* ties to Maréchal Philippe Pétain, the leader of the Vichy regime and a reputed member of the Cagoule prior to the war. This organization explains why the documents related to the investigation of Marx Dormoy's assassination can be found alongside copies of those deriving from Pétain's trial in this vast series of documents, over six meters, about the Cagoule.

The research for the book began in 2010 and the sources were consultable only with special permission (a *dérogation*) from the French government. Archives often engage in periodic evaluation of their holdings and inventory systems. While we were writing and editing our manuscript, the Archives de Paris reorganized and renumbered the PEROTIN documents. This process took several years and was not completed until the summer of 2019. By then our book was in production. Most of the documents related to Marx Dormoy can now be found in 134W 130–132 (formerly PEROTIN 212/79/3/49–51) and the material on the *Amicale de France* is in 134W 124 (formerly PEROTIN 212/79/3/47). The archives have removed, however, the titles of the dossiers in these boxes such as "Affaire Dormoy" and "Dossier Montélimar," and consolidated the dossiers. Since we did not want to introduce errors into the documentation of the sources we used to write the book and the recoding came too late to change our manuscript, we opted to list the corresponding new codes in the bibliography but use the older codes in our endnotes to reflect more precisely the research that we conducted. The archivists sent us the permissions for our images using the new call numbers; all the rest of our citations refer to the older call numbers. Our derogations for the PEROTIN documents, which will remain restricted from the general public until 2024, state that we had permission to view PEROTIN 212/79/3. Our notes and bibliography correspond to these call numbers. Anyone desiring to retrace our steps will find everything we used in the archives even though the documents have been reorganized and placed in renumbered dossiers.

INTRODUCTION

26 July 1941: Explosion

At 1:50 a.m. on 26 July 1941 a powerful explosion rocked the stately hotel Le Relais de l'Empereur in the city of Montélimar, awakening everyone, including the hotel's owner, Madame Louise Vilnat, who resided on the premises.[1] She immediately telephoned the hotel desk clerk and instructed him to call the police.[2] Vilnat then made her way to the third and highest floor, where the blast took place. The third-floor hallway was dark and smoky, but there were no flames, only a strong odor of gunpowder. Vilnat called out to the other guests, telling them to stay in their rooms with their doors closed until the police arrived, in case there was a second bomb. The outside lights shining through the windows at the end of the hall illuminated the corridor as Vilnat groped her way toward the site of the blast.[3]

As she approached the room, #19, identifiable as the center of the explosion by its half-destroyed door and a halo of dust, feathers, and debris on the hallway floor, she detected a new odor competing with that of smoke and gunpowder – the smell of blood and scorched flesh. The blast had destroyed the bottom panel of the door and shattered the deadbolt inside. A single floor lamp, its bulb miraculously still flickering, lay on the floor. Vilnat peered through the doorway. Through the thick veil of dust and feathers from exploded pillows floating in the dim light she saw shattered furniture scattered around the room. Despite the nearly ten-foot-high ceiling, there was also a hole that went through the roof and opened the room to the night sky. Vilnat called out to the room's tenant, but no one responded. Her eyes were drawn to the pile of crumpled bed sheets and coverlet on the floor. A single glance at the mangled body lying half-naked, its feet still tangled in the sheets at the foot of the bed, its head, or what was left of it, on the floor near the top of the mattress, revealed that she need approach no further. The part of the head still attached to the body lay at an unnatural angle. Vilnat screamed, backed out of the room, and stood paralyzed in the hallway. But she was made of stern stuff, the proprietor of a hotel with a responsibility for her guests. She needed to act – now. Vilnat stiffened her shoulders and strode back down the hall to the room of another guest, the sister of the man who was now lying dead on the hotel floor.[4]

Vilnat's brother-in-law, Émilien Behuret, a firefighter from Paris, resided at the Relais with Vilnat's younger sister. He was in the lobby and rushed upstairs when he heard Vilnat's scream. With his firefighter training and military experience, Behuret knew it was vital that no one enter the crime scene until the police arrived. He phoned a local physician, Dr. Chapuis, the acting city coroner on duty that night. Behuret also took the initiative to herd the guests and hotel staff out of the hallway and downstairs to the lobby while Vilnat pounded frantically on the door of the room down the hall where the victim's sister, Jeanne Dormoy, was staying. Jeanne emerged, shaking and in tears. She knew her brother was in danger and most likely was the target of the blast even before Vilnat delivered the grim news. The desk clerk, Louis Pinard, who had now also made it to the third floor, threw his arms around Jeanne and held fast to keep her from running to her brother's room.[5] When the police arrived, they were able to investigate a relatively clean crime scene where, except for Vilnat's fingerprints on the door panel and her footprints just inside the threshold, visible in the pattern of feathers and debris on the floor, nothing had been disturbed since the explosion.

The first policeman to arrive at the Relais was Marc Fra, a superintendent of police at Montélimar, who rushed to the scene with at least two constables at around 2:15 a.m. Fra inspected #19, took a statement from Vilnat, and returned to police headquarters to author a report. The victim was lying at the foot of the bed, where the force of the explosion had thrown him. The cause of death was apparent as he was partially eviscerated and nearly totally decapitated. The walls around the bed were fissured and badly scorched; it was apparent to Fra that the bomb had been powerful. He knew this was going to be a lengthy and potentially ugly investigation, not only due to the nature of the crime, but because of the victim's identity. As the police report stated, the deceased was: "DORMOY, Marx, born August 1, 1888 at Montluçon. Mayor of Montluçon. Senator. Residence at Montluçon. Under house arrest at Montélimar since March 20, 1941 by ministerial decision."[6] Dormoy had been a prominent Socialist, an interior minister of the Third Republic, the parliamentary republican system of government in France from the mid-1870s to 1940. Most recently, he was a political detainee interned at Montélimar and ordered to reside at the Relais by a decree of the *État français*, the new government established in the town of Vichy in 1940. Maréchal Philippe Pétain, leader of the authoritarian Vichy regime, signed the directive himself.[7] Dormoy was no ordinary victim, and his death was clearly an assassination.

A FORGOTTEN HERO: FRANCE'S FIRST MARTYR OF WORLD WAR II

At the time Dormoy was murdered, France was struggling under German Occupation, and much of the world was enmeshed in World War II. Despite the investigation that Police Superintendent Charles Chenevier and Investigating Magistrate Jean René Marion carried out for nearly two years, no one was ever punished for Marx Dormoy's murder. After the war, between 1945 and 1950, Jeanne Dormoy did her best to engineer the apprehension and trial of her brother's assassins, to no avail. By 1950, France was focused on healing the wounds the war and occupation had caused the country's economy and society. The case was closed, and the surviving perpetrators remained safely in exile, for the most part in Spain and South America. Marx Dormoy had been laid to rest and most people seemed content to leave it at that.

In 2010 we published *Murder in the Métro: Laetitia Toureaux and the Cagoule in 1930s France*. In this book we told the story of the murder of Italian immigrant Laetitia Toureaux and of the right-wing extremists, members of a secret terrorist organization, the *Comité secret d'action révolutionnaire* (CSAR) or, more popularly, the Cagoule, who killed her. As we researched Toureaux and the Cagoule, a very politically sensitive topic when we began the project, we were struck by the parallels in the deep divisions between right and left in France and Europe in the 1930s, and the economic inequality and ensuing political polarization developing in the United States and Europe in the 2000s. Although the political conflicts in the United States under President Trump and a Great Britain struggling with "Brexit" command the most attention from English-speaking audiences today, France too at this moment is much more divided socially, economically, and politically than many observers – including many in France – acknowledge.[8]

We came across the story of Marx Dormoy while researching the Cagoule for *Murder in the Métro*. We found in Dormoy's murder an excellent opportunity to follow up our analysis of France's extreme right and political struggles during the 1930s with an investigation of the same themes during World War II. As we worked on *Murder in the Métro* we became convinced that scholars had not taken seriously enough the threat the Cagoule posed to the French government. The leaders of the Cagoule were violent men and women, dedicated to their goal of a "National Revolution" that promoted an authoritarian state, reactionary Catholic values, and a nostalgic mystique about France's past, which idealized rural peasants even while promoting elite technocrats.[9]

The Cagoulards were also terrorists who were not afraid to shed blood to achieve their ends. They were educated, intelligent, and extremely sophisticated in their ability to manipulate the media and use terrorism to communicate with the public in a way that gave them power, even as a clandestine organization, to effect political change. The Cagoulards firmly believed they were terrorists. Their theorist, Aristide Corre, wrote of their mission: "[T]here is no alternative but terrorism. But a scholarly terrorism, studied, transcendent, that will strike only the heads of the regime, but strike them without ceasing at any time, in any circumstance in order to render all government impossible so that they (the leaders of the Third Republic) are obligated to concede."[10]

As right-wing terrorists, the Cagoulards were also content to leave the public in doubt about their true identity. This strategy increased the impact of their terrorism if the public and the police were faced with waves of violence from an unknown source. The Cagoule had a political ideology, but deeds were their discourse with the French public, what their leader Eugène Deloncle called "a taste for action."[11] Such was the Cagoule's strategy in 1936–7.

The Cagoulards and their supporters in politics and the press succeeded in controlling the discourse surrounding their organization. The story they told was of a group of patriotic conservatives banded together to fight the Communists who they believed posed the real danger to French liberty. The right-wing press supported the Cagoule by making a joke of them and downplaying their crimes once they were exposed, a process made all the easier given that the Cagoulards failed to achieve a coup, in part because the French government unmasked the organization and arrested its leaders in 1937. The journalists' story stuck. A tiny group compared to other political organizations and leagues of the era, the Cagoule seemed to many pre- and postwar scholars an insignificant blip on the enormous radar of pre-World War II France. These scholars failed to understand the power the Cagoule wielded as right-wing terrorists and their contribution in the late 1930s toward shifting public opinion to favor an authoritarian model of French government, using fear to discredit the Third Republic, and preparing the way for Vichy.[12]

Our research has led us to a very different interpretation of the Cagoule. The Cagoule did not disappear in 1937–8. The organization may have been forcibly disbanded – although that is by no means clear – but the men who led it regrouped during the war in a new political party, the *Mouvement social révolutionnaire* (MSR), based in Occupied Paris and ensconced at the heart of Vichy. The man who headed the investigation of the Cagoule in 1937 was Marx Dormoy and the people behind his death in 1941 were the same people who led the Cagoule and never forgave Dormoy for combatting them before the war. Dormoy paid a high price for going after the Cagoule. By recounting the story of his duel with France's extreme right we expand two narratives. First, we continue our analysis of the impact of the Cagoule on French history, extending our study to 1950. Second, we resurrect the memory of a courageous but nearly forgotten man who in many ways was France's first resister and martyr of the war.

On Sunday, 9 December 1945, Dormoy was buried in the city of Montluçon (see Figure 0.1). Despite the freezing temperatures, thousands of people lined the route through the Bourbonnais region and then Montluçon's streets as his funeral cortege traveled from Montélimar, where Dormoy had been hastily inhumed in 1941, to Montluçon's cemetery-west, where his remains would be interred. When Dormoy's funeral cortege wended its way through Montluçon, hundreds of people were waiting in front of the Hôtel de Ville to pay their respects, including Mayor René Ribière and Henri Ribière, deputy for the Department of the Allier in the French National Assembly. Léon Blum, head of the Socialist Popular Front government before the war, led a delegation that included Félix Gouin, the president of the Constituent Assembly responsible for creating a new government for post-war France. Also attending were Vincent Auriol and André Blumel, stalwarts of the Popular Front and old friends of Marx and Jeanne, as well as other politicians representing Charles de Gaulle and the post-war French government. At about 1:30 p.m. the speeches in Dormoy's honor began.[13]

Three men spoke at the ceremony, Gouin, Blum, and Henri Ribière, who had all known Dormoy before the war. Each of them lamented the loss of a courageous man, a committed Socialist who had fought to the end against the rise of fascism in France. His death was a terrible blow to their party and to the

Figure 0.1. Marx Dormoy's Funeral Cortege, Sunday, 5 December 1945. AD Allier, 64/J/136, "Fonds Marx Dormoy, Photographies et autres documents figurés."

Republic, and his 1941 inhumation, which the Vichy government prevented most of them from attending, was an insult to his memory. But why had he been murdered? Here too, the speakers agreed: Dormoy had been the ferocious enemy of the Cagoule. As interior minister in Blum's government, Dormoy had tracked this organization, infiltrated it with police spies, unmasked its leaders in 1937, and foiled their plot to overthrow the Third Republic and put in power an autocratic regime that would have either chosen the path of neutrality during the war or entered the war on the side of the Axis. The war had forced the closure of the Cagoule case, but now, Gouin assured his listeners, the Cagoule file had been "reopened" so that those responsible for its crimes, including Dormoy's assassins, could finally be hunted down and punished.[14] But what exactly was the Cagoule, why were Blum, Gouin, and Ribière convinced that its members had engineered Dormoy's murder, and why were they also certain that the Cagoule had posed a real danger to the Third Republic in the years prior to the war? To answer these questions, one must understand the trajectory of Dormoy's life.

On 26 July 1940, one year to the day before his murder, Dormoy was dining at his home in Montluçon with friends and fellow Socialists (and wartime

Resistance leaders) Daniel and Cletta Mayer. Dormoy had just returned from Vichy, where despite their best efforts he and Blum failed to prevent the rise to power of Maréchal Pétain and the collapse of the Third Republic in the wake of the German invasion. Pétain, with the crucial support of Pierre Laval, a former Socialist politician who embraced the political right in the pre-war years, established in its place an autocratic government to rule France, the État français, with its capital in Vichy. Dormoy and his dinner guests were discussing the recent Armistice with the Germans, Pétain's new autocratic regime, and what these events portended for France. Suddenly Dormoy declared: "In one year, I will either be a minister, or I will have been shot by a firing squad."[15]

He had good reason to be worried. Dormoy had long opposed authoritarian ideologies such as that upon which Pétain's regime was founded. His vocal opposition to Pétain's dictatorial rule in July of 1940 was thus nothing new. Even before the police had identified the perpetrators, therefore, French people at home and abroad assumed that Dormoy's death was a political assassination tied to Vichy. Worse, it seemed to signal the beginning of a wave of bloody reprisals against individuals such as Dormoy, a Socialist, a friend to France's Jewish community, and a Freemason. The Freemasons are a secret fraternal order that many European conservatives feared was plotting to take over the world. Extreme right politicians targeted Freemasons for repression because the organization supported liberal democracy. Dormoy, who had fought to preserve the ideals of the French Revolution, was what we would call today a champion of human rights. His murder was part of Vichy's revenge for the Popular Front.[16]

A born militant, Dormoy held strong convictions and defended them with zeal. He was genial in temperament, with a long face, dark hair and eyes that sparkled as if he was always on the verge of telling a joke, a handsome man with or without the bushy beard that became his trademark. While not tall, he was robust and unafraid of throwing punches, verbal or otherwise. First and foremost, Dormoy was a political man, not just because he made a successful career as a politician, but because he viewed the world through the lens of his Socialist ideology. For Dormoy, politics was a means to an end, and for him that end was improving the lives of his constituents in the Allier, and of the working classes everywhere in France. Dormoy possessed excellent political instincts and more intelligence than his enemies often realized. He was also an effective orator, a capable administrator, a loyal friend, as well as a courageous warrior in the political arena.

Following World War I, Dormoy became a leader in the *Section française de l'internationale ouvrière* (SFIO) or the French Socialist Party founded in 1905. After becoming mayor of Montluçon in 1925, Dormoy was elected to the French Chamber of Deputies in 1931 and subsequently senator from the Department of the Allier in 1938.[17] Dormoy was a close friend and staunch supporter of SFIO leader Léon Blum, and he served as an undersecretary of state in Blum's first government in 1936. When Blum's interior minister, Roger Salengro, committed suicide, Blum chose Dormoy to replace Salengro. During his brief second government that began in June of 1937, Blum again kept Dormoy on as interior minister.[18] With the fall of the second Popular Front government in April of 1938, a new, conservative government under Édouard Daladier took power and Dormoy returned to looking after the interests of his constituents as senator from the Allier and mayor of Montluçon.

As minister of the interior, Dormoy clashed with groups on the extreme right in France. This earned him the ire of the *Parti populaire français* (PPF) leader, Jacques Doriot, as well as the Cagoule head, Eugène Deloncle. Dormoy pursued his fascist opponents using every legal method available to him, and as the French national police were under the authority of the interior ministry, he had both the power and the responsibility to track down threats to the security and stability of the French state. When the French Republic was on the verge of collapse he opposed the Armistice with the Germans that Pétain and his supporters on the right foisted on France. By 1940, therefore, Dormoy was a beloved political figure in the eyes of many ordinary French citizens, but he had also made bitter enemies who would not be sorry to see him eliminated.[19]

MEMORY AND THE LEGACY OF MARX DORMOY

Our quest to understand Marx Dormoy's murder raised another question. Why has Dormoy's memory remained as quietly laid to rest as his corpse? It is true that a Parisian metro stop in the 18th arrondissement was named after Dormoy, and streets and squares bear his name, especially in the Department of the Allier. But most works on France during World War II either relegate him to a footnote or, at best, accord him a paragraph or two. This lacuna surprised us when we began work on *Assassination in Vichy*. Dormoy never led the Socialist Party or became prime minister, as did his friend and mentor Léon Blum. Yet Dormoy played a significant role in the Socialist Party in the 1920s and the 1930s and in the French Popular Front government, 1936–8. His political career, including his courageous resistance to dismantling the French Republic after the German victory in 1940 – not to mention his assassination – should have garnered more attention than it has received. Instead, historians seem almost embarrassed by Dormoy – his working-class origins and lack of university education, and his ignominious demise. But most of all, we think that most historians, and France, have been content to let Dormoy slumber for the same reason that they have been content to downplay the Cagoule.

Dormoy is irrevocably linked to the Cagoule, and the Cagoule is a very difficult subject in French history because once one scratches the surface of the organization, it becomes apparent that the Cagoule exemplifies the deep political polarization in 1930s France. A significant minority of French people chose to collaborate with the Germans during the war. France was neither a "nation of resisters" as Charles de Gaulle declared, nor a nation of collaborators as later critics of the country's wartime record alleged. Most French people, before and during the war, were consumed with the struggle to survive economic depression, war, and occupation.[20] French politics were polarized between left and right, and many French people feared Communism at least as much as they feared fascism. That is why so many acquiesced to Pétain's authoritarian regime. The elderly Maréchal, renowned for his military success in World War I, seemed to offer a bulwark not only against the Nazis occupying much of France, but against the Communists and the Soviet Union as well, and even if his regime was essentially a dictatorship, at least it was French. After the war the French, under the leadership of Charles de Gaulle, were convinced that only by forgetting those pre-war and wartime divisions could the country unite, heal, and prosper. Marx Dormoy, as much a victim of Pétain as of the Cagoule, never lived to take part in France's reconciliation. Instead he remained, and remains, a symbol of France's divisions during a terrible period of French history. His grave symbolizes the tomb in which the most painful memories of wartime France have been interred.

But we are historians, and historians by nature are gravediggers. We disinter the past, poke around the remains, ask questions and revive memories that are often uncomfortable. World War II France, collaboration, and the Cagoule, have become less sensitive topics in the twenty-first century. Most documents from the era that were classified during the second half of the twentieth century have since been opened to the public. Our research took us to multiple archives in France and the United States, most significantly in Paris, Montluçon and Moulins, but we also traveled to the sites associated with Marx Dormoy's life, imprisonment, and assassination. The latter involved climbing over weed-covered walls just to get a good glimpse of the hotel, abandoned in 2010, where he died. We also followed in the steps of his killers, from Paris to Marseille, to better understand the places and spaces in which they lived. We are by no means the only scholars who have been rattling the bones of France's extreme right before and during the war.[21] But we hope in *Assassination in Vichy* to approach the topic in a unique way: through the story of a brave man whose death, ironically, helped to ensure the exposure, if not the punishment, of the people who sought by killing him to avenge his victory against them in 1937, efface the record of their pre-war terrorism, and take advantage of the German Occupation to construct a France around their nationalistic, authoritarian, and antisemitic ideals.

This book is about those who murdered Dormoy, and those who tried to solve that crime, bring his assassins to justice, and preserve his memory. Our goal is to understand the motivations of those involved in the crime and what their ideals, political agendas, and personal hatreds can tell us about wartime France. Because the fortunes of the investigation of Dormoy's murder depended upon the trajectories of World War II and the German Occupation of France, these stories – that of Dormoy and that of the war – cannot be separated, and thus we weave them together in this book.

Who was Marx Dormoy and why was he killed? These are questions that few historians have explored extensively. Only three biographies of Dormoy have been published. Dormoy's friend and personal secretary, Georges Rougeron, wrote the first in 1956.[22] The late historian André Touret published the second in 1998, and Daniel Dugléry, former mayor of Montluçon, authored the third in 2013.[23] The need remains for a comprehensive biography of Dormoy that assesses his career in light of recent scholarship on the Third Republic. *Assassination in Vichy* is not that book. While we do summarize Dormoy's life in our first chapter, this book is not a biography. Rather, we use his wartime assassination and the subsequent investigation of that crime, carried out in the face of great danger and difficulty by Police Superintendent Charles Chenevier and Investigating Magistrate Jean René Marion, as a lens through which to understand the deep conflicts between the political right and left within France prior to, during, and after the war.

These conflicts, Henry Rousso, Julian Jackson, and other historians contend, can be characterized as a French "civil war," albeit one waged as a "cold war" rather than as a violent conflagration akin to that which wracked Spain from 1936 to 1939.[24] Some historians, notable among them Serge Berstein, have argued that political conflict in France during the interwar period was a "simulated confrontation." Due to their attachment to France's democratic traditions, the French public rejected outright violence by privileging symbolic rhetoric over street-fighting and thus rendering France "allergic" to fascism.[25] Historian Chris Millington rejects Berstein's emphasis on the rarity of violence in interwar France and exposes France's civil conflict as very much a violent, ideological battle over French identity. Ideological conflict brought World War I veterans and young, right-wing extremists into the streets, where they clashed with trade unionists, Communist students, and workers. While the lethality of this violence was relatively low – approximately 100 people died between 1918 and 1940 due to street fighting – the civil conflict continued during and after World War II and claimed more lives.[26] Political violence also weakened, perhaps fatally, the already unstable Third Republic even before the Nazi invasion of France in 1940.

Dormoy was a victim not of Nazi depredations, but rather of home-grown French violence. His extreme right-wing killers envisioned themselves as "terrorists of the National Revolution," enjoined to "save" their country by punishing those who had corrupted it with the foreign ideologies of socialism and Communism and failed in their duty to prepare France for conflict with Germany. Dormoy's assassins understood themselves as soldiers in a French and European struggle between the left and the right, between "Bolshevism" and "traditional" nationalistic values. We can understand their actions and events in France from 1936 through 1950 only if we permit ourselves to explore their mindset, as well as that of their opponents, even if their interpretations of their times and their actions do not coincide with ours.

The 1930s was a crisis-ridden decade for a France weakened by the Great Depression and threatened by the rise of fascism and the expansion of Bolshevism.[27] The French government refused to devalue the franc even after the British and Americans had devalued their currencies. The value of French exports collapsed and governmental budget deficits rose. Factory owners manipulated wages while agricultural prices plummeted, setting the stage for social unrest. Extra-parliamentary political groups, often known as "leagues," drew supporters, especially on the right where Colonel François de La Rocque headed up the *Croix de feu* (CF), a veterans organization that grew to include over 300,000 adherents by 1935. Members of these leagues proclaimed themselves ready to fight the Communists. Other right-wing leagues and parties included a revived *Action française* (AF), with its pro-Catholic ideologue Charles Maurras, who appealed to a respectable bourgeois audience, Pierre Taittinger's *Jeunesses patriotes*, Marcel Bucard's *Parti franciste*, and François Coty's blue-shirted and beret-wearing *Solidarité française*. All of these leagues pressed for more authoritarian government and some were drawn to fascism. French historians dispute the nature of France's relationship with fascism, though most seem to agree that Jacques Doriot's PPF was a fascist organization.[28] "The leagues' self-conscious styling in the image of foreign fascism reminds us," Chris Millington observes, "that France was not isolated from the extremist politics of its European neighbours and nor was there a uniquely French attitude to violence."[29] The French government, fearful of the violence the leagues were inciting, dissolved them in 1936. Upon the dissolution of the leagues many of their former members gravitated to the remaining right-wing political parties, especially the PPF. At this point, the CSAR or Cagoule was also founded as a clandestine organization comprised of the most radical members of the AF, expelled from that organization in 1935 because of their penchant for violence and regime change.[30]

Political tensions exploded on the night of 6 February 1934, a date Julian Jackson, professor of history at the University of London, associates with the opening of the "French civil war."[31] Thousands of right-wing leaguers and war veterans congregated in the Place de la Concorde and attempted to storm the French parliament building to protest the perceived corruption of Edouard Daladier's government and the Republic in general.[32] Communists, fed up with the right and hoping to prevent a fascist coup, were also in the crowd. Fighting with the Police mobile guard ensued and the latter, often called the "bludgeoners of the people," opened fire on the crowd, killing fifteen and wounding hundreds of others. The government's use of force against its own people brought down Daladier's government and led to the short-lived ascendancy of conservative Gaston Doumergue. The most significant outcome of the February 6 riot, however, was the decision of left-wing and center-right leaders to unify in an attempt to salvage the Republic. These efforts culminated in the election of the first Popular Front government, an alliance, albeit fragile, of the left-wing Socialist, Communist and Radical parties, in June of 1936 and the rise of Marx Dormoy to national prominence. After 1936 he also became the focus of heightened right-wing animosity, and in the years leading up to the war endured both physical and rhetorical attacks.

For many observers, Marx Dormoy was, if not the first victim of wartime political conflict in France, its first martyr. Dormoy's dearest friends, Socialist politicians Félix Gouin and Léon Blum, proclaimed this during their eulogies for Dormoy on 9 December 1945.[33] Pierre Cot, Dormoy's friend and colleague in the Popular Front government of 1936–8, declared two weeks after the murder that Dormoy's assassination revealed the "moral decadence of the Vichy Regime."[34] Cot surmised that Dormoy, "one of the most influential leaders of French democracy," was murdered precisely because his enemies feared Dormoy's staunch opposition to the rise of fascism in Europe and of fascism's proponents in France. Dormoy's assassination was a political crime, the first bloodletting in a bloodbath that France's extreme right planned in order to wipe out the "champions" of French democracy and the legacy of the French Revolution. They were determined that France should remain under an autocratic regime even if it meant allying with the Nazis. Despite the pre- and post-war tensions between the Communists and Dormoy's Socialists, the Communist leaders who seized control of Montluçon when the city was liberated in September of 1944 told the American forces occupying the city that Marx Dormoy was a heroic victim of wartime fascists.[35]

Assassination in Vichy begins with a summary of Dormoy's life and murder. Subsequent chapters segue back and forth between the progress of the war and that of the investigation into the crime, led by Superintendent Chenevier and Investigating Magistrate Marion, two courageous men who at great personal risk insisted on completing a thorough rather than a cursory examination of the crime. Convinced that the roots of the crime could be found in the highest levels of the Vichy regime and in the collaborationist circles in Paris, neither man was willing to give up on calling to account those who plotted Dormoy's demise. The lives and motivations of the assassins themselves are also analyzed. Through our study of Dormoy, his defenders and his killers, we illuminate the deep political, social, and cultural tensions that divided France before, during, and even after the war. Our book offers a new perspective on Dormoy and on wartime France, told through a narrative of a crime, its victim, its perpetrators, and two men who sought to bring the latter to justice. Finally, *Assassination in Vichy* is also a story about a struggle over memory, not simply the memory of a man, Marx Dormoy, whose legacy his adoring older sister fought valiantly to protect, but also the ideals and flaws of Third Republic France, of the actions, noble and ignoble, of the people of France during the Occupation. In that respect the story of Marx Dormoy's life, death, and legacy is also the story of the struggle over the ways in which French people chose to remember, or forget, the last decade of the feeble Third Republic and the terrible war years as they sought to build a new France after the Liberation, a France that, it must be remembered, exonerated many, if not most, for their wartime crimes.

CHAPTER ONE

1888–1941: Marx Dormoy and the Fall of France

Marx Dormoy (see Figure 1.1) liked to say that he was "born on the baptismal font of socialism" and in fact this was no exaggeration.[1] His father, Jean Dormoy, was born in 1851 in Montluçon's industrial suburb of Ville-Gozet. A steel worker in Montluçon's factories, Jean Dormoy was a union organizer, convinced that only through solidarity could workers improve their lot. Despite his minimal formal education, Jean Dormoy read widely. He became an early follower of Jules Guesde, a journalist and political figure known for his devotion to Marxism and uncompromising attitude toward capitalism. Under Guesde's inspiration, Jean Dormoy organized the workers of Montluçon and wound up in prison in 1883 alongside Guesde and another revolutionary Marxist, Paul Lafargue, Karl Marx's son-in-law.

These political and personal ties to Marxists and trade unionists propelled Jean Dormoy into the political arena and leadership of the *Parti ouvrier français* or French Worker's Party. His activism provoked the anger of factory owners in Montluçon and he lost his job in 1880. In 1892 Dormoy was elected the first Socialist mayor of Montluçon, which at least afforded him a salary sufficient to support his wife and children. He died just six years later, at the age of forty-seven.[2] Marx was only ten years old but he had already learned from his father the power of political convictions to change the world and the absolute moral responsibility of every person to fight to defend them.

Jean Dormoy fathered four children: Françoise (b. 1876), Érnestine (b. 1882), Jeanne (b. 1886), and finally René Marx (b. 1888), named after Jean Dormoy's political idol, Karl Marx. Françoise died in 1881 and Érnestine in 1883, the latter

Figure 1.1. Portrait of Marx Dormoy. AD Allier, 64/J/138, "Fonds Marx Dormoy, Photographies et autres documents figurés."

Figure 1.2. Marx and Jeanne Dormoy as children in 1896. AD Allier, 64/J/136, "Fonds Marx Dormoy, Photographies et autres documents figurés."

while Jean Dormoy was in prison. The surviving children, Jeanne and Marx, were thus raised in the shadow of their deceased siblings, who died before they were born.[3] Although infant mortality was higher in nineteenth-century France than it is today, the deaths of Françoise and Érnestine marked Marx and Jeanne emotionally, in their relationships with their parents and each other, causing Jeanne to adopt a protective role toward her younger brother. Figure 1.2 shows the siblings in childhood around the ages of eight and ten. Jeanne leans her right arm on Marx's left shoulder reflecting their mutually dependent and close emotional relationship that continued for the rest of their lives.

Jeanne was an attractive woman who resembled her brother and shared his fierce convictions, but her temperament was more serious, as behooved an older sister upon whom much responsibility fell, especially after the premature death of their father. More studious than her brother, Jeanne completed her formal education at the local *lycée* (a secondary school similar to an American high school) and became a school teacher and then director of the local orphanage. Her job provided an apartment within the building housing the orphanage in Montluçon, which she shared with Marx. Neither sibling married. They resided together most of their lives and Jeanne was fiercely devoted to her brother. Marx's letters written later in life indicate that he depended on his sister for her practical advice and moral support. Following his assassination in 1941, the devastated Jeanne spent her remaining years until her death in 1975 fighting to preserve and defend her brother's memory and bring his killers to justice.[4]

According to his friend and colleague from the Allier, Henri Ribière, "the young Marx Dormoy was raised in this atmosphere of political struggle. His father made him read the classics of socialism: Fournier, Proudhon, Marx and, above all, Guesde, which he assimilated with a precocious intelligence."[5] Life became more difficult for Jeanne and Marx after Jean Dormoy died. Marx had to leave school at the age of twelve as his earnings were needed to supplement the family income. He labored as a bench hand and metal fitter in Montluçon's factories but Dormoy's "real life was elsewhere," at the meetings he attended of the youth branch of the Socialist Party, the *Jeunes socialistes* of the Allier, and later within the ranks of the party itself.[6]

Jeanne and Marx benefited from their excellent relationship with Paul and Laura Lafargue, who frequently invited the Dormoy siblings to stay with them, nurtured them intellectually, and helped provide for their material needs. Paul Lafargue was a doctor who was as militant a Socialist as Jean Dormoy. Lafargue married Laura Marx, the younger daughter of Karl Marx. At Lafargue's home in Draveil, Marx Dormoy became a self-taught young man during the hours he spent studying in their library.[7] Dormoy joined forces with Paul Constans, one of the founders of the SFIO in 1905, and began writing for Socialist papers like *Le Combat social* and became secretary of the Union of Metal Workers, whose members formed his earliest base of political support just as they had for his father and uncle. In 1905, with Constans' help, Dormoy became secretary of the Montluçon wing of the SFIO. Mobilized in 1914, Dormoy was stationed in French Algiers during World War I, where he started a Socialist magazine, *La lutte sociale*.[8] His courage under fire earned him numerous medals. Just before he was demobilized in 1918, a colonel congratulated him on his bravery and conduct, but at the same time lamented that Dormoy was a Socialist. Dormoy responded, "What would you have me be? I was born to it!"[9]

After the war Dormoy returned to politics. Elected to the municipal council of Montluçon in 1919, by 1926 Dormoy was mayor of the city and shortly thereafter he took the place of Constans as president of the regional council.[10] Dormoy, now a deputy from the Allier to the French National Assembly, became embroiled in the major ideological conflict that literally tore apart the SFIO.[11] The 1917 Russian Revolution created a crisis for the party, even as it benefitted from new recruits the revolution inspired. Expansion brought in its wake a rift between those members who sought to unite the SFIO with the Communists by joining the Moscow-based Third International and those who feared a drift toward Bolshevism.[12]

Dormoy belonged to the faction of SFIO stalwarts who rejected the authoritarianism of Lenin's brand of Communism and firmly believed that French Socialists needed to stand apart from the Communists. In attendance at the Party Congress at Tours in 1920 as a representative of the Allier, Dormoy mourned the split in the SFIO that resulted when the majority of delegates voted to join the Third International, a move that eventually led to the creation of the French Communist Party in 1920. Dormoy sided with Léon Blum, a member of the SFIO Executive Committee who represented Paris in the National Assembly. Blum led the reconstituted SFIO following the schism with the Communists and headed it throughout the 1920s and 1930s.[13]

Born in 1872, Blum came from a family of wealthy Alsatian Jews. After studying law at the Sorbonne, Blum joined Jean Jaurès' SFIO in 1904. Jaurès was assassinated in 1914 and although his fate haunted both Blum and Dormoy, it opened the way for Blum to rise in the party ranks to become its principal theoretician as well as the editor of the Socialist newspaper, *Le Populaire*.[14] Blum and Dormoy were opposites in many ways yet got on well and were political allies. Jeanne Dormoy also became a part of Blum's inner circle. Dormoy's close association with Blum from 1920 on evolved into one of the most important relationships of his life. The two men developed a friendship that endured until Dormoy's death. Blum became a political mentor to the younger Dormoy, and Dormoy repaid Blum's support and patronage with an unshakeable loyalty. During difficult times, Blum once wrote to Dormoy, "your friendship makes me a better man."[15] Blum exerted a great influence on Dormoy who even took to wearing the distinctive wide-brimmed hats Blum preferred.[16] Far from succumbing to the antisemitism that was rife in French society, Dormoy was a vigorous defender of the rights of Jews in France, which prompted some of his political opponents to target him with antisemitic slurs. Much of the public thought Dormoy was Jewish, especially since most of his closest friends, like the men in Figure 1.3, were Jewish.[17]

In 1936, after a succession of conservative governments proved unable to revive the French economy or stem the rise of German militarism across

Figure 1.3. Undated picture of Marx Dormoy (right), Léon Blum (center), André Blumel (left), and an unidentified woman, "Suzanne," probably Blumel's sister, Suzanne Weill. AD Allier, 64/J/137, "Fonds Marx Dormoy, Photographies et autres documents figurés."

the Rhine, the French elected new leaders in the form of the Popular Front alliance of Socialists, Communists, and Radicals. Conservatives, horrified at the election of Blum as the first Socialist and the first Jewish prime minister, fomented riots in the streets in an effort to overthrow the fledgling government. The Communists also proved uncooperative. Workers across France, inspired by the accession to power of the Popular Front, struck to improve their pay and working conditions. Desperate to find a way to satisfy at least some of the workers' demands and get French factories in operation again, Blum brokered a series of meetings that resulted in the Matignon Accords (7 June 1936), which for the first time mandated a forty-hour workweek and paid vacations. Even after the Accords, however, many workers remained on strike, often at the instigation of the Communist trade unions jealous of the success of their rivals on the left, the Socialists. These massive strikes stymied Blum's initiatives to revive France's economy, threatened his ability to ramp up France's armament industry in the face of the rising Nazi threat, and discredited him and the Popular Front in the eyes of many French people.[18]

On 16 March 1937 Dormoy made a fateful decision to permit right-wing Colonel de La Rocque and his *Parti social français* (PSF) to hold a meeting in a theater in Clichy, the traditional Communist center of Paris. Whether deliberate or not, La Rocque's choice of Clichy predictably outraged Parisian leftists and was likely to goad them into staging a demonstration that everyone knew could easily erupt in violence.[19] But Dormoy's firm belief in freedom of assembly induced him to allow the meeting to proceed. A riot involving some 9,000 people ensued and when someone discharged a weapon, the panicked police began firing as well. Dormoy reacted to the crisis with his usual courage. He hurried to Clichy, still in his white dinner jacket, and personally confronted the rioters. Together with André Blumel, the head of Blum's cabinet, Dormoy "threw himself between the demonstrators and the bullets of the police."[20] The situation was extremely dangerous; Blumel was shot three times.[21] Five people died and 367 more were injured.[22] Dormoy initially suspected that the Communists had fomented the tumult in order to embarrass the Socialists, but in fact *agents provocateurs*, some from the Cagoule, had infiltrated the crowd. They instigated brawls in order to provoke the police to do exactly what they did – open fire. Their goal was to discredit the Popular Front government.[23]

Because the police had fired on Socialist and Communist protesters, the riots undermined Blum's support within his own party.[24] Communists and some in the SFIO blamed Clichy, and Dormoy, for the disarray and political weakness of the Popular Front in the summer of 1937. One supporter of the Popular Front castigated Dormoy as "a traitor" who had "sold his country out for money" and "made suffer the little guy who had voted for the Popular Front."[25] The great irony of these accusations for Dormoy must have been that he had repeatedly urged Blum to refrain from using force against strikers occupying the factories urgently needed to prepare France for the coming war with Germany.[26] On 6 July 1938 Dormoy and Blumel were accosted at an SFIO Congress in Royan. As Dormoy reached the entrance of the meeting hall, a group of people wearing the insignia of the SFIO surrounded him, chanting "Dormoy at Clichy! Dormoy at Clichy! Dormoy to prison!" Blumel shouted that he too had been at Clichy, where he had "taken three bullets," but nevertheless the protesters attacked Blumel and Dormoy, who managed to shake them off. Once inside, Dormoy and Blumel received a standing ovation and Dormoy was asked to take the podium.[27]

Dormoy's words that day illustrate his sorrow over Clichy, his conviction that nevertheless he had done the right thing, and his pride in his history as a militant for the Socialist cause.

> Clichy! Clichy! ... That night we fully accomplished our duty. Now that we understand the truth about the affair, I repeat, and with even more

force, "Yes, we did our full duty" ... We went [to Clichy that night] to try to ensure that no one fired on the workers and André Blumel was wounded ... Dormoy at Clichy! I know of no graver insult to a militant Socialist such as I, or you ... I have belonged to the Party since my earliest childhood. I have served it with my entire soul, my entire heart. I will not accept these insults. I demand that our lives as militants be respected.[28]

Dormoy must have felt vindicated when it became apparent from the police investigation that the situation at Clichy had spiraled out of control as the result of a deliberate effort on the part of the extreme right to overturn Blum's government. From that point on, the gloves were off for Dormoy, who was now determined to rein in the growing power of demagogues such as Jacques Doriot and Colonel de La Rocque. The Spanish Civil War broke out in July of 1936 and from the outset the Popular Front was divided between the Communists and Socialists, who urged France to intervene on behalf of the Socialist-dominated *Frente popular* government (the Republicans or "loyalists"), and the majority on the center and the right who urged either non-intervention, or intervention on the side of Francisco Franco's Nationalists. Blum's government officially adhered to the Non-Intervention Pact the British championed. In light of the growing Nazi threat, Blum's centrist colleagues in the Popular Front felt that France needed above all to preserve its alliance with Britain. But some members of his cabinet, such as Pierre Cot, minister of aviation, urged Blum to offer clandestine aid to the Republicans. That Blum allowed at least some weapons to trickle from France into Spain was an open secret. The support for the Republican cause of many Socialists infuriated Franco's sympathizers on the French right. Tensions over the Spanish Civil War remained extraordinarily high and it is possible that only Franco's victory in March 1939 and the outbreak of war with Germany on 3 September averted a French civil war.[29]

Except for France's policy on Spanish Civil War refugees, Dormoy was not directly involved in the struggle over Spain in Blum's cabinet, although he did speak out against the lopsided results of Non-Intervention that advantaged the Nationalists.[30] But there is no doubt that from Dormoy's perspective, Clichy and the struggle over Spain confirmed that France too was locked in a battle between left and right that threatened to tear the country apart. Dormoy, always a fighter, was determined to keep the French Republic from falling prey to the forces of reaction that seemed to be triumphing everywhere else in Europe. He focused his attention, therefore, on tracking the proliferation of right-wing groups in France whose support of Franco and opposition to the Popular Front were evolving into dangerously seditious rhetoric and terrorist acts.

In May of 1937 Dormoy ousted Jacques Doriot from office as mayor of the Parisian suburb of Saint-Denis. Dormoy accused Doriot of mismanagement of funds and fiscal malfeasance, which may have been accurate, but the real reason Dormoy decided to act against Doriot was political. "Le grand Jacques," as Doriot's followers often called him because of his height, girth, and larger-than-life personality, was a World War I hero who joined the Communist Party after the war. He was twice elected mayor of the working-class Parisian suburb of Saint-Denis, a traditional hub of Communist unions. But in 1934 the Communists ejected Doriot, in part due to his growing fascination with fascist ideology. Doriot founded his own political party, the PPF, in 1936 which split his constituency in Saint-Denis, although he continued to have a large following, especially among veterans of World War I and young men attracted to the aura of power and social renewal surrounding Nazism and fascism. A classic demagogue, Doriot grew increasingly pro-German in the late 1930s. Convinced that Doriot's PPF posed a real danger to the Republic, Dormoy did not hesitate to force Doriot out of office, an injury that "le grand Jacques" never forgot.[31]

After an extensive investigation Dormoy also dismantled the Cagoule and arrested much of its leadership. He initially downplayed the Cagoule when he first announced its existence to the French public in September of 1937. On the morning of 23 November, however, Dormoy issued a statement explaining that a plot to overthrow the French Republic had been unearthed and the perpetrators arrested.[32] At that moment a shocked public learned of the existence of the Cagoule and its links to a succession of murders and terrorist acts. In January 1937, Russian economist Dimitri Navachine was stabbed to death in the Bois-de-Boulogne. In July two Italian anti-fascist exiles, Carlo and Nello Rosselli, were gunned down in Normandy and in September bombs devastated the headquarters of two major business associations in Paris, killing two police officers in the process. When the police broke the case, Blum informed the public that Dormoy had saved France from the dangerous terrorist organization, committed to fascist rule, behind this crime wave. The police discovered mountains of weapons and ammunition, over two tons of explosives including 9,000 grenades, 24 machine guns, 259 automatic rifles, and an anti-tank gun, along with proof that the Cagoule was stockpiling more weapons in Spain near the border at Hesdin.[33]

The leader of the Cagoule was a wealthy naval engineer and inveterate plotter named Eugène Deloncle (see Figure 1.4). Deloncle and his followers shared extreme nationalist and antisemitic convictions as well as a horror of Bolshevism. He attracted the support of active military personnel, veterans, engineers, journalists, bankers, and industrialists who vehemently opposed the Popular Front. Like Franco's Falangists, Deloncle's Cagoulards were willing to destroy the Republic in order to "save" France. The organization earned its nickname from a supposed penchant for wearing hoods resembling those of the Ku Klux Klan during meetings to disguise members' identities – a *cagoule* is a hood in French. The name also reflected the clandestine nature of the Cagoule, which Deloncle organized as a self-proclaimed underground group, committed to terrorism in order to achieve a "national revolution" that would bring to power an autocratic government in France. They viewed such terrorism not as criminal, therefore, but rather as politically motivated, an extreme form of patriotism. Ostensibly Deloncle formed the Cagoule as an auto-defense militia designed to prevent a Bolshevik uprising in France. He secured funding from industrialists, among them Eugène Schueller, the founder of the cosmetics giant L'Oréal, as well as executives at the tire manufacturer Michelin, aperitif distributor Byrrh, car maker Renault, and cooking-oil producer Lesieur, who shared Deloncle's hatred of Communism. This revenue kept Deloncle and his circle of elites awash in money that funded the purchase and stockpiling of illegal arms, supposedly for self-defense, but really to seize power. Although the Cagoule's leadership was concentrated in Paris, where Deloncle resided, the Cagoule was tied to extreme right groups throughout France. Most notable were the Cagoule's strongholds in the south, including Nice, where the ultra-militant Joseph Darnand was in charge, and Marseille, which became a hotbed of right-wing extremists. In these and numerous other cities Cagoule representatives recruited angry young men and furnished them with training and weapons.[34] "You have to build up an explosive force," Deloncle explained, "that could explode – and explode well – on the day of peril."[35]

Like Doriot, Deloncle imagined that after toppling the Third Republic he would replace it with a dictatorial regime modeled on Benito Mussolini's Italy, with himself in Mussolini's boots, of course. On more than one occasion the Cagoule attempted to assassinate Léon Blum. Deloncle liaised with Mussolini's government, from which he received funds and weapons. The Cagoule formed militias in major cities throughout France, most notably in Cannes, Nice, Bordeaux, Lyon, Toulouse, and Marseille, and Deloncle claimed to have hundreds of thousands of adherents. His supporters more likely numbered in the tens of thousands. Even so, Deloncle's Cagoule successfully carried out a surprisingly large number of terrorist acts. His agents instigated street fighting on multiple

Figure 1.4. Eugène Deloncle, circa 1940, AN (France), Z/6/808, dossier 5672.

occasions, including at the Clichy riots of 1937. The goal of the violence was to incite fear and thus persuade the French media and the public that a Communist uprising was imminent, and that Blum's government was unable to maintain order or ensure the security of the French state. Deloncle also cultivated ties to World War I hero Philippe Pétain. Pétain cautiously refused Deloncle's offer to make him a dictator, but likely gave the Cagoule his unofficial support.[36]

On the night of 15 November 1937 Deloncle attempted to provoke a Communist uprising in the streets of Paris. The goal was to force military intervention against the "Bolsheviks" that would dwarf the Clichy riots and lead to the fall of Blum's government. The plan went awry, however, as the Communists, and Marx Dormoy, got wind of the plot. It was the excuse Dormoy needed to reel in the Cagoule. Over the next several weeks the French police acting under Dormoy's instructions arrested and incarcerated Deloncle and other key Cagoulards although some, such as the Cagoule's chief assassin, Jean Filliol, and the man in charge of procuring its enormous arsenal, Gabriel Jeantet, managed to slip through Dormoy's net and escape to safe houses they had established in Italy or Spain.[37] In *Le Combat social*, Dormoy announced, "I can safely say that through these attacks the authors and those who are behind them [demonstrate] that they have no other goal than to provoke a civil war in France which could perhaps drag us into a foreign war."[38] Dormoy's use of the term "civil war" indicates how well he understood the Cagoule's terrorist threat to divide and even destroy the nation.

Dormoy should have been recognized as a hero whose foresight and bold action had saved the democratic order in France.[39] But instead the well-funded conservative newspapers launched a massive campaign of fake news that blunted the effects of Dormoy's triumph. Right-wing journalists embraced the Cagoulards and demanded that Dormoy order their release. The royalist newspaper *L'Action française* declared that Dormoy had imprisoned the Cagoulards as part of a government-sanctioned plot against the entire political right by using scare tactics to drum up sympathy for Socialist-Communist policies. These journalists rejected the coup allegations as fiction and began referring to the whole Cagoule episode as "Fantomarx," a delusion of the paranoid interior minister. *L'Echo de Paris* announced on 25 November 1937 that whereas the Cagoule plot was a joke, indeed there *was* a "particularly dangerous man in France" – Marx Dormoy![40] Most of these publications insisted that Dormoy was obsessed with phantasms and portrayed conservatives as the genuine defenders of France against the true threat to French liberty – Communism. *L'Action française* characterized Dormoy as "that fool."[41] A key Cagoulard, Aristide Corre, stated in November of 1937 that conservative journalist Maurice Pujo was using ridicule to persuade the French public that the Cagoule was a figment of Dormoy's imagination.[42] Political cartoons also satirized him. One pictured Dormoy running around Paris finding bombs he had planted himself and wearing a black hood while taking aim at innocent conservative targets. In another the strands of his famous beard composed the word "plot" (*complot*). Andre-René Charlet's cartoon for Jacques Doriot's newspaper, *L'Émancipation nationale*, 24 September 1938, is typical of the ridicule Dormoy faced when he exposed the Cagoule. Charlet depicted Dormoy wearing a hat and black suit with a stereotyped Jewish nose, making him look more Jewish even than Léon Blum, who was pictured in the third cell of the cartoon. Conservatives thereby could dismiss the Cagoule as a delusional conspiracy conjured up by a group of Jews and designed to damage the right.[43] Dormoy's portrayal in the media as Jewish was thus well established before World War II and was used as a rhetorical strategy to diminish the relevance of his exposure of the Cagoule and his influence on public opinion. An interesting interplay thus occurred between the Cagoule, which used terrorism as a means of communication with the public, and the right-wing journalists who ensured the Cagoule's success by convincing the French there was nothing to fear except perhaps Dormoy himself.[44]

No stranger to controversy, Dormoy never shied away from a good fight. This was evident on 5 April 1938 when an incident occurred in the *Chambre des députés*. During a debate over finances, taxes, unemployment, and how to prepare for the war on the horizon, conservative deputies attacked Pierre Mendès-France, the undersecretary of the treasury. Mendès-France was Jewish and antisemitic insults began to fly especially from members of the far right. When a deputy from Brittany made a menacing gesture and yelled, "Down with the Jews," and "France for the French," Dormoy leaped to his feet and bellowed in reply "What a bunch of bastards! A Jew is certainly worth as much as a Breton!"[45] To avert chaos, the *président de la chambre*, Édouard Herriot, suspended the session.

Dormoy's declaration was particularly controversial. To compare a Jew favorably to a Breton was tantamount to sacrilege in the eyes of many French people. Brittany was a staunchly Catholic region, an oft-romanticized land of peasants and traditional French values. This was in sharp contrast to the popular stereotype of the urban, cosmopolitan, and money-grubbing Jew. Dormoy's statement reflected his devotion to the values of the French Revolution that emancipated and gave citizenship to France's Jews, but it mired him in more controversy and derision in the papers. Right-wing opponents quickly compiled demographic information from World War I to compare the number of Jews and Bretons who died in that war and calculated that in fact one Breton was worth 236 Jews.[46] The walls of the stock exchange were covered in caricatures of Blum wearing traditional Breton dress, and the antisemitic propagandist Charles Legrand attacked Dormoy, saying, "You ignore Brittany, land of the Druids, for the land of Judas.... A Breton, Mr. Dormoy, is French: your Jews aren't of our blood. They're not of our race."[47] The right-wing daily *Le*

Nouveau Cri proclaimed, "A Breton is home here, but a Jew is nothing but a leech from the Dead Sea."[48] Thus Blum's government and Dormoy's days as interior minister ended in a maelstrom of political conflict and antisemitism.

Dormoy, like Blum, knew it was unrealistic to believe that France could avoid war with Germany. In a speech he gave in March 1939, Dormoy debated those members of his own party who criticized Blum for supporting Prime Minister Édouard Daladier. Blum and Dormoy, while lamenting Daladier's repeal of many of the economic reforms the Popular Front had enacted, agreed with Daladier's increasingly tough stance toward Germany and efforts to mobilize the French economy for war.[49] Dormoy stated that he was willing to fight to the end for peace. But, he said, even though some Socialists dismissed the need to rebuild France's military, they were people who would "accept any sort of capitulation" whereas "we will not accept servitude" to Germany.[50] "What are you going to do? One would have to be truly naïve to think that if war breaks out, France could somehow remain neutral." To preserve the peace, it was necessary to mobilize for war, and if France took bold action, the situation might still be saved. But across Europe, Dormoy said, "The greatest problem is that of liberty, which is the most precious of our possessions." Prescient words indeed.

DORMOY IN THE CRUCIBLE

Dormoy's forced residence at Montélimar in 1941 was ultimately tied to one of the darkest chapters of French history, Germany's humiliating defeat of France and the Armistice signed on 22 June 1940 that established the État français in Vichy under Pétain.[51] When war broke out in 1939, the French initially were certain that the Allies would win the war. The French had good reason to be confident. Despite the bloodletting of World War I in which 1.3 million Frenchmen lost their lives with over a million more disabled, the French economy expanded during the interwar period until the advent of the Great Depression in 1929. In 1939 France still represented a potent economic and military rival to Germany. Recent scholarship indicates that the fall of France in 1940 resulted primarily from poor decisions on the part of France's military leadership that led to the country's defeat. Observers throughout Europe and the Americas were shocked at the precipitous collapse of a country many admired as a beacon of Western culture and values.[52]

France during the first six months of the war settled into a period of inaction often referred to as the "*Drôle de guerre*" or "Phony War." Then, on 10 May 1940, the Germans invaded France, erupting with their tanks from the Ardennes on 15 May and driving to the coast by 20 May, thereby cutting the Allied Army in two and forcing the massive evacuation of British and French soldiers from Dunkirk. Although many French soldiers fought valiantly, they were outgunned and demoralized, and much of the French army broke ranks and retreated, often in chaos, before the advancing Germans. Hundreds of thousands of soldiers were captured and sent to German prison camps. The speed and magnitude of the debacle stunned everyone in France and observers worldwide. By late May nothing lay between the Germans and Paris.[53]

Paul Reynaud became prime minister in March of 1940. Although Reynaud was center-right in his politics he had shared Blum's and Dormoy's insistence in the late 1930s on a hard line against Germany. As it became apparent in May that the Germans were advancing on Paris, Reynaud, with the blessing of fellow center-right politician President Albert Lebrun, began shuffling generals, replacing Maurice Gamelin with Maxime Weygand in a desperate effort to find someone who would hold firm against the Germans. These generals, veterans of World War I, were convinced that France could not prevail against the superior might of the German military. The generals, well aware of the deep political divisions in France before the war, knew that many French troops were fighting the Germans out of a sense of duty but were sympathetic to the Nazi argument that only Germany could save Europe from the threat of Communism. Weygand continued to focus on defense and devoted much of his political capital to devising ways for the military to avoid being blamed for the defeat that he believed was only a matter of time.[54] Reynaud then reorganized his cabinet and asked Pétain to join his government, a serious mistake given that Philippe Pétain shared Weygand's defeatism and had already declared publicly that the war was lost. Panic ensued as refugees from Belgium and northern France began fleeing south before the German onslaught, clogging the roadways with cars, trucks, carriages, bicycles, carts, and columns of slow-moving people. No one, it seemed, had planned for an evacuation, and local institutions collapsed under the strain. Panic-stricken civilians were essentially left to their own devices.[55]

As it became evident that the shattered French army could not stop the German advance toward Paris, even government officials, municipal and national, abandoned the city and joined the throngs of people fleeing with whatever possessions they could carry. Six million civilians jammed the roads and made troop movements almost impossible. Many French soldiers also went south. The government declared Paris an open, undefended city and fled. On 14 June the Germans marched into Paris. That same day, the French government reassembled in Bordeaux. The next day, 15 June, the overwhelmed Reynaud turned in his resignation to President Albert Lebrun. To the general relief of the great majority of French people, including Lebrun, Pétain was waiting in the wings, ready to replace Reynaud and with a list of cabinet ministers tucked into his pocket. His fatherly demeanor, steely blue eyes, and reputation forged in World War I reassured people that in Pétain, France would at least have a leader of sufficient stature and resolve to negotiate a just peace with Hitler. Few among France's pre-war politicians felt able to oppose Pétain. The defeat had shocked them and shaken the faith of many in the Republic. Some stalwarts, such as Georges Mandel and Pierre Mèndes-France, tried to flee to North Africa aboard the *Massilia*, where they hoped to re-establish the legitimate French government and continue the fight, but more resigned themselves to defeat and an armistice with Germany, the solution Pétain favored.[56]

On 22 June General Charles Huntziger signed the Armistice on Pétain's behalf, which had been dictated to him by the Germans with little or no room for negotiation. He did so in the same railway car near Compiègne where the defeated Germans had signed the Armistice that ended World War I. Hitler insisted on this spectacle, his revenge for the despised Treaty of Versailles. By the terms of the Armistice, France was divided with the Germans taking the larger and more industrialized regions in the north and along the Atlantic coast (see Map 1.1). Vichy retained control over about one-third of the nation's territory in the south and partial authority over the civilian population in the Occupied Zone. The Germans assumed responsibility for France's defense and the French army was demobilized. Vichy retained the important Mediterranean port cities of Marseille, Toulon, and Nice, but no Atlantic ports. From that point on, the Line of Demarcation became another means to keep France quiescent, as the Germans threatened to invade the unoccupied territory, as they ultimately did late in 1942.[57]

The National Revolution was the new regime's ideological program, although many of its tenets were conceived prior to the war. Grounded in a deep opposition to the democratic Third Republic (1870–1940), the National Revolution demanded moral and political renewal designed to restore France to an imagined idyllic, pastoral, and more Catholic and moral past. Many Vichy politicians were certain that France had become decadent under the Third Republic. Rejecting individualism, Vichy leaders exalted family and

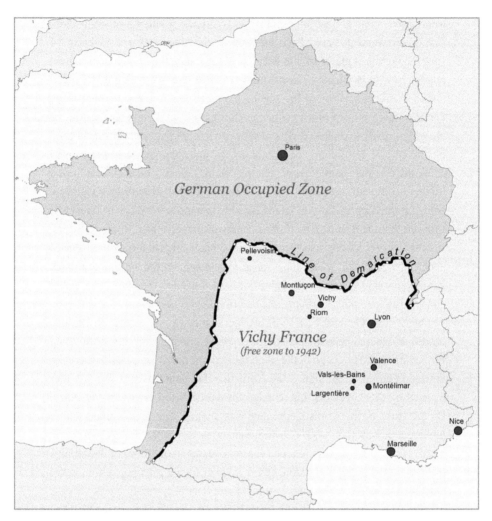

Map 1.1. France and the Line of Demarcation, 1940]. Thomas Chapman, ODU Digital Cartography Lab. Data Source: Stanford University Spatial History Project.

motherhood, work and community, the Catholic religion, and the traditional values they associated with agrarian France prior to the French Revolution. Vichy's motto, seen on posters and propaganda throughout wartime France, was *"Travail, Famille, Patrie"* or "Work, Family, Fatherland." Vichy added to the agenda of the National Revolution a cult of personality surrounding Pétain, who was depicted as France's stern but kindly *pater familias* (father of the family). National Revolution ideology also included state-sponsored antisemitism that eventually led to collaboration with the Germans in deporting

Jews from France. Historian Julian Jackson notes that "Vichy was a regime of persecution and repression" whose leaders were determined to punish people they deemed responsible for France's defeat in 1940.[58] Although the National Revolution cost many lives, it was never enacted as a coherent program because its proponents, most notably conservatives in Vichy and collaborationists in Paris, developed competing political agendas that rendered it moribund, although this reality was not apparent in 1940–1.

Pétain chose the spa town of Vichy as his capital, primarily because it had adequate hotel space to house the government officials and their staff. Vichy was also safely distant from the Line of Demarcation and was politically conservative. France was to pay the costs of the Occupation, which the Germans calculated at exorbitant levels designed to impoverish France while funding the German war effort. French troops remained ensconced in German prisoner-of-war camps, hostages to ensure France's compliance with the Armistice's terms. Pétain explained that he decided, even at his advanced age of eighty-four, to sign the Armistice and accept leadership of the French state because the alternative, direct German occupation of all French territory, would be even worse. Meanwhile, he would share the suffering and humiliation of ordinary French people and eventually lead France to renewed glory. Most French people saw him as a hero who had saved the country from the worst ravages of defeat, and many who had opposed the war from the beginning rejoiced that it was now finally coming to an end.[59]

General Charles de Gaulle, by contrast, was not yet viewed in 1940 as the heroic liberator he became at the end of the war. De Gaulle vehemently opposed the Armistice and capitulation to Germany. When it became apparent that the French leadership had rejected his call to carry on the war from outside of metropolitan France, principally from the French colonies, de Gaulle made the fateful decision to go into exile in Great Britain. As Julian Jackson explains, "The core of Pétain's appeal to the French people in 1940 was his decision to remain on French *soil* to defend his compatriots, to defend French lives, while de Gaulle left France to defend what he later called his '*idea* of France.'"[60] In fact, although Pétain stripped him of his rank and ordered de Gaulle condemned to death in absentia, many French people suspected that the two men were secretly acting in tandem to save France (which was untrue). On 18 June the day after he arrived in London, de Gaulle made a fateful speech, a reply to Pétain's statement the previous day announcing an armistice with Germany. De Gaulle's speech, broadcast on the British BBC radio network, called upon French men and women to continue to resist the Germans, by rallying to de Gaulle's side in London if they could, and if not, by clandestine acts of resistance in France. Few French people heeded de Gaulle's appeal in 1940 because most were dubious about the prospects of successfully resisting the Nazi juggernaut and preferred to put their faith in Pétain. The 18 June speech, however, did establish de Gaulle as a principal figure in the nascent French Resistance.[61]

The French public blamed the politicians who had led France in the 1930s, and especially the Popular Front, for what historian Marc Bloch called France's "strange defeat."[62] The Third Republic and its politicians were accused of having ignored the rising German threat in the years preceding the outbreak of war and of hewing too closely to the "appeasement" policy of Great Britain. France's leaders had spent too much time uselessly bickering among themselves while putting their faith in a British ally that could not be trusted to defend France's interests. They ignored the advice of right-wing politician Marcel Déat, that Frenchmen should not die to save Danzig, and when the Germans invaded Poland, France honored its treaty with the Poles and declared war on Germany. The pro-war *bellicistes*, many people in France were convinced in 1940, had thus hurled their country into a conflict for which France was totally unprepared, when they would have done better to have jettisoned the British, made their peace with Hitler, or even joined with him in his crusade to crush the Bolsheviks and remake Europe along National-Socialist lines.[63]

In fact, Blum and Dormoy had been very worried about the German threat. As interior minister, Dormoy contended with German and Italian spies who worked to undermine French war preparations and bolster the power of fascist sympathizers in France. The Popular Front initiated a rearmament policy in 1936, but was hampered because the Socialist leaders were beholden to a rank-and-file membership that included many devoted pacifists who opposed rearmament.[64] In 1940 when France paid the price for the political disarray and poor military decisions that led to the swift collapse of the French defenses against Germany, it was not the generals and their unwarranted faith in the outmoded "Maginot Line" but rather the Popular Front and the Socialists that many French people blamed.

Despite the contempt that the right heaped upon Blum and Dormoy, the pair exhibited exemplary courage during the final days of the war. They were two of the last French leaders to abandon Paris and then only under great duress. Blum felt duty bound to remain in Paris as long as possible, hoping for a miracle and reluctant to abandon his beloved City of Lights to the German invaders. As late as 9 June, even as his friends, aware of the danger he incurred as a Jew and a Socialist in lingering, tried to persuade him to leave Paris, he could not believe that other ministers whose lives were less at risk than his own would flee. Blum wrote: "And yet departing did more than wound me in my most cherished sentiments; in my eyes it was also symbolic in a sense. To leave home, leave Paris; but when would I again see my house and my city? Wasn't leaving, for me as for others, an admission to oneself of defeat; and did it not in some fashion render that defeat irremediable?"[65] Blum's good friend and former minister of agriculture, Georges Monnet, telephoned him repeatedly to pressure him to leave Paris. Finally, late in the night Blum agreed to depart. He reached Montluçon near daybreak on 10 June where Dormoy was waiting for him.[66]

Blum and Dormoy didn't stay in Montluçon for long, however. They returned to Paris on the 11th to find the city-center abandoned. They expected, even at this late date, to find the French leadership still in place. Desperately they telephoned the offices of the various ministries and got no response. No one answered at Reynaud's office or at his private residence. They hunted down William Bullitt, the United States' ambassador to France, who was rushing to get American citizens out of the city before the Germans arrived. Bullitt's citizenship rendered him safe from German reprisals, but he advised his French visitors to depart. Blum and Dormoy became increasingly demoralized.[67]

They went to the Chambre des députés. When they entered, they found the building entirely deserted, save for a lone legislative page whom they asked, "Well, everyone has left then?"[68] The fellow responded that yes, everyone was gone. Blum and Dormoy could not believe their ears. "There is really not a single person here?"[69] The young man replied that there remained a lone staff member who had stayed behind to oversee the building. They could find him on the third floor. Blum and Dormoy climbed the stairs and located the employee, whom Blum described with irony as "abandoned as a hostage or a guide" for the advancing Germans. He informed Blum and Dormoy that the legislators and ministers were headed to Bordeaux. At this point the two men separated, as Dormoy needed to go to a working-class neighborhood of Paris, Belleville, near the Père Lachaise Cemetery, to fetch the mother of one of his staff members. Dormoy had promised to bring the woman with him when he left Paris.[70]

Blum returned home, where he spent an hour in his office collecting his papers, the last time he would work amidst familiar surroundings and possessions, as the Germans later ransacked his Paris residence and destroyed or dispersed his belongings. Dormoy returned from Belleville, struck by the contrast between the suburb, which he found animated and in a celebratory mood now that the war was finally coming to an end, even if it was an ignominious one, and the desolate city center. He and Blum ate a hasty meal and left Paris, each in his own chauffeured vehicle. Dormoy had packed many of his personal papers in his car and asked his chauffeur to take them to the chauffeur's home so that they would be safely out of the hands of Dormoy's enemies, German or French. Dormoy selected, however, several hundred especially sensitive documents that he stuffed into a briefcase and took with him. Dormoy and Blum reached Montluçon on the morning of 12 June.[71]

By 15 June the pair were in Bordeaux, where the panicked French government had reassembled. Blum and Dormoy knew their enemies would be gathering like vultures, waiting for the Third Republic in its death throes to pass away. Deputy Prime Minister Camille Chautemps introduced a resolution to the National Assembly calling for talks with the Third Reich on terms for ending hostilities. His resolution won widespread support even though Lebrun was against it. Reynaud, who vehemently opposed the armistice resolution, resigned and Lebrun appointed Pétain in Reynaud's place. Most people, even opponents of Nazism, seemed to have concluded that Britain's downfall was imminent and that France needed to sue for the best peace terms possible while there was still time.[72]

In early July the French government re-convened in Vichy. Blum and Dormoy, who were inseparable at this point, arrived in Vichy on 4 July and went straight to one of the casinos where the Socialists were holding meetings. There they tried to persuade the members of their party to vote against the Armistice, although they only won over a minority of them. Meanwhile, they endured continual threats and harassment from "ultras" on the right such as Doriot and his PPF foot soldiers, who cornered Dormoy on the afternoon of 9 July outside the casino. Doriot yelled in Dormoy's face, "I will have your hide."[73]

The matter on the table before the National Assembly was a proposal to revise the French Constitution. On 9 July Pierre Laval, who was closely allied with Pétain, announced on the casino floor that he spoke for Pétain in calling for constitutional reform. Laval, who had begun his political career as a Socialist but drifted to the right during the 1930s, served two terms as France's prime minister, January 1931 to February 1932, and June 1935 to January 1936. He never forgave Blum or the Popular Front for evicting him from power in 1936 and was delighted in 1940 to have the opportunity to punish his political enemies while bringing to a close the Third Republic that he considered to be hopelessly corrupt and outdated.[74] In the casino at Vichy Laval roundly condemned the Third Republic and argued that France could only be revived through an authoritarian government under a strong leader – Pétain – whom Hitler would respect, and with Laval as Pétain's chief minister, of course. German success in the war derived from the Nazi reforms of government, and the future of Europe was German leadership. If France was to have any hope of taking part in this new order in any role other than as a conquered nation, she would have to imitate Germany in order to partner with her. Horrified at Laval's open advocacy of dictatorship and repudiation of the values of the French Revolution, Dormoy demanded the floor, and asked for a resolution in support of the Republic. Laval opposed vehemently Dormoy's motion. Many of Dormoy's staunchest allies were missing, trapped on the ill-fated *Massilia* and even Dormoy's former foes, the Communists, who would have rejected Laval's measure, had been banned from the National Assembly. On 10 July 1940 the National Assembly voted 569 to 80 (with 12 abstentions) to give Pétain full authority to revise the constitution, effectively ending the Third Republic.[75] Blum and Dormoy were among the minority who voted against the constitutional revision. Blum wrote, "What a scene! How I wish that the memory of it could be erased; how I wish, above all, that I could forget it myself."[76] Chaos ensued and Blum's and Dormoy's lives were threatened. Dormoy ushered Blum out of the casino through a secret door using his strong arms to protect his friend. At that point the two defenders of the French Republic separated. Dormoy returned to Montluçon while Blum retreated to a friend's home near Toulouse.[77]

On 17 July 1940 – thus only a week after assuming power – Pétain ordered the arrest of a group of politicians from the now defunct Third Republic. In Montluçon, Dormoy continued to function as the city's mayor until he was ejected from office on 14 September and arrested on the 25th of the same month. As the 1st of October issue of the official bulletin of the Vichy Ministry of the Interior noted, Marx Dormoy, along with Vincent Auriol, Jules Moch, Salomon Grumbach, and Abraham Schrameck, all stalwarts of the Popular Front, had been placed under "administrative internment" in Pellevoisin, which is in the Department of Indre, about halfway between Angers and Montluçon in central France.[78] Dormoy spent all but an hour a day locked in *Chambre* #28, in solitary confinement. Prisoners were forbidden to speak with each other, even during meals, and were permitted only one short walk in the garden per day. Friends and relatives had to receive permission from Vichy to visit and the poor conditions of hygiene were deplorable. Prisoners had to be escorted to the toilet and there were no showers available, and no heat.[79] The prison was strictly guarded, bars were placed over the windows, passers-by were warned not to approach the building, and any attempt to escape would result in the escapee being shot. Perhaps most painful for Dormoy, however, aside from the severe tooth infection which threatened his health, was that Jeanne was refused permission to visit. Dormoy complained in one note to the warden that he had not seen his sister in over sixty days. In another he asked that she be allowed to visit after a hard-won visitation had been revoked due to an "unfortunate incident that I regret," probably an outburst of some sort resulting from Dormoy's frustration over the conditions at Pellevoisin.[80]

The expulsion of Pierre Laval from Pétain's government on 13 December 1940 led to an improvement in Dormoy's situation. Pétain ordered Laval expelled from his cabinet and arrested because Laval was pressing him to collaborate more closely with the Germans than Pétain knew the French public was willing to accept. Laval had engineered a handshake between Pétain and Hitler when the two men met at Montoire in October, and most of the French population reacted with horror. Pétain preferred to jettison Laval rather than risk his own reputation. Also, Laval had a bad habit of blowing cigarette smoke in Pétain's face during cabinet meetings, which annoyed him to no end.[81] Neither the Maréchal nor his new vice-president of the Council of Ministers (Pétain was head of state and president of the council), Pierre-Étienne Flandin, bore any particular fondness for the detained politicians.[82] Still, Flandin and Admiral François Darlan, who replaced Flandin in March of 1941, like Pétain, were unwilling to trade the lives of the political prisoners too cheaply. Instead, they intended to use them as bargaining chips. Vichy insisted that unless the Germans relaxed the terms of the Armistice rather than ratcheting up their enormous economic demands, Vichy would refuse to hold the show trials the Germans wanted.[83]

Between January and March 1941, as it became evident that the Germans were not going to make any concessions, the Vichy government made a triage among the Third Republic prisoners it had arrested the previous autumn. Those whom Vichy considered to be more dangerous, prominent, or compromised in the debacle of the Third Republic and France's defeat, such as Léon Blum and Paul Reynaud, were to be put on trial. The "smaller fry," including Marx Dormoy, who were too important to be released but not important enough to feature at the show trial at Riom except as witnesses, were restricted to house arrest. Léon Blum was held at the Chateau de Burrassol in Limoges, which had been converted into a prison. To send the message that Vichy could, if it wished, release Dormoy and the others should the Germans continue to interpret the Armistice as harshly as possible, Vichy decided to move the prisoners from Pellevoisin to somewhat more comfortable accommodations at Vals-les-Bains. On 1 January 1941 they were taken to the thermal station town in the Ardèche Mountains.[84] After two weeks in Aubenas waiting for a new prison to be prepared, on 13 January Dormoy and his fellow prisoners were transferred to the Grand Hôtel des Bains in Vals-les-Bains. It offered improved conditions in rooms equipped with central heating, but this was of little consolation to Dormoy who missed Jeanne and complained he would die of boredom. On 20 March 1941 Vichy eased the terms of Dormoy's confinement further. He was transferred to the Relais de l'Empereur in Montélimar, where he was no longer guarded day and night and could walk around town and take his meals in the hotel dining room. By May Jeanne was even allowed to visit regularly. In July she was permitted to reside at the Relais and took a room on the same floor as Dormoy. Things were far from perfect, but at least Dormoy had a little more freedom. Even so, he worried, with good reason, that he was vulnerable and might be targeted for assassination.[85]

CHAPTER TWO

1941: A Long, Hot Summer

Late in the afternoon before he was killed, Dormoy had strolled through the streets of Montélimar on his way to the barber shop where he had his hair cut. Montélimar is a pleasant town, with winding streets and alleys, as well as a tree-lined central boulevard, and a small wooded park that Dormoy would have had to pass on the way to his barber. The sweet smell of nougat would have wafted over the city; Montélimar was known then and now as the "nougat capital of France." The stroll, however, would not have been entirely relaxing for him, as agents of Vichy discretely shadowed him wherever he went. His face and famous bushy beard were instantly recognizable to most French people. Dormoy knew he had few friends or supporters in Montélimar, and townsfolk not infrequently heckled him with cries of "bandit!" and "delinquent!" when he ventured out to purchase a newspaper or stop in a local café.

Montélimar had not been Dormoy's choice as a place of residence.[1] He had wanted to be permitted to live in his beloved Montluçon and the home he shared with his sister Jeanne. He knew that was unlikely, however, because Montluçon was a bastion of socialism as well as his political power base. In Montluçon his devoted constituents would have offered him a measure of protection from supporters of Pétain who were hostile to him. He may also have been better able to resist Vichy's agenda for France, a possibility that Pétain would never entertain. Dormoy had submitted to Vichy a list of cities where he preferred to reside, including Lyon, Toulouse, and Clermont-Ferrand. Pétain rejected them all, and instead opted for Montélimar, a small and politically conservative city whose leaders were noted for their enthusiastic support of the National Revolution. By July Dormoy ventured from the Relais much less often than he had when he first arrived.

As he headed alone back toward the Relais after his haircut in the late afternoon sun on 25 July, Dormoy likely pondered his situation and that of France. Even during his darkest days of incarceration at Pellevoisin, Dormoy exchanged dozens of letters with Léon Blum in which the two old friends and political allies discussed at length the catastrophe of the French defeat, the division and occupation of France, and the disastrous trajectory of the National Revolution. Their conversations via letter continued while he was in Montélimar.[2] Their correspondence reveals not only the prescience and intelligence of both men, but also how they attempted to bolster each other's spirits while incarcerated, Blum near Riom where he awaited trial on charges that could ultimately bring him the death sentence, and Dormoy at Vals-les-Bains, where in February he was subpoenaed to testify at Blum's trial. The expectation of facing hostile questioning before a kangaroo court in Riom, where he would be pressured to incriminate his old friend, must have been a frequent preoccupation. Still, Dormoy faced more immediate and pressing concerns about his own safety in Montélimar.

While interior minister in 1937–8, Dormoy was the target of frequent death threats. Although he was a popular figure within the Socialist Party, many conservatives in France despised Dormoy. The more fanatical the conservative, the more extreme was their venom toward Dormoy. The primary reason for that hatred was Dormoy's battle against the "ultras" of the AF and its violent offshoot, the Cagoule.[3] Now Dormoy was vulnerable, marooned in a city filled with supporters of Pétain who bore a visceral hatred of all Third Republic politicians, those *barbus* (beards) on whose shoulders they placed the blame for France's defeat in 1940. Such conservatives had a special animus toward Socialists like Dormoy, whom they conflated with the despised "Bolsheviks" they were certain menaced the very foundations of French civilization. Vichy's agents tailed him but gave no sign that they intended to shield Dormoy from potential attackers who might be stalking the streets of Montélimar. Nor were Dormoy's fears of assassination mere paranoia. His worst enemies, including Jacques Doriot and former Cagoulard Robert Jurquet de la Salle, who in July of 1940 had publicly threatened Dormoy in Vichy, were now working for Pétain or heading their own political parties and paramilitary bands in the Occupied Zone.[4] Dormoy might not be on trial for his life like Blum (yet) but he could be put on trial at any time and, what was probably worse for Dormoy, he was going to have to testify at Blum's trial – assuming he wasn't assassinated in Montélimar first.

Figure 2.1. Le Relais de L'Empereur. ©Fonds Combier Musée Niépce Chalon-sur-Saône.

The Relais (see Figure 2.1), Dormoy's home and prison in Montélimar, was an imposing gray stone building constructed in 1758 as a relay post at a strategic crossroads linking Paris, Lyon, and Marseille. The hotel became known as Le Relais de l'Empereur after Emperor Napoleon Bonaparte lodged there four times, including in 1814 on his journey into exile on the island of Elba. In 1941 the Relais was a privately owned hotel commanding one of the principal *places* of Montélimar. Its austere exterior, especially on the side adjoining the sidewalk and boulevard, gave the long, rectangular building a fortress-like appearance. It boasted large windows for the guest rooms and a dining room that looked out on a walled courtyard with a parking area, a small garden, and a patio with chairs, tables, and a trellis, where guests could smoke and sip coffee or aperitifs when the weather was warm. The hotel's interior had a rustic ambiance, more like a rural inn than an urban hotel, with dark ceiling timbers on the first floor. The tables and chairs of the spacious dining room were simple, wooden affairs, but it was pleasant, clean, and well lit, with an imposing stone fireplace at the end of the room, where Dormoy preferred to sit, his back toward the fireplace. From there he could keep an eye on the guests who came to sample the food in the hotel's restaurant, which enjoyed a strong reputation for its excellent cuisine and wine cellar. The Relais was known for its lavender-flavored cocktails and iced nougat parfait, regional specialties that in better economic times attracted locals and tourists alike to its restaurant. The rooms had their own bathrooms and toilets, luxuries compared to the amenities at most French hotels in 1941 and certainly better than the conditions Dormoy endured at Pellevoisin.

Most of the hotel's forty rooms were empty, not surprising even though it was the height of the French vacation season. Few tourists from the northern Occupied Zone were flocking to Montélimar to buy nougat and sightsee before heading to the resort cities of the Côte d'Azur. Despite the relative calm in 1941 France, Europe remained locked in a conflict between right and left, fascism and socialism, authoritarianism and democracy, that Vichy France could not hope to escape indefinitely. Anxiety and distrust spread throughout the country like a bad odor carried on the warm breezes of summer. As the mounting costs of the Occupation emptied the wallets of those fortunate enough to have jobs, and with food and other basic necessities rationed, few French people, in Occupied France or in the Vichy Zone, had the money or the inclination to travel for pleasure in the summer of 1941. The atmosphere at the hotel must have been tense, as most of the dwindling number of guests were staying there on their way to somewhere else, or because, like Dormoy, they had nowhere else to go.[5]

As was his habit, at 1:00 p.m. on 25 July Dormoy came downstairs to the dining room to have his midday meal. Jeanne joined him, as did Bretty Dangel, who frequently shared his table. Bretty was the mistress of Third Republic politician Georges Mandel. Mandel was not a Socialist and Dormoy and Mandel had not always seen eye-to-eye during the Popular Front government toward which the more conservative Mandel bore serious reservations. Bretty had not been permitted to follow Mandel to prison where he, like Blum, awaited trial. Instead, she, along with Mandel's adolescent daughter, Claude, and the family's Senegalese manservant, Baba Diallo, were ordered to reside at the Relais. When Dormoy arrived in Montélimar, he formed an alliance with Bretty, who was happy to find an intelligent and supportive friend in Dormoy. As Jeanne observed to the police after Dormoy's death, he always made a great effort to project patient, friendly good humor toward those around him. He and Bretty watched out for each other and now, with the addition of Jeanne to their circle, there was another pair of eyes that could keep a look out for suspicious visitors.

After the meal, at about 3:15 p.m., Jeanne and Marx went up to his room to listen to an English radio program, which technically was illegal. No one hindered them, however, and Marx continued to nurture a keen interest in the course of the war and the political situation in France, of which he kept apprised via visits and letters from his old friends, political allies who were still free to circulate in the Vichy Zone, and the newspapers and magazines he read as well. At the conclusion of the program, Jeanne retired to her room to rest and Marx went out to get a haircut. When he returned that evening, he, Jeanne, and Bretty had a light supper and sat on the patio basking in the evening air. No one knows what they discussed, although it is likely that worries for their own safety put a damper on their enjoyment of the long summer twilight. Finally, at about 10:00 p.m., while the last of the twilight glow still lingered, Jeanne decided to go to bed. Marx asked her to fetch the *Journal de Genève*, as he intended to sit on the patio a bit longer. When she didn't come down for some time, he grew worried and went to find her. Fortunately, it was a false alarm – she simply couldn't find the *Journal* amidst the many other newspapers, magazines, and papers that littered his room. Before bidding him good night, Jeanne remarked on the chirping of the crickets, which seemed quite loud that evening. Marx shrugged off the comment, then picked up the *Journal* to read downstairs. Jeanne headed to her room. It was the last time she saw her brother alive.

WARNING SIGNS

In June and July of 1941 France was awash in rumors of threats against the lives of Third Republic ministers, especially toward former politicians from the Socialist and Radical parties, who had played prominent roles before the war. German Ambassador Otto Abetz was reflecting Hitler's views when he insisted that Pétain punish the "warmongers" who had urged France to declare war against Germany. The "big fish" such as Mandel, Blum, and Édouard Daladier were to be put on trial. "Lesser" ministers such as Dormoy would be imprisoned indefinitely as hostages to ensure France's good behavior. The Germans and their supporters in the press demanded that the trials begin as soon as possible and result in executions. Heads needed to roll for France's audacity in "forcing" Germany into war.[6] None of these detainees, pawns in the hands of Vichy and the Germans alike, were safe. Ironically, however, those still incarcerated, such as Mandel and Reynaud, were more secure during the summer of 1941 than those permitted greater freedom like Dormoy, and Vichy knew this because Pétain's ministers and the *Sûreté*, the French equivalent of the FBI, had been warned.

RESTIVE CAGOULARDS AND COLLABORATIONISTS

On 21 May 1941 the police searched the offices in Vichy and Paris of Dr. Henri Martin, the inveterate plotter who had run the "intelligence services" (2e bureau) for the Cagoule in the 1930s. Martin was a medical doctor and a freelance trafficker in intelligence. Far to the right in his politics, Martin could match even Eugène Deloncle, whom he knew well from his years in the Cagoule, in the plots he hatched. In 1941 Martin was expanding his already voluminous collection of files and notes on pretty much everyone on the right or the left. Martin's hatred of the German occupiers overcame the fear and disgust he felt toward the left in his own country. During the war he spied on his former friends in Paris, including Deloncle, and on the government in Vichy.[7]

Dr. Martin added a note to his files stating that his sources had recently informed him that Deloncle was planning on sending "punitive expeditions" to Vichy, to assassinate in particular former ministers, such as Vincent Auriol, Marx Dormoy, and Georges Mandel, who had opposed the Armistice. Martin furnished this information to his contacts in Pétain's cabinet, but those surrounding the Maréchal "unfortunately did not want to believe it."[8] By 21 May, however, Martin reported that the police had received further intelligence that confirmed Martin's original notification. According to Martin, "a certain disquiet" resulted in Vichy, although that unease did not lead to any police protection for Dormoy.

The anxiety in Vichy was understandable. If Deloncle was behind plans for an assassination or a coup, everyone knew that he would follow through. Deloncle had founded and headed the CSAR, and although he failed to overturn the Popular Front in 1937, it was not for lack of trying. As Deloncle himself expressed in his 1941 manifesto, *Les idées et l'action*, ideas were fine in their place, but at heart he was a man of action.[9] Deloncle was present for the fateful session of the French National Assembly on 10 July 1940, when the Third Republic he so despised ended. That very day he wrote in a letter to his wife that he was "full of joy" because "the Republic is no more. Today I watched these puppets kill themselves. I observed their agony, me, whom they persecuted. My dream is half-realized, that for which you and I suffered so much. If you had seen their faces grimacing with fear, sweating with infamy, how great would have been your joy."[10] The question now was how he intended to fulfill his dream to create a strong, autocratic French government modeled upon and allied with those of Italy and Germany that he so admired. As he boasted to his wife, he had played a role in "the affair" and helped to bring about this triumph, the collapse of the Third Republic. In the spring of 1941, everything he wanted seemed finally to be within reach.

The creation of the Vichy regime meant, however, that Deloncle and his Cagoulard allies, as well as other pre-war leaders of extreme-right movements, such as Colonel François de La Rocque and Jacques Doriot, faced thorny strategic choices as they simultaneously cooperated to achieve their political agendas and competed to advance their own careers. The problem was that there were now two sources of patronage and funds, Vichy and the German occupiers, but it was impossible to curry favor with the one without the risk of incurring the wrath of the other. Pétain and those closest to him were preoccupied with advancing the "National Revolution," the conservative renewal of French society and culture that they believed would lead France out of the morass of defeat. For Pétain, softening the terms of the Armistice, obtaining the liberation of the two million French prisoners of war in Germany, and safeguarding the French empire in Africa required a delicate balance. Vichy needed to meet the escalating German demands for French money and labor without sacrificing an iota more of what remained of French sovereignty than was necessary to keep the Germans at bay. Convinced that Germany would win the war, Pétain recognized the need for and the advantages of collaboration. But collaboration for Pétain was a matter of expediency. He intended France to partner with Germany, and the National Revolution to be a uniquely French style of autocratic government based on traditional French values and history.[11]

Neither the Germans nor the French collaborationists in Paris shared Pétain's vision of collaboration. The Germans promoted collaboration when it was in their interests, but the Reich had no intention of allowing France to renew itself as a united, strong partner in the new Europe that the Germans were creating. Rather, they wanted to keep France a weak and humiliated source of manpower and resources for the German war effort. And they needed a calm and stable France as they waged the "Battle of Britain" and prepared for the invasion of the Soviet Union. Pétain and the collaborationists in Paris alike were deluding themselves. No type of revolution, "National" or otherwise, was part of the German program for France. Hitler did not want France as a "partner" in Europe's "New Order," but rather intended to keep France subjugated after the war ended. The Germans used the collaborationists as a threat with which to pressure Pétain when he made too many demands or seemed to be getting overly independent – the Germans could, after all, change horses and elevate one of the collaborationist leaders to head the French state in place of Pétain.[12] Such a "regime change" was exactly what men such as Deloncle dreamed of, their reverential rhetoric about "our venerated Leader Maréchal Pétain" notwithstanding.[13]

A few former Cagoulards, most notably Commander Georges Loustaunau-Lacau, fled to London and joined forces with General Charles de Gaulle. Others, such as Gabriel Jeantet, Raphaël Alibert, Colonel Georges Groussard, and François Méténier, remained by the side of the Maréchal, believing that Pétain's program of renewal would succeed. Deloncle initially placed his hopes in the Maréchal as well. It quickly became apparent, however, that Deloncle was too addicted to intrigue to gain Pétain's trust or win a position in the Vichy government. Finding himself unemployed in Vichy, he instead pursued German patronage in the City of Lights.[14]

In Paris Deloncle rounded up some of the remaining stalwarts such as Jean Filliol, Jacques Corrèze, André Tenaille, and General Paul Lavigne-Delville, who shared his disappointment with Vichy, and on 1 September 1940 created the *Mouvement social révolutionnaire*. The MSR was "the first collaborationist movement established in Paris during the German occupation."[15] The organization's ideology was both nationalist and Socialist, in conscious imitation of German National Socialism, but it was also defined by what it sought to expunge from the "true" France: Freemasons, Jews, capitalism, individualism, and the three hallmarks of the French Revolution, liberty, equality, and fraternity. Like Pétain's National Revolution, Deloncle's MSR had little use for anything in French culture since 1789, including the emancipation of the Jews.[16]

In his quest for German patronage, Deloncle drew closer to Pierre Laval. Laval, architect of the Armistice and the Vichy regime, had taken refuge with his German sponsors in Paris after his expulsion from Pétain's cabinet on 13 December 1940 in what the Germans called the "Putsch of Vichy." In 1941 Laval sought allies among the collaborationist movements – Deloncle's MSR, Doriot's PPF, and Marcel Déat's *Front révolutionnaire nationale*, although Laval never managed to persuade Doriot to join him. With the blessing of the Germans, irritated at Pétain's unexpected show of independence, Laval organized the disparate collaborationist movements in Paris into a single coalition, the *Rassemblement nationale populaire* (RNP), created on 1 February 1941. Meanwhile, during the summer of 1941, Deloncle was able to realize another cherished project when he and Déat created the *Légion des volontaires français contre le bolchevisme* (LVF), which staged its first rally on 18 July in Paris' main indoor arena, the *Vélôdrome d'Hiver*. Deloncle, president of the LVF, officiated.[17] In order to hold together his unruly, radical, and violent followers in the MSR, Deloncle needed to do more than preside over quasi-military parades.

Figure 2.2. Charles Chenevier in his office. Amis de la Fondation pour la Mémoire de la Déportation de l'Allier, http://www.afmd-allier.com/PBCPPlayer.asp?ID=776564 (accessed 14 March 2019).

He needed to demonstrate his power. What better way than to assassinate a prominent enemy in the Vichy Zone?

Vichy received another alert regarding the danger that collaborationists and their extremist foot soldiers posed to the interned politicians from the Third Republic, and perhaps even to the Vichy government itself. This warning came from a more creditable source than Dr. Martin. In late June of 1941 Superintendent Charles Chenevier was on assignment in Paris (see Figure 2.2). According to the terms of the Armistice, the Vichy regime retained broad authority to govern the lives of French civilians throughout France, including in the Occupied Zone. In reality the ability of Pétain and his ministers even to travel across the Line of Demarcation, let alone exercise power on the other side of that border, depended on the occupiers. But most of the time it was in German interests to allow French officials to bear the burden, and the onus, of policing civilian affairs throughout France. French officials, including members of the various branches of the Sûreté, the French National Police, worked in Occupied Paris. Chenevier, as a senior officer of the Sûreté before the war, followed his superiors, Pierre Mondanel and Jean Belin, to Vichy in June of 1940, but continued to investigate crimes all over France. He often worked in Paris because he had been based there before the war and still had an excellent network of contacts and informers among the criminal underworld.

Charles Chenevier was born on 2 November 1901. His father, Cyril Chenevier, joined the military and when Charles was born Cyril was stationed in Montélimar. Charles was an only child, and although his father was something of a disciplinarian, both parents doted on their son. Charles was proud of his father, who received the decoration of the Légion d'honneur before he died. Cyril Chenevier had insisted that his son follow an athletic regimen resembling that of the recruits he trained, and learn marksmanship as well; Charles Chenevier later credited these skills with advancing his career and on more than one occasion saving his life.[18]

Like his father, Chenevier tended to be an "old school" conservative, traditional in his lifestyle and moderate in his politics. Patriotism, personal honor, and devotion to the Republic were his highest ideals. Chenevier preferred a down-to-earth approach to life and police work. Ideologues, whether to the right or the left, repelled him. And, like most police officers, Chenevier preferred stability and calm in the streets over agitation, even for a good cause. It was these values, and especially the premium he placed on keeping order and fighting crime, that induced him to follow his superiors to Vichy and continue his police work there for Pétain's regime. These values likewise prompted Chenevier to join the Resistance by 1943 as it became apparent that the true cost of the "order" Pétain had purchased for France with the Armistice and the National Revolution was enthrallment to Germany. Chenevier paid a high price for his wartime choices as the Germans eventually arrested him and interned him in a prison camp.[19]

Chenevier had always wanted to be a policeman, and he joined the force in 1925.[20] He flourished in the police. Of medium height, dark-haired, stocky in build, and somewhat taciturn in personality, Chenevier had hooded eyes and a gaze both enigmatic and piercing at the same time. He commanded attention and exuded an air of authority, even while still a young policeman. Thanks to his father's training, he was tougher than he looked, and a redoubtable boxer. He was also disciplined, methodical, tenacious, and a good strategist, humble enough to learn a great deal, even from the dullest work pursuing minor criminals, and ambitious enough to take whatever opportunities presented themselves to shine before his superiors. Most important, he got results. Chenevier became known for his ability to outwit his quarry and "get his man." In 1928, he attracted the attention of Superintendent Jean Belin, and when Belin was named in 1934 to a high position in the Sûreté, Chenevier came with him. The two men worked under the director of the *Services de police criminelle*, Pierre Mondanel.[21] Chenevier's reputation continued to improve under the tutelage of Mondanel and Belin, and he participated in some of the most sensational investigations of 1934, one of the most tumultuous and troubled years in French history, including the Stavisky and Prince affairs, and the assassination of Alexander I of Yugoslavia. Moreover, as pre-war espionage in France accelerated, Chenevier and Belin frequently found themselves entangled with Russian, German, and Italian spies as well.[22]

Chenevier participated in the pre-war investigation of the Cagoule and in 1941 it no doubt rankled him that the Cagoulards arrested in 1937 had never faced justice. It was Chenevier's intimate knowledge of the workings of that secret terrorist organization, and the informers within it with whom he carefully nurtured relationships, that uniquely equipped him to hunt down the assassins of Marx Dormoy.[23] As Chenevier explained in his memoir, the French police in the 1930s and 1940s relied much more than their American counterparts on informers without whom very few crimes could be solved. Hence even though he knew that the practice was frowned upon in some quarters as "dishonest" or unseemly, Chenevier cultivated informants, often prostitutes, petty criminals, or illegal immigrants whose "irregularities" and minor crimes he would "overlook" in return for information. The intelligence Chenevier and his colleagues obtained from informants, along with the vast database of files that the Sûreté maintained and constantly updated, far more than forensic science or "stakeouts," permitted them to make most of their arrests.[24]

After his return to Paris following the war, Chenevier gave a deposition, dated 3 January 1946, related to the investigation of the Dormoy case. When asked what he knew about the assassination of Marx Dormoy, Chenevier offered the following statement:

Toward the end of June 1941, while I was on assignment in Paris, I learned through a political informer that a violent act was going to happen soon between Lyon and Marseille. I was not given any explanation regarding the nature of this crime, nor did my informer mention Dormoy's name or talk to me about an assassination, but he did inform me that the violent act was to be organized by the MSR and in particular by Eugène Deloncle, Filiol [sic] and someone called by the first name of "André" and whom I was later able to identify as André Erard. My informer was able to furnish me with further information forty-eight hours later, but I had to return immediately to my post at Vichy and was unable to return to Paris. I made a written report of this in a note addressed to the General Secretary of the Police [Mondanel] at Vichy.[25]

In the same deposition Chenevier explained that he learned about the Dormoy assassination on 26 July and given the intelligence his informants had passed on to him in late June, he received permission to head back to Paris as soon as possible. He discussed the case with Mondanel in Vichy and, while making his way to Paris, stopped in Montélimar on 3 August, where he inspected the crime scene with Superintendent Georges Kubler of the branch of the Sûreté based in Lyon. Although Chenevier took control of the investigation, he was impressed by what Kubler had achieved so far in Montélimar and left the younger man to continue his work there. Kubler was already showing photos of known Cagoulards to witnesses in town. Meanwhile, Chenevier focused his efforts on Paris and Marseille. Chenevier's informant had indicated that the roots of the crime would be found in the French capital and the perpetrators themselves had most likely gone underground in France's second largest city on the shores of the Mediterranean, Marseille.[26]

CHAPTER THREE

26–30 July 1941: Anatomy of a Crime Scene

By 3:00 a.m. of 26 July 1941 Inspector Marc Fra, head of the police in Montélimar, had notified Georges Bonnet, who was the substitute investigating magistrate for the official administrative districts of Montélimar and Nyons, about Dormoy's murder. Bonnet had been appointed to stand in for the vacationing Jean Marion. As part of its legacy of Napoleonic law, France has a very different system of criminal investigation than do the United States, Canada, or Great Britain. In France, as in the US, the police investigate most misdemeanors and other, less serious crimes. But in France serious felonies are "transferred" into the hands of an investigating magistrate who oversees every step of the investigation. Investigating magistrates are expected to be neutral, acting neither for the prosecution nor for the defense. They may issue warrants, grant or deny bail, and interrogate defendants and witnesses. In some cases they arrange "confrontations" among defendants to tease out the truth. In these "confrontations," the judge interviews the defendants in each other's presence and/or in the presence of witnesses, and then permits the defendants to refute or affirm the testimony. The investigating magistrate may decide to dismiss a case because the evidence is too weak to hold up in a trial. If prosecution is warranted, the investigating magistrate turns the dossier over to the state prosecutor who from that time forward represents "the People" in the criminal trial under the supervision of a trial judge.[1]

Bonnet arrived at the Relais in the company of a deputy public prosecutor. They prohibited anyone from entering or leaving the hotel and carried out a preliminary investigation with Mark Fra and Dr. Chapuis. Since there are photos

Figure 3.1. Crime scene photograph of Dormoy's cadaver. AP 134W/130 Dossier Marx Dormoy.

of the crime scene and corpse *in situ* still extant (see Figure 3.1), there must have been a police photographer present as well. When Bonnet and the others went up to #19, two police officers guarded the door. Assured that no one had entered since the explosion, Bonnet examined the room, which reeked of gunpowder. The blast had been powerful – Bonnet found a fragment of cerebral matter on the sill of a window in the hallway next to the room. Dormoy's body still lay "on the floor, on the same axis as the bed, direction north-south."[2]

It was obvious that Dormoy had been in bed asleep when the bomb exploded. Bonnet's report contained a sketch of the room showing that #19 sat at the end of a hallway. There were two windows in the room that faced out into the courtyard garden and another window in the hallway right next to #19 that also overlooked the courtyard. It was on this sill that Bonnet found a fragment of brain matter. Both windows in the bedroom and the hall window were shattered. The room itself was large, about 15 meters long, and probably contained about 200 square feet, with high ceilings, over three meters (ten feet) high. It is testament to the force of the blast that it punched two holes in the thick stone wall of the room and blew a hole in the ceiling that compromised the roof.[3]

The iron bed frame was twisted and broken, the pillows were shredded, and the mattress was ripped open with a huge hole where the pillows would have been. The painted wallpaper at the head of the bed was scorched with black powder burns that fanned out from the approximate height of the pillow, and with bits of bone and brain matter visible at the edges of the scorches. And everything, absolutely everything in the room, including the bedframe, the walls, and the furniture, was covered with feathers and gore, not surprising as "the corpse was almost completely decapitated, a sea of blood spread out from the end of the neck."[4] Dr. Chapuis announced the obvious, that medical intervention would be "useless."[5]

After this preliminary inspection, Bonnet ordered an official autopsy, which Dr. Chapuis was not qualified to perform in such an important case as this. Bonnet telephoned the 10th brigade divisional chief of the police mobile at Lyon, whose officers would investigate the crime under the authority of Jean Marion, the investigating magistrate for Montélimar, once he returned from vacation. Bonnet assigned the autopsy to a Dr. Rigaux, the official coroner at Montélimar, and notified the Marseille police and the Prefecture of Drôme, whose offices were in Valence. It was already clear to Bonnet that the trail of this investigation would lead to Lyon, Marseille, and even further afield, if for no other reason than that the main train line and roadways from Paris to Marseille went through both Lyon and Valence, and then Montélimar, before reaching Marseille and Nice. Since Lyon and Marseille were the most populous cities in France after Paris, and the most important cities in the Vichy Zone, with the largest and most professional police forces available to Bonnet, it was inevitable that detectives from Lyon and Marseille would take center stage in the investigation.

Bonnet next questioned the hotel staff and guests. These interviews took most of the night, but it was vital for the police to obtain statements and track the movements of everyone on the scene while the crime, and memories, were still fresh. There were thirty-four rooms in the hotel, but not all of them were occupied on the night of 25–26 July. Most of the guests were ordinary travelers passing through Montélimar on their way to visit family or conduct business in the region. After verifying their identities, the police sent most of the guests on their way.[6]

Besides Dr. Chapuis, there were five people whose statements Bonnet most urgently wanted to get on record: 1. Louise Vilnat, the owner of the Relais;

2. Louis Pinard, the hotel's night watchman and desk clerk; 3. Ernest Ceccheto, the hotel's porter, who also cleaned rooms, including that of Dormoy; 4. Madame Béatrice "Bretty" Dangel, a member of France's national theater, the *Comédie française*, and 5. Baba Diallo, a male domestic servant. Bonnet's focus on Dangel and Diallo is evidence of his realization that the politics of Vichy likely played a role in the crime.[7] Forty-three years old and a widow in 1941, Bretty's maiden name was "Bolchesi" and her professional name was Béatrice Bretty.[8] Bonnet knew she would be an excellent witness. As Mandel's mistress she was used to moving in the labyrinthine circles of French government and detecting subterfuge and deception in those around her. Bonnet suspected that had Dormoy noticed someone suspicious, he would have mentioned it to Bretty, who kept a close eye on all the comings and goings at the Relais. As it turned out, there had been an unusual guest in the hotel, one who had troubled not only Bretty but also Vilnat and her staff as well.

WHO IS MADEMOISELLE GÉRODIAS?

By the time the Lyonnais police arrived in Montélimar at 6:30 a.m., Fra and Bonnet's interviews had already yielded results. They had zeroed in on a likely suspect, a woman who had arrived at the Relais several days earlier and, by her striking behavior and appearance, drawn the attention of everyone at the hotel. But she had checked out during the night a few hours before the bomb exploded. All the police had to go on was the information she had provided when she registered at the hotel, along with the number of her official identity card, and the interviews with those who had interacted with her or remarked on her movements in the days preceding the crime. It was these witnesses who pointed out the woman as a suspect.[9]

According to her identity card, Florence Gérodias was born in Lyon in 1914, making her twenty-seven years old at the time of the murder. She was a professional model residing in Paris, at 43 Avenue Niel, and the photo on her identity card showed a woman thin but athletic, and attractive enough to enjoy a modeling career. She had stayed at the Relais before, in June, and returned on 25 July, taking Room #35, but this time she did not spend the night. Bonnet inspected her room, which was "still in the state in which the occupant had left it at her departure."[10] Bonnet and the police noticed "nothing remarkable" in Gérodias' room during that preliminary inspection. Witnesses, however, had noted some remarkable things about Mlle. Gérodias and her behavior at the hotel.

In her second statement, given during the morning of 26 July to the Lyonnais police, Vilnat described Florence Gérodias this way:

> On June 19 there arrived at the hotel a young woman whom I did not know and who registered under the name of Mlle. GERODIAS, Florence ... This person seemed to be aged less than thirty years old, tall, slim, platinum blond hair, dark eyes, wearing makeup, resembling a model. She arrived in the afternoon. She did not give me any explanation [for her stay]. She was lodged in Room #17, on the second floor. In the evening, she sat at the table facing M. Dormoy. She slept here the nights of the 20th and 21st of June and left during the night of the 22nd.[11]

Gérodias had attracted Vilnat's attention not only due to her striking appearance and evident charm, but also because of her curious behavior during her second stay at the hotel. Gérodias arrived at the Relais at 5:00 a.m. on the morning of 25 July. She had taken the night train from Marseille to Montélimar, by itself not that unusual. The young night clerk and watchman, Louis Pinard, greeted her. Gérodias was evidently rather breathless when she got to the hotel and made a point of telling Pinard that her train was a half hour late and asked him for a room "where she could rest." Pinard recognized her from her earlier stay at the Relais and offered her the same room she had taken before, #17. She refused that room, however, claiming that during her previous visit the neighbors had watched her get undressed, a statement that Pinard and Vilnat both found strange given that although her room did have an outside window, it was equipped with shutters and a curtain. Gérodias insisted that Pinard give her room #35, which unlike #17 was on the same floor as Dormoy's room. She was carrying a small dark blue suitcase decorated with metal strips around the edges.[12] Gérodias went up to her room and settled in to get some rest.

Kubler questioned everyone who had seen Gérodias. He was particularly interested in Gérodias' interactions with Dormoy, and any attraction toward her that Dormoy might have shown. A bachelor, Dormoy was reputed to be something of a ladies' man, and the police tracked down one of his former mistresses, an actress and model named "Flo" who was living in Avignon in 1941 but normally resided in Paris.[13] Kubler reasoned that Dormoy might have tried to strike up an acquaintance with the attractive new guest at the Relais. Witnesses' recollections differed, as some seemed to believe Gérodias was openly flirting with Dormoy, and that Dormoy had responded in kind. Others, however, like Vilnat, claimed that Dormoy had shown little interest in Gérodias.

According to Vilnat, when Dormoy first arrived as a "pensioner" at her hotel, "he went out in the evenings to take a short walk."[14] But more recently, no doubt due to his growing nervousness about his own security in town, Dormoy had "only been going out to get his newspapers and make some small purchases." He "did not frequent anyone in particular," but "he was very sociable and spoke with everyone in the hotel," according to Vilnat. From her perspective, it was to be expected that Dormoy occasionally exchanged a polite word or two with Gérodias, as it was his custom to chat a little with everyone at the Relais. Dormoy was a politician by trade, and he knew how to work a room. He also was a veteran of the ferocious struggles between right and left in France before the war, and as interior minister had investigated cases of espionage and home-grown terrorism, so he was well acquainted with subterfuge and subversion and was a decent judge of character. His political survival before the war had depended on those qualities, and his life depended on them now.[15] By the same token, Vilnat pointed out, Jeanne Dormoy had moved into the Relais three days earlier. Dormoy would hardly have carried on an affair with Gérodias under the watchful and disapproving eye of his sister.[16]

Dormoy had demonstrated some curiosity about Gérodias, however, and he noted her interest in him during her earlier visit in June, despite her attempts to appear nonchalant about it. Vilnat admitted that after Gérodias arrived at the Relais, Dormoy "looked her over carefully" as she walked by him on her way up to her room.[17] He then asked Vilnat, "What is it with this woman? Surely she's someone sent by *Gringoire* [a popular literary and weekly magazine that was editorially pro-Vichy] and one of these days, you'll see an article in *Gringoire* about me." Dormoy never spoke to Gérodias in Vilnat's presence, and Vilnat insisted that "Mlle. Florence" paid little attention to Dormoy and behaved properly around him. "I did not have the impression that Mlle. Florence tried to establish a relationship with M. Dormoy. During meals, she did not seek to profit from her place [seated near him] to do that. On the contrary, she sat with a book in front of her." Vilnat conceded, however, that Gérodias took her meals at a table close to where Dormoy and Bretty habitually dined.

Other guests and hotel staff were not so discrete or reticent. Bretty Dangel was convinced that "Mlle. Florence" was spying on Dormoy and listening in on his conversations. "I remarked that the blond lady in question, during her last stay at Montélimar a while ago, seemed to be interested in the conversation in the [hotel] dining room. She stayed seated there even after she had finished eating, and she seemed to be listening to our conversation, as if she was listening to other people. I pointed out the fact to M. Marx Dormoy, who responded to me that he didn't attach any importance to her, who [struck him] as a woman of questionable morals who had proposed a rendez-vous with him."[18] Bretty described Gérodias as "very chic" and stated that Dormoy considered Gérodias to be a "tart" who would "easily offer a man a rendez-vous." Several people at the Relais were convinced that she had given one to Dormoy, and that he had accepted.[19] During the June stay of "the blond lady" Baba Diallo, Bretty's manservant, saw Dormoy leaving Gérodias' room at about 3:30 in the afternoon. This led Diallo to assume that Gérodias was Dormoy's mistress.[20] Bretty also seems to have suspected that Dormoy had responded to Gérodias' flirtations, although she claimed that once she had warned him about the woman, she paid no further attention to whether or not he slept with Gérodias since "it was none of her affair."[21] Bretty did, however, notice that Dormoy spoke with Gérodias privately on a couple of occasions, although, no doubt much to her chagrin, Bretty could not overhear their conversations.[22]

Whether or not Dormoy had flirted with her, it soon became clear that Dormoy's interest in Gérodias related more to her strange behavior and the "friends" who began showing up to visit her, which also attracted the notice of everyone in the hotel. Dormoy cultivated the friendship of the barman at the Relais, Louis Chevet. During Gérodias' stay in June, Dormoy asked Chevet to help him investigate Gérodias. "Mlle. Florence," as everyone at the Relais called Gérodias, checked in on 19 June and Chevet stated that she had immediately struck him as "rather a tart."[23] The next day, Chevet spotted Dormoy speaking with her in the hotel's courtyard just before lunch. That afternoon, Dormoy asked Chevet to search her room to "find out who she was." Chevet waited until she left and then entered and opened her suitcases, in which he found letters and some crime novels. The blue suitcase bore a tag that read "Florence GERODIAS, 43 avenue NIEL, Paris."

Two days later, during the night of Sunday, 22 June to Monday, 23 June, at around 2:00 a.m., Gérodias received a visitor. A fellow of medium height, about thirty years old, dressed in a dark suit with a "soft hat," probably a fedora, and wearing espadrilles, entered the hotel and asked the receptionist to call "Mlle. Florence." Chevet was on duty at the desk. The man's sudden appearance in the middle of the night and request to see Gérodias unnerved Chevet, who went in search of Vilnat. She came down and asked the fellow who "this Mlle. Florence" was, presumably to ascertain whether the stranger really knew her guest or was an interloper.[24] The man "responded in a soft voice," said Chevet, with the manner of someone who was "afraid to speak," that he was seeking a "young blond woman who had been at the hotel for three days." This evidently satisfied Vilnat, who said "that's Mlle. Gérodias" and instructed Chevet to go and fetch her after the man responded, "Yes, that's the one." Chevet asked the man how he should announce his presence to Gérodias. The response was "M. André, her friend." Chevet immediately went up to Gérodias' room and did as he was bidden. To his surprise, he found her strolling in the corridor, still in "city clothes." She seemed surprised to hear that she had a caller, but after a moment said to Chevet, "Oh good. Tell him that I am coming down."

Chevet headed back downstairs. Gérodias soon followed him down to the lobby. When she spotted "M. André" waiting for her at the reception desk, she appeared happy to see him and said, "There you are."[25] The two shook hands and spoke together so softly that Chevet was unable to hear their conversation. Then they went up to her room together. They were up there for about forty-five minutes, after which they came back down, each carrying one of her suitcases. She settled her bill, including paying for a café au lait she'd ordered from Chevet at the bar that evening, and the pair headed out of the hotel in the direction of the train station.

Dormoy had noticed the strange comings and goings of "Mlle. Florence," as well as the arrival of her nighttime visitor. After they left, while Chevet was in the hotel lobby, he heard Dormoy softly call his name. Dormoy, standing on the staircase landing, fully dressed, asked who had just gone down the stairs. He had heard sounds on the stairs and in the hallway as M. André and Gérodias were going to and from her room. Chevet told Dormoy that "the young blond woman" had made the noise and added that she had checked out in the company of a man who had struck Chevet as rather suspicious.[26] Dormoy told Chevet to go to her room to see whether she had left anything that might be "useful," which Chevet did although he found nothing. Dormoy then said, "Good, that's fine. Good evening, kid," and went back to his room. Chevet and Dormoy were not the only ones whom Gérodias and her visitor in June had unnerved. Even Vilnat found "M. André" disturbing and his late-night visit odd. Like Chevet, she remarked on the espadrilles M. André wore, evidently a sign of a dodgy character in her eyes, although it was his "sinister face" that bothered her more. The following day Vilnat made a point of telling Dormoy that "Mlle. Florence" had had a visitor during the night, a criminal type who had frightened her. Dormoy made no comment.[27] But he cannot have been happy about Gérodias' return to the Relais in July.

THE ASSASSINS' BOUQUET

When the police questioned Jeanne Dormoy, she insisted, "never did my brother confide to me any fears that he had regarding [threats to] his life."[28] Like Bretty and the hotel staff, Jeanne also noticed Gérodias, who had returned to the Relais at about 5:00 a.m. on the 25th and dined in the hotel restaurant at noon, along with the Dormoy siblings and Bretty Dangel. Jeanne stated that "having noticed the presence in the dining salon of a young blond woman, I asked my brother who this person was." Marx responded that Gérodias was "someone who crosses the Line of Demarcation for 150 francs and that she says she is a model." Jeanne then asked him what Gérodias was "doing there" – presumably Jeanne was inquiring as to why Gérodias, a Parisian model, would have been staying alone in a provincial town like Montélimar in the Vichy Zone.[29] Dormoy shrugged and suggested that Jeanne should "ask Madame Vilnat."

Bretty stated that Dormoy seemed wary but not overly worried, either about the mysterious blond woman who seemed so eager to arrange an assignation with him, or about the situation in the hotel. She also assured the police that Dormoy "never confided to me any menacing letters or fears regarding his life. On the contrary, he seemed quite content."[30] Still, she added, "One time, he did speak of significant affairs that took place while he was Minister of the Interior, and notably, related to a question I had posed to him, he spoke about the affair of the 'Cagoule' and of its importance and of the discoveries he had made regarding it." Bretty hinted that Dormoy should have shown rather more concern about the activities of Mlle. Gérodias. An actress herself, Bretty quickly sized up "Mlle. Florence" as an imposter. Her suspicions about the blond woman were turning out to be quite prescient.

Had there been any doubt on the part of the police, the forensic evidence they gathered from Dormoy's room demonstrated conclusively that he had been killed by a powerful time bomb placed in a hole in his mattress at the height of his pillow. On the floor beneath the bed and following the trajectory of the debris, the Lyonnais police found fragments of the bomb itself, including parts of the pocket watch that had served as the timer. They also found "shards of white wooden debris, painted on one side with the color 'tango' [a popular orange-red color]. To certain of these shards adhered pieces of paraffin. On the other side of the shards multi-colored paper was glued, indicating that the box from which these wood shards came originally held a child's toy."[31] Bonnet ordered this evidence sealed and sent by express train to the police forensics laboratory in Lyon. In addition, the police forwarded a towel and a small drinking glass they found on the nightstand of Gérodias' room. By the morning of 26 July the police knew that Gérodias' identity card was false.[32]

It is a sign of the importance the Vichy authorities attached to the case that the chief superintendent of the Lyonnais Police mobile personally inspected the crime scene in Montélimar on 26 July and sent a lengthy report to the head of the Judicial Police at Vichy on 28 July.[33] By now the police officer overseeing the investigation in Montélimar was Georges Kubler, a superintendent of the police mobile at Lyon. Kubler was still relatively young, only twenty-eight years old in 1941, but he was intelligent, competent, and ambitious enough to earn the confidence of Charles Chenevier. Chenevier trusted Kubler to handle things in Montélimar, while Chenevier worked angles in Paris and Marseille.[34]

Kubler searched Dormoy's room and confiscated his personal effects. The results of this search were reported in two statements, one by the chief superintendent of the Lyonnais police, and one from Kubler himself.[35] There is an interesting and potentially consequential divergence between the two reports. The chief superintendent stated that the police found the following things in Dormoy's room, all of which were sealed in the presence of witnesses and then deposited for safekeeping at the Registry of the Civil Court of Montélimar:

- The sum of 26,320 francs in bank bills of 5,000, 1,000, 500, 100, and 20 francs, and three $100 bills in American money;
- A briefcase containing diverse identity cards, notes, letters, etc.;
- Other manuscript letters found in the baggage or the furniture [evidently Dormoy had hidden them to conceal at least some of the letters from hotel staff or others who might get access to his room]; and
- A rubber stamp of the City Hall of Montluçon.

Kubler, however, reported that he had also found among Dormoy's personal possessions various classified papers without describing these papers further. What was in these papers? Were they the documents that Dormoy had taken with him from Paris in June of 1940? Why did the chief superintendent fail to mention them in his report to Vichy on 28 July, and might those documents have played a role in Dormoy's death? These questions re-emerged when Jean Marion ordered Dormoy's papers unsealed in 1942 and discovered that the classified papers were missing.

On 28 July, once the forensic evidence had been expedited to Lyon and Dormoy's possessions stored under lock and key in the courthouse at Montélimar, Kubler sealed the windows and door of Dormoy's room and awaited Chenevier's arrival.[36] After Dr. Rigaud had performed the autopsy, Jeanne hoped that her brother could be inhumed in Montluçon. But by the early morning hours of 26 July, the Vichy government had already decided otherwise. News reports about Dormoy's death were limited and censored. Newspaper headlines on the 27th announced: "An attack against M. Marx Dormoy, Former Interior Minister. A Bomb Placed in the Room of the Former Interior Minister Explodes, Killing Him Instantly."[37] After the 27th, there was little further coverage of the crime or the investigation, in Paris or Vichy.

Pétain and his ministers had no choice but to investigate, much to their chagrin, given the spectacular nature of the crime and the outcry in France and abroad at such a brazen murder. But Vichy had no intention of allowing Dormoy to be made a martyr, and insisted that he be inhumed in a provisional grave at Montélimar, with a small ceremony. The inhumation took place on the 28th, too soon for many of Dormoy's friends to be alerted, let alone get there in time to attend the ceremony. Only a dozen or so people showed up, and the chief superintendent noted in his report for Vichy who came to "express their condolences to Mademoiselle Dormoy, sister of the victim."[38] Félix Gouin, Monsieur and Madame Isidore Thivrier, and Henri and René Ribière, all pre-war friends and political allies of Marx Dormoy, were among the mourners.

The inhumation over and the chief superintendent on his way back to Lyon, it was now up to Kubler and Chenevier to track down Florence Gérodias and the several unidentified men who had visited her at the Relais in June and July. The police knew Gérodias and her visitors were involved in the crime because of another piece of forensic evidence. On 27 July Kubler found another shard of white wood with "tango" paint on one side, identical to the one recovered from under Dormoy's bed. But this fragment came from another hotel, the Hôtel de la Place d'Armes, whose owner, Madame Lurol, had rented a room to one of Gérodias' male visitors in Montélimar, a room in which Gérodias and three men spent the afternoon of Friday, 25 July.[39] The police learned from Lurol about the three young men, two of whom paid a visit to Gérodias at the Relais the evening of 25 July. Like M. André in June, the men stood out among the guests at the hotel. For the next two weeks, Kubler and his team focused their efforts on tracking down Gérodias, M. André, and her other three friends.

The first indication the police received that Gérodias had received callers on 25 July came from Vilnat and her staff at the Relais, who related how two men interrupted "Mlle. Florence" during dinner. According to Vilnat, at about 8:30 p.m. on the 25th, while Gérodias was in the hotel restaurant "finishing her soup," Louis Pinard entered the restaurant and alerted Gérodias that she was wanted in the lobby.[40] Marx and Jeanne were also in the dining room, eating as usual with Bretty. According to Vilnat's brother-in-law, Émilien Behuret, the smaller of the two men looking for "Mlle. Florence" was just under five feet tall, thin, with brown hair combed back away from his face, clean shaven, with slightly tanned or brown skin. He was wearing a gray suit and light-colored gloves, odd attire for a warm summer evening. Behuret thought he was about thirty years old. The second man was taller, about five feet seven or eight inches in height, and had large eyes and an intense stare. Marie Behuret described him as "medium weight and dressed a little like a gangster."[41]

The trio seemed delighted to see each other. When Gérodias came into the lobby, the smaller fellow said, "There's Florence."[42] Gérodias, meanwhile, focused on the taller man, whom she hugged, whereas she only shook hands with the shorter fellow. The taller man presented her with an enormous bouquet of red and white carnations and gladiolas. "Mlle. Florence" thanked him but said he should not have gone to the trouble. He also had a box of Montélimar's famous nougat for her. Gérodias told the men, "Because you've been so nice, I want to give you something in return," and then led them upstairs to her room. They were upstairs for only ten minutes. When they came back down and were saying their goodbyes, Gérodias realized that the smaller man was carrying her blue suitcase and declared, "Oh, no jokes! Don't take my suitcase. Leave it in the corner and I will take it with me when I leave." The man sheepishly handed her the suitcase. She placed it at the foot of the stairs in the lobby and they all had a good laugh, after which they said their goodbyes and parted.

As soon as Gérodias finished eating, she checked out. She chatted with Vilnat while she was paying her bill, repeating the story that she lived in Paris, was a model but was out of work, and frequently crossed the Line of Demarcation near Chalons by bribing the police at the frontier with 150 francs. She and Vilnat discussed the issues worrying everyone in France at that time – food supplies, life in Paris versus the provinces – and Gérodias added, perhaps by way of explaining her two trips to Montélimar that summer, that she was seeking lodging for her mother for the coming winter. The implication was that her mother, like many French people, was a refugee in the Occupied Zone who needed to find somewhere to live until she could return home. Gérodias remarked on how encumbering the bouquet would be for the train trip she was about to make. Vilnat claimed that it was she who suggested to Gérodias that she leave it with Vilnat, although Vilnat warned Gérodias that if the latter "ran into those fellows again, they might be surprised not to see her with the flowers."[43] Such a bouquet was an expensive gift in wartime France. Gérodias answered that she would simply tell the men that she'd left it, along with her suitcase, with the porter. She handed the bouquet to Vilnat who offered Gérodias a glass of chartreuse in exchange, which Gérodias downed before leaving the hotel. Louis Pinard, who observed the encounter with the two men, remarked on the taller man's haircut "au bol rasé," meaning shaved up the neck and then in a "bowl cut," with the bangs brushed back, a style typical of gangsters and militant young men of the era.[44]

The police were increasingly suspicious of "Mlle. Florence" and her visitors, especially as further testimony indicated that her behavior during the day on 25 July was also odd. Her abrupt arrival at 5:00 a.m., her announcement to Pinard as soon as she entered the lobby that her train from Marseille was a half hour late and her insistence on being given a room on the same floor as Dormoy all stood out as unusual. Chevet served Gérodias at noon in the dining room on 25 July. Soon after that meal, some ladies from the Red Cross whose car had broken down in the courtyard of the hotel asked Chevet to summon Ernest Ceccheto, the hotel's porter. When Chevet reached the third floor in his search for Ceccheto, he spotted Gérodias "leaning out the window in the hallway, next to the door to the entrance to the room of M. Dormoy. She was looking into the courtyard."[45] Chevet suspected she was attempting to peer into the nearby window of Dormoy's room. He continued his search for Ceccheto, however, and as he started back down the hallway on the third floor, he saw Gérodias go back into her room. He noted that Dormoy's room had not yet been cleaned.

The fundamental problem facing the police was how, and when, the assassin had gotten the bomb into Dormoy's room, and why no one had noticed it being planted, or later, when the room was cleaned. Ceccheto's 27 July statement was suggestive. At around 1:00 p.m. Chevet had gone in search of him. According to Ceccheto, he cleaned Dormoy's room at about 1:30 p.m. that day. Dormoy had, Ceccheto stated, "firmly told me not to touch his papers, letters, etc. that were in his room. Most of the time he put them securely into his armoire that could be closed with a key. But he also frequently left them lying on the table. I never had any curiosity to read any of them."[46] Dormoy rarely locked the door to his room, but rather left the key in the lock. This was not as surprising at it might seem, as Dormoy surely knew that there was a skeleton key that opened all the hotel's rooms in a drawer of a small table in the hallway, and thus was easily accessible to anyone in the hotel.[47]

When Ceccheto cleaned Dormoy's room on the 25th, he lifted the mattress. Under it, near the head of the bed, he discovered a rectangular package, "about the size of the sheet of paper on which you [the policeman taking his statement] are writing, about 5 to 10 centimetres thick" (about eight by eleven inches in length and width, and about two to four inches in depth).[48] It was wrapped in gray paper. Since Dormoy had warned Ceccheto not to touch his papers, Ceccheto, assuming that it contained notes that Dormoy was trying to hide, left the package under the mattress. He added that he did not hear any "tick-tock" from the packet and that he never told Dormoy about it. Ceccheto's testimony thus suggested that the bomb, or part of it, had already been under Dormoy's mattress by 1:30 p.m. in the afternoon of 25 July. The police later discovered that Ceccheto had indeed seen a bomb, but that it was defective (hence no "tick-tock"), thus necessitating the killers' elaborate ruse with the bouquet that evening to replace it. Gérodias carried the defective bomb out of the hotel in her suitcase.

THE INVESTIGATION INTENSIFIES

Between 27 July and 14 August, Chenevier and Kubler focused on tracing the movements and tracking down the real identities of Gérodias and her visitors. This became imperative once they discovered that the two men who had visited Gérodias at the Relais on 25 July, as well as a third man who joined them, had been in Montélimar during the exact same days when Gérodias had made her previous trip to the city. Kubler set out to discover when the men had arrived in Montélimar, by what train, and where they had stayed. But first, he tracked down the bouquet of flowers Gérodias' visitors had presented her with on the night of 25 July. Such a large and expensive bouquet, which could only have been purchased in a small number of shops, was sure to have attracted the attention of witnesses who saw the men carrying it to the Relais. Montélimar is not large and it did not take Kubler long to find both the florist and the hotel.

Mlle. Marie Salgon ran a flower shop on the rue des Quatre-Alliances. When the police interviewed her on 26 July, Salgon immediately recognized the flowers as a bouquet that a client had picked up in her store the preceding evening, 25 July. The client, a young man, ordered the flowers at about 2:30 p.m. He requested a spray of white flowers, but when Salgon discovered that they were intended for a "young lady," she suggested red and white roses instead.[49] She asked him how much he wanted to spend and mentioned that 50 francs would be appropriate. The fellow was willing to spend a lot, 75 francs, but rejected roses in favor of carnations and gladiolas which would make a much larger bouquet for the price. Evidently in this case, size did matter. Given the profit she stood to earn, Salgon rushed to make the bouquet. At around 8:10 p.m., the client picked it up.[50] Two men residing near Salgon's shop also saw two men pass by on foot, one of them carrying flowers. Both witnesses and Salgon described the fellow holding the bouquet in very similar terms – a clean-shaven, brown-haired young man, wearing a brown suit and a Lacoste shirt.[51] He was clearly the same man who later presented that enormous bouquet to Gérodias at the Relais, and who spent the afternoon with her in another hotel in Montélimar.[52]

On 27 July Kubler interviewed Madame Marie-Rose Lurol, who owned the Hôtel de la Place d'Armes, rue Aristide Briand, in Montélimar. Lurol's husband, like that of Vilnat, was absent, and she managed her hotel with the assistance of a few employees and her 14-year-old daughter Raymonde.[53] According to Lurol, on the morning of Friday, 25 July, as she was standing on the terrace of her hotel between 7:00 and 7:30 a.m., she saw a man heading toward her from the direction of the train station, lugging a small suitcase. He seemed to be talking to himself, and when he saw the sign for her hotel, she heard him say something along the lines of "hey, there's a hotel," suggesting that he had just arrived in town and intended to grab the first hotel room he could find for a short weekend holiday. Lurol described the man as aged about 26 to 28 years old, wearing a gray suit and a "soft hat," and she sensed that he was a "gangster type." She followed him into the hotel café and asked him what he wanted. He requested a room "to clean up in," presumably from the train trip, and indicated that he would not be spending the night. Lurol accompanied him to room #2 on the second floor. She did not request that he check in, which suggests that her hotel specialized in transient clientele and "working girls." That seems to have suited her new guest quite well, although it later meant that the police did not have the benefit of even a false identity from the hotel's registration book to go on as they tried to track down the young man who had rented the room. He informed her that "people at Montélimar" would be showing up at the hotel looking for him and sure enough a half hour later the man in the brown suit with the brushed back short brown hair and intense stare showed up at Lurol's hotel with another young man. In the afternoon a young woman matching Gérodias' description joined them.

When the two men came to Lurol's hotel between 7:30 and 8:00 a.m. on 25 July, they were surprised to discover that the fellow who had rented the room had just arrived that morning in Montélimar. Their meeting seemed amicable enough, however, and Lurol returned to the lobby. At about 9:00 a.m. the trio came downstairs, had something to drink in the bar and left. It was Lurol's daughter Raymonde who had served the young men at the bar.[54] Later in the morning and after the men left, Raymonde went up to their room to clean the sink and, most likely, to snoop. She noticed an "open suitcase" on a table near the window although given its contents it is doubtful that its owner left it lying open when he departed the hotel. "Pushed by curiosity," Raymonde went over and peered inside it. Rather than clothes and toiletries, it contained only an empty box, about 17.5 inches by 2 inches (45 × 5 centimeters) that had once held a child's construction toy, resembling an Erector set. On the box was glued a rainbow-colored label that said, "construction toys." Raymonde recognized the box immediately because she had seen one before, at the home of an acquaintance. She also saw in the suitcase a cylindrical packet wrapped in newspaper. There was nothing else in the room except for a tube of Dentol toothpaste and a toothbrush on the mantelpiece. When she cleaned the room on the following day, Saturday, the newspaper had been crumpled into a ball and lay on the floor. The guests had left nothing else behind.[55] Once Lurol alerted Kubler to the construction box, he searched room #2 and discovered on the floor under the table a fragment of white wood with orange paint identical to the one found in Dormoy's room, confirming his suspicion that the young men were Gérodias' accomplices.[56]

Kubler also learned that on 25 July at about 3:30 p.m., the three young men returned to the Hôtel de la Place d'Armes, in the company of a blond woman who appeared to Mme. Lurol to be about thirty years of age. Mme. Marthe Barnier, who worked for Lurol doing laundry and mending, and who sometimes waitressed in the hotel's café, also saw the young men and the woman, whom she described as "platinum blond, tall, thin, rather a tart, wearing a corsage and a dark coloured skirt."[57] The woman's shoes also impressed Barnier, as they were "modern," beige mule-style sandals with wooden soles that "clicked on the ground, because the shoe wasn't held on by any strap. I paid close attention to them."

Barnier had plenty of time to observe the woman and the young men, as they entered the café, ordered beer and lemonade, and asked for a deck of cards. Lurol agreed to lend them the deck of cards and let them bring it, the beer, and the lemonade up to their room. At around 5:30 p.m. Lurol went out to run some errands, warning Barnier not to permit any of the guests to leave without settling their bill. While she was out, the group in room #2 came downstairs, one of them carrying the small suitcase. The tall young man ordered a glass of Vichy water, drank it on the spot, and paid with a 50-franc bill. The woman remarked that she had "really taken them" while playing cards.[58] After they settled the bill for the room and departed, Lurol went up to #2 to "see if they took anything away in the suitcase." When she inspected the room, Lurol found the bed "completely unmade," which led her to suspect that "they had been doing more than playing cards up there."[59] Barnier remembered that Lurol told her, when she came back down to the café, "Well, you know! I think that all three of them 'did it.' The bed is a mess!" Neither woman saw where the foursome had gone, nor did they return to the hotel that night.

The police were "particularly eager to research where the three men ate their meals during the course of the day of July 25," as they knew it was not at the Hôtel de la Place d'Armes.[60] Kubler's team tracked this information down when they interviewed Madame Lucienne Ceyte, owner of another hotel in Montélimar located on the Boulevard Marre-Desmarais, who recognized the young men from the police description. Ceyte had served meals to the tall young man and his companions several times because they had been in Montélimar in June, at the time of Gérodias' first stay at the Relais, and again on 25 July.[61]

According to Ceyte, at around 10:00 p.m. on the evening of Sunday, 22 June, two men came to dine in her restaurant, the Brasserie Delhoste. She mentioned that one of them was about 25 years old, with a strong Marseillais accent.[62] The second man was shorter, with a medium build, chestnut hair, a round face, and light skin. He was wearing a light-colored suit. She remembered them because when she asked them whether they were satisfied with her menu they were unenthusiastic, although they did order a meal. Then they proceeded to complain about the wine and asked for a better bottle, at which point Ceyte remarked to them, "You are quite difficult to please, so you must come from at least as far away as Marseille." They responded that they were indeed from that city. After dinner, they drank two liqueurs on the patio, paid, and left.

Ceyte was not the only person to notice the two men. She employed a waitress at the brasserie, Mlle. Lucie Bisazza, who also served the men in June. According to Bisazza, "These two men had me serve them two meals. They drank two or three bottles of old wine and told me that this was to celebrate Russia's entry into the war. They added that they hoped for a Russian victory and seemed to be very happy. Both had a Midi accent and they told me that they came from Marseille, but they did not tell me what they were doing [in Montélimar]. My employer, Mme. Ceyte, also noticed them because she served them the aged wine. They attracted our attention because we immediately thought that they were 'gangster types.'"[63]

On 25 July, at around 7:00 a.m., "at the moment when the maid opens the establishment," the taller man returned to Ceyte's restaurant in the company of two friends, neither of whom she recognized as the man who had dined with him in June.[64] Given the early hour, it was obvious that their train had just arrived in Montélimar. One of the two companions of the original guest was about his height, thus rather tall, with a strong build, but dirty, with "uncombed blond hair," "messy in appearance," and "vulgar looking," albeit with an "intelligent mien." The other fellow was short, with blond hair, and medium in build, unremarkable in appearance or behavior. Bisazza was again waitressing, and it was she who first noticed the men making their way toward the Brasserie Delhoste from the direction of the train station. The men asked if they could get some breakfast despite the early hour, preferably something hearty with cold meat. Given the rationing situation in France at the time, Bisazza reminded them that it was forbidden to serve meat, but said she could offer them eggs, cheese, and fruit. They sat down and each ordered two eggs, bread, fruit, and coffee with milk. Still hungry, they asked if they could order more food. Bisazza asked Ceyte, who had come downstairs to the restaurant in the meantime, if it would be permissible to serve them more breakfast. Ceyte agreed to bring them more eggs.[65]

At that point Ceyte recognized the tall fellow from his visit in June. The resulting exchange struck both Bisazza and Ceyte as strange, to say the least. The man seemed "very surprised and somewhat unhappy" that Ceyte recalled him.[66] Bisazza, seeing his expression, asked, "Does it bother you that we recognized you?" The man turned toward her and asked, "You also, you recognized me?" Bisazza replied, "Oh, one doesn't have to be a physiognomist to do that." The smallest of the trio then interjected, "Me too, you should know me because I was there too." Despite their discomfort, the three men told Ceyte before they left the restaurant that they would return at noon. Just as they were leaving, both Ceyte and Bisazza noticed that the tall man was carrying a small, light blue suitcase. Bisazza also thought they had a small, square box with them. When they returned for lunch, at about 12:30 p.m., they no longer had either the box or the suitcase. They insisted on sitting near the back of the restaurant, where the tall fellow and his companion had eaten in June. They spoke in hushed tones and, Bisazza said, stopped speaking whenever she approached their table. Neither she nor Ceyte ever saw them again after that lunch.[67]

Kubler's investigation appeared to have stalled at this point, except for one possibly important lead. The police had questioned everyone in Paris, Lyon, and Marseille they could find named "Gérodias," to no avail. No one with the name in Paris or elsewhere fit the description of "Mlle. Florence" or knew anyone who did, and the Parisian address on her identity card was false.[68]

Interviews with the personnel at the Montélimar train station had also yielded little fruit. The clerk and the porter at the station had issued tickets to a variety of people the evening of 25 July, but none of them closely matched the three men who had been in the room of the Hôtel de la Place d'Armes. Moreover, due to a shortage of staff, no one at the station checked tickets during the night. Passengers who purchased their tickets in advance could get onto the platform and board the train without being perceived. Still, the porter did state that on 25 July, when he was working on the train that left Montélimar at 10:33 p.m. and headed for Lyon, he noticed a woman fitting Gérodias' description. What drew his attention were her platinum blond hair and noisy, wooden-soled mules. She was carrying a small package wrapped in paper, and he first saw her sitting on a bench at the station at about 10:00 p.m., so she must have purchased her ticket in advance, as the clerk issuing the tickets did not remember her. She was in the company of two young men who fit the description of the men who had visited Gérodias at the Relais. None of them had any luggage and they all boarded the train for Lyon.[69]

On 30 July Kubler finally did get a break in the case, when he identified a man who witnesses remembered visiting Gérodias at the Relais in June: Ludovic Guichard, aged 27, a businessman from Marseille. By 2 August the police had obtained a statement from Guichard, whom they tracked down at his residence in Marseille. He admitted that he had stayed at the Relais in both June and July of 1941, but insisted that he did not know Gérodias and had nothing to do with the death of Marx Dormoy. Guichard bought and sold food, including dry and frozen vegetables, for a wholesaler in Marseille. He claimed that he traveled to Montélimar in June to investigate purchasing a factory for drying vegetables. Upon his return to Marseille, Guichard looked back fondly on his stay in Montélimar. Of a nervous disposition and in poor health, he felt he needed a break from Marseille's cloying heat, so he again booked a room at the Relais, which he found to be a pleasant hotel. Guichard stated that he had little to do with any of the other guests, however, including Dormoy, except to offer a polite "bonjour" in passing. The police remained suspicious of Guichard despite his story, if for no other reason than that they soon discovered that he was a member of Jacques Doriot's PPF and thus a follower of one of Dormoy's most vicious enemies.[70]

CHAPTER FOUR

14 August 1941: A Bombing in Nice

On 29 June 1941 Jeanne Dormoy filed a civil suit for damages in the case of her brother's murder.[1] By now she had rented rooms on the rue Laveret in Montélimar, a sign that she was in for the long haul. She would spare no time or expense in the pursuit of justice. French law allows for the protection of the interests of a crime victim by permitting the victim or other individuals who have been harmed, such as a family member in a murder case, to file a civil suit in which they seek reparations from the perpetrator. Victims or their representatives may also file suit as a civil participant in the criminal investigation and trial, in which case their lawyer represents their interests during every stage of the investigation and trial to ensure that the investigating magistrate is acting impartially and conscientiously to uncover the truth.[2] Jeanne Dormoy did not hesitate and the day after her brother's body was laid to rest she chose Félix Gouin to file on her behalf. Gouin was an experienced lawyer and politician who had been a Deputy in the French Legislature. He proved a trustworthy and tenacious advocate in Jeanne's quest for justice, during and after the war. He immediately contacted a colleague in Montélimar to monitor the progress of the investigation, since Gouin was based in Paris. This lawyer, J. Richard, kept an eye on the evolution of the case and represented Jeanne in the Montélimar courtroom.[3]

 Everyone involved in the case knew that the inquiry threatened to be long and arduous. Few doubted that the roots of the crime went far beyond Montélimar, if for no other reason than the murder had been meticulously planned and expensive to carry out. The political situation was far from ideal, given that Marx Dormoy's enemies held power in both Paris and Vichy. Supporters of Pétain's National Revolution all over France were celebrating Dormoy's assassination. Nor were the Germans enthusiastic about pursuing the assassins. German Ambassador Otto Abetz instead was determined to prosecute those French politicians who, like Dormoy, prior to the war had advocated for a strong French stand against German aggression in Europe.[4] For appearances' sake Pétain might be willing to allow the investigation to proceed, but there were also prominent individuals in Vichy who wanted the affair smothered, not least because they feared that the assassins' trail would lead to them and might even end at Pétain's own doorstep. Her civil suit would be costly for Jeanne Dormoy, not only because of the potential threat to her personal safety, but because of the considerable legal expenses entailed. Ultimately, her struggle for justice consumed the rest of her life.[5]

Kubler enlisted the aid of colleagues throughout France in the manhunt. The most tantalizing leads hinted at the involvement of former Cagoulards based in Paris and Vichy, but as yet Kubler had nothing solid to go on beyond hearsay testimony. Chenevier thought the information he had received from his informants was plausible, given the bad blood between Dormoy and Deloncle and the Cagoule's reputation for avenging itself against its enemies. He relayed the intelligence to his superiors in Vichy and to Kubler.[6] Chenevier traveled to the Relais and inspected the crime scene on 3 August, but neither he nor anyone else could make much headway unless they could track down the four young men witnesses had seen at Montélimar, and the real identity of Florence Gérodias. Despite an extensive search that reached from Paris to Marseille they had not yet succeeded.[7]

Dr. Locard, a well-known forensic scientist based in Lyon, was examining the evidence from Montélimar. By 3 August he had sent Investigating Magistrate Jean Marion a bill for 1,000 francs but no report. The delay irritated Marion, especially given the size of the bill.[8] The fingerprint expert in Paris examined the prints on the drinking glass in Gérodias' room at the Relais, but could not find a match in the police files.[9] The police had taken a statement from Ludovic Guichard, the odd little businessman from Marseille who had stayed at the Relais and who witnesses thought was a friend of "Mlle. Florence," but they couldn't hold him without evidence linking him to the crime. Meanwhile, Vilnat was fretting over the repairs to her hotel, delayed because Dormoy's room remained a crime scene. She called in an architect to assess the damage to the roof over room #19 and petitioned Marion to permit her to make repairs before the winter rains arrived or the damage would lead the wall of the hotel to collapse entirely.¹⁰ The summer was passing quickly and every day that went by increased the likelihood that the trail would go cold. Unless something broke in the investigation, Chenevier and his file on the Cagoule would be sent back to Paris. The police needed a break in the case – soon.

That break came on 14 August, when at ten minutes before midnight another bomb exploded, this time in the public garden in the city of Nice. Three young men were sitting on an iron bench in one of the broad alleys of the park. One of them had brought a small suitcase containing the components of a time bomb, which the trio intended to deploy against one of Nice's synagogues. While he was attempting to set the timer, the device detonated unexpectedly with enough force to blow the three of them to pieces, scattering their remains over dozens of yards.¹¹ The bomb bore an uncanny resemblance to the one that killed Marx Dormoy. Both were time bombs, powerful but simple affairs that used a common explosive called "cheddite" and watch or clock parts for a timer.¹² The Marseille police immediately suspected a connection between the crimes.

The police managed to locate the identity cards of the three victims, Lucien Guyon, Horace Vaillant, and Maurice Marbach. They were already known in Marseille as militants of the extreme right. Trained as an engineer, Guyon was 27 years old, a native of Marseille who still lived there, working as a mechanic and residing with his mother on the rue Ruffi. Horace Vaillant was born in St. Tropez in 1909. Unmarried like Guyon, he resided alone in Marseille, where he earned his living driving taxis. Maurice Marbach was also single and a native of Marseille, although in 1941 he worked in Toulon at the naval arsenal there, where he built explosives. It was Marbach who possessed the expertise and access to explosives needed to construct the time bomb in Nice.¹³ On 7 April 1941, the police in Marseille had arrested Guyon and Vaillant for defacing sidewalks with antisemitic graffiti, in the company of two other men, Guy Fontes and Yves Moynier.¹⁴ Kubler showed pictures of the three dead men to witnesses in Montélimar. Bisazza, the waitress at the Brasserie Delhoste and her employer, Ceyte, as well as Lurol, owner of the Hôtel de la Place des Armes, all recognized at least two of them. All three women, and another witness, truck driver Camille Burgaud, recognized Maurice Marbach as one of the men who came to the city in both June and July.¹⁵

A search of the dead men's residences proved fruitful. In Marbach's home they found Ludovic Guichard's name and address as well as a veritable arsenal of weapons and explosive materials.¹⁶ There were four bombs ready to be used, and at least nineteen detonators, indicating that Marbach and his friends were planning a series of bombings resembling the one that had killed Dormoy.

Besides destroying synagogues, it was rumored that the young men intended to kill other Third Republic figures.[17]

Marseille Police Inspector Elie Tudesq interviewed Guichard again. This time, he thoroughly searched Guichard's five-room house on the rue Pastoret in Marseille.[18] In the cabinet of the dining room the police found a set of documents that included a list of names and addresses, including that of Marbach, a notebook with "Patria" [Fatherland] on the cover containing the results of "inquiries and stakeouts," and a black folder, divided into alphabetical compartments, containing Guichard's correspondence.[19] Guichard stated that he and Marbach had been acquainted for years, since their student days at the Lycée Thiers in Marseille, but claimed he had lost touch with Marbach until the two men ran into each other by accident in Marseille. Guichard avowed that he had last seen Marbach several months earlier when the two men had another chance encounter on the Canebière, the historic street where people from Marseille frequently went to stroll and window shop. Guichard also was "slightly" acquainted with the other two victims of the bomb in Nice. But he insisted that even though he shared the political views of the three bombers and occasionally met up with them at rallies and meetings, he knew nothing about their violent political activities.[20]

In this same statement, dated 17 August 1941, Guichard stuck to the account of his activities he had offered in his original deposition, maintaining that his first stay in Montélimar resulted from his need to contact a M. Teste, who manufactured jam, and two salesmen from the Soubeyran nougat factory. Unfortunately, when Guichard arrived in town, Teste was on vacation, so Guichard only stayed in Montélimar for two days, because he had to get back to the hair salon in Marseille he and his wife had purchased on 5 June 1941. Guichard explained that he returned to Montélimar on 8 July and stayed at the Relais for eight days, in rooms #5 and #6, this time for a vacation. During both visits, he saw Marx Dormoy daily in the dining room but paid no attention to him and during his second visit to Montélimar "did nothing there but rest."[21] Even though both of his stays at the Relais directly preceded the arrival at the hotel of Florence Gérodias, Guichard claimed not to know her and insisted that he had chanced upon the Relais by accident.

Given that Guichard's name figured in Maurice Marbach's address book, and all three dead men in Nice were in Guichard's, Kubler was not inclined to accept his story. It simply was not possible that Guichard's presence in Montélimar in June and July of 1941 could have been a coincidence, and Kubler concluded that "the participation of Guichard in the crime at Montélimar, at least in terms of its preparation, seems to be without doubt."[22] Even more damning were the notes he found along with the address book and other materials in the cabinet in Guichard's dining room, one of which read:

> In the affair of the Cagoulards, while good Frenchmen pay with long days in prison the price for having dared, only the P.P.F. has carried on a truly dignified campaign [of action]. Due to fear, the A.F., the P.S.F. and many others who have the right ideas have on the contrary condemned the victims.[23]

The second note was even more telling: "All you've done, Dear Simon, by raising yourself up through your tenacity, and by your ardour for battle, is to have gained the hearts of many, of which mine is honoured to be among them."[24] "Simon" was the code name of Lucien Guyon, for whom Guichard had drafted a eulogy of sorts.

Ludovic Joseph Guichard was born on 30 June 1914, in Marseille, the only son of a wealthy businessman who had also held the municipal post of controller of commercial weights and measures. Guichard's parents were well into middle age when he was born and they clearly doted on him.[25] Guichard was a small and rather nervous man with a high forehead, dark eyes, and an aquiline nose (see Figure 4.1). Intelligent, he assumed the airs of an intellectual, although he came off as more eccentric than brilliant.[26] He also suffered from an anxiety disorder since childhood and epileptic seizures and delusions as an adult. In October of 1934 he volunteered for military service in the 141st Alpine Infantry Regiment based in Marseille, but only lasted a month, after which he was discharged for unspecified psychological problems. He was not called up again when war broke out in 1940 even though at age 27, he was still young enough.[27]

Guichard's emotional problems began when he was a teenager. From 1924 to 1930 Guichard attended the École Libre de Provence, from which he was expelled "due to his rebellious spirit."[28] Apparently Guichard had joined a clique of students who "did not accept the school's discipline." His instructors at the *Institut Leschi*, an elite private school still operating today in Marseille, described Guichard as "a fairly intelligent student but sombre, temperamental and of a very nervous temperament. Some of his behaviour suggested that he was slightly emotionally disturbed." While in law school in his early twenties, he suffered from "crises d'aggréssivité," as a result of which he spent two months in confinement in a hospital under the treatment of a Monsieur Volle.[29]

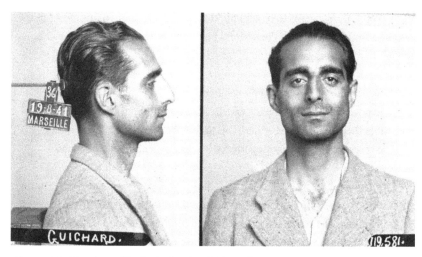

Figure 4.1. Mugshot of Ludovic Guichard, Marseille, 19 August 1941. AD Bouches-du-Rhône, 1269/W/77, "Dossier 936: Assassinat de M. Dormoy (1941)."

As his legal troubles related to the Dormoy case mounted, Guichard sought to use his history of emotional problems to claim diminished responsibility for his role in the affair. He had been in treatment with a psychiatrist since July of 1939, and in 1941 obtained a certificate to that effect. He also requested a psychological examination, which the police arranged with an eminent doctor of neuropsychiatric medicine from Montpellier, Luis Tarbouriech. While Guichard certainly held some strange beliefs in "supernatural manifestations," Tabouriech affirmed that despite Guichard's odd ideas and nervous temperament, he seemed lucid and of average intelligence.[30] Still, Tarbouriech declared that "like all obsessive, anxious persons, Guichard is very suggestible. This is not a passionate person who obeys extreme sentiments, but an undecided person who allows himself to be influenced by someone with a stronger will than his own."

Yet the police uncovered another side to Guichard as well, one that indicated a more resourceful and determined person than he wanted the authorities to perceive. Chenevier noted during his interviews that Guichard seemed to take an almost "malign pleasure" in wasting Chenevier's time for hours on end during interrogations.[31] Despite his problems at school, Guichard managed to obtain his baccalaureate degree from the Institute Melizan in 1931, and he then earned a law degree at the *Faculté Libre de Droit de Marseille* in two years, although he never passed the bar.[32] After his aborted stint in the military, Guichard found work as a salesman and then as manager for a food wholesaler in Marseille, "La Fraternelle de Provence, société d'alimentation," probably through the influence of his father, a principal shareholder in the company.[33] In October 1938 Guichard married Julienne Gensul, and in 1941 they were childless.

The lengthy period of stability in Guichard's life came to end in December of 1939, when "La Fraternelle de Provence, société d'alimentation" went bankrupt. Guichard's parents lent him 60,000 francs to tide him over despite the strain that the bankruptcy must have placed on their finances as well. Guichard got another job, probably again with his father's help, as a customs officer for a private company that collected customs duties in Marseille, a position he held from December 1939 until May of 1940. The German invasion in May of 1940 ended Guichard's new job and he once again was at loose ends.[34]

From 1940 on, like many disaffected young men in France in whom the defeat and Occupation had bred a righteous fury against the "bastards" of the Third Republic who they were convinced had brought about the disaster, Guichard's politics became the determining factor in his future. Guichard had long been a member of two political organizations associated with France's extreme right. The first of these, the AF, was the venerable royalist party that had for decades been under the control of Charles Maurras, who delighted in using his considerable skills as a writer, journalist, and orator to fling invective against the Third Republic. Born as a reaction to the Dreyfus Affair of the 1890s, the AF represented an older generation of conservative thought, steeped in hatred of the legacy of the French Revolution. The second organization to which Guichard belonged was Jacques Doriot's PPF.[35] The latter, which attracted a younger cadre of followers, was by far the more dangerous.[36]

Guichard's political associations had led him, like many other unemployed young men adrift in the wake of the Armistice with little mooring left in their lives except for their anger and their political convictions, to join the Marseille branch of Colonel Georges Groussard's newly created *Groupes de protection* (GP). The GP was meant to be an elite corps of young men devoted to Philippe Pétain who would dedicate their lives to "protect" the National Revolution and the Maréchal against "counter-revolutionary" forces. Guichard himself admitted that he was a "militant" in both the AF and the PPF. But it is perhaps even more indicative of where Guichard's real talents lay that the leader of the GP in Marseille, a Corsican ex-soldier named Antoine Marchi, recruited Guichard to work for the *Centre d'information et d'études* (CIE), the wing of the GP dedicated to gathering intelligence. Both Marchi and Guichard had belonged to the Cagoule. Moreover, it was apparent that in the Marseille GP

Guichard had rubbed shoulders with all three of the young men killed by the bomb in Nice, and their friend Yves Moynier, also a former Cagoulard.[37]

Given that Moynier's whereabouts, and possible involvement in the Dormoy murder, were unknown, and the other three men involved, including the person who most likely fashioned the murder weapon, were dead, Kubler knew that he had to squeeze more information out of Guichard if he was going to break the case. This was not going to be an easy task, however. Kubler confronted Guichard with the mounting evidence that Guichard was involved in the Dormoy assassination and asked whether he had been assigned to spy on Dormoy in Montélimar and, if so, by whom. Guichard refused to answer and said simply, "I cannot respond."[38] Kubler took this to mean that Guichard was bound by an oath of silence.

Guichard's stint with the CIE ended in December of 1940. The Germans, incensed because the GP had arrested Ambassador Otto Abetz's protégé Pierre Laval, forced Pétain to dissolve the GP. Kubler became curious as to how the unemployed Guichard raised the capital in June of 1941 to purchase a hair salon in Marseille, called "Conchita," which Guichard's wife managed. Given that Guichard had already run through the 60,000-franc loan from his parents the previous year, and had worked only intermittently since the bankruptcy of his wholesale food enterprise in January of 1940, where did Guichard find the money to buy the salon? Although they paid their son a monthly stipend of 1200 francs, his parents denied that they had given him the 20,000 francs in cash he had used to purchase his salon.[39] Guichard had a mistress, Zöe Hosch, a waitress in a restaurant in Marseille who had been seeing "Ludo" since October of 1940 and must have also cost Guichard at least some money.[40]

The issue of funding was crucial because Kubler knew that the multiple trips of the assassins to Montélimar, including Guichard's extended stay at the Relais in July, for which he paid 90 francs per night, had been expensive, especially for a group of young men in their twenties, only one of whom, Maurice Marbach, held a regular, full-time job. If "Mlle. Florence" participated in the murder, her trips to Montélimar had to have been costly. The two men who dined at the Brasserie Delhoste and ordered bottles of "aged wine" had money to burn. Guichard might have received funds from his parents, but none of the three dead men came from affluent families. Kubler and Chenevier knew that the source of the funds was likely also the instigator of the crime.

Guichard had found a business partner in the spring of 1941, Roger Mouraille, a native of Marseille and the owner of a trucking company. Mouraille's name also figured in the address book Kubler discovered in Guichard's home, and the two men had known each other while members of the AF, the PPF, and the GP. When the police pressed Guichard about his sources of income, he stated that at the beginning of June 1941 he had sold his share in Mouraille's company, along with a truck, for 30,000 francs. It was this money that had paid for the salon, and, so he claimed, for his trips to Montélimar.[41] The Marseille police found Roger Mouraille's telephone number, along with that of Guichard, on the body of Guyon, and a quick check showed that the 28-year-old Mouraille had also been a member of the GP and the CIE in the fall of 1940. Marchi and Mouraille had been ardent supporters of the extreme right prior to the war, and both had lengthy police records.[42]

Kubler thus had good reason to suspect that Roger Mouraille and Antoine Marchi were party to Dormoy's assassination. Marchi was the link tying together the suspects that Kubler had identified so far. It was clear now that they had been recruited from the milieu of the extreme right in Marseille, and Marchi as founder of the Marseille GP was the obvious candidate for the ringleader. Chenevier's informant in Marseille asserted that Marchi organized the crime at the behest of a former member of the Cagoule, now an influential figure at Vichy, Gabriel Jeantet. A close friend and advisor of Pétain's personal physician, Bernard Ménétrel, Jeantet had been general secretary of the Amicale de France, a propaganda organization tied to the GP and the CIE and, like them, created in the autumn of 1940 and based in Marseille. The Amicale, GP and CIE were not official entities in Pétain's government, but rather were designed to work in tandem to advance Pétain's National Revolution. Former members of France's interwar extreme right, including the Cagoule, comprised most of the recruits for the Amicale, GP, and CIE. With Jeantet at the helm of the Amicale, and ex-Cagoulards Georges Groussard and François Méténier running the GP and the CIE, the three organizations together reconstituted the Cagoule in southern France. In addition, from the inception of the État français Jeantet was charged with establishing centers of propaganda for Pétain's civil cabinet. In February and March of 1941 Jeantet established propaganda centers in French West Africa at Pétain's behest. From September 1941 to January 1942 Jeantet acted as a liaison between the civil cabinet and the propaganda service within the information ministry. His formal title during that period was inspector of propaganda. The investigation seemed to be heading toward the highest echelons of the Vichy government and to Occupied Paris. Either direction was fraught with danger for Kubler and Chenevier. Before they could move against Marchi, who was well connected within Vichy political circles and in the Occupied

Zone, they would have to unearth compelling evidence. And for that, they needed to locate Roger Mouraille.[43]

Arresting Mouraille would be a more difficult and dangerous task than dealing with Guichard had been. Roger Albert Marius Mouraille was born in Marseille on 10 June 1913.[44] He was well educated, having attended the Institut Leschi and the Lycée Thiers and then having received a diploma from the *Institut commercial Colbert*. In October of 1931, aged 18, Mouraille joined the 22nd Regiment of the Colonial Infantry based at Aix-la-Chapelle. He returned to civilian life two years later and worked for six months at the Maison Rémington. Swept up next in the fervor of the Spanish Civil War, Mouraille was among the few Frenchmen who had fought for General Franco's Nationalists rather than for the Republicans and belonged to an even smaller cadre among the French volunteers who had gained the respect and appreciation of the Nationalist military commanders and contributed significantly to the Nationalist victory. Franco's gratitude was such that despite the prevalent distrust among the Nationalists toward all things French, Franco personally authorized Mouraille to maintain a branch of his trucking business in Spain.[45]

Mouraille demonstrated in Spain that he was a risk-taker with a talent for espionage. He joined the French Socialist Party (SFIO) and the Barcelona Red Cross in order to obtain the necessary credentials to access Spanish Republican territory, including the Republican stronghold of Barcelona. Mouraille had a truck driver's license, and under the cover of transporting supplies to the Republicans he garnered vital intelligence that he passed on to the Nationalists. He also helped to smuggle Franco sympathizers out of Republican territory, which earned him accolades from Franco, although Mouraille's "cover" as a supporter of the French Socialists and Spanish Republicans obliged him to return to Spain after the Nationalist victory to defend his record from the suspicions of members of Franco's entourage. Mouraille joined the Cagoule in Marseille during the 1930s. A mere six months prior to the outbreak of war with Germany in 1940 (and thus a good two years after the French police had supposedly dismantled the Cagoule), Mouraille tried to recruit a childhood friend to join the Cagoule.[46] During the summer of 1939, Mouraille visited, on multiple occasions, the villa in San Sebastian, Spain, where Jean Filliol and Aristide Corre were holed up in exile. Mobilized at Marseille in the autumn of 1939, Mouraille by all accounts fought bravely until he was demobilized shortly after the Armistice. He was credited with rescuing priests and nuns after an Italian bombing raid over Marseille. An ardent Catholic and supporter of Pétain's National Revolution, Mouraille joined the GP and soon became the head of the CIE at Marseille, where he reconnected with Guichard, whom he brought into his trucking business as a partner. Commissaire de Police Mobile Spotti noted that of all the suspects, Mouraille was considered "the most dangerous, audacious, and reflective."[47]

Mouraille owned a rural property in the village of Allauch, just east of Marseille, and Chenevier's informant had told him that Mouraille could be found there. When Kubler showed up at Allauch late in the day on 18 August, Mouraille surrendered peacefully. With Mouraille was Yves Moynier, a former postal worker at Marseille who had worked for Mouraille's trucking company in 1941. Moynier closely matched several witnesses' descriptions of one of the young men who took a room at the Hôtel de la Place d'Armes and presented the bouquet to Gérodias at the Relais the afternoon before Dormoy was murdered. Kubler arrested both men (see Figure 4.2 and Figure 4.3). He got to Allauch just in time, as with Mouraille's help Moynier was planning to flee Marseille that very night. Both men knew about the deaths of Guyon, Marbach, and Vaillant and the arrest of Guichard.[48]

Yves Moynier was 27 years old in August of 1941, single and a native of Marseille. He was less educated than either Guichard or Mouraille, having attended lycée for only one year. It was at the Institut Leschi that he had first met Guichard. Moynier enlisted in the army when he was 18 and after his discharge in 1933 got a job with the post office. He reenlisted when war with Germany broke out in 1939, served with distinction, and was demobilized in 1940 with the rank of sergeant. In September of 1940 he joined the GP. At loose ends upon the dissolution of the GP in December of 1940, he went to work for Roger Mouraille, whom he knew from the GP and the Amicale de France. Moynier was a firm supporter of the National Revolution who like Guichard and Mouraille belonged to both the AF and the PPF in Marseille.[49] After his arrest on 18 August Moynier freely admitted his role in the assassination of Marx Dormoy and authored a detailed statement of how the assassination was plotted and carried out. In fact, he was eager to confess and determined to persuade the police that his crime was a justified political execution.

The only problem was that the police knew that while many of the details Moynier offered regarding the crime were accurate, much of his confession was a lie. Not only did Moynier steadfastly refuse to give the police the real name of the woman who had spied on Dormoy and helped the assassins get the bomb under Dormoy's mattress, but Moynier also insisted the he alone had organized the crime and recruited the other participants.[50] He maintained that Roger Mouraille had played no role other than sheltering him after the fact,

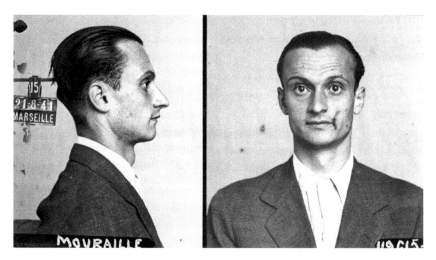

Figure 4.2. Mugshot of Roger Mouraille, Marseille, 21 August 1941. AD Bouches-du-Rhône, 1269/W/77, "Dossier 936: Assassinat de M. Dormoy (1941)."

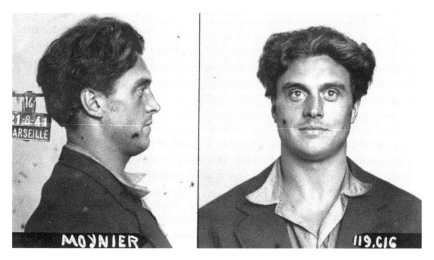

Figure 4.3. Mugshot of Yves Moynier, Marseille, 21 August 1941. AD Bouches-du-Rhône, 1269/W/77, "Dossier 936: Assassinat de M. Dormoy (1941)."

and that no one at Vichy or in Paris had masterminded the crime or offered him any financial or logistical assistance. It was obvious that Moynier was lying, not only because Chenevier's informants in both Paris and Marseille had stated otherwise, but also because it wasn't hard to see that Moynier simply was not equipped, emotionally, intellectually, or financially, to have plotted and carried out the assassination. Although his level of education was not high, Moynier was by no means stupid, but he was clearly emotionally unstable. Moynier was an ideologue, a fanatical supporter of the National Revolution, and more a foot soldier than a mastermind, a man of action rather than of strategy. After interrogating him on 21 August Étienne Mercuri of the Marseille police described Moynier as "a sort of ascetic for whom earthly pleasures mean little. He lives only for his nationalist ideals and exclusively for himself. The revival of our country is his obsession. Ardent nationalist, he joined two [officially] recognized groups, l'AMICALE de FRANCE and the PARTI POPULAIRE FRANCAIS. But the political nuances of humans mean little to him. He nurtures a cold hatred toward those whom he considers responsible for our misfortunes ... He is a man of action, athletic and of a powerful vitality."[51]

Moynier dreamed of punishing the Third Republic politicians whom he viewed as responsible for the debacle of the French defeat. An impulsive, angry young man who grew up fatherless – Moynier described himself as a "war orphan" because his father was killed in World War I and Moynier never knew him – Moynier explained his motivations in this way:

> Two bloodlettings in twenty years, once again the young Frenchmen sleep cold and bloody on the ground of their poorly defended land. Who is at fault? Was it fatal, ineluctable, that this poor country be transformed into a cemetery? To whom should the responsibility for this disaster, this defeat belong? All our Jews with their long-hooked noses and our corrupt and venal politicians belong before a firing squad, a just punishment of these traitors, because it is an insult to our dead, to our wounded and amputees, to all our young twenty-year-old Frenchmen now cadavers forever, that this situation still continues. They promised us, these venal traitors, but it is French people who pay and not them, they who will perhaps once again escape forever the just punishment their acts merit. I admit to this action, carefully conceived of my own initiative, which brings me only honour.[52]

Prior to the Dormoy assassination, Moynier's most significant brush with the law was his arrest on 7 April 1941. He and a couple of friends, including Lucien Guyon and Horace Vaillant, were caught at 3:30 a.m. painting "Death to the Jews" on the storefronts and sidewalks of Marseille's fashionable Canebière, a long avenue with many shops and cafes in the city's Old Port quarter. While spending the night in jail together, Moynier, Vaillant, and Guyon discussed their frustration with mere vandalism and their desire to strike a more significant blow against the enemies of the National Revolution. That night they hatched a plot to blow up the Jewish synagogue in Marseille and recruited the help of Maurice Marbach, who had access to and experience with explosives. Marbach was able to build them a bomb and they attacked the synagogue a couple of weeks later.[53] Even so, until the Dormoy assassination, Moynier had not committed any crimes beyond defacing or destroying property. Moynier was no trained assassin. For all his fiery rhetoric, he was also a young man who still lived with his mother, spent most of his spare time at the gym, was unemployed at the time of his arrest, and lacked the money to fund the trips to and from Montélimar required for the murder. Kubler and Chenevier were convinced that someone with more wealth, experience, and emotional toughness had to have organized the crime, and thanks to their informants and careful detective work using the police files on members of France's violent extreme right prior to 1940, they had a solid list of suspects. What they needed was evidence but amassing that was going to be difficult unless they could get Guichard, Moynier, or Mouraille to reveal who had recruited them.

Mouraille denied any involvement in Dormoy's murder. Mouraille and Guichard concurred that they had hired Moynier in the spring of 1941 out of sympathy and abhorred Moynier's extremism and penchant for violence. Mouraille stated that he did not discuss politics with Moynier because Moynier's political views "disgusted him." Moreover, Mouraille claimed that he fired Moynier after a few months because Moynier often failed to come to work in the morning, offering as his excuse that he'd been up all night putting up propaganda posters for the Maréchal. Mouraille knew that Moynier had been arrested for painting graffiti "insulting to Jews" but was willing to shrug off Moynier's vandalism as simply the hijinks of an excitable and politically ardent young man. Mouraille claimed to know nothing about Moynier's role in the attack on the synagogue in Marseille.[54] Again, however, the police had evidence that Mouraille and Moynier were lying, because they knew that Mouraille and Moynier had traveled to Paris together during the second week of August.

When confronted with the evidence, Mouraille and Moynier both admitted to having made the trip to Paris. According to Mouraille, he ran into Moynier around 2 August on the Canebière. By then, Mouraille had heard about Dormoy's assassination but had responded to the news with indifference. "I thought, 'There's one less jerk.'"[55] Mouraille was already planning a visit to Paris to, so he claimed, repatriate funds from his business interests in Spain. When he told Moynier about the trip on the 2nd, Moynier, who had not revealed his role in Dormoy's death, asked if he could go along, and Mouraille was happy to have his company on the train. It made sense that Moynier would be eager to travel with Mouraille, as the two men had to find a way to sneak across the Line of Demarcation separating the Vichy Zone from the Occupied Zone, since neither had the required German permits to cross.

On 7 August 1941, Mouraille met Moynier at the Saint-Charles train station in Marseille and they took the 11:45 p.m. train to Paris. They disembarked at Saint Florent, in the Department of Cher, about 12.5 miles (20 kilometers) from the crossing point at Bourges, and traversed the Line on foot at night in a rural area where it was lightly patrolled. Mourailles' extensive military and espionage experience dating from the Spanish Civil War equipped them with the skills to evade the border guards and forego assistance from a guide, although Mouraille had gotten an itinerary of where to cross from "someone." They arrived in Paris on 10 August, which suggests that it took them at least 36 hours to cross the Line, reach the nearest town with a train station, and board another Paris-bound train, probably in Bourges. There the two men supposedly went their separate ways for most of the week they spent in Paris. It was only after they had returned to Marseille that Moynier revealed to Mouraille his part in "the affair at Montélimar" and asked Mouraille to shelter him at Allauch and help him get out of the country.[56]

The police knew, however, that Mouraille and Moynier had a very different agenda for their trip to Paris. The pair headed back to Marseille on 13 August and decided to stay on the train for the return voyage. At 11:30 p.m. they were arrested at Louhans while trying to re-enter the Vichy Zone without a pass and, when questioned by the police prefect at Saône-et-Loire, admitted that they were on their way back to Marseille from Paris.[57] The police at Louhans discovered twenty copies of Eugène Deloncle's manifesto *Les idées et l'action*, essentially MSR propaganda, in a suitcase. After confiscating a copy, the police let Mouraille and Moynier go on their way.

The two men arrived in Marseille on the afternoon of 15 August and arranged to meet again a half hour later at the Brasserie des Danaïdes near the train station. But when Moynier showed up at the brasserie, he wasn't alone. With him was their mutual acquaintance from the GP, Corsican ex-soldier Antoine Marchi. It was then, according to Moynier, that Marchi informed Moynier in Mouraille's presence that "things aren't going well," because their mutual friends Marbach, Guyon, and Vaillant had accidently blown themselves up the night before in the public garden in Nice. Moynier admitted to his role in the assassination of Dormoy, to the supposed surprise of Marchi and Mouraille, and informed Mouraille that he had gone to see Eugène Deloncle at the MSR headquarters in order to escape the police by joining Deloncle's LVF. Since he had some reservations about the LVF, Moynier decided to return to Marseille and think over his decision. Once it became apparent that the police were closing in, Moynier decided that he no longer had a choice and appealed to Mouraille for assistance. Mouraille agreed to let Moynier hide out at his rural property, because the two shared "nationalist ideas," and to help smuggle Moynier out of Marseille. Mouraille sent Moynier to Allauch and stayed in Marseille to arrange Moynier's flight via the German-controlled port. Mouraille had a pass to access the port because he loaded his trucks there. On the morning of 16 August "a friend of Moynier['s]" went to Allauch and confirmed the demise of Guyon, Marbach, and Vaillant. In this version of events, when the police arrested them both on 18 August, just hours before Moynier intended to return to the Occupied Zone, Mouraille was guilty only of aiding Moynier after the fact, and Marchi had nothing to do with the affair.[58]

Again, however, the police had their own information about the trip to Paris, and confronted with what the police already knew, the two men's stories began to diverge. Moynier and Mouraille admitted that they had not separated in Paris but rather had stayed in the same hotel. Mouraille accompanied Moynier to the MSR offices and the meeting at the Brasserie immediately after their arrival in Marseille on 15 August. Mouraille claimed not to know who Marchi was – a lie given that both Moynier and Mouraille had been team leaders in the Marseille GP, which Marchi had founded and led.[59] Once both men realized that Moynier would not be able to shield Mouraille entirely, they concentrated their efforts on protecting Marchi, which of course confirmed the police suspicion that Marchi was deeply involved in Dormoy's death. Their determination to keep Marchi out of it is apparent in Mouraille's refusal to describe to the police "the man who came to the Brasserie des Danaïdes to tell Moynier about the death of his friends."[60] Curiously, however, already on 19 August Mouraille admitted that he and Moynier met in Paris with a man named André "Hérard" (sometimes spelled Erard or Evrard), who worked for Deloncle in the MSR. By the 20th, once he realized that the police knew the truth about the trip to Paris and about Hérard, Moynier also gave up Hérard, but neither Marchi nor the name of his female accomplice. Perhaps Mouraille and Moynier reasoned that because Hérard was in the Occupied Zone and under Deloncle's protection, he would be out of the reach of the Vichy police, whereas if Marchi was still in the Vichy Zone, he would be more vulnerable.[61]

Thus in their "revised" version of the trip to Paris, they admitted that Moynier visited the MSR headquarters and had a "brief" meeting with Deloncle and a more extensive conversation with Deloncle's lieutenant, André Hérard, on whom the police had an extensive file that would only get thicker when Hérard went to work for the Gestapo in 1942.[62] Mouraille claimed that he had arranged to meet Moynier at the Napolitaine Café on the Parisian "Boulevards" to take an aperitif, "as was the custom in the Midi." Much to his surprise, Moynier showed up in the company of "André" with whom, it just so happened, Mouraille was already acquainted, because the two had met while in the AF's youth organization, the Camelots du roi, in Marseille. Mouraille offered the police a description of "André" and insisted that he had no idea why Moynier had brought him to the Napolitaine. The police, of course, knew that the 33-year-old Hérard was one of Deloncle's chief lieutenants in the MSR and Chenevier's informant in Paris had indicated that Deloncle and Hérard were involved in the Dormoy assassination. Mouraille's testimony confirmed Chenevier's conviction that the trail of the crime led to the MSR. Moreover, it did not take the police long to guess that Hérard was the "Monsieur André" who had paid Florence Gérodias a visit at the Relais in June, a suspicion that would be confirmed when they showed photos of Hérard to the witnesses in Montélimar.[63]

On 20 August Moynier also admitted to having met Hérard in Paris, and that, like Mouraille, he knew Hérard because they had been in Marseille's Camelots du roi together prior to the war. The circles of young men in Marseille's extreme right, relationships developed well before the formation of the GP, were the recruiting grounds for Dormoy's assassins and everyone connected with the crime. Moynier still denied that Hérard or anyone else had helped him organize the assassination, which only he and his deceased friends Guyon, Marbach, and Vaillant had carried out. But the noose was tightening. In the course of questioning Moynier, the police showed him a photograph of a couple in "swimming clothes" and walking a "black dog."[64]

"Do you recognize anyone in this picture?" they asked.

Moynier's response was "I give up. The woman is no other than the 'Annie' who I have spoken to you about, but I refuse to give you any other information about her or her address." The police were closing in on the real identity of "Florence Gérodias."

CHAPTER FIVE

Summer 1941: Recruiting the Assassins

> An inventory of the discourses in Je suis partout during the Second World War reveals a host of revenge fantasies: revenge against the weak and decadent Third Republic; revenge on those deemed responsible for the debacle of 1940; revenge on the liberated woman imagined by modern feminism; revenge on socialist and liberal bien pensants deemed to have held cultural power in France since the 1789 Revolution; revenge on "modernity" and all that it signified.
>
> Joan Tumblety, "Revenge of the Fascist Knights: Masculine Identities in Je suis partout, 1940–1944."[1]

ANNIE

Charles Chenevier caught up with the blond woman calling herself "Florence Gérodias" purely through a stroke of good fortune, after she had eluded the police for nearly a month.[2] On 19 August Chenevier telephoned his superior at Vichy to relate the news of the arrest of Yves Moynier and Roger Mouraille the preceding evening. The telephone services in the Vichy Zone were both unreliable and frequently monitored. An "officer of the telephone control" decided that the call had been going on too long and cut off the line. Infuriated, Chenevier called back and upbraided the officer for terminating such an important conversation. Word of the dispute quickly percolated up the Vichy chain of command, not surprising given the significance of Chenevier's news and the fact that he had been reporting it to Pierre Mondanel, head of the Judicial

Police for the entire Vichy Zone, when the call was terminated. Chenevier's complaint reached the level of Pétain's military cabinet, where it drew the attention of an unnamed "military officer" who recognized Roger Mouraille's name. By now the police had learned from Moynier that Florence Gérodias' real first name was "Annie," and the military officer recalled that a woman named "Annie" and matching Gérodias' description had been decorated with the *Croix de Guerre* for her heroism in driving a truck to and from the front lines in May and June of 1940.

Armed with this information, Chenevier soon tracked down "Annie," whose real name was "Anne Félice Mouraille."[3] Mouraille was a theater actress who had adopted the stage name "Annie Morène." A photo from the program for a 1937 production of Jean Cocteau's *Les Chevaliers de la table ronde* shows a handsome blond woman with fine but not delicate features, a rather aquiline nose, a hint of a smile, and an intense gaze focused not on the camera but into the distance. She has a scarf wrapped tightly around her neck, her hair is shoulder length, smooth, wavy and swept back, and her head is tilted slightly forward, as if she is leaning into a breeze. The impression the photo conveys is of a confident, composed, intense young woman preoccupied by thoughts inaccessible to the viewer and impervious to the regard of the camera. She is perhaps a bit headstrong and certainly not at all self-conscious, a woman determined to march to the "sound of her own drummer."[4] Although Mouraille's name is often confused with that of Roger Mouraille, Chenevier was emphatic that the two were not related and that the correct spelling of Annie's name was "Mouraille." Annie herself subsequently also emphasized that she was not related to Roger Mouraille.[5]

Although residing in Nice during the war, in late August Mouraille, a member of the troupe *La Comédie en Provence*, was in Vichy acting in a popular French comedy, *Ces dames aux chapeaux verts*, and it was there that Chenevier arrested her on 24 August, backstage in her dressing room at the theater (see Figure 5.1). The police found in Mouraille's handbag twenty-two documents pertaining to the case, among them a telegram from Yves Moynier.[6] Mouraille first tried to bluff her way out of trouble, but once the police had the letters, she readily confessed to participating in the crime. "Not only did she describe precisely her role in the affair, but she revealed that certain members of Pétain's entourage were compromised as well," Chenevier stated.[7] Her cool reaction to her arrest and willingness to implicate powerful accomplices indicated that Mouraille would not easily be cowed or controlled, and that she was confident of both the righteousness

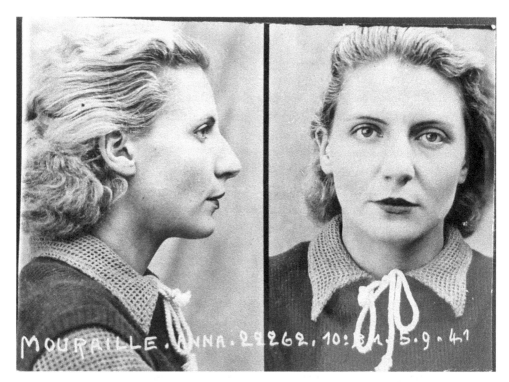

Figure 5.1. Mugshot of Anna Mouraille [sic], Marseille, 5 September 1941. AD Bouches-du-Rhône, 1269/W/77, "Dossier 936: Assassinat de M. Dormoy (1941)."

of her cause and protection from those whose names she dropped in that initial interview. From the outset, she showed neither the slightest regret for her part in the murder, nor the slightest doubt as to the justice of her actions and those of her co-conspirators.

Chenevier and his men searched her apartment in Nice, 20 rue Meyerbeer. They discovered two additional telegrams from Moynier, sent from Marseille on the 2nd and 17th of July and addressed to "Annie Morène" at the Palais de la Méditerranée in Nice. The police found two other letters and a telegram, also from Marseille and dated July, and, most damning, a map of the city of Montélimar with the name "Florence Gérodias" written on it, and another map drawn in pencil illustrating the interior of the Relais de l'Empereur. They also spotted two colorfully wrapped boxes of Montélimar's famous nougat, souvenirs from her trip to the city in July to assassinate Dormoy. These last three finds indicate her confidence that those who organized the crime would shield her from prosecution should the authorities track her down.[8]

Figure 5.2. Annie Mourraille in Nice, probably with Antony Carretier, undated. AD Bouches-du-Rhône, 1269/W/77, "Dossier 936 Assassinat de M. [sic] Dormoy (1941)."

The police also unearthed in her apartment a stamped and notarized act concerning the sale to "Annie Morène" and one Antony Carretier, of a yacht, "L'Ami," registered on the tax rolls of Nice, along with a boating permit. They tracked down Carretier, a 33-year-old actor residing at his villa "Toi et Moi" on the Côte d'Azur near Cannes.[9] According to Carretier, although the two were lovers, they had an "open relationship" where each of them was free to date other people and neither "would ever pose the least question to the other."[10] Carretier knew about Mourraille's close relationship with Moynier. In fact, she had introduced the two men, and Carretier added that Moynier seemed "handsome enough," albeit in the "genre of Tarzan."[11]

The police obtained a photo of Mourraille out for a stroll near the Mediterranean in Nice (see Figure 5.2). She is tall and athletic, and her muscled arms reflect her swimming prowess – she was a French champion of the crawl.[12] Walking with a man, probably Carretier, she holds a black dog on a leash. She is wearing men's pants and, most unusual for the era, she is topless except for what appears to be a bikini. Witnesses claimed that she fashioned this provocative style of dressing and sewed the tops herself.[13] The photo shows a beautiful woman, tanned, the picture of health and vitality. As in her theater headshot, Mourraille looks resolutely away from the camera, toward the ocean, uninterested in the photographer's gaze, or that of the other people on the boardwalk, a woman in motion, moving confidently toward her destination, with a man, but not holding his hand and clearly not belonging to him. The formidable woman in the photo fits perfectly Carretier's depiction of Annie Mourraille.

Carretier admitted that he also knew his mistress had "pretty significant" involvement in "political activities."[14] According to Carretier, Mourraille was very "antisemitic" and "anti-Gaulliste." He found the political passions of his lover mystifying. "For my part, each time she raised these subjects for discussion, I tried to dissuade her and make her understand that there were other means than brute force to express her point of view. For example, I told her to refuse to work with Jews, refuse to shake their hands if need be, but that would be sufficient for the moment." Annie Mourraille had a more violent solution to France's "Jewish problem" in mind than what Carretier was suggesting. Her militancy unnerved him, although not enough for him to end their affair.

While Chenevier was searching Mourraille's apartment, Victor Chauvin, divisional superintendent of the Judicial Police, Paris, interrogated her in Vichy on 25 August. During the subsequent days, the police amassed a considerable dossier on her background.[15] Anne-Félice Mourraille, whom her family sometimes called "Anice," was born on 24 September 1913 in Lyon, the youngest of four children.[16] Her father, Léon Mourraille, was mayor of the city of Gattières, in the Alpes-Maritimes not far from Marseille, a post he had occupied for almost four decades by 1941.[17] Evidently he was largely an absentee mayor, as until the German invasion the family resided in or near Paris much of the year. An artillery commander in his youth, Mourraille was named a *Chevalier de la légion d'honneur*, most likely for his service during World War I.

Léon Mourraille wed Annie's mother, Mathilde Lamouroux, in 1896. Annie was raised in Paris, where her parents resided in an apartment in the 7th arrondissement on the upscale Avenue de la Bourdonnaise, which runs parallel to the Champ de Mars and ends at the École Militaire about a mile from her family home. Annie loved Paris. Her mother, however, was always happiest in Gattières and found the family's frequent displacements that Léon Mourraille's career necessitated extremely tiring. Mathilde noted in her journal in 1908 her joy at returning "back to the large house with its friendly furniture, back to the woodland and back to the meadow! More than that, I am back to the existence I love! Peace and quiet at last, and no travelling! Let us hope it stays this way!"[18]

The contrasting influences of her parents played a central role in shaping Annie Mourraille's personality. Mathilde Lamouroux's journal reveals a well-read woman with literary talent who was emotional, something of a romantic who doted on her children. Léon rarely figures in Mathilde's journal entries; he appears to have been an absent father much of the time, regardless of whether he was away on business or at home. Older than Mathilde, he was already middle aged when Annie was born. There is no sense in Mathilde's memoirs that Léon had a strong emotional connection with any of the children, not even his son. Annie was a latecomer to the household, nine years younger than her closest sibling, Jean. Her older sisters were both teenagers during her childhood, and Annie and her mother developed an extremely close bond that seems to have surpassed their emotional relationships with anyone else in the household. Annie's birth gave Mathilde, whose children were the center of her existence, a new purpose in life. In 1915 she described Annie's arrival on the scene this way:

> Two years earlier, when it had felt as if there were no children left in the household, Anice had come along. She had become our sovereign overnight. When she was one day old, Mother had never felt so maternal! When she was one month old, we were all her servants – devotees to her adorable little hand because it was such a perfect work of art! When she was one year old, she had no equal among her peers, having taken to walking like a fledgling takes to flying. With her round cheeks, golden locks and large blue eyes, she was our little doll – the goddess of smile and the goddess of grace.[19]

In a passage added in 1917, Mathilde stated that Annie "is now aged four and she is still our queen."[20] Annie grew up to be confident in her own beauty and abilities, but also appears to have been the classic spoiled child who as a teenager became rebellious. She remained close to her mother throughout her life, and while she was in prison between 1941 and 1943 she exchanged numerous letters with her mother, albeit not a single one with her father. Mourraille shared her mother's flair for drama and penchant for writing yet rejected her mother's focus on domesticity and children. She was highly sexual and strongly attracted to men, but she eschewed the standard feminine gender roles of her day and at times even wore men's clothing. Fit and engaged in sports, she was deeply imbued with the culture of youth, physical fitness, and "virility" that pervaded interwar France.[21] Mourraille was willing to use her looks and charisma to charm men. But no man – not her father, not her lovers, not her husbands, and not Chenevier – was going to dominate her. Despite her father's emotional absence in her life Léon Mourraille appears to have shaped Annie's self-image, aspirations, and career – or at least her career as an assassin. Annie loved her mother, but in many ways, it was her father whom she admired and sought to emulate.

Annie Mourraille spent much of her youth literally and figuratively in the shadow of the École Militaire, the symbol of her father's career. After grammar school Annie's family enrolled her at the *Maison d'éducation de la légion d'honneur* "Les Loges" de Saint-Germain, a boarding school for children of members of the Légion, where she was admitted in August 1925. In July 1928, she left "Les Loges" and entered the *Maison d'éducation de la légion d'honneur de Saint-Denis*, from which she graduated the following year with a *brevet elémentaire*, the equivalent of a high school diploma. She was fifteen years old. Her instructors both at "Les Loges" and at Saint-Denis reported that she was "undisciplined, independent, turbulent" in her conduct, and of "mediocre" intelligence.[22] Later observers would use the term *exaltée* to describe her. Mourraille had an exaggerated opinion of herself and her prospects and was something of a fantasist, convinced she was more intelligent than most people. Chenevier took full advantage of this trait when he interrogated her and solicited her testimony against other suspects in the Dormoy case.

On 12 July 1932 Annie Mourraille married Charles Pascale. A few years older than she, Pascale worked for Annie's brother Jean Mourraille in Paris. They had no children and divorced in 1934. After marrying they had moved in with Pascale's mother, and the two women did not get along. Madame Pascale insinuated that Annie had loose morals and had cheated on Charles.[23] Witnesses, even those favorably inclined toward her, emphasized her "bohemian" lifestyle and willingness to flout sexual mores and gender role expectations of her day. Paullette Menard, stage name "Paullette Pax," the director of the Théâtre de l'Oeuvre on the rue de Clichy in Paris, met Annie Mourraille in 1932. Pax was convinced that Mourraille was both intelligent and talented, and noted her "athletic" good looks. She found Mourraille to have "lots of imagination," and to be very independent and determined to "look after her own needs."[24] Pax arranged for Mourraille to take acting lessons at a conservatory, at no cost because Mourraille was "poor," which suggests that she was receiving little if any financial help from her parents. Pax noted that Mourraille was often in the company of a painter named Anatole Soungouroff, with whom Mourraille resided. Mourraille passed off Soungouroff as her "brother" or her "cousin" and insisted that the relationship was entirely platonic, which likely was true since he was the gay Russian painter Antonin Ivanovitch Soungouroff (1894–1982). Soungouroff's paintings were often homoerotic, of sailors, harlequins, and handsome young men in shirtsleeves, and he specialized in depicting the homosexual lifestyle in France.[25]

René Simon, who gave Mourraille acting lessons in 1934, also recalled a "beautiful and strong girl who was in magnificent health" and "very agreeable to interact with but also very bohemian and above all very boyish."[26] Simon was unenthused about Annie Mourraille's acting talent, because even though she was very "artistic," she lacked the "expressiveness" to carry off classical theatrical roles. In 1934 Simon sponsored Mourraille for a place in a theatrical conservatory, but she failed to obtain a slot due to her "lack of femininity."[27] Moreover, according to Simon, Mourraille was "always running hither and yon in different theatres, starting projects but never accomplishing them due to her unstable character and lack of perseverance to follow them through." Because she had trouble paying her rent in her small apartment in the Passage de l'Union in Paris, Mourraille moved to the rue Clerc, also in Paris, and took in Soungouroff as a roommate. Nevertheless, Simon stated that it was well known that Annie "received many visits from men and it often happened that these visitors spent the night with her." Soungouroff slept upstairs in a loft while Mourraille was entertaining her overnight "guests."

It is interesting to note that in 1938 Mourraille moved again, with Soungouroff still in tow, to a more affluent neighborhood on the rue des Acacias in the 17th arrondissement of Paris. No one was able to explain how she could afford the new apartment, which had a much higher rent, 10,000 francs per month, than her previous one. It is possible that by 1938 Mourraille's acting career was successful enough to afford her a more comfortable lifestyle. But given her subsequent involvement with Dormoy's assassination, by then she may have also developed political connections with well-financed leaders of France's extreme right, men such as Eugène Deloncle, who had access to substantial funds and were subsidizing her. Although it is unclear when she developed her extreme right convictions, she socialized with supporters of extreme right political organizations in Paris and Nice during the 1930s and joined the Cagoule in 1936. Soungouroff was mobilized in the French military early in 1940, and after the Armistice Mourraille ended up in Pau prior to relocating to Nice at the end of the year. She had by then lost track of Soungouroff, who was a prisoner of war in Germany. In 1941 Mourraille appears to have had access to plentiful funds unlikely to have originated solely from her acting career. She and Antony Carretier were co-owners of the yacht "L'Ami"; clearly, she had prospered since her days as a struggling actress residing in her mother-in-law's Parisian apartment.

Chenevier questioned Léon Mourraille on 26 August. Mourraille's description of his wayward daughter is enlightening: "Very independent, she has lived her life as she wanted."[28] Léon Mourraille insisted that he knew little about his daughter's "nationalistic" political views. It is telling that Annie "never had her own room" at the family home in Gattières and always shared her mother's room. It suggests an intense intimacy between mother and daughter, but also indicates that Gattières was not in any way Annie's home, and that Léon Mourraille did not go out of his way to encourage her to spend much time there. Although Mourraille was silent on his political views he disapproved of his youngest daughter's militant support of the National Revolution and the Germans, not to mention her lifestyle.

And yet, despite her rebellion against the bourgeois milieu of her family, Annie also seems to have wanted on some level to emulate her father's military career. Even as she rejected the French Third Republic her father served, Annie had a brilliant tour of duty in the military in 1940 and performed courageously under fire, earning the Croix de Guerre for her heroism and a gushing appraisal in at least one admiring article in a French newspaper. Among the first things she told the police during her interrogation on 25 August, the morning after her arrest, was: "I did not belong to a woman's section at all, but during the month of June 1940, I was assigned [to drive] a truck on behalf of the Ministry of Arms to transport, a number of times, anti-tank mines. On June 13 I evacuated the last of the wounded in the Val-de-Grace. Later I retreated with a number of units and I rendered the most services possible to numerous officers. I was given the citation of the Order of the 54th Infantry Regiment."[29] The police verified her citations and her service, and there is no doubt that she took great risks evacuating wounded soldiers from the front. Marcel de Renzis, news editor of the Marseilles newspaper *Le Petit Provençal*, wrote an article about Annie Mourraille in the first half of 1941 entitled "Andromache behind the Steering Wheel: A Heroine of the Theater after Having Been a Heroine in War."[30] After she was demobilized, Mourraille reunited in Aix-en-Provence with many of her theater friends who had also fled Paris and joined the theatrical troupe Comédiens en Provence based in Aix.

Like her male co-conspirators in the Dormoy assassination, Annie Mourraille was too young to have participated in World War I. Her father was a war hero, however, and her generation was steeped in continuous propaganda, emanating especially from the conservative press, about the moral superiority of the veterans of that war. Moreover, mobilizing women was crucial to the war effort in both World War I and World War II even though the wartime role of women, especially in the armaments industry and as support personnel behind the front lines, seemed to contradict the romanticized and domesticized ideal of womanhood that conservatives held up as a role model during the interwar period. Once the Armistice was signed in June of 1940, the Vichy leadership returned to the gender discourse identifying women with domesticity. It is unlikely, however, that women like Mourraille who had served in the military were all willing to give up their jobs and return home, even had France's economic situation and the nearly two million French men trapped in German prisoner-of-war camps rendered such a reversal possible.[31] Women could and did accept virility as a model, and throughout Europe there were women who subscribed to what historian Julie Gottlieb has called "feminine fascism." Some of these women even took part in the same sorts of violence, including street brawls, as the men whose political views they shared.[32] Such women may have been in the minority, but they did exist, and Mourraille was one of them.

Annie Mourraille was an *exaltée*, who embellished her accomplishments and capabilities. But she was also a "modern woman" who did not lack nerve.[33] Her exploits, real and imagined, suggest a woman who rebelled against the sexual and gender conventions of her day and who also wanted to impress her father and her male companions through her own heroism on the battlefield. In her statements related to the Dormoy assassination it is evident that Annie Mourraille saw herself, no less than her male co-conspirators, as a soldier in the National Revolution. She walked a fine line regarding the crime, portraying herself in a more traditional gender role, as a femme fatale ordered to spy on Dormoy and use her feminine charms to lure him from his room, and yet simultaneously insisting that she shared the ideology of her male co-conspirators and was just as devoted to the National Revolution as they.

YVES: RECRUITING A TEAM OF ASSASSINS

Yves Moynier and Annie Mourraille each made prompt confessions to the police soon after their arrests. Their statements are interesting both for what they have in common – the details of how the assassination was planned and committed – and for where they diverge and what they leave out. At the outset both insisted that Moynier alone had organized the team of assassins. Annie Mourraille was merely an accomplice. Three members of the group Moynier had assembled to carry out the crime, Maurice Marbach, Lucien Guyon, and Horace Vaillant, were dead, killed in the explosion in Nice. Only Moynier and Ludovic Guichard were still alive from the original conspiracy.[34]

Proud of her role in the plot, Annie Mourraille struggled to frame her participation within the traditional gender stereotype of a passive sexual lure unaware of the violent actions the "guys" intended to take once she had played her part. In her first official statement she claimed that Moynier told her that the men were only going to "chastise" Dormoy by beating him.[35] But she also evinced far too much knowledge about the plot and its financing to make that version of her participation believable. "In spite of everything, I do not believe that it was Moynier who was the instigator of the attack because, on several occasions, he led me to understand that he and his friends were under the command of a leader who lived in Vichy or received his orders from Vichy."[36] Yet Moynier was emphatic that no "boss" had directed him or financed the crime, and that he and his male accomplices had conceived and executed the entire murder from start to finish. As it became increasingly clear that Moynier intended to "take the fall" for the "higher ups," Mourraille realized that only decisive action on her part could save them both, and that would require not only revealing more about her part in the crime, but also taking the lead in the negotiations – as she saw them – with the authorities.

Neither Moynier nor Mourraille clarified how the two of them had met. By the time of their arrest, they were already lovers. Moynier was much more forthcoming regarding the circle of men from whom he recruited his male co-conspirators. If the motive and inspiration for Dormoy's murder originated among the leaders of France's extreme right in Vichy and Paris, those who carried out the crime came from the lower echelons of these same extremist circles. Mourraille put it very succinctly when she told the police, "As I have already told you, my friends Moynier, Guyon, Vaillant, and Marbach were great patriots, very antisemitic and very anti-Popular Front. They believed that it was people from the extreme left who had caused the war and our defeat."[37] What motivated Dormoy's assassins, fundamentally, was the desire to punish him and men like him for their politics, which in the killers' eyes had led to France's defeat in 1940. This motivation was linked to a crisis of masculine identity that was a powerful force in French and European culture during the interwar era.

Moynier and the other Dormoy suspects shared a culture that revered, even fetishized, youth, masculinity, and violence. They embodied the worldview and obsessions of many French young adults in the 1920s and 1930s. To understand Moynier and his male co-conspirators, therefore, and what drove them to militancy and violence, they must be viewed through the lens of the interwar discourse of masculinity dominant not only in France but throughout Europe and in the United States as well. The roots of this discourse, and its power, lay in the traumatic impact of World War I. The Depression of the 1930s and France's defeat in 1940 only strengthened its resonance for French men and women.[38]

The veterans of World War I were adulated for their patriotism, courage, and sacrifice for the nation. Soldiers represented the ideal of patriarchal masculinity, moral as well as economic heads of their households just as the generals during the war, and especially Philippe Pétain, had been father figures to the ordinary soldiers who served on the battlefield.[39] Despite the powerful currents of pacifism in a France bled dry by World War I, there was also a strong sense that veterans possessed a moral mandate derived from their experiences in the trenches that had rendered them "truer representatives of the people than was the political establishment," which was comprised of old men who had sheltered behind the front lines during the war.[40] This "veteran's mystique" afforded veterans the high moral ground in politics since they were the survivors of a generation that included 1.3 million who had perished fighting for France.[41]

Interwar France experienced a profound "crisis of gender identity" that reached far beyond the discourse of the extreme right. Intellectuals and politicians from both the left and the right worried about effeminate, "weakling" men and sought to fashion "new men" who would boldly carry the banner of their political ideals into the streets and onto the battlefield. It was not only the excessively "masculine" modern woman that worried people. If French women appeared to have jettisoned their essential femininity, French men seemed to have abandoned their virility, physique, and moral character. "The Great War not only traumatized men at the front, it also unleashed a plethora of fears about male homosexuality, which was thought to flourish in the trenches."[42] Moreover, the "veteran's mystique," far from assuaging the crisis of masculinity, exacerbated it for many men who, like Roger Mouraille or Yves Moynier, were too young to have fought in World War I. How were they to live up to the exploits of their veteran fathers, especially if those fathers were absent from their lives?[43]

A self-described "war orphan" (because his father was killed in action during World War I), Moynier shared some of the cachet of the veteran's mystique.

He and his mother were considered (and considered themselves) especially deserving of financial support and official sympathy and recognition because of the sacrifice Moynier's father had made. Moynier never let slip an opportunity to reiterate his special status as a war orphan in his various statements to the police upon his arrest and in letters to the warden when he was incarcerated.[44] Paternity was at the heart of debates about gender during the interwar years and the Vichy era. Fathers and fatherhood, paternal authority and its link to citizenship were fundamental to political and social discourse, not just among nascent fascists in France, but across the political spectrum. Masculinity and paternity were inextricably linked, and those on the right assumed that all "true" men would be fathers.[45]

Yet fatherhood became increasingly problematic in 1930s France, as the economic crisis exacerbated the difficulties working-class fathers faced in providing for their families. Unemployment further depressed the French birth rate at a time when the German population, already much larger than that of France, was rebounding after the effects of World War I. Unemployed men found themselves cut off from the pride and dignity of working and from the traditional masculine camaraderie of the workplace, unable to support their families and at times even dependent on the income of a working spouse or forced to live at home instead of striking out on their own and starting their own families.[46] At the time of Marx Dormoy's assassination, Yves Moynier was still living with his mother, and one of his accomplices lived at home as well. None had children. Their economic insecurity and difficulty finding stable jobs inhibited them from progressing toward economic independence and respectable fatherhood.

Even though he wasn't a father, however, fatherhood was a central facet of Moynier's identity. His status as war orphan, at least in his own mind, gave him a special authority, almost akin to that of an actual veteran of World War I, to criticize the weakness and immorality he perceived in France, and to demand a reform of government and society along the lines of Pétain's National Revolution. He was not a war martyr, but he was the son of one, in his own estimation required to carry on his father's legacy. His identity as a war orphan also placed a distinct burden on Moynier. He was obliged to live in the shadow of a father whose example he could never fully emulate, a man who he never even knew. Moynier's quandary was that even though he had fulfilled his mandatory military service in 1932, until the outbreak of war in 1940 when he was finally able to "see action" and be decorated for his courage under fire, he simply had no battlefield upon which to equal or surpass his father. Absent that opportunity, he could never be the man that his idealized father had been during an era when "the emergence of national consciousness and the rise of military service, particularly in France and Germany, turned the experience of battle into the defining element of the masculine ego, the ultimate test of male self-confrontation, forming the male self-image along aggressively virile lines."[47]

The response of interwar France to this dilemma of gender identity was oddly paradoxical. Even while nourishing an entrenched pacifism, a deep reluctance to become embroiled in an actual war, France sought to turn young men into soldiers in peacetime, to cultivate in them physical strength, steadfast courage, and youthful virility.[48] This adulation of youth, fitness, and virility was ubiquitous in popular culture and spanned the political spectrum.[49] It was a means of protesting against a deep distaste for what those throughout the political spectrum perceived as the decadent politics of the aging and degenerate Third Republic.[50] Both the Communist and the fascist versions of the "new man" prized "physicality, youthfulness, manly camaraderie, and discipline," qualities designed to militarize civilian men in anticipation of when they would be called upon to fight the enemies of the nation on the battlefield.[51]

The spaces where men were expected to build up their bodies and their characters were sports arenas, gyms, and paramilitary formations, all of which figured significantly in the lives of Moynier and the other Dormoy assassins. French popular and scientific culture was flooded with publications about the male body and physical fitness, and "a range of competitive sports and athletic leisure activities now touched the lives of men and women across a range of social classes."[52] Sports and physical exercise prepared politicized young men for the escalating street fighting that took place in interwar France often promoting a toxic masculinity.[53] Moreover, the virile new man was a central motif of the National Revolution Vichy sought to enact in France.[54]

This vision of a renewed France dominated by "new Frenchmen" seduced Moynier, and he and his accomplices tried to embody it in their own lives. It is significant, therefore, that they spent a great deal of time together not only in political activities, but in local gyms. On 21 August 1940 Marius Gandie, a 29-year-old pastry maker in Marseille and good friend of Moynier, gave a statement that revealed how Moynier, the other male Dormoy assassins, and Gandie met and socialized frequently through a local gym. The owner and manager of the gym, Monsieur Anglade, a conservative nationalist, brought the young men together at the gym to strengthen their bodies and discuss politics. Anglade was also a leader of the Marseille branch of the GP, Colonel Georges

Groussard's paramilitary formation organized to protect Pétain and advance the National Revolution. Anglade recruited Gandie, Moynier, Guyon, Vaillant, and Guichard, who all joined the GP. According to Gandie, "All four of us [Gandie, Moynier, Guyon, and Vaillant] had similar attitudes, a community of spirit coming certainly from our love of sports. We hung out together frequently and we got together especially at the gym and the big swimming pool of the Catalans, our habitual establishment."[55]

As was true elsewhere in Europe, French politics during the 1920s and, especially, the 1930s, experienced a "totalitarian drift" that has been well-documented and studied. Movements such as the CF were clearly, if not "fascist," then "fascistic." Their members emulated the fascist exaltation of physically fit bodies, especially masculine bodies, toned and strengthened through athletics. They sought to inculcate camaraderie and military discipline in their recruits and to prepare them mentally and physically for the coming battle for France and for Europe against Bolshevism, hedonism, and decadence.[56] Moynier and the young men who helped him to murder Dormoy envisioned themselves as soldiers in a war that began well before Hitler's armies invaded Belgium and by no means ended with the Armistice in 1940.

BATTLEFIELDS OF A "NATIONAL REVOLUTION"

Moynier nurtured dreams of revenge against a society and political order that he believed had orphaned him in childhood, abandoned him on the battlefield as an adult in 1940, and attempted to destroy his future and that of his beloved "fatherland." One cannot grasp how or why he and his fellow assassins of Marx Dormoy had banded together to plot and carry out this murder without understanding the fantasies of revenge that motivated them to commit a series of escalating violent acts against individuals and institutions that they perceived to embody the cancer eating away at France, rendering their country ripe for defeat in 1940. The heart of the National Revolution was a utopian vision that Pétain and the men surrounding him drew upon in order to unify a defeated France and rally the country around the Maréchal. The utopia Vichy's leaders sought to incarnate drew upon the values of a communitarian, peasant, and Catholic France that they imagined existed prior to industrialization and bourgeois liberalism.[57]

Figure 5.3 is a propaganda poster that demonstrates how adherents of Pétain's National Revolution understood the causes of France's decline. Engulfed in red

Figure 5.3. "Révolution nationale," a poster originally designed ca. 1941–2 by R. Vachet for the Centre de Propagande la Révolution Nationale in Avignon. By Atrix20 – Own work, Public Domain, https://commons.wikimedia.org/w/index.php?curid=70404898 (accessed 14 March 2019).

ink, symbolizing both Communism and the blood on the hands of the corrupt leaders of the Third Republic, the "house" of France is collapsing, undermined from below by moral and physical forces that have surged upward like a cancerous tumor. The "tumor," in which Jews, Freemasons, and the corruption and weakness of Third Republic politicians figure prominently, feeds in turn off a deeper layer of moral corruption – laziness, demagoguery, and internationalism. The house can only be righted and cleansed through the program of the National Revolution, in which women and female domestic virtues played a prominent role. Hence a woman is shown on the right, opening the shutters of the reconstructed France in which she has apparently participated, albeit hidden from view, on the inside, cleansing and repairing. Moynier and his accomplices would have strongly agreed with the diagnosis of the causes for France's collapse pictured on the left side of this poster, and shared the hopes embodied on the right for a restored, orderly France founded on the National Revolution's program of "Work, Family, and Fatherland." But they rejected the Pétainist recipe to achieve France's recovery.

Vichy propaganda urged French men to wage the National Revolution peacefully, through fatherhood to rebuild France's population, through moral virtue to resurrect the country's traditional Catholic values, and through hard work to rebuild its economy and infrastructure. Martyrdom was a powerful theme in interwar France and was central to Pétain's conception of the National Revolution as well. World War I soldiers had been martyred on the battlefield, and their families martyred through the loss of the paternal breadwinner and moral compass of the family.[58] The plough, not the gun, would be the tool of resistance and revival in a France that the Armistice had disarmed and that the Occupation was impoverishing. "Constructive work, rather than war, was to be the keynote of the new man."[59] For men and women like Moynier, by contrast, only "direct action," if necessary violent, including punishment for Third Republic wrongdoers, rather than penitence from all French citizens, was required. France had first to pass through a spasm of retributive violence before France's house could be put in order. The program of extremists like Moynier differed radically from what Pétain envisioned for the National Revolution.

The assassins of Marx Dormoy were convinced that they had "executed" Dormoy for treason against the "real" France. Zealous supporters of the Maréchal, they avowed that they were defending France from the Communists and Socialists whose Popular Front government had left the country vulnerable to German invasion. Moynier explained why Dormoy had to die this way:

> With all my heart I approved of the National Revolution. I believed that the men responsible for the defeat would be immediately chastised. Unfortunately, I realized that justice was too slow. I thought that in order to create a true revolutionary spirit it was necessary to strike and to help the course of justice, as the price for the revival of my country.[60]

For Moynier and his comrades, there was a terrible contrast between their wartime battlefield in 1940, which ultimately proved through no fault of their own to be a field of dishonor and humiliating defeat, and that of their fathers' generation. Veterans of World War I suffered heroically, but they also won a great victory that brought them veneration, honor, and accolades from a grateful France. For French soldiers of the "Class of 1932," there were no such glorious battlefields upon which to establish their manhood. Rather, they were forced to endure the ravages of the Great Depression and watch their country fall under the control of their foes, Socialists, Communists, Jews, and cowardly old men. Street battles against leftists failed to assuage their wounded honor or renew their nation.[61] The National Revolution seemed to offer opportunities to restore their threatened masculinity and revive France. But as Moynier stated, it soon appeared that the politicians surrounding the Maréchal at Vichy were impeding the wheels of justice. How could the National Revolution succeed if those responsible for France's defeat remained unpunished?

THE ANATOMY OF A MURDER

Moynier was proud of having accomplished Dormoy's murder, and he gave a detailed confession that, together with forensic work and interrogation of the witnesses, allowed Chenevier to assemble an accurate account of the crime.[62] According to Moynier, he, Horace Vaillant, Lucien Guyon, and Guy Fontes first resolved to take "direct action" to further the National Revolution in April of 1941. Moynier had a friend from his school days in Marseille, Maurice Marbach who, having worked in an arms factory, had access to explosives and some skill in the construction of time bombs. Since Moynier knew that Marbach shared his political views, he invited Marbach to meet him on the Canebière in Marseille, where he persuaded Marbach to join their team. Marbach's help was crucial in building the bomb. In May, Moynier met with another old school chum, Ludovic Guichard, who agreed on the need for an "immediate chastisement of those responsible for our disasters" and accepted Moynier's offer to "join our little group."[63] A few days later, they were delighted to learn from a newspaper article the whereabouts of "one of those whom we considered to be responsible for our misfortunes, Marx Dormoy."[64] Dormoy was alone, accessible, and vulnerable in Montélimar.

The first step was to launch surveillance of Dormoy. In early June, Guichard traveled to Montélimar where he gathered information on the Relais de l'Empereur, Dormoy's habits and movements, and the feasibility of smuggling a bomb into his hotel room. Guichard told the plotters about Dormoy's "weakness for the feminine sex," having observed Dormoy flirting with young women in town.[65] This, according to Moynier, was why they decided to recruit "a young woman," Annie Mourraille, with whom Moynier was acquainted and who Moynier knew shared their political views. Mourraille stated that in May of 1941 Moynier, whom she'd been seeing since October, told her, "One of these days I will have need of you; it will be a question of doing a big favour for me – will you agree to that?" Mourraille told him she would, "without asking him any other questions." This suggests that Moynier was already thinking of involving Mourraille in the plot prior to Guichard's first trip to Montélimar.

On 2 June and 15 June Moynier sent Annie Mourraille two urgent telegrams asking her to meet him in Marseille. Mourraille agreed to spy on Dormoy for Moynier and made her first trip to Montélimar on 18 June, under the identity of "Florence Gérodias." She claimed that Moynier indicated only that she was to lure Dormoy out of the hotel so that Moynier and his friends could "beat him up."[66] It was Moynier who told her to register under the name Gérodias, although he was not the person who supplied her with the false identity papers.

Mourraille claimed that soon after her arrival at the Relais, Dormoy noticed her and began making advances. She asserted that Dormoy went so far as to enter her hotel room the second afternoon she was there and ask to have sex with her immediately. She brushed him off, claiming that she was going out to visit friends in the area, although she was really heading by train to Lyon to report to Moynier. In Lyon the group of assassins planned the murder and then returned to Montélimar as a group later that night to carry it out.[67] Annie Mourraille asked Dormoy to meet her at the train station at 11:00 p.m., where the assassins conspired to attack him in the station or while he was walking her back to the Relais. According to Mourraille, the group arrived in Montélimar, but when Dormoy failed to show at the train station, they went to the public park in town to discuss their next move. Mourraille claimed she told them that she would no longer spy on Dormoy since he was "profoundly enamored" of her. Moynier and the others wanted to follow her back to the Relais and, with her help, get into Dormoy's room and beat him up there, but she demurred and told them that she no longer wanted to be involved in the plot, and then returned alone to the hotel, leaving them in the park to "argue among themselves."[68] Clearly the group needed a better plan. Mourraille's version of events is implausible. Dormoy was forbidden to leave the hotel after sunset and would have known better than to meet Mourraille in a train station late at night, not only due to the risk of an attack on his person, but because he might be arrested.

Moynier's version of events differs from that of Annie Mourraille at several significant points. According to Moynier, it was he who gave Mourraille the false identity papers, although not until her second trip to Montélimar, in July, and he did not reveal how he obtained them. He does not mention her trip to Lyon on 21 June, but rather states that he and the other plotters stopped in

Montélimar while returning to Marseille from Lyon, where she met them in the public park. There Mourraille informed Moynier that she "was lodging on the same floor as the Sieur Dormoy and that she had not been able to enter into contact with him."[69] Since it was apparent that they could not carry out their plans under those circumstances, as they needed to find a way into Dormoy's room in order to plant the bomb unobserved, they decided to delay until they could rethink their strategy. They broke up into two groups and went out to dinner in Montélimar. Mourraille returned to the Relais, where at 2:00 a.m. Moynier indicated that Vaillant went to fetch her, and they all took the train back to Marseille.[70] Although Dormoy may have gone to Mourraille's room for amorous reasons, he more likely was trying to find out more about her, given that immediately after Mourraille left the hotel in the early hours of 22 June Dormoy came downstairs and asked the bartender to search her room for him.[71] Mourraille, ever the exaltée, was surely embellishing her story to the police. Dormoy was suspicious rather than enamored of her, and with good reason.

On 20 July Moynier again sent Annie Mourraille an urgent telegram asking her to meet him immediately in Marseille. He wanted her to return to Montélimar to help him and his friends "chastise" Dormoy. Despite her supposed reluctance to take further part in Moynier's scheme, Mourraille left Antony Carretier's villa in Nice on Thursday, 24 July and had dinner with Moynier at his mother's home in Marseille. The couple then went to Vaillant's place, where they met up with Guyon. They had already sent a letter to Marbach arranging for him to construct a bomb and meet them in Marseille with it, which he did on the evening of the 24th. He had packed the bomb into a wooden box. The cheddite was not yet attached to the bomb, nor was the timer set. Moynier, Marbach, Vaillant, and Mourraille then headed out for Montélimar during the night of the 24th, arriving at 4:30 a.m. on the 25th. Mourraille went to the Relais and managed to get a room on the same floor as that of Dormoy. Meanwhile the three men checked into the Hôtel de la Place d'Armes. For most of the morning the trio wandered around the town on what was a fine summer's day, all the while leaving the bomb in their hotel room. Annie Mourraille slept in at the Relais. After lunch the men ordered an enormous bouquet of flowers from a local florist, and in the mid-afternoon Mourraille joined them in the park. They returned to the Hôtel de la Place d'Armes where they "played cards" and "took a siesta" while Marbach set the timer on the bomb. Mourraille returned to the Relais at about 5:30 p.m. with instructions to expect Moynier and Vaillant to call on her at about 8:30 with the bouquet, in which part of the bomb would be hidden.

As planned, Moynier and Vaillant showed up that evening at the Relais while Mourraille was in the dining room and asked for "Mademoiselle Florence." The timer already set, Marbach waited for them in the park. Moynier had brought the bouquet and a box of nougat in which, most likely, he carried the actual explosive material. As is evident from the untimely demise of Guyon, Marbach, and Vaillant in Nice the following month, it was extremely dangerous to carry a time bomb around with the explosives connected to the apparatus. Any unexpected jostling that advanced the clock or loosed a spark from the battery would set the bomb off prematurely or cause it to malfunction. Because the bomb they had already planted in Dormoy's mattress was defective, they had to find a way to get into the room when Dormoy was out to replace it, correctly attach the explosive material and ensure the device was operational, while someone acted as a lookout. That meant finding an excuse to get Moynier and Vaillant upstairs. The hotel staff was reluctant to allow unaccompanied non-guests access to the guests' rooms. Hence the need for Annie Mourraille to return to Montélimar, check in again as "Mademoiselle Florence," and then invite her friends to her room to "thank them" for having brought her such a lovely bouquet of flowers and box of candy.

Everything went off smoothly. While Dormoy was in the dining room eating with Bretty and Jeanne, Mourraille brought Moynier and Vaillant to Dormoy's room. Getting into the room was easy as the door was unlocked. While Mourraille kept watch, Moynier switched the bombs, set the timer to go off at 2:00 a.m. and replaced the sheets and pillow. They disassembled the defective apparatus in Annie's room and put the pieces in her suitcase. A few minutes later, they went back downstairs, where Vaillant, evidently flustered, almost departed with it. Moynier left this detail out of his first statement because it revealed Annie Mourraille's true culpability in the crime. Mourraille's nerves were stronger than Vaillant's. She reclaimed her suitcase, deposited it in plain sight in the lobby with the bouquet perched on top and the bomb inside and left it there until she checked out. Moynier and Vaillant re-joined Marbach in the park while she finished her dinner at the hotel. They all boarded the 10:30 p.m. train to Valence, although they traveled in different compartments. At Valence they split up, Mourraille heading to Lyon while the men got on a train for Marseille. According to Moynier, when the Marseille-bound train retraced the route back through Montélimar, he and the others had the satisfaction of hearing the bomb that killed Dormoy explode just as their train was passing through the Montélimar station.[72]

Chenevier knew he had caught Dormoy's assassins, although he was convinced that they were mere operatives, part of a larger scheme. He also realized that his investigation was only beginning rather than ending. Even before Dormoy was killed, Chenevier's informants in Paris and Vichy had warned him that an assassination and possibly a coup attempt against Pétain were imminent. Witnesses in Montélimar had testified about other men, a tall, elegant, light-haired stranger who visited Guichard on 12 July and inspected the hotel, "M. Andre" who clearly was not Vaillant and who came for Annie Mourraille at Montélimar at 2:00 a.m., and the "gangster type" at the Brasserie eating with Moynier, Vaillant, and Marbach. Nor had Moynier revealed how he had obtained the Vichy identity card for Annie Mourraille or the money to fund their trips to Montélimar. Moynier had traveled to Paris in the company not only of Roger Mouraille but of another man, one of the persons who also had met him and the others in Montélimar. In her initial police statement Annie Mourraille indicated that the origins, funds, and logistics of the plot reached much higher than an unemployed postal worker from Marseille. Roger Mouraille made much the same assertion, and even Moynier conceded that the roots of the crime lay in Vichy. According to Annie Mourraille, a "leader" who received his orders from Vichy had organized Dormoy's assassination, supplied the money – 40,000 francs – and her false identity card issued by the "Sûreté Nationale Vichy." She testified Moynier told her that "Vichy wanted to draw attention to those responsible for the war so that they would be punished and that the Dormoy affair would bring about a change of Minister."[73]

Annie Mourraille seemed to be hinting that the assassination was part of a plot to force Pétain to replace his chief ministers and return Pierre Laval to power. When Chenevier asked whether she had heard Moynier or the others mention someone named "Jeantet," a leader of the Vichy propaganda organization the Amicale de France, she responded that indeed "Moynier and his friends spoke several times to me about Jeantet with whom they were in contact."[74] If Annie Mourraille was telling the truth, of which Chenevier could not be certain, the trail of Marx Dormoy's assassination was leading to exalted and dangerous territory, possibly to the very corridors of the Hôtel du Parc at Vichy, the seat of power of Pétain's regime.

CHAPTER SIX

August–October 1941: The Net Widens

Even before the bomb that killed Marx Dormoy detonated, Charles Chenevier knew that the assassination plot emanated from much more powerful men than Moynier or Roger Mouraille. Chenevier's informants had indicated that the trail led to Deloncle and the MSR in Paris, but the logistics of the crime, including Annie Mourraille's false identity card, strongly suggested that influential people associated with Pétain's government at Vichy, perhaps even members of his inner circle, were implicated. The connections between the assassins and the Amicale de France, headed by former Cagoulard Gabriel Jeantet, were clear by mid-August 1941. In Nice, the police investigating the accidental deaths of Maurice Marbach, Lucien Guyon, and Horace Vaillant found papers that survived the blast and linked the men to the Amicale. More Amicale documents surfaced in their hotel room in Nice.[1] Thanks to Dormoy's efforts to dismantle the Cagoule prior to the war, and the dogged police work to untangle the thread of the Cagoule's networks throughout France, Chenevier and Kubler had a roster of likely suspects, former Cagoulards in Paris, Vichy, and Marseille, about whom they already knew a great deal. Moreover, when they arrested them in August of 1941, the police discovered that three of Dormoy's assassins, Annie Mourraille, Yves Moynier, and Ludovic Guichard, all figured on the famous list of Cagoulards that Aristide Corre, Eugène Deloncle's childhood friend and secretary in the Cagoule, had compiled and Dormoy's police had discovered in September of 1937. Roger Mouraille joined the Marseille branch of the Cagoule and worked with the Cagoulards in Spain in 1939. The police had an ample dossier on him as well.[2]

The difficult task would be connecting these people, and especially Jeantet, to Dormoy's murder. Deloncle, known for his ruthlessness, made little effort to hide his role in various assassination plots. During the course of 1941 he only became more daring and violent.[3] Jeantet, more careful and more anxious about his reputation than Deloncle, did not conceal his prewar links to the Cagoule, but ensconced in Pétain's cabinet in 1941, he eschewed any ties to Deloncle and his other former Cagoule associates who were now collaborating with the Germans. Not only did Jeantet declare his aversion to collaboration, but he knew that most of the French public opposed rapprochement with the Nazis, which would undermine the legitimacy of Pétain's leadership, at home and abroad.[4]

A skilled detective with years of experience interrogating witnesses and criminals, Chenevier realized he would struggle to uncover evidence that would hold up in court implicating Jeantet in Dormoy's assassination. The closer that he got to the organizers of the plot, the harder it would be to elicit testimony from witnesses who were either, like Moynier, determined to remain loyal to the cause and their comrades until the bitter end or, like Guichard, more frightened of their leaders in Vichy and Paris than of the police. Men cast in the mold of Eugène Deloncle knew how to reward loyalty and even better how to punish "traitors."[5] They also knew how to use other people to do the "dirty work" and to cover their tracks. Chenevier's best chance of unearthing the roots of the plot was to get the accused to turn on each other. It was clear from the outset that the suspects had their own agendas and fully intended to shape their testimony to serve their interests. He thus had to exploit the points where those agendas diverged.

CHENEVIER'S QUARRIES

Chenevier was going to find it difficult to indict either Deloncle or Jeantet. Both had long experience eluding French justice going back to their Cagoule activities prior to the war. Moreover, in 1941 the two men were based in different locations in France hundreds of miles apart and separated by the Line of Demarcation. Although Vichy nominally policed French civilians in the Occupied Zone, the Germans were in control there, and especially in Paris. If the Germans chose to protect a suspect or impede a criminal investigation, there was little the Vichy police could do. The Germans possessed effective means of pressuring Pétain when the Maréchal's government seemed to be getting out of control. Jeantet had powerful backers at Vichy, while Deloncle remained physically and politically out of reach in Paris. Just to depose each of them, Chenevier needed to amass enough evidence to convince Investigating Magistrate Marion to issue a subpoena. He initially focused on Gabriel Jeantet.

Jeantet was born in 1906 to a bourgeois family with strong ties to the French publishing business. The family originated from the region of Pomponne and owned property, including a small chateau, Saint Lupicin, and other property in Switzerland. Jeantet studied literature at the Sorbonne and political science at the *École de science politique* – the "nursery" of almost all French politicians – but he never received a diploma because he and his journalist brother Claude became caught up in the tumultuous politics of the 1920s and 1930s in France, along with their close friend and fellow Cagoule sympathizer, François Mitterrand, the future Socialist president of France. Ultra-Catholic and supporters of the extreme right, Gabriel and Claude wrote articles for *L'Étudiant français: Organe mensuel de la Fédération nationale des étudiants d'Action française*, the newspaper for the royalist *Fédération nationale des étudiants d'Action française*, in the mid-1920s.[6] Despite his cool and cerebral manner, Gabriel Jeantet also had a violent side that showed itself early; in 1928 he was jailed for participating in a protest at the French Ministry of Agriculture.[7] Jean Védrine, who knew both Jeantet and François Mitterrand well, reminded Mitterrand in 1944, when the latter had changed his political allegiances and joined the Resistance, that Jeantet was essentially fearless: "Jeantet, who hesitates before nothing, will have you cuffed [arrested] without raising an eyebrow."[8]

Jeantet and his friend Michel Harispe became members of a dissident faction of the AF in 1931 and joined the Cagoule in 1936.[9] Jeantet, who planned to make a career in politics, was one of the creators of the Cagoule and under Deloncle was its chief arms smuggler.[10] He prided himself on his patriotism, no matter how misguided and corrupt he considered his government to be. When war broke out in 1939, he enlisted and fought, ironically, under the command of then Colonel Charles de Gaulle. A tall, fair-haired, and handsome man, Jeantet by nature was an intellectual, cool and calculating. He did not share Deloncle's opportunism and lust for power at any price. After he was demobilized, Jeantet went to Vichy to witness with satisfaction the dissolution of the Third Republic and the creation of the Vichy regime.[11]

Jeantet was a close friend of Dr. Bernard Ménétrel, Pétain's personal physician and confidant. Through Ménétrel's support Jeantet obtained the post of "Inspector General of Propaganda in the General Secretariat of Information, of the Vice-President of the Council of Vichy."[12] At the moment of the French defeat and armistice with Germany in the summer of 1940, Jeantet opted for Pétain and Vichy. "I could not imagine another option besides that of the Maréchal," Jeantet subsequently testified.[13] Jeantet put his journalistic talents to good use as secretary-general of the Amicale de France. Pétain ordered the Amicale disbanded soon after Dormoy's assassination, most likely because rumors were circulating that linked Jeantet to the crime. Pétain was careful from the outset to distance himself from Dormoy's assassination.[14] Jeantet remained an influential figure in Vichy even so. He founded a new publishing house for Vichy, *les Éditions de l'État nouveau*, which published the newspaper *France, revue de l'État nouveau*.[15] In July 1941 Jeantet had the political clout to obtain a false identity card for Annie Mourraille and a large budget for the Amicale from which he could divert money to fund an assassination.

Deloncle, by contrast, had established himself in Paris, where he reconstituted the Cagoule as the MSR with former comrades in arms such as Jean Filliol, Jacques Corrèze, Jacques Fauran, and Jean Fontenoy, all violent men associated with murder, terrorism, and antisemitism.[16] Deloncle's MSR jostled for power and Nazi patronage with other extreme right French political parties operating in Occupied Paris, including those of Marcel Déat and Jacques Doriot.[17] Deloncle threw himself wholeheartedly into collaborationism, including with the Gestapo, with whose help he orchestrated the bombing of seven synagogues in Paris on 3 October 1941.[18] He developed close relationships with influential Nazis.[19] Deloncle was also an eager participant in the looting of Jewish property and the appropriation of Jewish homes and businesses in Paris. The headquarters of the MSR had been confiscated from Jewish owners.[20]

Many ex-Cagoulards – Deloncle, Filliol, Corrèze, Fauran, André Hérard, Henri Deloncle (Eugène's brother), and Joseph Darnand, among others – had regrouped in the MSR. "The 'neo-Cagoulard' character of the Amicale de France is apparent in the regrouping [within the Amicale] of those people who, the day after the Armistice, founded at Marseille an organization whose leaders 'GABRIEL JEANTET, VAUDREMER, DAUSSIN, BAGARRY, BARON, BERTHIER, DERCHEU, DUNGLER, etc.' were all notorious royalists who figured on the list 'Corre.'"[21] Dr. Henri Martin, well-acquainted with that organization's membership prior to the war, warned the Vichy authorities that the Cagoule had not disbanded but rather had mutated into branches of the Vichy bureaucracy.[22] Georges Richier, Commissioner of the Parisian Judicial Police, claimed in 1946 that the Amicale under Jeantet's direction had been packed with former Cagoulards, to the point that it constituted a "second Cagoule."[23] The problem Chenevier faced was how to connect Deloncle and Jeantet.

Deloncle and, especially, Jeantet, along with their fellow Cagoulards at Paris and Vichy were, according to historian Pierre Péan, well positioned to "control and direct the France of Pétain."[24] The key was to avoid the appearance that they were collaborating and in control. On 1 October 1940, the two men ostensibly had a heated argument at Vichy in front of witnesses and from that point forward each of them insisted that they had broken all contact with each other. The quarrel was over strategy, and especially Deloncle's determination to head his own political party.[25] Jeantet vehemently opposed Deloncle's plans to wrest power from Pétain, whom Deloncle characterized as too weak to control his own ministers, many of them Third Republic holdovers. The National Revolution and the policy of collaboration with the Germans that Deloncle insisted were the only paths by which France's fortunes could be revived and the country's honor restored, had to be the work of younger men who were ardently patriotic but also dedicated to Hitler's New European Order. They had to collaborate with the Germans and resort to violence in order to save their country.[26] None of this sat well with Jeantet who historian Valerie Deacon concludes was "a Pétainist through and through."[27]

At the end of September 1940, Deloncle received provisional authorization from the Germans to constitute the MSR. He declared that the organization would be collaborationist and might even engage in a "march on Vichy" modeled on Mussolini's famous "March on Rome," with the goal of "rescuing Pétain" from the ministers surrounding him who were venal and tepid about collaboration. Jeantet was virulently anti-German.[28] Upon leaving a meeting with Deloncle, probably in late September, Michel Harispe reported that Jeantet told him that "just the sight of a German uniform made him want to vomit."[29] According to Harispe, in October Jeantet contacted him with the request to publish in the Parisian press a note Jeantet had authored announcing the cessation of his relationship with Deloncle and disavowing the MSR. Out of loyalty to his old friend, Harispe saw to it that Jeantet's note was published even though Harispe knew that this would deepen the schism over collaboration among the former Cagoulards, most of whom had rallied around Pétain in an informal grouping, "the Friends of the Maréchal." A minority, about a quarter of the Cagoulards, supported Deloncle in Paris and collaboration with the Germans. At that point, Jeantet supposedly "ceased all relations with Deloncle" because Jeantet was adamantly "opposed to the creation of a political party in the Occupied Zone."[30]

Jeantet objected to Deloncle's plan to use the MSR to challenge the authority of the new Vichy regime.[31] It did not help matters that Deloncle intended to create armed militias in the Occupied Zone to act as political police charged with the task of keeping an eye on Vichy civil servants working in the Occupied

Zone who showed insufficient loyalty to the National Revolution. Deloncle was negotiating with the Germans early in 1941 to establish his militia and ensure that its members had modern weapons, which would have made them better armed than the French police. Worse, Deloncle's close collaborator in the MSR, Jacques Corrèze, declared in a speech to MSR members on 16 January 1941 that "we operate in complete agreement with the Germans, we are armed and the Germans know it, we have a list of the principal communists in the region of Paris and we will bring them down in one night."[32] Corrèze asserted that the MSR planned to enact a "new Saint Bartholomew's [massacre]" in December of 1940, but had held off at the request of the Germans who were, nonetheless, on board with the idea.[33] Meanwhile, Deloncle demanded in a speech he delivered on 14 February 1941, broadcast on Radio-Paris, that "the National Revolution finally will be enacted, not with [empty] decrees, but all those unworthy [to exercise power] will be swept away, and there will be no more Jews or Freemasons still able to live. We want all those responsible for the defeat to be chastised."[34]

Chenevier's informant in Paris had stated even before Dormoy was murdered that the trail of the crime would lead straight to Deloncle. Still, the deed was committed in Vichy territory, and all the assassins had strong connections with the Marseille branches of the GP, the CIE, and/or the Amicale de France, and all of them, except Annie Mourraille, originated from the region around Marseille. She had longtime family and professional connections in the south as well, especially in the region of Nice, a hotbed of the Cagoule in 1936–7.[35] Deloncle had no position in the Vichy government and no formal or institutional ties to the Vichy organizations promoting the National Revolution. Moreover, Deloncle ostensibly was *persona non grata* at Vichy, especially after he began to support Pierre Laval. Deloncle's speeches supporting Laval, while calculated to win favor with Laval and his German protectors, did not gain him any friends in Vichy.[36]

Pétain had prohibited the MSR from operating in the Vichy Zone, but Deloncle nonetheless managed to establish branches in Montpellier, Toulouse, Nice, Lyon, and Marseille, under the leadership of two operatives who recruited former Cagoulards and other pro-German individuals. The leader of the MSR in Marseille was Dr. Pierre Dercheu, a member of the Amicale de France; Dercheu's membership in the Amicale did not inhibit him from receiving several visits from Deloncle.[37] The meetings between Dercheu and Deloncle are important, because they demonstrate that Deloncle traveled to the Vichy Zone frequently. Dr. Martin's spies kept track of Deloncle's comings and goings and noted that Deloncle was in Marseille 20–5 April 1941, where he met with MSR leaders in the Vichy Zone. He returned to Marseille in July of 1941, where he had every opportunity to meet with Dormoy's assassins.[38] He was in the city of Vichy on 2 August, a week after Dormoy's murder, and again on 21 August 1941, two days after the arrest of Yves Moynier and Roger Mouraille. He most likely consulted at least once with Jeantet while in Vichy. Deloncle met with Pétain and members of his cabinet during this trip and suggested that Pétain designate him as the intermediary between Pétain and the Germans. Deloncle returned to Vichy in October of 1941 after the synagogue bombings.[39] It would not have been difficult for Deloncle to have met with a representative of Jeantet, such as Antoine Marchi, who remained in contact with both men.[40] The police, who were also watching Deloncle and Jeantet, were convinced that they were more closely "attached" than ever by February of 1941 and were coordinating their activities via intermediaries such as former Cagoulard Joseph Darnand.[41] When Dormoy disrupted the Cagoule in 1937, its leaders managed to remain in contact with their followers in hiding outside of prison, including those such as Jeantet and Aristide Corre who had fled to Spain or Italy. Among the most important intermediaries ensuring these contacts were the lawyers the jailed Cagoulards had engaged.[42] Deloncle and Jeantet could thus have used their lawyers or their underlings in the offices they administered in Paris and Vichy in much the same way in 1941.

Deloncle and, especially, Jeantet, were careful, and Chenevier knew he would not find evidence of direct communication – letters, phone calls, or witnesses – putting Deloncle and Jeantet in the same room together. Whether or not their quarrel in the park had been real or staged, it was in the interests of both men to maintain to the world that they were estranged. Deliberate ambiguity served Jeantet well. He could keep his options open and develop his contacts among those in Vichy opposed to collaboration with the Germans but still enthusiastic about the National Revolution, and even with some members of the Resistance like ex-Cagoulard Georges Loustaunau-Lacau.[43] Deloncle took the collaborationist route, cultivated the Germans, especially the Gestapo, and attracted the MSR collaborationists enamored of Nazi ideology and disenchanted with Pétain's effort to chart a course between the Allies and the Axis powers. In this way, if Jeantet and Deloncle were still working together, the Cagoule would retain and develop its networks of supporters on either side of the Line of Demarcation. The organization could play a central role in shaping the course of France under the Occupation and even after the war that most still expected would end in a Nazi victory.

Whatever their differences, Deloncle and Jeantet engaged in similar efforts to harm Jews. Both supported cadres of antisemites in Paris and Vichy. Deloncle's ties were with the Gestapo, particularly the German ambassador Otto Abetz and the ardent antisemite Fernand de Brinon, an architect of the collaboration. Deloncle worked with Paul Sézille to create a "Section Juive" inside the MSR in April of 1941 dedicated to solving France's "Jewish problem," which included raids on Jewish property. Deloncle's key MSR agent and an associate of Sézille, André Hérard, resided in an exquisite apartment in Paris confiscated from a Jewish man named M. Sack. When the French owner of the apartment refused to allow Hérard entry, the latter threatened to send the man to a concentration camp via his Gestapo connections and so Hérard took possession of the property.[44] In addition, it was Deloncle who organized the synagogue bombings in Paris in October of 1941. Jeantet, meanwhile, worked in the Amicale with André Daussin, director of the economic Aryanization operations in Marseille, along with Daussin's deputy Henri Place, a former Cagoulard. Daussin and Place both became major figures in the *Commissariat général aux questions juives* (CGQJ) under Vichy. The lower level operatives in their circles, Guichard, Moynier, Annie Mouraille, and Roger Mouraille, were well known to the police as vehement antisemites who defaced Jewish property early in the war and had escalated by 1943 after their release from prison to engaging in theft and extortion from Jews in hiding.[45]

Chenevier needed to unravel the identities of the emissaries linking the assassins to Paris and Vichy and that meant getting one or more of his suspects in custody to talk, and soon. The French and German authorities wanted the case to be resolved quickly and would happily accept Yves Moynier's story that he alone had organized the assassination. Chenevier could not be sure the mandate he had been given to investigate Dormoy's murder would not disappear due to a shift in Pétain's cabinet or its relationship with the Germans. Should the Germans soften their stance in their negotiations with Vichy, Pétain's interest in prosecuting Dormoy's assassins could quickly evaporate.[46] Nor could Chenevier be sure of his own safety, especially given that he was already either in the Resistance or at least in touch with its members, as was his assistant, Kubler. Given the risks, Chenevier's determination to follow the crime's trail to the heart of Vichy and to Occupied Paris was itself an act of resistance.

CHENEVIER'S DILEMMA

By the time they interrogated Moynier and the others, Chenevier and Kubler had acquired a great deal of information the suspects did not know the police possessed. The problem was that the suspects also had an advantage – time.

They had all obtained high-powered lawyers who were petitioning Vichy on behalf of their clients.[47] It was thus reasonable for the suspects to assume that if they held out long enough Chenevier's superiors would close the case without a trial. But if one of them cracked, he or she could bring down the rest and those in Vichy or Paris who were behind the crime as well. To break the suspects' resolve, they had to be held incommunicado as far as possible, for as long as possible. It was especially important, therefore, that the suspects be denied their repeated requests to be freed on bail. Fortunately, however, Investigating Magistrate Marion held firm. Chenevier's advantage in this game of "cat and mouse" was the suspects' growing realization that Vichy might let them hang in order to confine the parameters of the investigation.

The suspects were well connected in Marseille and Nice, and their families and clandestine supporters helped them pay for lawyers. At the arraignment M. Franceschi from Marseille represented Annie Mourraille, Moynier, and Guichard.[48] Roger Mouraille hired two lawyers of his own, Messieurs Bergasse and Delormo, also based in Marseille.[49] It was obvious that the suspects were convinced their contacts in Vichy would come to their rescue.[50] Their initial strategy was to maintain the tight solidarity that had linked them as they plotted and carried out the murder. But by October, Guichard and Annie Mourraille, like Roger Mouraille, had hired their own lawyers. Guichard had several, in fact, Messieurs Franceschi, Gbonsaide, and Carboni, all from Marseille, as well as a M. Ansaldi.[51] Each of them began to importune Marion repeatedly to release them on bail. Marion refused to yield and ordered them detained in the prison at Valence. But the suspects had another "angle" to work. Within a week of his arrest Moynier petitioned Marion to change his status, and thus the conditions of his detention, from that of a common criminal suspect to that of a political detainee, which in French law is someone whose crime derived from their political convictions.[52] Under French law political prisoners were granted a special status that allowed them greater rights than those afforded ordinary criminals. On 25 August Moynier wrote to a friend, "I am waiting for a response to my [request for] status as a political prisoner. Work at it from your end. We don't lack any contacts who could, if necessary, intervene."[53]

Yet, below the surface Chenevier also sensed fear. The suspects expected a quid pro quo for their silence. From the outset and at each step in the investigation, when deciding how much to tell the police, they had to weigh their faith in their leaders at Vichy and Paris against their fear of being abandoned. As time passed and they remained in prison their anxiety about abandonment would only grow. Kubler came to believe that Guichard was more afraid of those who had recruited him for the crime than he was of the police.[54]

All the suspects, even Guichard, possessed a great deal of nerve. But that did not mean that they would be willing to die for their cause. To get them to talk, Chenevier had to undermine their sense of being protected and therefore inviolate. If he could impress upon them that the people who had organized the crime would be willing to sacrifice those who had carried it out in order to save themselves, fear would gradually replace confidence, and eventually one of them would break. It was Roger Mouraille, the most experienced of the suspects, who first talked to the police, most likely because he understood the stakes better than the others. It was Annie Mourraille, however, who was the most forthcoming. She talked to Chenevier not for her own sake, but because she was desperate to save her lover, Yves Moynier, from the noose.

THE GO-BETWEENS – ANTOINE MARCHI AND "MONSIEUR ANDRÉ"

On 16 August, three days before the arrest of Moynier and Roger Mouraille, Mme. Lurol, owner of the Hôtel de la Place des Armes in Montélimar, recognized a photo of Maurice Marbach as the man who had come to her hotel asking after another man whose photo she also now recognized – Antoine Marchi. Although one of Chenevier's informants may have tipped him off regarding Marchi, the Corsican soldier's career and involvement with Marseille's extreme right organizations also made him a suspect. On 17 August Guichard admitted that he knew Marchi, not surprising because the two men traveled in the same circles in Marseille. On the 19th the police questioned Moynier, who refused to discuss Marchi but did admit that while in Paris he and Mouraille had visited the offices of the MSR and met with André Hérard. Marion immediately contacted the Parisian police to ascertain "what relations exist between the sieurs DELONCLE and HÉRARD on the one hand and the sieur JANTET [Jeantet] on the other."[55] Moynier thus was willing, when confronted with what the police had already uncovered, to give up Hérard, a go-between linked to Deloncle, although at first he insisted that Hérard was not the "M. André" who had visited him and Annie Mourraille at Montélimar. Hérard was Deloncle's secretary in the MSR, a Gestapo agent, and also worked directly with Filliol gathering information on MSR enemies. Hérard also had deep ties to both Marseille and Spain and was known for arms smuggling, like Jeantet, before the war, although his closest ties were to Filliol, the most violent member of the Cagoule and its chief assassin. The police knew that if they could put Hérard in Montélimar, they would have a direct connection between Deloncle and the murder.[56]

The patterns in which Moynier and Roger Mouraille revealed some of their collaborators are telling. The Paris contacts seem to have been less off limits for Moynier than for Roger Mouraille. Moynier evinced much greater loyalty to his contacts in Vichy. He stubbornly refused to give up Marchi. Moynier clearly was closer to the Marseille branch of the Cagoule than to the Parisian branch in 1941 and did not trust Deloncle to look after his interests. Moynier remained certain Marchi would repay his loyalty by saving him and his friends. Roger Mouraille was willing from the outset to point the police in the direction of Marchi and even of Jeantet. Their contrasting testimonies may offer a clue as to the primary loyalties of each man. Mouraille seems to have been more tied to Deloncle and the MSR, not surprising given his close pre-war ties to Deloncle and Jean Filliol, whereas Moynier's contacts were primarily with Vichy, via Marchi, under whose command he had served in the GP and the CIE in 1940. Roger Mouraille was also the first of the suspects to implicate Jeantet. On 25 August Mouraille stated that Moynier and his friends spoke to him "several times about Jantet [sic] with whom they were in contact."[57]

Annie Mourraille is a more complicated case. Her ties to the extreme right based in Paris, Marseille, and Nice pre-dated the war. Yet her involvement in the plot to assassinate Dormoy seems to have derived from her relationship with Moynier. They both claimed that he recruited her to spy on Dormoy and neither of them, nor any of the other witnesses, suggested that she had masterminded the plot or had her own ties to Jeantet or Deloncle. That said, her military service, the medal Pétain's government awarded her in 1940, and the fact that it was a Vichy official who tipped off Chenevier about her identity, all suggest that at the least she was no stranger to many of the military officers and bureaucrats in Vichy. She likely knew a great deal more than her often deliberately vague and hesitating depositions would suggest. She was a good actress and her performances when under interrogation attest to her skill.

Almost from the outset, during her 25 August interrogation, Annie Mourraille contradicted her lover's testimony, insisting, "I do not believe that it was Moynier who was the instigator of the attack because, on several occasions, he led me to understand that he and his friends were under the command of a leader who lived in Vichy or received his orders from Vichy."[58] She claimed to have seen this man in Lyon at the Brasserie Georges after the crime and then proceeded to offer the police a description of him. "He is about thirty-five to forty years old, fairly tall and fairly hefty without, however, being fat. When I saw him he was wearing a hat but I believe nevertheless that I remember that his hair was brown and his eyes were light coloured. He was clean-shaven with a fairly round and full body type, [and] his nose was pretty big. He was neatly and appropriately dressed." Moynier and the others told her that this man was their leader whom she "understood" gave them their orders and funded the "expedition" to Montélimar. They had "mentioned," Annie Mourraille said, "the sum of 40,000 francs." Moreover, it was this "leader" who provided her with her fake identity card, "on which had been glued a picture of a woman who rather vaguely resembled me." She asserted that she "examined the document pretty closely and saw that it was covered in a black folder on which was printed SÛRETÉ NATIONALE VICHY." After they had planted the bomb, she returned the "document" to Marbach on the train.

Annie Mourraille went even further on the 25th, essentially giving up all her accomplices, dead or alive. When asked if she had heard anyone talk about someone named Jeantet or the Amicale de France, she responded that Moynier had spoken about Jeantet on several occasions and was in regular contact with him, via Marchi. Although her "friends" had mentioned Roger Mouraille, she claimed never to have met him and to know nothing about his involvement in the crime. This answer again would suggest that Roger Mouraille was, along with Hérard, the Parisian liaison with the assassins, and thus not part of the "loop" within which she was operating, at least not before the murder took place. She insisted that Marbach had also stayed at the Relais and was the one who informed her about the skeleton key that would open Dormoy's room. She wasn't sure whether Marbach had registered at the hotel under his own name because she knew that he and the other accomplices had received false Vichy identity cards like hers. "I even saw in Marbach's hands a card of Inspector of the Sûreté Nationale." According to Annie Mourraille, Dormoy's murder was part of a political plot hatched among the rival factions around Pétain. "During my second trip to Montélimar, Moynier told me that Vichy wanted to draw attention to those responsible for the war, in order that they would be punished rapidly and that the Dormoy affair would bring about a change of Prime Minister."

When Pétain came to power in the summer of 1940, most French people supported him. The Maréchal was a war hero from World War I, a respected fatherly figure in the minds of many French men and women who, in agreeing to lead France in 1940, had "sacrificed his person" for France. In the summer of 1940 most French people accepted this narrative and were ready, albeit some with more enthusiasm than others, to follow the Maréchal's lead.[59] By December support for Pétain began to waver, however, and many in his government blamed this on Laval. The crux of the issue was the same as had divided the Cagoulards from within in August and September. Few French people at this point in the war supported the nascent Resistance in France or followed de Gaulle's call to join him in London. Except among France's remaining Communists, support for the Resistance did not rise significantly until the German invasion of the Vichy Zone in November 1942, when it became clear that the Germans would never permit France, even under Pétain's rule, any meaningful autonomy.[60]

But well before 1943 the question of collaboration – how far Pétain and the État français should go in collaborating with the occupiers – was a central preoccupation for French political leaders. Pétain's most ardent desire was to repatriate the 1.5 million French prisoners of war still being held in Germany. His cooperation with the Nazis was designed primarily to extract concessions and, in particular, the release of the prisoners.[61] In 1941, nearly everyone at Vichy was convinced that the imminent Nazi victory meant that France had no choice but to collaborate with the Germans to ensure France a "place at the table" in Hitler's Europe after the war, and to lessen the burden on the French in the meantime. The conflict within Vichy hinged more on tactics. Convinced that close collaboration was the safer strategy, Pierre Laval arranged the 22 October 1940 meeting between a reluctant Pétain and Hitler at Montoire. The handshake between Pétain and Hitler on that occasion horrified many patriotic, anti-Nazi supporters of Vichy. Pétain acquiesced to Laval's insistence he meet the Fuhrer in person, but the encounter failed to yield the German concessions Laval had promised, a major factor in the arrest of Laval and his expulsion from Pétain's cabinet on 13 December. Laval became irrevocably linked with the hated collaboration with the Germans.[62] Pétain's repudiation of Laval was thus by no means an outright rejection of collaboration on the part of Pétain's government, but rather a result of political rivalries within the circle around Pétain and his sense that Laval was willing to concede too much to the Germans without extracting enough in return.[63]

At Laval's urging, in January of 1941 Marcel Déat founded the RNP to unite the collaborationist groups in Paris, including Deloncle's MSR. Doriot refused to join the RNP, but Deloncle agreed, in part because he hoped to evince Déat and assume control of the organization.[64] In July 1941, despite the rivalry between Deloncle and Déat, Deloncle and Laval were still allied in an effort to engineer Laval's return to power in Vichy. Annie Mourraille's claim that Dormoy's murder was part of a plot to change the power structure in Vichy, probably by bringing down Admiral François Darlan and Laval's other rivals at Vichy, thus may have had some truth to it.

TAMING THE TIGER: THE ARREST OF MARCHI

On 28 August 1941 Antoine Marchi checked into a hotel near Paris' Austerlitz train station.[65] The next day, in Montélimar, Jean Franceschi made a surprising request to Marion on behalf of Yves Moynier. Aware that the police had sequestered documents found in Dormoy's hotel room after the assassination, Franceschi demanded that the papers be unsealed in his and Moynier's presence. Although Marion did eventually yield, his response in August was that because Jeanne Dormoy had filed a civil suit, and thus also had a legal interest in the outcome of the case, he could not allow Franceschi to see the papers without her permission.[66] These two events are linked in that by the end of August, both Marchi and his co-conspirators in custody in Valence were beginning to get nervous that Vichy was going to abandon them to the wheels of justice in order to keep the investigation from reaching any higher into the ranks of Vichy officials. On 29 August Guichard for the first time admitted to having "seen" the man Annie Mourraille described as Antoine Marchi.[67] Mourraille in particular had realized that if she could not induce the police to apprehend Marchi, he had little incentive to help her and the others already in custody, and every reason to lie low and let Moynier and his "band" take the fall. Marchi's trip to Paris suggests that her suspicions were correct.

On 5 September Marchi "put himself under Deloncle's protection" by joining the MSR.[68] Marchi had decided that the time had come to change patrons and hoped that Deloncle's connections with the Germans would supply him with the protection that Vichy would not. Annie Mourraille's goal was to offer Chenevier and Marion enough information to permit them to issue a warrant for Marchi's arrest. Nor would she hesitate to implicate Jeantet if that proved necessary to induce Vichy to intervene in the police investigation. During their interrogations on 26 September, Annie Mourraille and Moynier continued their previous tactics, with Moynier steadfastly refusing to implicate Marchi even when confronted with Annie Mourraille's testimony, while Mourraille repeated and embellished her previous testimony to Chenevier regarding both Marchi and Jeantet.[69] Moynier's stubbornness infuriated Annie Mourraille, who stated in her diary at one point, "Yves insists that he will claim sole responsibility for having organized the affair, like a fool taking all the blame, faithful to the promises he made without taking into account the risk he is running, because I know, myself, that we have been abandoned."[70]

Chenevier affirmed to Marion that his informant in Marseille had told him in August that Marchi was the leader of Moynier's band, and that "the person who had put all these people into action was the man named Gabriel Jeantet of Vichy."[71] Chenevier assured Marion that witnesses had seen Marchi meet with Maurice Marbach while waiting for the train that would bring Marchi to Montélimar a second time. Other witnesses had seen Moynier, Marchi, and Jeantet meet in Marseille. Once the assassination had been accomplished, the entente among Moynier, Marchi, and Jeantet quickly deteriorated. According to Chenevier's informant, "for some time after the assassination of M. Dormoy, Marchi appeared discontented with the new attitude taken by Jeantet," who had become "more fearful regarding the consequences" of the crime. Thus, the meeting at the offices of the MSR in Paris among Marchi, Moynier, Roger Mouraille, Hérard, and Deloncle "was the result of the intervention of Jeantet who seems to have no longer wanted to finance an action that would turn into direct action."[72]

Annie Mourraille knew that the key to her and Moynier's survival lay in Marchi and, beyond him, Vichy. As she stated in her diary, "certainly there are things that we must forget, names that we will never utter, but he [Moynier] is risking his head to cover up for some jerks who are going to let him take the fall in the hope that he will disappear as soon as possible ... the only hope is that when it's his turn he [Marchi] will talk...."[73] She insisted that Marchi was one of the conspirators who planned Dormoy's murder.[74] Moreover, she asserted that Marchi had told her that he was acting as an intermediary between Moynier and a "certain person" whose identity she did not know but who occupied a high position in the Vichy government. When asked whether the "person to whom you have alluded may be named Jeantet," she responded:

> In effect, I heard my friends use the name and [they said] that Marchi had gone to see Jeantet about the Dormoy affair. During the preparation of the affair, it was for that reason that my friends said that Vichy was interested in having the affair succeed. I don't believe that Jeantet was the only person in the loop and whom Marchi had seen at Vichy. Marchi was eager for the affair to succeed. According to what my friends said, at Vichy people had at the least promised Marchi a great

boost up in the National Revolution if the Dormoy affair succeeded. This boost was to be material assistance permitting them to carry further their cleansing work. They were going to form some sort of group or team that would work in close collaboration with the government.[75]

The last part of this declaration would have been especially chilling for Chenevier and Marion, as it implied that Dormoy's murder was to be merely the opening salvo in a campaign to "execute" many other former Third Republic politicians who had "escaped" a punishment they well deserved. Annie Mouraille stated on 26 September that Vichy viewed the elimination of Dormoy as urgent and was pressuring Moynier to take action and bring the affair to a close in July. If true, this would suggest that someone at Vichy saw Dormoy as a danger. The most likely threat Dormoy could have posed in the summer of 1941 would have been if he had testified at the upcoming trial at Riom of Léon Blum and the other defendants, such as Paul Reynaud and Georges Mandel, whom the Germans were insisting be judged and condemned.[76] If subpoenaed to testify, which he surely would have been, Dormoy would have discussed at length the activities of the Cagoule prior to the war. Moreover, he may have backed up his testimony with papers from the Ministry of the Interior that he or his sister had brought to the Relais. Such testimony would have resurrected skeletons that former Cagoulards at Vichy wanted to keep buried.

Although he still maintained that he was merely a bystander rather than a participant in the crime, Roger Mouraille stated on 26 September that he had heard Moynier and the others "talk about Jeantet among their comrades and of the fact that Marchi was going to meet Jeantet regarding the subject of the Dormoy affair."[77] Mouraille also asserted that he "understood that our comrades told me that Vichy was very eager for this affair to happen." Everything he knew, Mouraille insisted, was from conversations he had overheard. And note that he said only that Jeantet and Marchi were going to meet regarding the "Dormoy affair." That could be interpreted to mean that Jeantet was going to encourage Marchi to act or, equally, that Jeantet intended to dissuade Marchi from going forward. And when Mouraille stated that "Vichy" was "eager" for the "affair to happen," he omitted Jeantet's name and did not specify the nature of the "affair" – careful testimony from a careful man. Moynier, meanwhile, retracted his declaration that Vichy was involved in the murder and refused to testify against Marchi.[78]

Even though Marchi was present during the "confrontations" of 26 September at Montélimar, his first official statement is dated several days later,

1 October 1941. Marchi proved from the outset to be an irascible, obdurate, and uncooperative suspect. Antoine François Marchi was born on 13 July 1907 at Vescovato in Corsica. He attended lycée in Marseille and joined the military in December 1927. In 1928 he was promoted to second lieutenant in the reserves and served in the French colony of Senegal. Demobilized in June 1929, he re-joined the military in 1931, was promoted to lieutenant and served until July 1939, when he was disciplined for unspecified infractions and decommissioned. Mobilized with the outbreak of the war in September 1939, he was captured in June 1940 but escaped the Germans on 9 July and made it to the Vichy Zone, where he was again demobilized on 27 July and awarded the Croix de Guerre with a Silver Star for his heroics on the battlefield.[79]

Marchi was a courageous and audacious soldier who earned five citations for bravery, including one that was assumed to be posthumous when he received it. An article about him in *Paris-Soir* dated Saturday, 17 August 1940 bore the headline "He Helped to Save the Honour of the French Army." It featured a large photo of Marchi and explained that the headline was a quotation from one of the citations given to a "French Lieutenant left for dead on the battlefield." The article described Marchi, with more than a little hyperbole, as "A man. A tough guy. Square-headed. Hard-headed. With muscles of iron. Of blood. Who looks you in the eye ... A leader. A professor of bravado."[80] According to the article, Marchi went missing from his unit in the heat of battle. Badly wounded, he was left on the battlefield because his comrades assumed him to be dead. The Germans captured him, but his wounds were so severe that they did not bother to guard Marchi, allowing him to escape and re-join what was left of his regiment. Even the Germans, the newspaper proclaimed, respected and feared Marchi for his many "exploits" against them, and Pétain himself pinned one of the medals to Marchi's chest.

There was another side to Marchi, however, and he seems to have been a more successful soldier than civilian. Marchi was the son of a customs inspector in Corsica. In 1941 Marchi's father was dead. He had left Marchi ample means, mostly in the form of property in Corsica and elsewhere that permitted his son to live comfortably without needing to work. Even so, Marchi was unmarried and childless in 1941, although he kept mistresses. When Chenevier arrested him, Marchi was residing in Marseille, where he had "no known profession" but owned two houses that brought him about 16,000 francs per year in income. Marchi was a violent man. On 29 September 1937 he was convicted of "outrages" against police officers in Corsica; he had insulted officers and gotten into fistfights with them on numerous occasions. In 1938 he was convicted for "outrages and violence," against the Corsican president of the bureau of elections and for carrying banned weapons. In February 1939 he was convicted of threats and assault, this time against his own father. In each case he merely received a fine, but there was a pattern of violent language and hot-headed behavior.[81] One of his commanding officers said of him: "Very self-assured. Lively temperament. Needs to be watched closely and [instructed] to be more balanced."[82]

Marchi was also a leading figure in the extreme-right organizations based in Marseille. In 1940 he joined the GP and assumed leadership of it. He joined the CIE and the Amicale de France and recruited Moynier and Guichard to the GP. Marchi was also affiliated with the PPF. Doriot put him in charge of organizing a brigade of "shock troops" for the PPF to use in violent riots. According to the CIE's official archivist, Marchi was "the man to go to when you needed a violent action."[83] Others characterized him as "vicious" and not a man to cross lightly, not only because Marchi himself was violent and unpredictable, but because he was well connected in the circles of the extreme right based both in Vichy and in Paris. This was the man from whom Chenevier set out in October 1941 to extract the truth regarding Dormoy's murder.

From the outset Marchi steadfastly denied everything and insisted that Annie Mourraille was a liar, even as, through his lawyer, the ubiquitous Jean Franceschi, Marchi also demanded the status of a political prisoner.[84] Moreover, Marchi declared to Chenevier and Marion, "Your intervention does not surprise me, because while in Corsica, from whence I have just arrived via hydroplane, I received a telegram explaining to me what has taken place."[85] Marchi freely acknowledged that he knew most of the people implicated in the murder, but asserted that none of them had told him about the plot to kill Dormoy. He claimed never even to have met Annie Mourraille. Jeantet, by contrast, he was acquainted with but there was "nothing special" about their relationship. Nor had he introduced Moynier to Jeantet, accepted funds from Jeantet to pay Moynier and the others to murder Dormoy, or met with Jeantet after the crime to complain about Jeantet's abandonment of those who had carried it out on Jeantet's behalf. One of Chenevier's questions at this point is revealing, as is Marchi's answer. Chenevier asked, "Did you not confide in your friends (MOYNIER, VAILLANT, MARBACH, AND GUYON) that these people [at Vichy] had encouraged you [but now] seemed ready to put all the responsibility for the crime on you?" Marchi's response was not denial this time but rather, "I have already told you that I would not respond to any of your questions." When Chenevier pressed Marchi further about his meetings with the suspects in Lyon, his rendezvous with Marbach in the Saint-Charles train station in Marseille and his trip to Paris where he again met with Moynier and Roger Mouraille, Marchi repeated, "Don't interrogate me any further because not only do I refuse to listen to you but I will not respond to any of your questions." He then demanded to be treated as a political prisoner.

The police had searched his pockets and discovered a letter admitting Marchi to the MSR and no less than 66,950 francs in 5,000, 1,000, 100 and 50-franc notes, money Marchi insisted came from his own savings but which more likely came from Deloncle. They also found a telegram addressed to Marchi in Marseille. It was signed only "CT 94," a code name, but which also referred to a sender. The telegram emanated from the "VICE PRESIDENT PROPAGANDA COUNCIL VICHY HOTEL ASTRID." It read: "Urgent. Take the FIRST TRAIN TO COME TO SEE ME IMMEDIATELY. FROM PIERRE VEAU."[86] Marchi claimed that Pierre Veau was "one of my contacts from the GP," that he had skipped the rendezvous with Veau, and that he had no idea why Veau demanded the "urgent" meeting in the first place.[87]

It is likely that Marchi did indeed know Veau, although probably not only from the GP. Veau worked at Vichy under André Daussin, the man in charge of Vichy's Aryanization program (liquidating Jewish property). Daussin was also the treasurer of the Amicale de France, and Daussin's boss was his close friend Xavier Vallat, who in 1941 was the head of the CGQJ. Like Marchi, Veau, Daussin, and Vallat all had belonged to the Cagoule, and Vallat was Deloncle's lawyer in 1938. The connections among these men, and between them and Jeantet, predated the war. Jeantet was working for the Ministry of Propaganda for most of 1941, and the telegram purported to have come from that office. Most likely it was Jeantet, always careful to remain in the shadows and shield his identity, who had ordered the telegram sent to Marchi, using the name of Pierre Veau, to lure Marchi to Vichy. Marchi may have been telling the truth about having skipped the meeting, since he may well have realized the danger that Jeantet would arrest him to keep him out of Chenevier's hands. For Chenevier and Marion, the telegram constituted yet more evidence that Jeantet and other figures at Vichy were mixed up in the Dormoy assassination. Moreover, Marchi, as well as several of the other Dormoy suspects, retained Jean Franceschi as their lawyer. Meanwhile, Roger Franceschi, also a lawyer based in Marseille, worked with Veau under the direction of Daussin.[88] Thus it is clear that Jeantet was a prominent member of a circle of antisemites in Vichy who were tightly connected to Marchi, and via Jean Franceschi had a direct line to the jailed suspects as well.

Vichy had good reason to want to rein in Marchi given the tenor of another letter the police found in Marchi's possession along with the telegram, a letter that drew a straight line between Marchi and the Dormoy assassins and, more importantly, a direct link between Vichy and the assassins as well. "My friend is ready to give his life for the triumph of the National and Social Revolution as we understand it following the Maréchal and following the team that we are forming. But he must be helped by every means possible. I am counting on you. Bring the boss up to date as far as you think useful. It will not come as a surprise to him after our conversations that you are talking to him about our friend, a former employee of the P.T.T."[89] The P.T.T. is the French postal service for which Yves Moynier had once worked and Moynier was clearly "the friend" to whom the letter referred. The identity of the "boss" remained unknown, but that of the letter's author, Pierre Bagarry, was significant. Bagarry, a native of Marseille, was a member of the technical council of the Amicale de France and knew Jeantet well, raising the distinct possibility that "the boss" was Jeantet. The letter supported Annie Mourraille's testimony about the identity and real intent of at least some of those who had organized Dormoy's murder.

Marchi was unforthcoming in his responses to the questions the police put to him, including those regarding documents they confiscated from his residence in Marseille. He did admit that he had made a number of "interventions" at Vichy on behalf of Moynier and the other suspects, not because he knew anything about the plot but because "I consider them all to be good Frenchmen, having appreciated them at the GP, where they gave me complete satisfaction."[90] The letter from Bagarry also indicated that "individuals" at Vichy were organizing a kind of strike team because it was "necessary that the État Nouveau demonstrate its strength and make a powerful impression."[91] Neither Pétain nor the German military would have looked with favor in 1941 on armed vigilantes who wanted to punish former Third Republic politicians, Communists, or Jews in the Vichy Zone. Such a strike team would have disrupted the fragile peace, so necessary for France to fulfill German demands for French reparations in the form of money, food, industrial products, and raw materials to feed the Nazi war machine. It would have also represented an intolerable challenge to Pétain's authority. Bagarry's letter thus helps to explain why officials at Vichy, whom Chenevier and Marion doubtless informed of its contents, were willing to permit the investigation to continue. Pétain too, at this stage, had a strong interest in uncovering and rooting out organizers of a vigilante "strike team" in the Vichy Zone.

Marchi was a man who made a habit of challenging authority. Brought before Marion on 2 October, Marchi announced that he expected "to be judged as rapidly as possible, and by a military court."[92] Marion ignored him, ordered his money confiscated and placed under seal in police custody, except for 3800 francs which Marion allowed him to take with him to prison, to pay Franceschi and for his "personal needs." Marchi then joined the other suspects in custody in Valence, and the next day was arraigned in the Office of the Public Prosecutor of Grenoble.[93]

By 1 October Chenevier had made significant strides in the investigation. He had linked the culprits to both Jeantet at Vichy and Deloncle in Paris through two intermediaries, Antoine Marchi and André Hérard, and obtained a wealth of evidence that Jeantet and Deloncle together had plotted the crime Moynier and the others had committed. He had managed to arrest one of the two go-betweens, although Hérard remained out of reach in Paris. So far, Vichy had not withdrawn its support for his investigation, and Marion had shown himself cooperative with Chenevier and firm in his attitude toward the suspects. Annie Mourraille's testimony had proved invaluable in helping Chenevier convince Marion to arrest Marchi, and Chenevier could reasonably hope that Marchi too, once he realized that neither Jeantet nor Deloncle could get him released, would testify and persuade Moynier to talk as well.

Still, the telegram and letter from Vichy would have disabused Chenevier of any doubts regarding the ruthlessness of his adversaries in Vichy and Paris, and their determination to quash the Dormoy case before it could lead to them. Moreover, Chenevier knew that the suspects, and especially Marchi, Roger Mouraille, and Annie Mourraille, were convinced of the righteousness of their cause and exceedingly well "lawyered up." All of them, even the seemingly cooperative Annie Mourraille, would not yield an inch to the police without something in return. If he could hold them in custody long enough to convince them that Vichy and Deloncle both were abandoning them, the suspects might cooperate. But even then, Vichy could intervene, by demanding that the suspects be tried without searching any higher for the origins and financing of the plot, or by ordering the suspects' release due to insufficient evidence. Chenevier knew that the odds were against him, but he nevertheless persevered.

CHAPTER SEVEN

October 1941–March 1942: The Waiting Game

On 17 June 1942 Marie Thérèse Payre, a widowed midwife incarcerated in the same prison in Valence as Annie Mourraille, testified before Investigating Magistrate Jean Marion regarding letters she had stolen from Mourraille and conversations she had overheard between Mourraille and the other suspects in the Dormoy case. Put to work in prison, one of Payre's jobs was to clean Mourraille's cell. Annie Mourraille had been regularly flouting the prison regulations, communicating orally and via written notes with the male suspects, and smuggling letters out of the prison to bypass the prison mail service (and censor). Payre handed over four notes she had collected from the many others she alleged the detainees were secretly passing to each other and informed the guards that Annie Mourraille kept a diary, which they found after searching her cell.[1]

Payre's testimony revealed how the Dormoy suspects, desperate to gain their freedom, coordinated their testimony, plotted to escape from Valence, and marshalled the support of influential figures beyond the prison walls. Even though Judge Marion and Charles Chenevier were trying to keep the Dormoy suspects incommunicado in solitary confinement, the prisoners were still finding ways to communicate. The prison guards confiscated two other letters Annie Mourraille tried to smuggle out, one to her mother and the other to Dr. Jean-Louis François Faraut, a former member of the Nice branch of the Cagoule and an influential figure in Vichy.[2]

Payre testified that she had overheard conversations among the detainees, including one in October of 1941, after Antoine Marchi's initial arrest. "The one called Marchi who happened to be in the courtyard taking his [exercise] walk, spoke to the woman Annie Mourraille, who was leaning out a window. Marchi said to her, "Who do you think denounced us?"[3] Annie Mourraille responded that she was sure it was Inspector Chenevier. Marchi's rejoinder was, "If it was him, well, it won't be long – he'll get his." Then Marchi added "We're going to go to the hearing. It is absolutely necessary that neither you nor Yves recognize [me]. Then you will have your part." According to Payre, Annie Mourraille and Marchi discussed money, between 70,000 and 120,000 francs, and Marchi also told Mourraille, "Don't worry about the dining hall – I will take care of your needs." During her second deposition on 27 August 1942 Payre reiterated her previous testimony regarding Antoine Marchi and Annie Mourraille and added that she knew the man in the courtyard with whom Mourraille was conversing from the window of her cell was Marchi because Mourraille called him "Toine."[4]

L'ATTENTISME OR THE WAITING GAME

In the autumn of 1941 the Germans were bogged down with the epic siege of Leningrad. Undaunted, on 19 October they launched an attack on Moscow. The opening of the Russian Front changed the war considerably for France, as it induced the Germans to ramp up their demands for French materials and labor to support the war effort.[5] To this point, the Vichy Zone had escaped the worst impacts of the defeat. Even in the Occupied Zone, the Germans were often polite and restrained in their treatment of the French populace, with the exception of the Jews, but the Occupation became increasingly harsh for the French from this point in the war forward.

The turmoil in Philippe Pétain's cabinet, meanwhile, continued throughout 1941. Pierre Laval bided his time in Paris, drawing ever closer to the Germans while waiting for the recall to power in Vichy that he surely believed was inevitable. Sporadic acts of resistance accelerated in the second half of 1941. Most of these were the work of members of the French Communist Party acting under the orders of Moscow, hoping that unrest in France would force the Germans to divert troops from the Russian front. Rather than putting more soldiers in France, the Germans resorted to a policy of escalating reprisals and hostage executions, substituting terror for military force and obliging the French judiciary and police to play a growing role in the repression of dissent. These changes coincided with a substantial reform and centralization of the structures of French policing and the development of special tribunals to handle resisters. General Otto von Stülpnagel headed the German Supreme Military Command (*Militärbefehlshaber in Frankreich*) or MBF in Occupied France until February of 1942. In his eyes, his mandate to minimize the German resources required to control France necessitated putting as much oversight of the French population into the hands of the Vichy government as possible and maintaining a low profile for the German forces to avoid creating tensions with the French. According to the Armistice, Vichy was to police the civilian population even in the Occupied Zone, and Stülpnagel was content to follow this strategy so long as the French were reasonably cooperative, as it reduced the demands on German soldiers and bureaucrats.[6]

Throughout the autumn of 1941 attacks, mostly small-scale and poorly coordinated, against German soldiers and officials, accelerated.[7] In 1940 military tribunals condemned 8 French people to death. That number rose to 51 between January and September 1941, and more than quadrupled to 236 between September 1941 and March 1942.[8] Initially neither the French police nor the German forces had much success in capturing the perpetrators of these attacks. The Germans therefore resorted to executing hostages – primarily Jews and Communists – that French authorities had detained for reasons unrelated to the assaults on Germans. German pressure on French authorities to bypass normal judicial procedures, including the right to a fair trial, was increasingly visible and deeply troubling to many French people. Even though Pétain at one point offered himself as a hostage in place of others in danger of execution, it was becoming apparent that the German promise to respect the sovereignty of the Vichy regime over French civilians was meaningless. Although most people were slow to lose confidence in Pétain, by the spring of 1942 anti-Pétain graffiti showed up more frequently in public spaces and complaints about deprivations in people's daily lives multiplied as well.[9]

On 21 August 1941 a young Communist militant, Pierre Georges, killed a German civilian employee of the German navy, Alfons Moser, in the Barbes-Rochechouart metro station. The Germans demanded that the French government designate six French hostages to be executed immediately. If the French refused, the Germans threatened to execute 150 interned French Jews themselves. A struggle ensued within Pétain's cabinet between Joseph-Barthélemy, minister of justice, and Pierre Pucheu, minister of the interior, over whether to accede to the German demands. Joseph-Barthélemy contended that complying would undermine any pretense of the independence of the French judiciary, whereas Pucheu insisted that cooperation with the

Germans was the only viable choice. Joseph-Barthélemy lost the argument.[10] On 7 September Pucheu authorized the creation of a new court, the State Tribunal, with two sections, one in Paris and the other in Lyon, with a mandate to handle cases involving national security and international relations; acts of resistance were under its purview. The Tribunal offered up three French hostages for execution, hoping this would satisfy the Germans. When the Germans refused to compromise, the State Tribunal handed down three more death penalty verdicts on 20 and 21 September 1941. The three additional hostages were executed immediately after the verdicts were pronounced.[11] Pierre-Étienne Flandin, a former Third Republic politician who briefly served as Pétain's foreign minister in December 1940, was horrified at the breakdown of respect for due process these executions signified. On 13 September Flandin wrote to Joseph-Barthélemy, "Is it possible that concern for legality and justice have disappeared at this point from the Councils of the government? How could you not have explained to the Maréchal the nature of the error that he is being induced to commit? No regime, in our recent history, has ever acted so arbitrarily; none has so deliberately suppressed the guarantees that are the safeguard of our citizens."[12] During this period Pétain also authorized the creation of special sections of the appeals courts to try Communists and anarchists. The Vichy regime was cracking down.

For growing numbers of French people, as the autumn wore into the second winter of the Occupation, the course of the war and its increasing impact on both Occupied and Vichy France began to erode confidence in Pétain and the inevitability of a German victory. Most French people seem to have been *attentistes*, unhappy with the Occupation but willing to give Pétain and his government the benefit of the doubt, especially as there seemed no viable alternative; for them it was a waiting game.[13] French people had more confidence in the Maréchal than in his government, but Pétain's subsequent inability to negotiate clemency for French hostages or the release of even half the total number of French prisoners of war held in Germany demonstrated his powerlessness in the face of German pressure. The Vichy regime also lost two stabilizing military figures in the autumn of 1941 with the accidental death of General Charles Huntziger on 12 November and the exile of General Maxime Weygand to North Africa on 18 November. Local-level police reports indicate that by the end of 1941 the Vichy regime was losing popular support, and that erosion of confidence worsened in 1942 and 1943.[14]

Even so, French people were unready to turn to de Gaulle. As historian Robert O. Paxton put it, "after the midsummer of 1941, most Allied successes seemed in France to involve French losses," as the Allies bombed French factories, such as the Renault plant in Boulogne-Billancourt shelled on 3 March 1942, and invaded French colonial territory in Africa and elsewhere.[15] To many, the Allied Forces seemed to pose as great a danger to French interests as the Germans. Despite Charles de Gaulle's optimistic creation in London on 24 September 1941 of a *Comité national française* that would form the nucleus of a French government once the country was liberated, most people remained wary of the general and his call to resist the Germans.[16] The French watched and waited as they struggled to maintain their standard of living. Food, clothes, and other necessities became increasingly scarce, and the Vichy regime seemed, during the first two years of the war, locked in what historian Philippe Burrin has called "permanent negotiations" with the Germans that produced little amelioration in the harsh conditions of the Occupation.[17] From August 1939 to July 1942 the cost of living in Paris rose by 65.5 percent. Despite the growth of a black market, Parisians and other urban dwellers were feeling the scarcity of food, coal, and other products. By the close of 1943 the Germans were appropriating over 50 percent of all French non-agricultural production. It was impossible for France to sustain industrial and agricultural production at the levels the Germans demanded and still adequately feed and supply the population.[18]

Worse, as German workers were drafted for the war effort, German demand for French labor also escalated. Even though most French people were reluctant to toil in German factories, the Germans managed to siphon off enough labor to create serious shortages in France just at the time the Germans were increasing production quotas. The Vichy government pressured workers to "volunteer" to work in Germany during 1942 via a system to draft workers known as the *Relève*, in return for the promise that for every three recruits who agreed to go to Germany the Germans would release one French prisoner of war. As it became apparent by the end of 1942 that not even liberating French POWs would motivate enough workers to meet German demands, on 16 February 1943 the Germans forced Pierre Laval, who had returned to Vichy as head of Pétain's cabinet, to introduce the *Service du travail obligatoire* (STO), a labor draft. The STO brought home to denizens of the Vichy Zone the realities of the Occupation. By the close of 1943 close to 650,000 French men and women were laboring in Germany. Even more than the German invasion of the Vichy Zone in November 1942, the STO eroded the legitimacy of the Vichy Regime for most French people.[19]

DEMANDS AND DELAYS

The autumn and winter of 1941–2 devolved into a game of cat-and-mouse for Chenevier and Marion, who continued to interrogate the suspects and gather as much additional evidence as they could to build a case against Gabriel Jeantet and Eugène Deloncle.[20] The suspects penned a flurry of letters entreating their friends, family, and connections at Vichy and Paris for help, and sent a continuous stream of petitions to Marion complaining about the conditions of their incarceration and demanding that he release them. Marion denied them all, but by the summer of 1942 he was becoming nervous as the mental and physical health of all the suspects, but especially that of Moynier, deteriorated.[21] Chenevier did make some progress, as he managed to depose Jeantet in March 1942. But Marion was obliged to release Antoine Marchi on bail in November and by the end of the year he had slipped beyond Marion's grasp, having joined Deloncle's LVF in Poland. Marion and Chenevier were forced into a position of *attentisme* resembling the waiting game in which France remained mired.

Still, they spared no pains in their slow and steady construction of a case justifying deposing Jeantet and Deloncle. On 2 October 1941, while questioning Marchi, Marion declared that "the gentleman Jeantey [*sic*: Jeantet] who knew you well through the Amicale de France esteemed you too ardent and often claimed that your comrades had to moderate your actions."[22] Marchi admitted that he knew Yves Moynier, Ludovic Guichard, Lucien Guyon, and Horace Vaillant but insisted he had nothing to do with Dormoy's murder. Marion then repeated Annie Mourraille's testimony, that Marchi was in fact the liaison between the assassins and Vichy. When Marchi responded that none of this was true, Marion told Marchi that Mourraille and Moynier had implicated him. Marchi's response is instructive. He stated that he knew that Moynier and Mourraille had changed their story that very morning and now agreed that they would testify that Marchi had played no role in the plot to assassinate Dormoy.[23] Despite Marion's efforts to control each witness' access to the others, his courtroom and private chambers, and the prison at Valence, leaked like sieves, permitting the suspects to communicate with each other and thereby manipulate the investigation. Marchi failed to persuade Marion to release him, however, because on 26 September 1941 Chenevier sent Marion intelligence from his informant in Marseille "who wished to remain anonymous" that tied Marchi and Moynier to Jeantet.[24] It sufficed to keep Marchi in custody a little longer.

Two other events took place on 2 October 1941 that would have an important impact on the Dormoy case. First, during the night of 2–3 October, Deloncle dispatched a team of operatives from his MSR to bomb synagogues in Paris, using explosives he had obtained from SS-Sturmbannfürher Hans Sommer, at the behest of Sommer's superior, SS-Obersturmbannführer, Dr. Helmut Knochen, a senior commander in the *Sicherheitspolizei und Sicherheitsdienst* (Security Police and Security Service – Sipo-SD) in Paris.[25] The perpetrators first bombed a prayer room on the Avenue Montespan at 2:05 a.m. Over the next few hours, they attacked five synagogues located at 21 rue des Tournelles, 24 rue Copernic, 13 rue Sainte-Isaure, 13 rue Notre-Dame-de-Nazareth, and 44 rue de la Victoire, home to the city's Grande Synagogue. The blasts injured several people and damaged adjacent buildings. At 3:50 a.m. the Paris police found an unexploded bomb in front of the synagogue at 10 rue Pavée. A German bomb squad detonated it later that morning in the presence of several French police commissioners. The synagogue attacks were spread across much of Paris, in the 3rd, 4th, 9th, 11th, 16th, and 18th arrondissements, home to the bulk of the city's Jewish population.[26] Deloncle had decided that absent any real support in Vichy, his best bet was to throw his lot in with the Gestapo. The bombings marked both the zenith of his power and influence in wartime France and the beginning of his downfall. They were also French terrorist acts that created a Holocaust landscape on the streets of Paris and sent a message aimed at Jewish destruction.[27]

The synagogue bombings help to explain why Marchi and the other suspects held out hope in 1942 that Deloncle would still assist them even though Jeantet had turned his back on them.[28] First, it is important to remember that Deloncle frequently visited Marseille to oversee the activities of the branch of the MSR based there. The suspects all had ample opportunity to meet Deloncle in person at least once prior to the Dormoy assassination in July and Moynier's and Roger Mouraille's trip to Paris in August.[29] Second, in 1941 Deloncle's rhetoric regarding the corruption at Vichy and the need for a "purge" of Jews, Communists, Freemasons, and figures from the Third Republic who were responsible for France's defeat in 1940 was becoming increasingly strident.[30] On radio, in print and in public addresses, Deloncle fulminated against Jews, Freemasons, capitalists, trusts, and other "occult" international powers that he believed wanted to destroy the National Revolution.[31] Deloncle also declared that those responsible for the defeat had to be chastised and Pétain's cabinet had to be purged of former Third Republic politicians. By May of 1941 MSR propaganda was again advocating a "march on Vichy," reminiscent of

Mussolini's "March on Rome," ostensibly to return Laval to power, although Deloncle clearly would have preferred that it was he who became head of the government.[32]

From the perspective of Marchi and the others involved in Dormoy's murder, Deloncle was the only leader in France willing to act rather than merely harangue, to carry out the purge they so desired and enact the National Revolution. Deloncle's demand that the remaining Third Republic politicians be swept from Pétain's cabinet, arrested if they were still at liberty, put on trial, and made to pay with their lives for the "treachery" and "incompetence" that had led to France's defeat, would have been music to the suspects' ears. They likely also knew of the generous subsidies that Deloncle was receiving from the Germans, some of which probably had found its way to their pockets.[33] The audacious synagogue bombings in October, which represented precisely the sort of "direct action" the suspects wanted and saw themselves as having committed in assassinating Dormoy, would only have confirmed their belief that Deloncle was on their side. If they could get word to him of their plight, he surely would pull strings with the Germans or engineer their escape. Much of this was pure fantasy. The October bombings set in motion a chain of events that rather than strengthening Deloncle's hand cost him most of his political support. The Germans no longer trusted him and neither did Laval.[34] But in October 1941 Deloncle still seemed a powerful ally.

The second event of 2 October was that Marion learned of the two letters that Annie Mourraille had tried to smuggle out of prison. These letters and her diary, confiscated at the same time, demonstrated the double game she was trying to play with Marion and Chenevier, a deception that Marchi's testimony on the 2nd revealed.[35] Her letter to her mother exposes Mourraille's strategy and the problems with which Marion had to contend:

> Maman Chérie, this letter is going out Sunday morning by courier and I can thus chat a little with you, freely and give you news that is not being watched. I was at Montélimar yesterday, brought there by car with Yves in order to get some results that I have already spoken to you about. I responded to the questions that I myself wrote for the Investigating Magistrate [Marion] as was already planned and I think that is going to put me a step forward. Yves did not say what he was supposed to but we were able to speak together for a long time by ourselves and he well understood I think where his interest and those of our cause [lie]. For us the situation is looking good. You know that I don't lose my head easily and from the

first moment, a month ago, I had prepared my system of defense and my first declaration did not contain any errors or anything not useful that could cause me problems now. My lawyer moreover told me that my declaration was "perfect" and that is very true because in these situations one says a little too much and things that are useless. From my perspective I think Yves and I have established exactly our responses down to the smallest detail reconstituting the facts. There is no risk that I will be tripped up in the details in my [assertion] that I was not informed [of the true nature of the plot]. The Investigating Magistrate was charming. I submitted my request to be freed with bail [provisional liberty] immediately after the reconstitution and that should happen now. I believe that things can be speeded up so that I can be free in about three weeks or a month.[36]

Annie Mourraille also revealed in the letter her devotion to the cause of the National Revolution and her understanding of what she and her comrades believed they had accomplished in assassinating Dormoy. "Now there will be a new minister, Laval, and that will be very good for us."[37]

In her letter to Faraut, Annie Mourraille complained that she was not being treated as a political prisoner and asked Faraut whether he didn't have friends in high places who could help her stifle the affair. Faraut had been implicated in the Cagoule before the war and was even arrested on 7 July 1938. He remained in prison until 23 December 1938, when the case against him collapsed, most likely due to witness intimidation and the support of businessmen and members of the government who sympathized with his views. When questioned regarding Mourraille's letter, Faraut denied having belonged to the Cagoule or more than a passing acquaintance with either Deloncle or André Hérard. Moreover, Faraut insisted that he had abandoned all political activities and professed to be mystified as to why Annie Mourraille wrote to him. He conceded that he had met her during the summer of 1941 while she was acting in the play "Britannicus" in Nice but declared that she was a woman with "too high an opinion of herself" and that he was "shocked that she dared to address herself to him for his help."[38]

About two weeks after Dormoy's assassination, Mourraille approached Faraut and, without admitting that she herself had played a role in the crime, expressed her concerns for her "friends" who were mixed up in it. Despite his denials Faraut was in fact an active member of the Cagoule in the 1930s and a collaborator who after the war was tried and condemned to a year in prison, confiscation of all his wealth, and loss of his civil rights. Witnesses who knew

Faraut claimed that he "had always benefitted from powerful interventions."[39] Faraut, a physician who moved in exalted circles in Nice, had connections in Vichy and the MSR and was connected before and during the war with a known German spy operating in France. It was not unreasonable for Mourraille to believe that he could lobby on her behalf. Annie Mourraille demonstrated through her missive to Faraut that not only was she was well aware from the outset that Moynier and the others intended to assassinate Dormoy, but that she had her own connections to figures tied both to Vichy and the Cagoule. This is unsurprising given that she had associated with extreme right figures prior to the war, including Cagoule leaders General Édouard Duseigneur and Deloncle.[40]

The moment was particularly sensitive because during the first two weeks of October Marion was trying to garner enough evidence to forestall granting Marchi bail. At this point in the investigation, Annie Mourraille was being obstructive, most likely because now that Marchi had been arrested he was pressuring her to retract her statements about him. Annie Mourraille's prison diary is highly revealing of the machinations among herself and her fellow assassins. In September 1941 she was convinced that the key to survival for her and the others was to get Marchi arrested and to push the affair "as high as possible," meaning implicating important figures in the regime. Initially she believed that Chenevier was sympathetic to her, and he was content to nurture this illusion.[41] Still, Mourraille doubted Chenevier's sincerity. In her letter to Faraut she asked about Chenevier: "Are you acquainted with Superintendent Chenevier? ... This guy seems to have an extremely friendly attitude and to be working for me and my friends, would you know whether he's a loyal fellow or a bastard?"[42]

Annie Mourraille was correct about one thing: she and Chenevier both wanted the investigation to implicate influential members of the Vichy government, perhaps even one or more members of Pétain's cabinet. "He too wants to climb as 'high' as possible and if our goals are not the same, we plan to take the same road to get there. He has promised in that regard to do everything in his power to get me out of here and to save Yves."[43] So long as it seemed that she and Chenevier were allied in their desire to implicate Jeantet, Annie Mourraille cooperated with the investigation. At the scene of one deposition, Mourraille later wrote, "We chat, and then the attack begins. C. and I win some territory; I clench my fists and play the part as planned."[44] Chenevier went out of his way to court her. During one of her trips from prison to the courthouse for an interrogation, for example, he ordered her an excellent lunch. She informed her lawyer, Joel Roche, that she was confident that Chenevier would help her to surmount any challenges to her testimony. Roche asked her why she had spoken of Marchi in a deposition. "Because I couldn't do anything else," she responded. She did not, however, inform Roche that she expected later to retract her allegations against Marchi although she did note this in her diary, along with her satisfaction that it was her testimony that had gotten Marchi arrested and only she could get him released, by changing her story.[45]

Once Marchi was in prison Mourraille did indeed retract her statements implicating him and Vichy figures in Dormoy's assassination. She had achieved her goal, as now that Marchi was in the same boat as she and Moynier, Marchi had to lobby on behalf of all of them or risk having her change her story yet again and implicate the people in Vichy Marchi was intent on shielding from prosecution. Given that Marchi tried shortly before his arrest to escape the police by joining the LVF and heading to fight in Russia, Mourraille was correct that Marchi would not keep his promises unless he too was incarcerated and facing murder charges. But once in prison with the others in Valence Marchi also could cajole them, and especially Annie Mourraille, to cease all cooperation with Chenevier and Marion.

Marchi soon went to work on Moynier to persuade him that Marchi was still his loyal ally and to get Moynier to pressure Annie Mourraille. Within a few days of Marchi's incarceration, Annie Mourraille met with Moynier and Marchi, most likely while waiting at court to be deposed. Mourraille took the opportunity to ask Marchi what he thought of Chenevier. Could they trust him? Was he really sympathetic to their cause? Marchi responded that Chenevier was a "bastard," to her great disappointment. Then Moynier assured her that they had not yet lost their case and that the most urgent matter was that Marchi regain his liberty. They agreed, therefore, that when she was confronted with Marchi in Marion's courtroom, she would "not recognize him." As she reassured Moynier, she "knew how to play in a comedy," and thus he could relax. She would get Marchi released.[46] As promised, in court that day she avowed repeatedly that she knew nothing of Marchi and that if she had previously testified against him it was because "his name had been furnished to her as that of the intermediary of whose existence she was certain." Marion knew that she was lying, of course, and this amused Annie. She congratulated herself on how her testimony had set Marion to muttering under his breath. She also enjoyed Marchi's even more dramatic performance as he alternately blustered and wept, insisting that he was innocent and that Chenevier and Marion were plotting to destroy him. Next, it was Moynier's turn and he too declared that neither Marchi nor anyone else at Vichy had helped him plan and execute

Dormoy's murder. After testifying, Annie Mourraille told Moynier that she had asked Marchi to give her his word that once released he would above all focus on obtaining Moynier's freedom (because she was terrified that Moynier would face the hangman's noose).[47]

Annie Mourraille's retraction succeeded. Marion had no choice but to grant Marchi's request for bail on 20 October. Félix Gouin, Jeanne Dormoy's lawyer, appealed this decision the same day. Chenevier also intervened. He asserted that Marchi was dangerous and a flight risk because Marchi had a history of violence and enough money to skip bail. Moreover, Chenevier pointed out that during a previous interrogation Annie Mourraille had testified that Marchi had played a central role in organizing Dormoy's assassination.[48] Mourraille's retraction was clearly a significant setback to the investigation, but all was not lost. On 25 October the public prosecutor filed a motion to rescind Marchi's bail and the Appeals Court in Grenoble granted the prosecutor's request. Ironically, it was to an indiscretion on the part of Annie Mourraille that Marchi owed this reversal of fortune, as the warden intercepted and passed on to Marion her letters in which she revealed her deceit in her most recent testimony about Marchi. Annie Mourraille acknowledged this in her diary, and averred that she was worried because she "couldn't remember" what exactly she had said about herself in her letter.[49] On 17 November, armed with a new warrant from Marion, the police rearrested Marchi at a café on the Canebière in Marseille. As usual Marchi insisted on a dramatic scene, demanding that the police handcuff him in front of the witnesses and yelling at one of the officers, "I'll have your hide in two months when I'm in power! You are all idiots!"[50] At the police station Marchi continued to yell: "You are all working for the Jews and the Freemasons!"

Nor would it be as simple as Annie Mourraille believed to retract her previous testimony against Marchi without risking perjury. Chenevier pointed out to Marion that he still could question her further and find other evidence to verify her original statements. In a way, Mourraille had done too good a job in making the case against Marchi in the first place. "If the lady Mourraille has gone back on her declarations," Chenevier asserted, "these were very detailed and must be meticulously verified because clandestine correspondence among the accused since the deposition of Madame Mourraille demonstrates that subsequent to her deposition the accused have agreed among themselves regarding the testimony they would give during the interrogations."[51] If Chenevier had been in any doubt regarding Mourraille's duplicity, this must have vanished once he intercepted her letters.[52] Even so, once again Marchi managed to get out on bail by the end of November 1941. He promptly joined the LVF and on 4 December shipped out from Versailles for Poland, headed from there to the Russian front.[53]

Annie Mourraille's letter to Faraut was also more revealing than she realized, given that in it she indicated that she and Roger Mouraille knew Deloncle as well. "Could you possibly help me reach sympathetic people who can smother this whole affair?" she asked Faraut. "Try to find out what Buchart [*sic*: the reference was perhaps to Marcel Bucard, co-founder of the LVF, but might have been to Henri Bruchet who was linked to Filliol, Hérard, and the Gestapo], Deloncle, André can do, my comrades have met with the latter two in Paris, a little before their arrest, one of them is named Mouraille like me, and I believe that Eugène knows him well."[54] She may have been "name dropping" in the letter, but her use of Deloncle's first name was her way of asserting that she, like Faraut, was closely acquainted with Deloncle. Whether she knew the fascist leader, Marcel Bucard, is unclear. But it is doubtful that she would have written to Faraut unless she was confident that he was aware that she and Deloncle knew each other.

A MYSTERIOUS VISITOR TO THE RELAIS IN JULY

Despite the setbacks, Chenevier and Marion were determined to forge ahead in their efforts to accumulate enough evidence to depose Jeantet, Deloncle, and Hérard. On 19 November Marion issued a warrant to the head of the criminal police at Vichy to investigate the connections between the suspects in custody and "diverse persons."[55] He and Chenevier also worked to establish the identity of a mysterious visitor to the Relais de l'Empereur on 12 July 1941. The man arrived at the Relais about 8:00 p.m., during the week (8–15 July) that Guichard was staying at the Relais and spying on Dormoy. According to Mme. Vilnat, the stranger requested a room "without specifying what floor."[56] Instead, as if inspecting the hotel to decide what room would suit him, "he walked up and down the corridors" and then came back down to the front desk. Meanwhile, said Vilnat, "there was Guichard who talked to me at the cash register, which was contrary to his habit." Vilnat became suspicious and telephoned the night watchman, whom she told to check on "what was going on in the hallways." When the stranger came back downstairs, "Guichard and the stranger came together to the cash register and seemed not to know each other." The stranger never filled out a registration card or took a room and instead simply left the hotel that same evening. Vilnat's description of this visitor whom Guichard pretended not to know but who clearly preoccupied Guichard was "tall, strong, elegant, well-dressed, light-coloured hair, a blond type. He gave the impression of being strong and agile." It is important to note here that this description does not fit any of the Dormoy assassins – those still alive in September 1941 or those killed in August – according to the testimony of multiple witnesses. Vilnat had the opportunity to see the only ones among them who could be described as "tall," Moynier and Horace Vaillant, and it is clear that neither man could be described as "elegant" or "well-dressed," and neither was the same man as this "stranger" who visited the Relais in July. Nor did the man fit the description of Hérard. Witnesses described both Hérard and Marchi as rather dark in hair and complexion, and Marchi as rather corpulent. In fact, there is only one man among Chenevier's list of suspects who does fit this description: Gabriel Jeantet. Given that Marion asked Annie Mourraille whether Jeantet had come to fetch her at the Relais, he and Chenevier deemed it quite possible that Jeantet visited Montélimar at some point to meet with the assassins.[57]

Marion and Chenevier were also trying to place Hérard in Montélimar at the time of Dormoy's assassination, and here they had more solid evidence. Despite Annie Mourraille's insistence that the "André" who had fetched her at the Relais on 22 June was not Hérard but rather Horace Vaillant, the other witnesses who were shown Vaillant's photo denied that he was the man they had seen.[58] By 22 December Chenevier had been to Paris, where he investigated Hérard, Faraut, and others, and reported back to Marion. On 27 January 1942 Marion received a discouraging response from Paris regarding the warrant he had issued on 19 November. "Messieurs Eugène Deloncle and Hérard dit 'André'" could not be questioned due to the "political role they played in the Occupied Zone."[59] Both worked for the Gestapo. In his 22 December 1941 report to Marion from Paris Chenevier concurred with this assessment. "Except for the indicated suspects [Marchi, Moynier, and the others], only the gentlemen Eugène Deloncle and Hérard are likely to be able to give us any further information. Still I have not believed it advisable to interrogate them due to the political role that they play in the Occupied Zone, at least not until I have a warrant to this effect from Monsieur the Investigating Magistrate."[60] Marion issued that warrant, but serving it and getting Deloncle or Hérard to comply were going to be difficult. With Marchi in Poland or Russia and Annie Mourraille and the others not talking, it seemed as though the case was stalled, perhaps permanently. Marion ordered that the suspects remain in solitary confinement through the winter and waited to see if time, harsh conditions, and their growing sense that they had been abandoned would wear them down. In February he did agree to allow them individual heaters to warm their cells.[61]

Marion's patience began to pay off during the winter of 1941–2. It was Roger Mouraille who first began to waver, not necessarily because he was breaking under the prison regime – Mouraille appears to have been the most seasoned and resilient of the suspects – but because he seems to have had both little faith in either Marchi or Vichy and a strong sense of self-preservation. In a letter dated 9 February, which the prison censors read as Roger Mouraille must have known they would, he wrote that "if Marchi is in flight, it is surely under orders, because of those of Vichy where the mouth will always be closed."[62] In the same letter Roger Mouraille indicated that Marchi had "broken their solidarity agreement." Annie Mourraille also began to realize around the same time that Marchi had fled as soon as he was released from Valence rather than lobbying Deloncle or Jeantet to help his accomplices. She and Roger Mouraille began to work on Moynier to persuade him to change his testimony and implicate Marchi, to whom he had remained steadfastly loyal up to this point.[63]

On 9 February the warden at Valence intercepted a letter Roger Mouraille wrote to Moynier, urging him to reveal "the true people behind the affair."[64] Mouraille knew that this note, like the letters to his wife and mother, would be confiscated and wrote it expressly to show the authorities that he was cooperating and trying to get Moynier to cooperate as well. The text of the letter is still revealing, however. Roger Mouraille averred that he was disgusted with the situation in which he found himself, implicated in a crime with which he had not been involved, simply because he had tried to aid Moynier and then traveled to Paris with him and Marchi.[65] He claimed that he "regretted" not having told the police immediately that Marchi had accompanied them to Paris, and that after everything that had happened, now that Marchi was out of prison, entirely due to Moynier's "generosity," Marchi had repaid Moynier by fleeing France, "surely under orders" from figures at Vichy, who had "panicked" and "broken" their agreements with Moynier and the others. Marchi, Roger Mouraille declared to Moynier, was "your leader" – Mouraille was careful not to imply that he was part of the plot in any way – and the "official liaison with the cabinet of the Maréchal or something along those lines." Roger Mouraille admitted that he now regretted having lied for Marchi because "it is cowardly to leave your friends in shit." "You," he told Moynier, "are a jerk to take care of bastards that let you be broken because you're a problem; don't you see that they are using you as a patsy and that you will pay for [in the place of] these cowards?"

On 14 February Annie Mourraille again changed her statement and declared that Marchi was indeed the liaison between Vichy and Moynier.[66] While Moynier was not yet ready to turn on Marchi, he wrote his mother around this time complaining of the harsh conditions in prison, where he was being kept in solitary confinement with inadequate heat and food. He called his prison regime "legal assassination" and insisted that "we are revolutionaries, nationalists, and we have become a problem."[67] Moynier did declare in court on 14 February, "I am certain about what I said that Marchi must have enlisted his former subordinates from the GP and then dumped them afterward."[68] He also admitted to doubts about whether or not Vichy was going to come to his rescue: "I am persuaded that I have become an encumbrance for several reasons."[69] He added that "if the police wanted to find out the identity of those really responsible in the Dormoy affair, they need to search at Vichy."[70] The following day Roger Mouraille stated that he had not revealed during his initial interrogation that Marchi had traveled to Paris with himself and Moynier because Mouraille was "persuaded that the former [Marchi] was a government agent. In addition, Marchi had a well-furnished portfolio." Roger Mouraille asserted that Marchi "often made trips to Vichy and in effect he led me to believe that he was a government agent. I also thought that the Dormoy case was an affair arranged by the government."[71]

Roger Mouraille was still not admitting culpability in the crime beyond abetting Moynier after the fact, but he was ready to turn on Marchi. Mouraille had always been more willing than Moynier to bring Vichy into the investigation, but by February of 1942 he was becoming desperate. Mouraille was a businessman and with his enterprise moribund while he was in prison, his bank had informed him that his associates in the trucking company could no longer send him any funds.[72] Something had to give. Roger Mouraille's testimony seems to have done the trick. On 14 February Marion again revoked Marchi's bail. Marchi was out of reach at this point, fighting on the Russian front, but eventually he would return to France on leave and when he did, the police would pounce.[73]

JEANTET'S STATEMENT

On 13 October 1941 Jean Franceschi, who Marchi, as well as Moynier and Guichard, had retained as his lawyer, asked Marion to unseal Dormoy's personal papers, which the police had confiscated the night of the murder.[74] Franceschi's goal in demanding access to Dormoy's papers, a demand that he reiterated in a petition to the Appeals Court in Grenoble in 1942, was to demonstrate that Dormoy was a traitor to France deserving of the punishment Franceschi's clients had meted out to him in Montélimar. The suspects were convinced that among Dormoy's papers Marion would find damning proof of "an unequivocal conspiracy that the former minister and his comrades had waged against the National Revolution," and they hoped that revealing Dormoy's supposed treachery would prompt Marion to drop the charges against them or at least prove a mitigating factor in their crime.[75]

On 27 February 1942 Marion acceded to Franceschi's repeated requests. He visited the Relais and searched Dormoy's room – and found little of interest – and then broke the seals on Dormoy's papers in the presence of Franceschi. Sixty-nine of those papers were of a personal nature. There were ten letters from Léon Blum, writing from his prison cell at Riom where Blum was preparing for his upcoming trial. In addition, there were thirteen documents someone had managed to smuggle to Dormoy while he was in prison, all related to the "Laval affair" of 13 December 1940. These sensitive documents provided Dormoy with an accurate account of the machinations behind Laval's fall. Their presence among Dormoy's papers demonstrates that even during the lowest point in his fortunes he must have had friends at Vichy who kept him informed about the politics there and the arrest of Laval.[76] Dormoy and his allies probably hoped that Laval's departure would prompt Pétain to pull back from collaboration with the Germans. It was the Germans and their collaborationist French allies who were most insistent on holding the trials at Riom and punishing former Third Republic politicians like Dormoy and Blum. Laval's exit could result in the delay or cancellation of the trials and an improvement in the conditions of incarceration of Dormoy and the others, which in Dormoy's case is precisely what took place. Marion also found in Dormoy's briefcase over a hundred documents related to the period of September 1937 through January 1938.

Franceschi must have been disappointed when he saw the contents of Dormoy's briefcase. None of the documents were particularly damning from Dormoy's perspective. There was no evidence in Dormoy's papers that he had behaved treasonously, taken part in any cabal to overthrow Pétain, or tried to undermine the National Revolution. "Among these documents," Marion stated, "there are none that implicate in a direct or violent manner either the National Revolution or the Head of State or the Admiral Darlan."[77] Marion added, "In no manner could such documents, even if they reveal a certain state of mind of the victim and a lack of comprehension of current events, justify the accused to raise themselves in judgment and 'chastise those people who they don't think are French.'" In Marion's view, while Dormoy did not fully support the National Revolution, he was neither a traitor nor a criminal, and nothing justified the suspects appointing themselves judge, jury, and executioners.

Marion's remarks do not rule out the possibility that certain people in Vichy and Paris, especially former Cagoulards like Jeantet and Deloncle, might have feared the contents of Dormoy's briefcase. In his report Marion was circumspect about the materials related to 1937 and 1938, stating only that there were many newspapers from this period. But he did find "manuscript notes from M. Dormoy related to his deposition before Monsieur the Investigating Magistrate of the Supreme Court" along with numerous letters that old political friends and allies had addressed to him. Marion does not indicate here to which deposition to the Supreme Court the notes referred, whether Dormoy had yet given the deposition, and, if so, when. Was this testimony he gave around the time of his arrest in September 1940, or did these notes refer to an earlier deposition from Dormoy, while he was still interior minister, and relate to the affair of the Cagoule in 1937 and 1938? We don't know from Marion's letter. Marion's goal in writing to the prosecutor in 1942 was to put to rest Franceschi's insistence that his clients should be freed because Dormoy deserved to die. Marion did not broach the issue of whether among Dormoy's papers in Montélimar there were documents that may have been problematic for the reputation and political careers of former Cagoule figures in Pétain's cabinet. It is likely, however, that Dormoy knew as early as that fateful trip to Paris in July 1940 that part of Léon Blum's defense strategy in any trial would involve discussing how the Cagoulards had undermined his government in 1937. Nor is it farfetched to suppose that Dormoy thus had selected materials related to the Cagoule investigation to bring with him to Montluçon. He knew he would be arrested and would need the materials to prepare his own defense and help that of his friend and ally Blum. He may have brought the papers with him to Montélimar, but Jeanne may also have carried them with her from Montluçon on one of her visits.

The unsealing of Dormoy's papers or the revocation of Marchi's bail on 14 February – perhaps both – may have been what motivated Jeantet to make a formal statement to Chenevier, who interviewed him on 11 March. It was quite possible that Marchi would meet his end on the Russian Front. No doubt some figures at Vichy fervently hoped this would be the case. If Marchi survived and the police did arrest and interrogate him again, however, Marchi might decide it was time to give up Jeantet. It was thus good strategy on Jeantet's part to submit to questioning before Marchi was caught and thereby discredit any testimony Marchi might later offer.

Jeantet was, as always, very careful and clever in his responses to Chenevier's questions. Given the information that Chenevier had amassed about his activities, Jeantet could not deny knowing Marchi without perjuring himself.

But Jeantet stated that he had "no particular relationship" with Marchi, although he did encounter Marchi a few times in Marseille while attending meetings of the Marseille branch of the GP that Marchi headed. Jeantet was also forced to admit that Marchi had traveled to Vichy often and on several occasions came to see him in his office on the rue Alquié, the same location where Chenevier interviewed him. Jeantet "saw" Marchi again in August, after Dormoy's murder, when both men were in Marseille for a conference, and also had "run into" Marchi in Vichy prior to a conference in early August, this time at the headquarters of the Propaganda Service of the General Secretary of Information at the Hôtel Astrid in Vichy.[78] Thus despite Jeantet's vagueness regarding the dates of the encounters, he met with Marchi at least twice within the weeks just after Dormoy's murder and prior to Marchi's first arrest. It likely was at those meetings that Jeantet turned down Marchi's request for further assistance, thus explaining Marchi's trip to Paris with Roger Mouraille and Moynier. It is quite possible that Marchi met with Jeantet right after the murder, and that Jeantet suggested to Marchi that he bring Moynier to see Deloncle and hopefully persuade Moynier to join the LVF and fight the Russians, which would have sent Moynier out of reach of the Vichy police. Moynier's refusal to cooperate meant that Roger Mouraille had to shelter him while Marchi returned to Vichy in August, consulted again with Jeantet and was again turned down for further help. Only then did Moynier finally agree to join the LVF, only to be arrested at Roger Mouraille's house hours before he intended to depart again for Paris.

Jeantet denied any discussions with Marchi about the crime before or after the fact. When Chenevier showed him Moynier's photo, however, Jeantet admitted that he was "pretty certain" that Moynier accompanied Marchi to Marseille for the conference held during the "first days of the month of August" – after the crime but before the duo's 7 August trip to Paris in the company of Mouraille.[79] He claimed not to recognize Roger Mouraille or Ludovic Guichard from their photos, or the deceased trio of Marbach, Guyon, and Vaillant. Annie Mouraille, Jeantet declared after viewing her photo, was "a complete stranger to me." Chenevier then asked Jeantet directly whether he was the Vichy official who supplied the false identity card that Marchi passed on to Annie Mouraille. Chenevier pointed out that the document was stamped "Sûreté Nationale Vichy." Jeantet's response was a succinct "no."

Chenevier next quoted several statements Annie Mouraille had made in court, including the assertion that the others spoke often of Jeantet's involvement in the Dormoy affair. Their reward for assassinating Dormoy was to be assistance in their work of "cleansing" Vichy, and to that end they had "formed a sort of group or team that would work in close collaboration with the government."[80] Once they were sure Dormoy was dead, Marchi was to return to Vichy "to bring the news to the persons who had encouraged him and lay the foundations for the prerogatives that had been promised him before." Annie Mourraille also asserted that she suspected that Jeantet, whom she did not consider particularly "ardent" about the whole affair, or powerful enough to authorize it himself, was probably fronting for someone else even more highly placed at Vichy. When confronted with Annie Mourraille's statement, Jeantet responded that he was "ignorant" of any role Marchi may have played in the murder, and that he "did not furnish Marchi with any assistance of any type, nor materials that might have facilitated an operation of this sort." And with that, Jeantet ended the interview.

Although Jeantet had so far avoided indictment, the suspects remained convinced that ultimately he would have to aid them. At the beginning of April Guichard's and Mouraille's wives together went to Vichy, where they met with Jeantet and begged him to help their husbands who were perishing in prison. When Chenevier questioned Jeantet about what prompted this visit if it were true that he had nothing to do with the case and had never met Mouraille or Guichard, Jeantet responded that the two women must have come to him because they "knew of him through his propaganda work" for the Amicale.[81] Chenevier found this answer less than convincing.

By the end of March 1942 Chenevier and Marion were locked in a stalemate with the suspects, whose mental and physical health was deteriorating in solitary confinement in Valence. Moynier was showing signs of severe mental breakdown. In a letter he sent to the chief warden at Valence on 13 April 1942, Moynier declared that "since the last time I was weighed I have lost seven kilos and my mental state is very bad. I feel that I am going mad and I absolve myself of any responsibility for what might happen as a result, since I am at times no longer as lucid as I might wish."[82] They knew that Vichy was content to allow them to rot there until they were tried and condemned, or simply died in prison. But Marion and Chenevier also knew that their window of opportunity to push the case higher, into the Vichy regime, was closing. Unless something changed, the case would remain open but unresolved until Vichy obliged Marion to close the dossier and release the suspects. What neither Marion nor Chenevier could have anticipated, however, was that in April 1942 a dramatic change in Pétain's government would alter the course of the investigation and, ultimately, precipitate a decisive German intervention in the case.

CHAPTER EIGHT

18 April 1942: The Return of Pierre Laval

If Eugène Deloncle was behind Paul Collette's attempt to assassinate Pierre Laval and Marcel Déat during an RNP rally on 27 August 1941, he made a grave strategic error and a dangerous enemy. Laval never accepted the MSR leader's insistence that he had nothing to do with the assassination attempt. During the winter of 1941–2 Laval and Deloncle were in a similar, frustrating situation, thirsting for power, recipients of German backing, but without a political office that would confer legitimate authority. On 18 April 1942 that all changed for Laval. Age, disillusionment, the treachery of the fractious members of his cabinet, and the multitude of power-hungry hangers-on in Vichy had weakened Philippe Pétain physically and politically in the nearly two years since the Armistice and the creation of the Vichy regime. In April, the old Maréchal finally swallowed his pride, succumbed to German pressure to oust Admiral François Darlan and recalled Laval from Paris to head his government in Vichy.[1] Deloncle thus far had refused Marion's repeated requests that he and André Hérard submit to an interrogation. It is likely no coincidence that the same day Pétain recalled Laval, Deloncle conceded to meet with Superintendent Weber of the Parisian police. Weber showed him the list of questions that Marion had formulated. Deloncle agreed to answer them, but requested a recess, which Weber granted, until the following Monday, 20 April, so that Deloncle ostensibly could "consult his notes so as to give them more useful responses."[2]

It is highly unlikely that Deloncle's cooperation in April was a coincidence. Three months after Chenevier had informed Marion that Deloncle was too important and dangerous to be subpoenaed, Deloncle went to the headquarters of the Parisian police to respond to the summons. Deloncle was not a man given to spontaneous changes of heart. More likely it was Laval who demanded the Germans yank Deloncle's chain. One thing Pétain, Laval, and the Germans had in common in 1942 was an ardent desire for the Dormoy case to be resolved before the investigation destabilized Pétain's regime. They were as aware as Marion that the jailed suspects, and especially Moynier, were finding it more and more difficult to maintain their resolve not to testify against Vichy figures. So long as Annie Mourraille was the only one who was cooperating, the case against Vichy remained thin. But if Moynier, the leader of the gang, testified, that would give Marion the ammunition he needed to indict Gabriel Jeantet and perhaps others close to Pétain.

The Vichy authorities faced a dilemma. They had just completed a major overhaul of the French court system, but now could not agree on the best court in which to try the suspects if things went that far. The new system was still fragile, and the threat that members of the extreme right would violently disrupt the trial was very real. Thanks in part to the remaining integrity of at least some of France's judges, and in part to the brilliant defense Léon Blum mounted for himself and his fellow defendants at Riom, the case against them was suspended in April 1942. The suspension of the process demonstrated that Vichy could not completely control France's judiciary, and the obvious German pressure behind the Riom trial undermined public confidence in the courts. The last thing the Vichy authorities wanted was a similar judicial debacle in the Dormoy case.

For the rest of 1942, while Joseph-Barthélémy and others at Vichy dithered over what to do with the Dormoy suspects, it was Laval and the Germans who held the key to the outcome of the stalemated case. In August they engineered the transfer of the suspects from Valence to the much smaller, more remote makeshift prison in the chateau of the small town of Largentière in the Ardèche. They then tried to facilitate a "spontaneous" escape that would look like the suspects and their "friends" on the outside – among those friends, Roger Mouraille, who was released instead of transferred – had engineered on their own. When that failed due in part to the refusal of the chief warden at Largentière to play along, it left Laval and the Germans with few remaining alternatives, none of them particularly palatable. They could allow the case to go to trial, with all the risks that entailed, or find a way to make the suspects "disappear" either through escape, death, or release.

RIOM

Divergent German and French ideas about who should be judged at Riom and why complicated the process and outcome of the investigation of the Dormoy assassins, and help to explain why it ultimately had to be suspended. During the summer of 1940, French people struggled with the question of why, after their victory in World War I, they had suffered an ignominious defeat. Many French citizens across the political spectrum demanded an investigation and condemnation of France's former leaders, whom they believed responsible for the collapse of the French military when confronted with the Nazi invasion. The idea of a trial appealed to many in Pétain's government, not least of them Laval, who saw an opportunity not only to condemn once and for all the institutions and leaders of the Third Republic, which he considered to be hopelessly bankrupt and outmoded, but also to gain revenge against former allies and foes alike who had driven him out of office in 1936. He bore a special hatred toward the Popular Front and its leader, Léon Blum.[3] From the perspective of Vichy, the trial that they ordered to be held at Riom would be a means of judging and condemning the failures of France's republican traditions since the French Revolution. The trial would thus bolster the belief that the regime at Vichy was far better suited to thrive in the New Order the Nazis were building in Europe.

On 30 July 1940 the Pétain-Laval government adopted Constitutional Act No. 5. This act established a Supreme Court of Justice with the power to judge former ministers and those who had served under them.[4] The mandate of the court was to proceed against those persons deemed to have "betrayed the duties of their office by acts which contributed to the passage from a state of peace to a state of war before 4 September 1939."[5] Pétain ordered General Maurice Gamelin, general secretary of the Ministry of War and Defense from September 1936 through March 1940; Pierre Jacomet, controller general during this same era; Édouard Daladier, former prime minister and minister of defense from June 1936 through March 1940; Guy La Chambre, minister of the Merchant Marine and a protégé of Aristide Briand; and Pierre Cot, Popular Front minister of the Air Force, to stand trial. Of them, all were arrested except Cot, who was in the US at the time and prudently decided to remain there, whereas La Chambre, also in the US when the indictments were handed down, returned to stand trial. Léon Blum and Paul Reynaud, premier in 1940, were added to the list of defendants.[6]

From the outset, the Germans and the Vichy authorities had quite different ideas about the charges that should be leveled and the purpose of the trials. In the eyes of the Germans, the French declaration of war in 1939 when Germany invaded Poland had been an unprovoked and illegal aggression. Hitler cast France as the aggressor in the war and insisted that French leaders such as Blum and Reynaud be condemned for their pre-war opposition to Nazi Germany. They, and not the Nazis, were responsible for France's misfortunes in 1940, and they needed to pay for their deeds. Hitler was also determined that just as the Allies, led by Georges Clémenceau, had forced the Germans to shoulder the guilt of having caused World War I, now he would oblige the French to accept the blame for the war between France and Germany in 1940.[7]

Not surprisingly, the Vichy regime by no means agreed with Hitler on the purpose of the Riom prosecution. For Vichy, it was impossible to broach the question of ultimate responsibility for starting the war because it would have been political suicide in France, even in 1941, essentially to put the country on trial. A verdict that France bore the guilt for the German invasion would have impugned France's honor and Pétain could not allow this. The process thus had to be about why France lost the war, not who caused it. It was obvious to most French people who had been the aggressor in the war: Germany.[8]

The great danger the Riom trial posed for Vichy, a danger Blum, Daladier, and the other defendants understood and exploited with much success when they took the stand in their own defense, was that the trial would veer into the period prior to the rise of the Popular Front in 1936 or would shift its focus to the military and French preparations for war. The proceedings had to be confined to civilian political decisions from 1936 onward, not an easy task given the pre-war political situation and reality of the role of military leaders in determining the state of France's defenses in the 1930s. For one thing, Pétain was minister of war in 1934, and was a member of the *Conseil Supérieur* in 1935. If France was ill-prepared for war in 1940, didn't politicians and generals who had opposed modernizing the French military bear some of the blame? It was imperative for Vichy that only civilian leaders, except for General Gamelin, stand trial. Gamelin's refusal from the outset to testify or mount a defense, a tactic intended to shield his beloved military and Pétain, to whom Gamelin retained a decidedly one-sided sense of loyalty, made it more difficult, but by no means impossible, for the other defendants to bring up the attitudes of military leaders such as Pétain in the 1930s.[9]

Neither Daladier nor Blum had any intention of confining their defense to questions about civilian political decisions regarding France's rearmament. For one thing, such partitioning was impossible. Decisions related to rearmament were inextricably both civilian and military because, as Daladier and Blum both pointed out, the civilian government voted for military funding, but military leaders decided how to use the funds allocated to them. It was military leaders – among them Pétain – who had refused to invest in the tanks and war planes the civilian strategists such as Pierre Cot and Georges Mandel insisted were necessary to modernize French forces sufficiently to counter the German threat. The Maginot Line was a military strategy derived from the experiences of France's generals in World War I. It took only a cursory overview of Germany's rebuilt military forces and the new *blitzkrieg* style of warfare the Nazis developed, heavily dependent on tanks and bombers, to realize that no amount of money would render French defenses capable of protecting the country unless the armed forces modernized. That required France's military leaders to reimagine how wars would now be fought and won, something most proved unwilling to consider. Pétain was one of the worst offenders in this regard.[10]

The ten magistrates of the new Supreme Court that was to hear the trial were sworn in on 8 August 1940 in Riom, a town north of Clermont-Ferrand. The presiding judge, Pierre Caous, opened an investigation that took testimony from hundreds of witnesses and amassed thousands of documents as evidence. An entire year passed, during which it became apparent to the defendants, Pétain, and the Germans alike that Caous was in no hurry to rush to judgment and did not intend to preside over a "show trial." This raised enormous anxiety in Vichy, which at any price did not want the defendants to be able to mount a rigorous defense. Because Vichy had initiated the trial, it could hardly suppress it, but the process remained adjourned for all of 1941 while the public prosecutor continued his investigation in preparation for the opening of the proceedings. In the winter of 1940–1941, meanwhile, Vichy, increasingly worried about the delays, promulgated Constitutional Act No. 7, which permitted the Maréchal under his own authority as head of state to investigate and punish present or past government ministers for acts he deemed to constitute a betrayal of their office. By August 1941 Vichy's patience with the delays at Riom was exhausted and Pétain invoked Constitutional Act No. 7 to appoint a Council of Political Justice. On 16 October he announced to the nation that the Council had found Daladier, Blum, and Gamelin guilty on all charges. Pétain sentenced them to life imprisonment and yet insisted that even so, the Supreme Court at Riom would still hold its own trial. The 16 October verdict, Vichy hoped, would placate Ambassador Otto Abetz, who was pressuring Pétain summarily to condemn and execute the defendants. But it put Caous and his court in a very difficult position because if the Supreme Court did proceed, it was trying the same defendants twice for the same crime, which was held to be illegal in the majority of democracies including, until recently, that of France. Caous was determined to proceed nonetheless and the defendants received copies of their formal indictments on 9 October 1941. Within five days they were each to present written statements outlining their defense.[11]

On the afternoon of 19 February 1942 the trial at Riom finally began. Among Blum's attorneys who flanked him in the courtroom was Félix Gouin. Caous announced at the outset that his court would not be prejudiced by the verdicts of 16 October. Caous was resolved to salvage his court's integrity by presiding over a relatively fair trial. He gave the defendants ample time to speak freely in court in their own defense, as well as to call witnesses and to cross-examine the witnesses for the prosecution. All the defendants except Gamelin took full advantage of this opportunity, and none more brilliantly than Blum. He and Daladier had been renowned during their political careers for their rhetorical skills, and it did not take either of them very long to turn the trial on its head, pointing out the absurdity of holding civilian leaders to account for not preparing the country for the war and excluding all mention of the military high command except Gamelin. Blum offered an impassioned defense of civilian government and the ideals of the Third Republic. The defendants successfully put Pétain on trial instead of the other way around. By 15 April Vichy suspended the proceedings. Blum and Daladier reveled in their victory, which they rightly saw as a triumph for their beloved Republic and its ideas. Still, they were well aware that none of them would be freed anytime soon.[12] Pétain and Hitler were both furious and four days after the suspension of the trial Darlan resigned and Laval returned to power at the helm of Pétain's government.[13]

LAVAL'S RETURN

Already by late autumn 1941 the winds of political intrigue began to shift at Vichy. Pétain was growing impatient with Darlan, who seemed to negotiate with the Germans a great deal but achieve little.[14] Meanwhile, Laval abandoned his effort to corral the squabbling Parisian collaborationists into a cohesive political party he could use as a power base. He returned to his estate at Châteldon, not far from Vichy, to recover from his bullet wound in August and began a campaign to regain Pétain's confidence. Laval already knew that he had the firm support of Abetz and Helmut Knochen and that most of the German high command by far preferred him to Darlan. Dr. Bernard Ménétrel, Pétain's closest friend and advisor, facilitated a rapprochement between Laval and Pétain via René de Chambrun, Laval's son-in-law. Ménétrel seems to have considered that a new cabinet under Laval would boost the flagging popularity of the aging Maréchal, or at least deflect blame as German demands made life harder for ordinary French people. Darlan did not put up much resistance and resigned although he remained in Pétain's cabinet as commander-in-chief of France's truncated armed forces. Laval consolidated his power by assuming several key posts, including the Ministry of the Interior. In addition, Constitutional Act No.11 promulgated on 18 April 1942, created a new office, head of the government of the French state, a position that Laval also occupied.[15]

Laval's policies upon his return to power were based on his conviction that he could use collaboration as an effective negotiating tool with the Germans, and unlike Darlan he never lost his faith in this strategy despite the intransigence of the Germans who refused him any meaningful achievements. Laval was even willing to make the damning declaration during a radio broadcast on 22 June 1942, one year to the date from the German invasion of the USSR, "I hope for a German victory, because without it Bolshevism tomorrow will install itself everywhere."[16] His statement may have pleased the Germans, but it did nothing for Laval's popularity or that of Vichy among the French populace. Most alarming to Pétain, the German demands on the economy were dragging France deeper and deeper into the Nazi war effort. But by April 1942 Pétain appears to have become resigned to the role of figurehead in the État français, willing to permit Laval wide latitude to take the risks and the fallout from running the state so long as the Maréchal, whose vanity was enormous, could keep his reputation and popularity intact. Better to be a beloved figurehead than a reviled politician.[17]

No group in France was more vulnerable than the Jews, and the *rafles* (roundups) of Jews in 1942 demonstrated that in this, as in other aspects of collaboration, Laval was willing to meet and even exceed German demands so long as he believed he could negotiate concessions from the Germans in return. The human toll was enormous, and the gains to France illusory – German demands for French resources and workers continued to mount and by the end of 1942 the German invasion of the Unoccupied Zone decimated any illusions of sovereignty left to the Vichy regime. During the first year of the regime's existence Vichy issued twenty-six laws and twenty-four decrees regarding Jews. But despite the regime's clear intent to make Jews into a subordinated group within France there seems to have been little enthusiasm to deport Jews until it became apparent in the summer of 1941 that the German agenda involved removing Jews from Nazi-controlled territory throughout Europe, including France.[18] By the spring of 1942, as it became evident that the road to collaboration with Germany ran through the deportations of Jews, French authorities began cooperating enthusiastically with the Germans in rounding up Jews. Although most of the Jewish deportees were refugees from elsewhere in Europe, by the end of 1942, the Vichy regime proved neither willing nor able entirely to shield any Jews, refugees or French citizens alike.[19]

In May 1942 Laval acceded to German pressure to replace Xavier Vallat, whom the Germans considered to be insufficiently zealous in performing his duties as head of the CGQJ, with Louis Darquier de Pellepoix, a rabid antisemite who would cooperate fully with the Germans in deporting Jews from France. At German insistence Laval also replaced Pierre Mondanel as head of the Vichy National Police.[20] He chose as Mondanel's successor the efficient young technocrat René Bousquet, who led the French police from April 1942 until December 1943, when the Germans took over policing Vichy. Of greatest concern to both Bousquet and Laval was to retain some semblance of autonomy for Vichy, even if that meant putting French police in charge of rounding up Jews in Paris and elsewhere in France. This devotion to autonomy explains why Bousquet was willing to use the French police forces in the hunt for Jews and resisters, despite the negative effect this ultimately would have on both police morale and public opinion in France.[21] The Vichy regime began aggressively to detain Jews in the Unoccupied Zone, especially as increasing numbers of Jews from the Occupied Zone sought refuge beyond the Line of Demarcation. The zeal of the French police in carrying out their orders to track and arrest Jews, and that of French officials who were willing to meet the German quotas for Jews, was indispensable for the success of the Final Solution in France. Their ardor was most evident during the notorious Vel d'Hiv roundup, when the French police arrested over 13,152 Jews in and around Paris on 16–17 July 1942. In addition, 8,160 of them, mostly women and children, were kept for five days in a bicycle stadium, the Vélodrôme d'Hiver, with almost no water and no food or sanitation before they were deported to various internment camps in France and then to Auschwitz-Birkenau.[22] Yet once again Laval's strategy of strategic concessions and collaboration with the Germans came to naught. On 5 April

1942 the Gestapo under Hugo Geissler established itself in the Vichy Zone. Laval's and Bousquet's maneuvering room was shrinking. It disappeared once the Germans invaded and occupied the Vichy Zone in November.[23]

The changes in Vichy that Laval's return initiated could not help but have a significant impact on the progress of the Dormoy case. Most important from the standpoint of Chenevier and Marion was the replacement of Mondanel with Bousquet, and the significant reforms of the structure and operation of the police that Bousquet carried out. Mondanel had backed Charles Chenevier and Jean Marion as they sought to identify and indict whoever in Vichy had funded and authorized Dormoy's murder.[24] Despite the institutional reforms of police structures in 1941, Mondanel and Chenevier had continued running the French police force from Vichy in much the same manner as they had before the war, and paid as little heed as possible to the Germans or Pétain's cabinet.[25] Mondanel's departure threatened to derail the Dormoy case entirely.

DELONCLE DEPOSED

Although Laval's ascent made things more difficult for Chenevier and Marion, one immediate benefit was that they were able to depose both Deloncle and Hérard.[26] Chenevier deposed Hérard first. Thirty-seven years old in 1942, Raymond Hérard listed his occupation as "political secretary" to Deloncle. Known by the pseudonym "André," he published under that name in the collaborationist journal *France-Europe*. Hérard admitted having met Roger Mouraille in 1935, around the time the Cagoule was created, when both men belonged to the AF and shared similar political views. Their relationship was "friendly," according to Hérard, who knew Mouraille's family, but Hérard "lost track" of Mouraille once Hérard moved away from Marseille at the end of 1938. Hérard had also met Ludovic Guichard in Marseille under similar circumstances but stayed in closer touch with him because Guichard "was a wine salesman" who "ran a wholesale food enterprise on the boulevard de la Madeleine" in Marseille. Hérard asserted that he lost contact with Guichard upon leaving Marseille. Likewise, Hérard also was acquainted with Yves Moynier, whom Hérard claimed he knew "mostly by sight" as he "only had occasion to meet him five or six times." Yet Hérard omitted a salient fact about his relationship with Roger Mouraille. The two men had in common their history of battling for Franco during the Spanish Civil War, and it is likely that they encountered each other in Spain. Moreover, both men maintained business and personal ties in Spain and to the Franco regime after the Civil War. Hérard's wife, Pilar Gallando, was from Santander. Although Hérard moved to Paris when the Spanish Civil War ended and resided for a time with his brother Maurice, an editor of the newspaper *Paris-Soir*, it is unlikely that he and Roger Mouraille ever really lost touch. They traveled in too many of the same political circles, in Spain and in France.[27] Hérard's assertion that he had "encountered" Jeantet only "two or three times" was equally implausible, especially since subsequent documentation proved Hérard had established a "reseau," or network, of agents in Marseille, operatives likely known to Jeantet.[28] Given that Hérard had a close relationship with Deloncle dating back to their years in the Cagoule and given Jeantet's leadership role in the Cagoule in the 1930s, it is highly likely that Hérard knew Jeantet far better than he was admitting in his statement. He was also well connected to the Cagoule chief assassin and MSR leader, Jean Filliol. The two shared an office at MSR headquarters.[29]

Hérard stated that he had never met Marchi prior to the latter's trip to Paris in August 1940 in the company of Roger Mouraille and Moynier. About "fifteen days or a month after the attack against M. Dormoy," to Hérard's "surprise," Mouraille and Moynier showed up at the MSR headquarters in Paris. The two men were equally "surprised" to find him there. Mouraille and Moynier announced that they "had come to see Doriot," and that they "wanted to meet Deloncle while they were there" (in Paris). Hérard's version of events seems implausible. It is not credible that neither Mouraille nor Moynier would have had no inkling that Hérard was a prominent member of the MSR who worked for Deloncle. MSR propaganda was widespread in the Vichy Zone, and Hérard was well known in Marseille, his hometown, where he kept operatives. Deloncle visited the Vichy Zone often to lobby for the MSR, and it is improbable that Hérard would never have accompanied Deloncle to Marseille (see Figure 8.1).[30]

Hérard also claimed that Roger Mouraille and Moynier raised the issue of Marchi with him during the meeting at the MSR headquarters. This contradicts Roger Mouraille's version of events, in which Moynier introduced Marchi to him at their meeting with Hérard in the café "Le Napolitain," and that Marchi and Hérard at that time seemed already to be acquainted. Mouraille insisted that he had never met Marchi and had no idea who he was when Moynier introduced them at "Le Napolitain."[31] Hérard claimed quite the opposite:

> They talked to me for a long time about their friend whose name they told me was Marchi, with whom they told me that they had come to visit

18 April 1942: The Return of Pierre Laval   159

Figure 8.1. Deloncle (center left) in MSR uniform gives the Nazi salute (circa 1942). Jean Vanor is on his right. Archives Nationales (France) Z/808/5672, "Dossier de Van Ormelingen dit Vanor."

Doriot. As I sensed that Moynier hesitated about whether to join our movement, I asked him if I could see this friend [Marchi], and I tried very hard to persuade him. They then told me that they were going to meet with him at a café, "Le Napolitain," and invited me to join them for an aperitif. That was how I made the acquaintance of Marchi.³²

The four men also had lunch together at the Paris-Soir restaurant, although Hérard was unable to tell the police whether that meal took place the same day as the aperitif or on another day. Marchi "definitely agreed" to meet with Deloncle, but Hérard asserted that Marchi never actually came back to the MSR headquarters. The topic of Dormoy's murder came up in their conversations but only because Hérard raised it, simply because he knew his companions were from the Vichy Zone and thus likely to be better informed than he about the progress of the police investigation. Hérard insisted that he had never heard of Annie Mourraille, under her own name or her stage name of Annie

Morène. He surmised that she had brought up "M. André" in her statements because he was "very well known in the nationalist milieu under this name." According to Hérard, not only was he not the "M. André" who had met with Annie Mourraille and the others in Montélimar, but he knew nothing about Dormoy's death, or at least nothing more than a reasonably informed person in the Occupied Zone might have discovered via the newspapers and gossip. He had played no part in the affair and was as surprised as anyone when the killers showed up on his doorstep asking for help.

While he was careful not to offer any information that might bolster the case against Marchi, unlike Moynier, Hérard was not at pains to protect Marchi either. Marchi was part of Moynier's group, according to Hérard, well known to Moynier and Roger Mouraille, and traveling with the two men in search of money and protection from the "nationalist milieu" in Paris. Hérard's testimony thus contradicted that of Marchi, Moynier, and Mouraille. Unfortunately, it also did little to help Chenevier close in on either Jeantet or Deloncle. Marchi was in Poland, and Hérard seemed content to let Moynier hang for killing Dormoy. Although Hérard didn't admit this, it was he, Marchi, and Roger Mouraille who tried to persuade Moynier in August 1941 to join the LVF and thereby put himself out of the reach of the authorities. That appears to have been the only help Deloncle was willing to offer Moynier.

When Deloncle gave his statement to the Parisian police in 1942, his "stock" had tumbled. It was his own political future that concerned Deloncle and his statement, like that of Hérard, was carefully calibrated to explain why Dormoy's killers had visited him in Paris shortly before the crime while exculpating himself from any involvement in the affair. Deloncle denied having ever met Annie Mourraille and professed to be mystified as to why she had mentioned him in her letter to Dr. Jean-Louis Faraut.[33] He admitted that he had met with Roger Mouraille and Moynier but denied ever having met Marchi. He recalled that Moynier was tall with "fairly long hair," and that the subject of their conversation was the desire of the two men to bring back to Marseille some "documentation" regarding the MSR, a request to which Deloncle gladly acceded. Deloncle intimated that if Annie Mourraille had written to him, it was because after Roger Mouraille and Moynier had visited him in Paris, perceiving that Deloncle might be sympathetic to their cause, she sought "to appeal for help from the politician that I am."[34] When asked about Jeantet, Deloncle responded that he had known Jeantet "well at one time," but had "ceased to have any relationship with him ever since 1 October 1940." As for the tracts Hérard had given to Moynier and Roger Mouraille to take back to

Marseille, such MSR propaganda was freely distributed to "anyone who asks for it." And at no time during his brief conversation with Roger Mouraille and Moynier in August 1940 had the Dormoy "affair" ever even come up.[35] Deloncle's deposition thus was even less informative than that of Hérard. Both men wondered why the police had bothered to follow up on Annie Mouraille's obviously unreliable testimony and hoped that Marion, stymied in his efforts to push the case further, would have to give up and order the case ready to proceed to a trial. When Marion showed no signs of closing the investigation, however, more drastic measures had to be taken.

THE ROAD TO LARGENTIÈRE

In July 1942, at the same time that Marion was deposing Payre regarding Annie Mouraille's letters, he received two others the warden at Valence had confiscated, one from Moynier to Mouraille and the other from Roger Mouraille to his wife.[36] After complaining that he had lost seven kilos, Moynier added in his letter that he had written to Justice Minister Joseph-Barthélémy and to the cabinet of the Maréchal as well. "If by June 15 there has not been an end to the instruction [investigation phase] it's the [hunger] strike to the end ... I know that I am at the end and ready to crack, or they will render justice." He could "no longer control" his "nerves," Moynier declared, and his "will" had been "used up."[37] Moynier also wrote a series of letters to Marion during this period, menacing and berating the investigating magistrate, who Moynier accused of trying to assassinate him. Moynier threatened to harm himself or others. "If at present you continue to hide me away in isolation and secrecy, it is because in this manner you can assassinate me more easily."[38] On 31 May Moynier suffered a breakdown in his cell, smashed all the furniture, and tried to kill himself. A medical exam Marion ordered on 11 June for Moynier and Mouraille confirmed that both men were breaking down mentally.[39]

Roger Mouraille did not profess to be in such a desperate state as Moynier, but he claimed not to understand why the investigation was dragging on. He continued to portray himself as innocent of any crime except trying to help out a friend and frustrated that the authorities didn't just let him go. "It is crazy that we still haven't finished at this point," even if it was necessary to hold the hearing before "the devil" if necessary, Mouraille declared. "You must write to the Minister of Justice," he instructed his wife, "and seal the letter without putting Barthélémy" on the envelope, or Marion would find out about it. He also told her to write to the chef du Cabinet Civil du Maréchal, in other words to Bernard Ménétrel, as well. Mouraille and Moynier continued to cling to their faith that ultimately Vichy, as instigator of Dormoy's murder, would step in and help them.[40] During the summer of 1942 their faith was finally rewarded, not so much because officials at Vichy were concerned about their welfare, however, as because Joseph-Barthélémy, among others, realized that the government needed to bring the whole affair to a close.

A "Note sur l'affaire Dormoy," authored by someone working for the Vichy Ministry of Justice, laid out the dilemma surrounding the Dormoy case. As of 21 July 1942, the date of the note, Marion had the depositions of Deloncle and Hérard, although no "confrontation" between the two and other witnesses such as Annie Mourraille had yet taken place (or was likely to happen). Nevertheless, "the investigation is in a state to be closed very soon."[41] The note's author pointed out the fundamental problem facing Joseph-Barthélémy: "there remains the question of which jurisdiction should pass judgement on this affair." This question was not as simple to answer in 1942 as it would have been in 1939 for two related reasons. The Vichy regime had recently completed an overhaul of the structures of the French police and justice system that entailed the creation of new courts and jurisdictions. These changes were neither well understood nor necessarily appreciated either by the magistrates themselves or the French populace. Moreover, the summary executions of hostages, arrests and deportations of Jews, and the fiasco of the trial at Riom, with two separate courts trying, and one sentencing, the same defendants for the same crimes, had undermined the faith of the French people in the courts, something the author of the July note on the Dormoy case recognized. The best way to hold the trial and terminate the whole affair was thus the subject of intense debate within the Ministry of Justice.

The public prosecutor based in Grenoble, who had oversight of Marion's court at Montélimar, advocated sending the case to the State Tribunal, the special court under Pétain's control that had judged three of the Riom defendants the previous October. The other option was to "allow the criminal procedure to follow its normal course, which would mean sending it before the Assizes Court of Drôme," which was fully competent to try a case such as the murder of Dormoy.[42] The underlying difference between these two options, although the July note did not spell this out, was whether or not to treat Dormoy's assassination as an "ordinary" murder, which would have entailed sending the case to the court that normally would have tried such a crime, at Drôme, or to treat it as a political assassination that threatened the security or legitimacy of the state. In the latter case, the trial would need to be heard before a higher court, or Pétain's tribunal. Marion contended that Dormoy's death was no mundane crime but rather a political assassination that compromised members of Pétain's own cabinet. Marion laid out his rationale for this approach clearly in his 28 July letter to the prosecutor at Grenoble although Marion wanted the case tried in the "regular" courts, but as a political assassination, not as a simple homicide. The prosecutor may not have agreed with Marion's proposed solution, but he understood Marion's argument and explained it to Joseph-Barthélémy.[43]

The prosecutor at Grenoble likely preferred a special tribunal because that would unburden him and his docket of a case that was politically dangerous. The suspension of the trial at Riom, followed within a few months by a guilty verdict against Dormoy's assassins, would have seemed to the Germans and their collaborationist allies to be a repudiation of Vichy's promise to collaborate with the Germans and purge Third Republic holdovers insufficiently supportive of the National Revolution and the Nazis' New Order. Some in Pétain's cabinet were content to view Dormoy's murder as just that, a simple murder carried out by misguided young people caught up in their revolutionary fervor. For Marion, Félix Gouin, and others who remained true to French Republican principles, Dormoy's death was a political assassination. The identity of the victim didn't matter. What did matter was that the murderers had struck a blow against the legitimacy of the state, and if they went unpunished, French institutions would be undermined further, with anarchy or complete autocracy as the only possible outcomes.

But either of the options, the "regular" court at Drôme or the State Tribunal, came with significant risks as well. By opting for the Tribunal, the Vichy regime would face the "inconvenience of transforming an affair which in itself merely has the nature of a banal assassination into a political matter."[44] In other words, the choice of the court itself would determine the way in which the Dormoy case was characterized. Moreover, "in taking the case away from its natural judges, the Government might [inadvertently] offer the impression that it is taking sides, even though this affair has no bearing on politics in general." This statement demonstrates that Pétain, Laval, and Joseph-Barthélémy wanted to define Dormoy's death as a simple murder, not as a political crime, which also explains why they had consistently ignored the appeals of the suspects to oblige Marion to treat them as political prisoners. Marion refused because he did not view Moynier and the others as true political prisoners, in jail because of their beliefs, but rather as murderers whose political views in no way mitigated, let alone justified, their crime.[45] Even so, Marion by no means wanted the case treated as a "banal" homicide because he knew this would mean that the men in Vichy he viewed as the real authors of the crime would not be prosecuted. Vichy and Marion thus held opposing views of the nature and significance of Dormoy's murder, yet shared an insistence that the suspects should not be treated as prisoners of political conscience.

But holding the trial before the State Tribunal posed another risk as well. As the author of the July note pointed out:

> At the time when the Government, by the law enacted on 25 November 1941 and in force as of 1 January 1942, to reform the jury system to render the justice system more efficient, to remove the Dormoy affair from the Assizes Court would seem to imply that the reforms decided upon by the Government were inoperable and that the jury, despite the structural modifications brought about by the legislation, remained incapable of ruling on an affair when it might appear susceptible to involve and raise political passions. The Dormoy affair must not become [an occasion] for the Government to contradict itself and under these conditions, it has been decided that the case will be submitted to the jurisdiction of normally competent common law: the Assizes Court.[46]

The July note also pointed out the risks of bringing the Dormoy case to trial anytime soon and another set of problems entailed in continued delay. On the one hand, it seemed to be "inopportune" to bring the case to trial immediately due to the "political passions" the case could "awaken." On the other hand, the continuing delays, besides raising the issue of due process before the law, were also resulting in serious economic, physical, and psychological damage to the accused, forced to put their lives on hold for almost a year while they sat in prison awaiting their day in court. In July Marchi was out on bail and fighting for the LVF, although within six weeks he returned to France and was again apprehended. As of 8 June 1942, Roger Mouraille had also been granted bail. This left Moynier, Annie Mourraille, and Guichard still in prison "protesting with vehemence" against their long incarceration without trial. The July note remarked on the suspects' numerous letters, along with those of their friends and family members, insisting that the government refused to try them because it intended for them to perish in custody. It also noted that Marion had subjected them to a harsh prison regime that was damaging their health and could not continue. Appended to the note were copies of letters the suspects had sent to Vichy, including one from Annie Mourraille addressed to Laval in which she asserted that Marion insisted on keeping them in solitary confinement because he "reserves all his sympathy for the attractive personality of the deceased former Minister," and thus, she implied, had much less sympathy for Pétain and the National Revolution.[47] The July note concluded with the recommendation that the justice ministry oblige Marion to accede to the suspects' demands to be released on bail.[48] Marion did not grant bail to Moynier, Annie Mourraille, or Guichard, but on 5 September the prosecutor at Grenoble ordered him to free Marchi. That same day Marion sent a telegram to the warden at Valence notifying the latter that Marion had set Marchi's bail at 50,000 francs and that the warden was to release Marchi upon receipt of the money, which Marchi had handed over by 8 September.[49]

It was Marion's staunch refusal to order the release of Moynier, Annie Mourraille, and Guichard, which the prosecutor at Grenoble evidently did not dare to or wish to override given the overwhelming evidence against the trio, that forced Joseph-Barthélémy and Laval to find another solution. The pressure on Joseph-Barthélémy was immense. The suspects were making life extremely difficult for him with incessant letters addressed to him and to Pétain (which Pétain just turned over to Joseph-Barthélémy), suicide attempts, and a stream of complaints from the suspects and their lawyers about their treatment in prison. The solution for which Vichy finally opted was to transfer the remaining incarcerated suspects sometime in August from the prison in Valence to a makeshift jail in the chateau of Largentière. Joseph-Barthélémy made this decision, he explained in his post-war memoir, to "get a little peace" while he waited for Laval to decide what to do with the suspects.[50] This move brought several advantages. First, although as the crow flies Largentière is no further from Montélimar than Valence, Valence is on a main road and railway line connecting Montélimar with Lyon, Marseille, and Paris, while Largentière is in the mountains to the west of Montélimar, in what today is the *Parc naturel régional des Monts d'Ardèche*. A picturesque town in which the chateau commands the heights of sheer cliffs overlooking the narrow valley of the Ligne River, it is connected to Montélimar, and the rest of the outside world, by the D5, a road through the mountains that can be difficult to navigate for those unfamiliar with the area. In 1941 it is likely that the town was more isolated than it is now. The air was much better than that of Valence, the prison rules clearly were less stringent, and the accommodations were more comfortable. The suspects thus benefitted from better conditions in Largentière, but at the same time Largentière was a place where they could also more easily be forgotten than in Valence. They were beyond easy reach of Marion, but they could find it more difficult to communicate with the outside world.

The fear of being held incommunicado indefinitely was at the forefront of the suspects' concerns. When Annie Mourraille heard that Marchi had been rearrested on 18 August, she wrote in her journal "Tx [her code name for Marchi] has been arrested again! My God, my God, we will never get out of this."[51] The suspects' mood remained bleak despite Marchi's release a few weeks later. Moynier complained that he was cold and could not get any aspirin to relieve his "anxiety." Still defiant, however, Moynier expressed his confidence that Dormoy deserved to die and that all the "Jews, traitors, assassins and deserters" ought to meet the same end. On 10 September the director of prisons in Nîmes sent a memo to the chief warden at Largentière ordering him to "suspend the incommunicado detention of the ones called Mourraille, Guichard, and Moynier," although the chief warden was also to "exercise over them a rigorous surveillance in order to avoid any incident so that, favoured by this new regimen, they do not try to put their project [of escape] into execution."[52]

The authorities had good reason to fear that their prisoners had developed a "project" to escape. One of Largentière's advantages from the suspects' perspective and, most likely, that of some officials at Vichy as well, is that the town's isolation ought to have made it much easier to engineer an escape and disappear before the Vichy authorities could intervene. This was exactly what the suspects tried to orchestrate on Monday, 19 October. According to the report from the Nîmes public prosecutor, sometime between 12:00 and 2:00 in the afternoon, with the "help of a person outside," Mourraille, Moynier, and Guichard tried to flee. "A knotted cord was thrown [over the wall] to permit them to get out of the centre of the prison. In addition, they got hold of a metal saw that permitted them to push aside two bars of the cell of the lady Mourraille. Someone also threw into the circular walking path [in the courtyard of the chateau] a bag of clothes for them to change into. The detainees were caught at the moment when, having reached the walking path, they tried to use the knotted cord to get out of the prison."[53] They needed to use the knotted cord because the "circular walkway" was in the courtyard of the chateau, surrounded by a high brick and stone wall. Once they were caught, the chief warden returned them to solitary confinement and opened an inquest for the crimes of attempted escape and complicity. Although no one was charged regarding the latter, the police reasoned that the "outside help" most likely was from Roger Mourraille, who had been released prior to the transfer to Largentière. It is also likely that he was waiting for them with a vehicle to whisk them into hiding once they had clambered over the wall.

On 26 October the Nîmes director of prisons reported to Joseph-Barthélémy that after receiving a fuller report on the escape attempt on 21 October from the chief warden, the director had visited the prison the following day. He observed that the escape attempt had been "carefully prepared" and with the "complicity of one or several persons outside." The guards had foiled it only because of the denunciation of another prisoner, a "woman ... pillar of the prison" who was serving a sentence of eighty years. Moreover, the prisoners had been able to communicate among themselves because the chief warden, lacking enough cells to keep them apart, had put Guichard and Moynier in adjoining cells and Annie Mourraille directly above them. Moynier and Guichard, who were on the ground floor, had passed to Mourraille a string that she hid under her mattress. She then used the string on Sunday, 18 October to pull the saw up to her room. During the night, she sawed through two bars on her window.[54]

These details are important because they suggest a real sense of urgency to escape from Largentière despite the obvious risk of being caught. The question is why the suspects chose that moment, in October, to take their chances with an escape attempt that, if it failed, could result in the loss of their newly won privileges. Moreover, Marchi had been freed in September and was thus in a position again to work on behalf of the remaining prisoners. The question, however, by October 1942, was to whom Marchi could turn for that help even if he was so inclined. Jeantet had clearly abandoned the suspects in the Dormoy affair. When the crime was committed, Admiral Darlan had been in charge of the government under Pétain. Despite Darlan's subsequent demotion and the elevation of Laval, after their October escape attempt Moynier and Guichard wrote to the admiral asking for help. They lamented that they had been held without trial for eighteen months and feared that they would never be tried.[55] That they wrote to Darlan rather than to Laval suggests that they had given up hope of assistance from the latter. Nor could they expect any further help from Deloncle who had been forced out of the MSR after being engulfed in a mire of his own making.

CHAPTER NINE

23 January 1943: German Intervention

DELONCLE DETHRONED

During the evening of 4 October 1941, the wife of the lock keeper at Marly-le-Roi on the Seine discovered a body that had floated to the surface even though it had been wrapped up in coal sacks and weighted down with large rocks and a cement block. Despite the poor condition of the corpse, which had been in the water for more than a week, the gendarmes of Bougival identified the remains as those of Mme. Antoinette Masse, née Béguin, wife of Jean Masse, a farmer at Nogent-le-Roi from whom she was separated. Béguin, who was Belgian in origin, had been living in Paris as "Tonia" Masse and was employed at 80 rue Saint-Lazare, as an administrative assistant for the Mouvement social révolutionnaire. Director of the Division of French Women's Assistance, her job was to distribute aid to needy families of MSR members and potential recruits, a responsibility that was extended to members of the RNP once the MSR merged with the RNP during the summer of 1941. Thirty-eight years old in 1941, Masse was a pretty woman, slightly corpulent, but a stylish dresser with a charming smile, and by all accounts an outgoing personality. She was also the lover of a younger man, Jacques Fauran, a close collaborator of Eugène Deloncle and, especially, of Jean Filliol, Deloncle's second-in-command and personal bodyguard in the MSR.[1]

On Tuesday, 23 September Masse told her colleagues at the MSR offices that she was going out that evening for a celebration, and that she had purchased a special gift for "Jacques." After an aperitif with Deloncle, she and Fauran were headed to the home of Fauran's parents, where he was going to introduce her to them and announce their engagement to be married. Masse left the office early, just before 4:00 p.m., to get her hair done. She announced at the salon that Jacques had told her that the evening would be "beautiful" and the "most wonderful day of her life," when their relationship would finally become "very official."[2] She also made ominous statements about the contents of her handbag and the documents it contained, telling her friends, "If only you knew what was in here." Masse left the salon at about 7:30 p.m., and headed back to 80 rue Saint-Lazare, where she was to meet Deloncle and Fauran. The trio went out to the Brasserie Garnier. Deloncle and Fauran claimed Masse left them at 8:15 p.m., alone. They did not know where she went and never saw her again.[3]

Masse's body resurfaced in the Seine approximately two weeks later. She had been beaten, knocked unconscious, and then strangled and stabbed as well. Her killers broke both her legs to fit them into coal sacks, which they filled with a "heavy piece of pavement," and wrapped with wire before tossing the entire bundle into the Seine. Meanwhile, after their aperitif with Masse, Deloncle and Fauran went out to dinner at a restaurant on the Champs-Élysées with Deloncle's wife Mércedès and daughter Claude, Jacques Corrèze, and Lucien Fromes, a captain in the German SS. Evidently it was a nice meal, as the bill came to 663 francs, which Deloncle paid.[4]

Not surprisingly, suspicion immediately fell upon Deloncle and Fauran. For one thing, whereas Fauran had led Masse to believe they were going to be married, it turned out that Fauran was already engaged, to none other than Claude Deloncle.[5] Casual observers informed about the crime assumed that this was the motivation for getting rid of Masse.[6] The police had some reason to be skeptical that thwarted romance was the only reason to eliminate Masse, especially given the violent, brutal manner of her murder. As one witness pointed out, "Mme. Masse could have been eliminated because of what she knew about the financial resources of the MSR."[7] The police certainly suspected that this was the case, as Masse's was not the only suspicious death associated with the MSR. On 19 October Auguste Jouanny, head of the Ratier Factory (*Usine Ratier*) and a prominent donor to the MSR, was found dead on a sidewalk. Jouanny's skull was fractured and the police decided that his demise most likely was an "execution," especially given that Jouanny had quarreled with Deloncle over Jouanny's MSR donations.[8]

The day before her murder Masse notified Deloncle that she was quitting her job at the MSR. She informed her secretary that she was going to meet with Deloncle and that if the meeting didn't "go well," she would "take him down," intimating that she had information about Deloncle that could destroy him.[9] The "information" to which Masse seems to have been referring related to financial irregularities. Deloncle and his cronies lived very well, and spent money freely and visibly, in part to establish themselves as well-funded German clients able to extend patronage and hand out cash, such as the thousands of francs the police found in the possession of Moynier and Roger Mouraille after their visit to MSR headquarters in August of 1941. Money comprised an excellent recruiting tool in a period of rampant inflation, rationing, and scarcity of cash. The MSR leaders also enjoyed living the high life.[10] Masse oversaw the social services funds of the MSR. Deloncle had been embezzling from MSR funds, including Masse's social services accounts. When he refused her request to replace it so that she could balance her books, Masse decided to resign and blow the whistle on Deloncle.[11] This was a threat Deloncle needed to take seriously. Masse was reputed to be a Gestapo spy and she socialized with German officers, with whom, according to one informant, she regularly used cocaine at "La Petite Chaise" on the rue de Grenelle and "organized orgies."[12]

In addition to his personal expenditures, Deloncle needed to recruit and arm as large a corps of fighters as he could, which was also costly. In March and April of 1941 Pierre Mondanel wrote to the prefect of the Parisian police with a warning that within the MSR Deloncle was assembling "groups of henchmen" who were potentially violent. Informers stated that Jean Filliol boasted in public that it was "necessary to eliminate" the leaders of Vichy, or "at least the Ministers, if not the Maréchal."[13] Other sources had also informed the police that Deloncle and Filliol were planning a coup against Vichy. Mondanel demanded the Paris prefect "instantly" verify this information, put both Deloncle and Filliol under close surveillance, and warn Vichy if either man entered the Vichy Zone. Meanwhile, the MSR's adherents patrolled the streets and made no effort to hide their weapons or their Nazi salutes.[14]

Deloncle's downfall can be traced to the decision he made during the spring of 1941 to merge his MSR with the RNP. The rivalry among the leaders of the main collaborationist parties in Paris – Deloncle, Marcel Déat, and Jacques Doriot – was vicious. Laval was confident that he could bring the collaborationists together in a single party, thus creating a political platform for himself. Many members of the MSR, Filliol among them, were leery of the RNP and, especially, of collaborating with Déat, a former university professor and Socialist whose sincere conversion to the political right they doubted.[15] In the early spring of 1941 Deloncle was already losing MSR recruits to his rivals, even given his pro-Laval, pro-RNP, and antisemitic stance.[16] The Parisian police, with or without the prompting of the Sûreté nationale, were tracking Deloncle and Filliol closely. At least some authorities, Mondanel chief among them, had not forgotten about Filliol's pre-war crimes as the chief assassin of the Cagoule.[17]

The police feared that Deloncle was using the "cover" of the RNP to create a domestic "combat force" as opposed to his LVF, intended to fight on the Russian front. Ostensibly designed to protect the RNP, in reality Deloncle planned to use this new *Légion nationale populaire* (LNP) to embed the best of his shock troops in the heart of the RNP, as a means to take over the RNP, use it as a base to catapult himself into power and, perhaps, even to overthrow Maréchal Philippe Pétain. Filliol was appointed head of the LNP despite the four outstanding warrants against him dating from 1938 and 1939. The LNP only had about 3,000 members in July 1941, but they were well armed and equipped, and well paid as well, with each member receiving 1500 to 1800 francs per month. The report concluded that although the LNP was formally part of the RNP, it was in reality entirely under the control of the MSR, and that it constituted "a combat organization whose possibilities should not be underestimated."[18] As the Parisian police noted in their report, Deloncle was determined that his MSR would take precedence over the other collaborationist parties in Paris, and that meant frequent public displays of his troops in full uniform.

Even so, by the summer of 1941, observers remarked that the number of soldiers the MSR could turn out for rallies and marches on important nationalist holidays such as the feast of Joan of Arc was falling even though Deloncle was paying 1800 francs per month to each soldier.[19] Deloncle was thus already under pressure from his own operatives before the murder of Marx Dormoy in July. Paul Collette's attempt to assassinate Laval and Déat in August most likely was Deloncle's bid to deliver on the promise he had made to the MSR membership in February that it would be the MSR that would take control of the RNP and not vice versa. That certainly was what Laval believed.[20] Whether or not he orchestrated Collette's attack, however, it turned the heat up on Deloncle, and helps explain the reckless actions he took in late September and early October, both the murder of Tonia Masse and the synagogue bombings, which again only worsened the situation.

The Dormoy suspects still hoped that Deloncle, who had given Roger Mouraille thousands of francs in August of 1941, would come through. Almost exactly a year after the discovery of Tonia Masse's corpse, in October 1942, Mouraille's wife paid a call on Deloncle's representative in the Vichy

Zone. She informed him that her husband had spent nearly all the cash he had received from Deloncle. Whether or not Deloncle had helped plan the crime, he thus was funding the suspects despite their testimony to the contrary. Mme. Mouraille complained that she was still waiting for an additional 10,000 francs her husband had been promised. The suspects had retained costly lawyers and none of them, with the possible exception of Guichard, had the financial means to pay their legal fees without outside help.[21] In her earliest testimony in 1941, Annie Mourraille had also mentioned funds to defray the costs of their "mission," 40,000 francs that Mourraille stated Marchi had mentioned and which she thought came from Vichy.[22] In her prison conversations with Marchi that Thérèse Payre overheard, the amount was even higher, 70,000 francs. By the autumn of 1942 those initial payments from Vichy were long gone and the spigot appears to have been shut off shortly after the murder.

Money should not have been an issue for Deloncle in 1941–2. The spring and summer of 1941 witnessed the peak of his power and influence. Deloncle's financial contribution to the RNP was substantial, even in terms of the devalued franc of the war years. When the RNP fell apart in the autumn of 1941, Deloncle received back 2,900,000 francs the MSR had contributed.[23] Deloncle, meanwhile, was receiving immense subsidies from the Germans, and the money he was taking in from them and his French sponsors, most of them bankers and industrialists, amounted to millions of francs.[24] One police report said that Eugène Schueller, the creator of L'Oréal, alone was giving the MSR a million francs per month.[25] In 1941 Deloncle had enough funds to offer a bounty of 15,000 francs for any British spy his men might identify or capture.[26]

Deloncle was also enriching himself and the MSR through his raids on Jewish property and confiscation of Jewish-owned apartments and buildings in Paris. In April 1941 he established a partnership with Captain Paul Léopold Sézille, head of an entity called *La Communauté française* that with German funding launched an antisemitic propaganda agency, *L'Institut d'étude des questions juives* (IEQJ). Both Deloncle and Sézille were especially interested in identifying wealthy Jews whom they could target for intimidation and robbery, and whose property they could aryanize.[27] It is clear that for Deloncle the financial benefits of his cooperation with Sézille were at least as satisfying as the ideological ones. On 9 April, for example, Deloncle and a group of his most trusted operatives, including Corrèze, Filliol, and Fauran, led a German-approved aryanization assault on a number of Jewish apartments and businesses in Paris, properties owned or rented by some of Paris' most prominent and wealthy Jewish leaders and businessmen who had fled prior to the German

Occupation.[28] The rapaciousness of Deloncle and his operatives was boundless. They confiscated for their personal use or sale furniture, paintings, statues, and household goods. When Jacques Corrèze raided 17 rue Desbordes-Valmore he even drove away from the site with his car full of bed sheets.[29] Deloncle should have been flush with cash in late 1941.

Rumors of Deloncle's money problems began to surface in the summer, however, and appear to have deepened the distrust that had always existed between Deloncle and Filliol.[30] Upon Deloncle's decision to merge the MSR with the RNP in April a group of dissident "hardliners" coalesced around Filliol.[31] Filliol, who was devoted to the ideals of the MSR and suspected that Deloncle was not, remarked in 1940 that if Deloncle showed himself unworthy of confidence, it would always be possible to "cause him a world of hurt."[32] What precipitated the bout of acrimony in 1941 seems to have been that once Deloncle merged the MSR with the RNP and turned over several million francs to the common fund of the latter, RNP and MSR members alike began to scrutinize the bookkeeping of the MSR more closely, and serious "anomalies" surfaced as a result. Evidently even by the lenient standards of the MSR, where Filliol was rumored to spend a thousand francs per day, Deloncle's spending and that of his closest cronies was becoming excessive. This cannot have pleased funders of the organization, including the German embassy.[33] The Germans were financing the MSR, but at least some officers in the German high command in Paris were also suspicious of Deloncle and by the summer of 1941 this likely resulted in less German money diverted to MSR coffers.[34]

Where was all the money flowing into the MSR going? When Deloncle created the MSR, he envisioned from the outset a fantastically high budget for what he expected would be a large political party with, essentially, its own army. His goal was "the unification of the two zones [Occupied and Vichy] under my sole command."[35] None of this would come cheap, of course, and Deloncle's budget was equally grandiose. He wanted 250,000 francs per month just to fund the military staff and the secret services under its control, 1,100,000 francs for the MSR's Parisian troops, and another 1,060,000 francs for the Parisian region (outside the city itself), plus 2,400,000 francs for the provinces. In addition, he demanded another twelve million for office space, staff, uniforms, and automobiles and twelve to fifteen million francs for weapons and ammunition.[36]

Graft within the MSR leadership was also a serious drain on funds. MSR leader Jean Goy made off with two million francs of MSR money that he used to buy jewelry for one of his mistresses.[37] Deloncle gave his daughter a dowry of a million francs (which helps to explain the rivalry between MSR members Jacques Fauran and Guy Servant, both the scions of wealthy French industrialists, for Claude's hand).[38] He also threw a party for his son Louis at the Michelin three-star Lapérouse restaurant that cost at least 20,000 francs (700 francs per plate).[39] Deloncle, Filliol and the other MSR dissidents complained, was living like an aristocrat off the donors' money while accomplishing very little toward furthering the National Revolution.

In that, Filliol was correct. The organization was hemorrhaging money without much to show for it. In November 1941 one of Dr. Henri Martin's spies remarked that "M. Deloncle's money worries now exceed his (ex)-worries about the revolution."[40] The same observer noted that Deloncle had traveled to the Côte d'Azur to meet with his banker, Renzberg, in late October, accompanied by Filliol. Deloncle's enemies, chief among them Déat, most likely with Laval's quiet backing, were stalking the wounded Deloncle, hoping to bring him down. Their most potent weapon was Tonia Masse. Whereas Deloncle may have hoped that her disappearance would soon be forgotten, as of mid-November the Germans were still "passionate" about the Masse case, as she evidently was a more important "asset" and agent for the Germans than Deloncle had realized. Déat began to attack Deloncle in the press and at rallies, accusing him of having ordered Masse's murder.[41] Deloncle's response was to separate the MSR from the RNP, which he did by November, but by then the damage to his reputation and authority within the MSR and Parisian collaborationist circles was grave.[42]

Laval returned to power in Vichy in April of 1942 and things came to a head in the MSR a month later. The police had a spy within the MSR and thus were well informed about the course of events. The fusion with the RNP had created rumbles of discontent, but the real problem lay in the "poor advice" that Deloncle was receiving from those around him. His leadership was becoming increasingly erratic as he lurched from scandal to scandal, and demonstrated what the police termed "an indecent opportunism."[43] During a meeting of the MSR executive committee and directing committee in the second week of May, Filliol alleged that Deloncle was discrediting the MSR because "everyone knew that he was being cuckolded by M. Corrèze," who was having an affair with Deloncle's wife.[44] The accusation was even more scandalous because it was true. Deloncle's protégé, Jacques Corrèze resided with the MSR leader and his family, and was thus carrying on the affair right under Deloncle's nose, probably with his tacit assent. Moreover, Filliol and his supporters declared, Deloncle seemed to confuse his position with that of a "tyrant" enshrined in power by "divine right."[45] The party was stagnating despite the devotion and "indisputable valor" of the militants comprising its base. Deloncle immediately banished Filliol from the party and threatened to have the Germans arrest him.[46] The next day, at an urgent meeting of the executive committee with the section chiefs, the majority voted to expel Deloncle, and the party split. Among those who sided with Filliol was André Hérard. Despite the brave face that both Filliol and Deloncle tried to put on the schism, it left the MSR in crisis, not least due to the debts of over 1,600,000 francs that Deloncle bequeathed the organization upon his departure.

Both Vichy and the Germans in Paris may have initially breathed a sigh of relief when Filliol ousted Deloncle, splitting apart the MSR in the process, but if they were not already aware, they soon realized that in Filliol they had a tiger by the tail. Laval certainly had no doubts about Filliol. When he was in Paris in May 1942 and was informed about the change in leadership of the MSR, Laval responded, "Deloncle had excellent ideas and, if I didn't much like his way of applying them, it is still evident that he is a good Frenchman." As for Filliol, all Laval had to say was, "Don't even talk to me about that one."[47] Laval may not have had much affection for Deloncle, but he knew that with Filliol in charge the MSR would become more unstable and dangerous, reflecting the tendencies of its new leader.

In November Laval ordered Filliol's arrest, not for his MSR activities, but based on the four outstanding Cagoule-related warrants from 1938 and 1939. The Germans were willing to stand aside and allow the police to carry out the arrest even though Filliol was working for them as an informer.[48] Laval ordered Filliol interned at Saint-Paul-d'Eyjaux (Haute-Vienne), near Limoges, where he remained until the spring of 1944.[49]

Thus, during 1942, while the Dormoy suspects jousted with Jean Marion and Charles Chenevier, Deloncle was far too preoccupied with his own problems to offer them much help. It was Laval, upon his return to power in April who, desiring to have the Dormoy case settled with the least amount of repercussions for the Vichy regime, arranged for the suspects to be transferred to Largentière in the autumn. He intended to warehouse them there while he decided how to put the case to rest and given the clear apprehension of his justice minister about trying the suspects a more radical solution was needed.

The suspects were getting more desperate. Annie Mourraille had declared to the chief warden the day of the escape attempt from Largentière "that they had to have left the prison before Tuesday or otherwise no one would concern themselves with them anymore."[50] The authorities at Vichy were also at their wits' end trying to figure out what to do with the Dormoy suspects. Even before the suspects were sent to Largentière, Pierre Pucheu had instructed Chenevier to hand the Dormoy file over to Marion and focus on other cases.[51] The suspects were set to be arraigned in Largentière on 26 January 1943 for their attempted escape. But arraigning them would only prolong settling the whole case. And the same "friends" who had tried to help them escape on 19 October threatened to stage a violent riot at the courthouse. Laval opposed sending the Dormoy case to trial because he was convinced that France was "too ill to endure such a trial."[52] Joseph-Barthélemy remonstrated with him, insisting that the trial should be allowed to proceed because Laval, as "master of the press" in France, could impose a shroud of silence over the verdict, and that Laval could always commute the suspects' sentences. But Laval refused to budge, and the suspects remained in limbo at Largentière.[53] The only bright spot, from their perspective, was that on 12 December the general prosecutor at Nîmes gave Moynier and Annie Mourraille permission to get married while still in prison, although they waited until August of 1943 to tie the knot.[54]

OPERATION TORCH

Everything began to change, for the war and for France, on 8 November 1942 when a combined British and American force landed at Casablanca in Morocco and in Algeria, in what became the first united British-American operation of the war.[55] Vichy's military response to the Allied invasion of North Africa was predictably weak. Some units refused to fight and welcomed the British and Americans, while other units attacked their future liberators. General George Patton captured Casablanca on 10 November after only two days of fighting. The Allies had planned to install the anti-Pétainist General Henri Giraud in power as the figurehead leader of the French forces that went over to the Allies. Delays in Gibraltar prevented Giraud's arrival so negotiations began with Admiral François Darlan instead who just happened to be in Algiers visiting his ill son. Agreeing to authorize the ceasefire, Darlan struck a deal with the American general Mark Clark and on 10 November was named the temporary head of the government of North Africa. Laval was apoplectic over the loss of North Africa because he rightly anticipated that the Germans would now invade the Vichy Zone to protect their control of France's Mediterranean ports. At 7:00 a.m. on 11 November German troops crossed the Line of Demarcation, thus ending the pretense of sovereignty of Vichy France. Pétain was unable or unwilling to take energetic action to try to stop the Germans. His protests to Hitler about the occupation of the south of France were ignored. As Julian Jackson observes, "[E]verything Vichy had salvaged from the catastrophe of 1940 was irremediably lost: the fleet, the Armistice Army, the Free Zone, and the Empire."[56]

Darlan's assassination on 24 December failed to stem the shift in French sentiment against Vichy that resulted from the German invasion of the Vichy Zone. The Nazi assumption of control in Vichy destroyed the dream to which many French people throughout the country had clung since 1940, that under Pétain's leadership France could be revived and function as a powerful counterweight to Germany once the war ended in a German victory. The Allied invasion of North Africa, the fall of Tunis in May 1943, as well as Darlan's and Giraud's abandonment of Pétain, signaled to French people that Vichy no longer had and, in reality, had never possessed, true sovereignty even as it undermined assumptions that the Germans would win the war. Darlan might have been dead at the end of 1942, but Giraud was very much alive and, under pressure from the Allies, joined forces with his rival, Charles de Gaulle. When the two men met on 22 January 1943 to discuss strategy, it ended de Gaulle's isolation. No longer could supporters of Vichy argue that de Gaulle was simply a minor refugee based in Great Britain and heading a chimera Resistance. People living in the Vichy Zone realized that the Germans were at their doorsteps rather than contained behind the Line of Demarcation and that soon the Allies could be advancing from the north and the south. With the creation of the STO on 16 January 1943, French workers also found themselves coerced in growing numbers into laboring in German factories and on German farms.[57] One result of the German invasion of the Vichy Zone was thus the end of the "waiting game" (attentisme) that had prevailed since the Armistice in 1940 and the creation of many Vichysto-Résistants, former supporters of the Vichy regime who now opted to join the Resistance.[58]

THE GERMANS AT LARGENTIÈRE

On 7 January 1943 Moynier and Guichard wrote to their lawyers expressing their indignation about how one of the wardens of the prison at Largentière, who was named Pons, and his wife had treated Annie Mourraille two days earlier. The occasion of the insult was the arrival at the prison of a German officer who came to "interrogate" the suspects. The officer, a first lieutenant, stood at the gates of the prison in the company of a German soldier and a French interpreter and informed the Warden Pons that he was there to question Ludovic Guichard, Yves Moynier, and Annie Mourraille. Both the officer and soldier were armed, and when Pons refused to allow them to enter, they threatened to blow up the door. Pons then brought the trio to his office and ordered his guards to fetch the suspects. The German officer spoke briefly with them alone, then called Pons back in and insisted that the chief warden hand custody of them over to him. Pons refused. As this was going on, Warden Pons' wife celebrated the Allied victories in North Africa with some of the prisoners while snubbing Annie Mourraille and hiding imprisoned resisters from the Germans, even as her husband was busy snubbing the Germans at the prison gates. After the Germans left, swearing and threatening reprisals against Pons, rather than being elated, the suspects appeared to be "completely depressed" about the visit and declared that the German proposal "was not what they had expected."[59]

A letter Moynier wrote describing the Germans' visit indicates the reason for their disquiet.

> Rumors are circulating, it is only a rumor, that doubtless will be proved wrong, of a transfer to an unknown destination to avoid any search [for us] on the part of the occupying forces ... Our friends, so mysteriously killed at Nice, were a problem since they were sincere revolutionaries, we ourselves equally [are a problem] – the fashion in which we have been treated since our imprisonment being but a long attempt to assassinate us, with premeditation, is obvious proof of this. So that under the pretext, under the cover of a transfer one can take advantage to reserve for us the same end as Thierry de Ludre, shot in the head in 1940 during his transfer under orders from the Jew [Georges] Mandel, then Minister of the Interior.[60]

Moynier concluded with the request that Jean Franceschi "inform the person of the Avenue Prado to whom we have written recently about this newly created situation." The Avenue Prado in Marseille was the home of the German Press service in the south of France. According to Roger Mouraille's post-war deposition, he worked for the Germans at the Avenue Prado, "gathering information related to politics."[61] Moynier's letter indicates that it was Roger Mouraille, with German help, who tried to organize their escape in October.

At 3:45 p.m. on 23 January the Germans returned to Largentière. Approximately twenty men, three Germans in civilian clothes, several German officers, and fifteen soldiers, under the command of Gestapo Captain Hugo Geissler, drove up to the prison gates. In January of 1943 Geissler was based in Clermont-Ferrand as a commander of the SS security police and intelligence office, the *Sicherheitspolizei* (SiPo) and the *Sicherheitsdienst* (SD) in the Vichy Zone. He commanded eighty officers of the German police charged with repressing resistance on the part of the French population. His close companion in this work was Joany (Jany) Georges Batissier, a corrupt French police officer who had been in Darlan's entourage in Vichy. On 23 January the Germans arrived in three vehicles, at least one of them a Mercedes and another a military troop transport truck. Geissler himself was commanding the group, and the soldiers were armed to the teeth, including with grenades.[62]

A German officer who spoke French rang the prison doorbell and asked to see Chief Warden Didelot. When Didelot came to the entrance, the German requested to "tour" the prison, which Didelot refused to permit. Didelot asked the German officer whether or not the latter had a written order. The German officer affirmed that he did but did not present it. Without the order, Didelot refused to let the Germans in, which elicited from the German officer a string of threats that he would knock down the door and arrest Didelot (the two men were speaking through a grate in the door). Didelot left the Germans standing outside and went to telephone his superior, the state prosecutor in Largentière, as well as that man's superior, the general prosecutor of the Appeals Court in Nîmes, and the penitential authorities in Nîmes, since his prison at Largentière was a branch of the Nîmes prison system. Didelot refused to budge until he heard back from them. His superiors telephoned Vichy and learned that it was none other than Joseph-Barthélemy who verbally had given the Germans the go-ahead to travel to Largentière, meet with the Dormoy suspects, and remove them from the prison if they wished. They then called Didelot back and told him who had authorized the Germans.[63]

At this point Didelot realized that it was time to open the gates, especially as the German soldiers were planting explosives around them in preparation for blowing up the prison walls. Once he opened the gates, ten Germans entered. While Didelot had been arguing with the Germans, his wife had taken the opportunity to ensure that any French resisters in the prison had been hidden in the kitchen where the Germans were unlikely to find them. The Germans made sure the prison guards were disarmed, and then went to Didelot's office, where they asked him whether there were any German prisoners on the premises. Upon receiving a negative response, they visited the cells. When they found Moynier, Guichard, and Annie Mourraille, they opened their cells and said, "Come with us, we're taking you out of here." The Germans escorted them outside. They put Moynier and Guichard in the military truck with the soldiers, but Geissler escorted Annie Mourraille to his Mercedes, and the whole group drove off in the direction of Aubenais. The "affair produced strong emotions among the population" of Largentière, which "in general disapproved of this manner of behavior." With typical German parsimony and efficiency, the Germans made sure before they left to take with them the clothes and personal effects of the suspects, including their ration cards, which, Joseph-Barthélemy lamented in his memoirs, still contained twenty-three unused tickets.[64]

Joseph-Barthélemy blamed the suspects' liberation on Laval, although it is unlikely that his role in the decision was as minimal as he claimed after the war. One day, Joseph-Barthélemy recounts in his memoirs, while he was complaining to Laval about his inability to conclude the Dormoy affair, and the headaches the suspects were causing him, Laval told him, "Wait. In a few weeks something is going to happen that will relieve you of your worries."[65] Then, several days before 23 January, Joseph-Barthélemy received a phone call from Laval, who was in Paris conferring with the Germans. Laval asked Joseph-Barthélemy where the suspects were. When Joseph-Barthélemy replied that they were still in Largentière, Laval responded, "Good. Leave them there."

KUBLER AND CHENEVIER: VICHYSTO-RÉSISTANTS

By the end of 1942, both Chenevier and his colleague Georges Kubler had joined the Resistance. Kubler joined the Gallia resistance network based in Lyon. Under the alias "Bernard de la Sûreté" he continued to work as a police officer while warning the local Resistance cells of police raids or informers who had infiltrated their network and, when possible, protecting them from arrest. He took over direction of the Gallia intelligence service early in 1944 when its director, Inspector Colle, alias "Julien," was detained. Later in 1944 Kubler was denounced, arrested, and deported to a camp in Germany, where he died in 1945 before he could be liberated.[66]

Chenevier was a classic Vichysto-Résistant, meaning someone who first supported Vichy and subsequently joined the Resistance. It was the collapse of the Vichy Zone that convinced Chenevier that Pétain's État-français could never become the nucleus of a free and sovereign France. A German bullet had killed his father during World War I, and Chenevier was deeply patriotic and bore little affection for Germans or collaboration. Moreover, he was well acquainted with German espionage in France prior to 1940, and as part of the police team working on the Cagoule case had tracked German spy Karl Boemelburg. Under cover of doing engineering work in France, Boemelburg was Deloncle's conduit to the Nazis, and helped furnish weapons to the Cagoule. Chenevier interrogated Boemelburg prior to the latter's expulsion from France shortly before the war broke out. Boemelburg returned to France in 1940 as an SS Sturmbannführer and head of the Gestapo. Installed in Paris at the Gestapo headquarters on the rue de Saussaies, it was Boemelburg who issued Chenevier, now working for the Vichy Judicial Police, an official pass to cross the Line of Demarcation freely in the course of his duties. When the two men again met in the autumn of 1940, Boemelburg was disappointed that Chenevier was not friendlier to him. But Chenevier despised the Germans, and when Boemelburg attempted on several occasions to recruit him to work as a collaborator for the Gestapo, Chenevier flatly refused.[67]

According to his grandson-in-law and biographer, Jean-Émile Néaumet, disgusted by the prominence of Cagoulards in Pétain's government whom he had tracked and arrested before the war, Chenevier joined the Resistance "de premiere heure" (almost immediately). He passed police intelligence to the Resistance network under the command of Pierre Paillole, who discusses Chenevier's activities in his memoirs, and to that of former Cagoulard Maurice Duclos, who joined de Gaulle in London immediately after the fall of France and then returned to create the Saint-Jacques network in August.[68] But it was the German invasion of the Vichy Zone that persuaded Chenevier formally to join the Saint-Jacques network in 1943.[69] In February of 1943, Boemelburg had the pleasure of expelling Chenevier from the Occupied Zone, after interrogating him at Gestapo headquarters. Chenevier remained under suspicion in Vichy and was arrested there and deported to Neuengamme in Germany on 11 November 1943. Geissler had Chenevier imprisoned and tortured before he was deported, although Chenevier, unlike Kubler, survived the war. He returned to France with his health broken and needed many months of recovery before he was on his feet again.[70]

FILLIOL IS UNLEASHED

Operation Torch and the German invasion of the Vichy Zone increased the pressure on Laval. Faced with the gradual defection of the more moderate members of his government (even Pierre Pucheu fled to Morocco in August in a doomed bid to join the Resistance), Laval was obliged by the end of 1943 to call upon the "hardliners" for support, including collaborationists such as Doriot and Déat. By now Laval was caught in a trap of his own making. The Germans no longer trusted Pétain, whom they feared would attempt to flee to North Africa, as had Darlan, and try to negotiate with the Allies, who were casting about for a replacement for de Gaulle, whom Franklin Roosevelt disliked. On 18 December Pétain suspended his cooperation with the Germans until they evacuated Vichy. The regime tottered on into 1944 with Pétain nominally still at its head but a virtual prisoner of the Germans. Every passing day de Gaulle's hand grew stronger and that of Laval weaker.[71] The imposition of the STO in the Vichy Zone on 14 January 1943 prompted many young French men and women to join the Resistance, not only out of patriotism but also because it offered a means to escape being sent to labor in Germany. The "French civil war" that had been simmering since at least 1934 returned to a boiling point as resisters targeted French collaborationists, as well as the occupiers and the Germans, and Vichy police stepped up their repression. Things were getting out of hand, and the Germans demanded that Laval act.[72]

Laval turned to Joseph Darnand, the celebrated World War I veteran and former Cagoulard who had headed the *Légion française des combattants*, a combat militia of French veterans charged with the defense of the Vichy government. As late as mid-1943 Darnand had made overtures to the Resistance, but his record as an extreme and violent anti-Communist who had formed the *Service d'ordre légionnaire* (SOL) in January of 1942 to defend the National Revolution induced Resistance leaders to rebuff him. The next year in January of 1943 the SOL was transformed into the Milice, a sort of fascist praetorian guard emboldened to enforce the political order and repress dissent. It quickly became tied to the Germans who used the *miliciens* against the Resistance. Although never including more than about 35,000 members by the time of the liberation, the Milice attracted young men loyal to Pétain but drawn more and more from rural France and committed to anti-Communist, antisemitic, and pro-Catholic ideals. The Milice grew in importance as the Resistance increased in strength. Neither the Milice nor the Resistance was well armed, but the clashes between them developed into a sort of civil war between supporters of the Maréchal and of de Gaulle. Because many of the Resistance networks had been founded by Communists, and Communists and Socialists continued to be prominent in their leadership, members of both the Milice and the Resistance often envisioned their struggle as a continuation of the conflict between the left and the right in pre-war France. Darnand joined the Waffen-SS in August of 1943, in part as a bid to induce the Germans to let him open Milice training camps and secure better arms for his men. He swore an oath of loyalty to Hitler and was awarded the rank of Obersturmführer, but this failed to translate into a significant increase in resources for the Milice. The Germans simply lacked any men or supplies to spare.[73]

By May 1944 Darnand convinced Laval to free Jean Filliol, who immediately joined the Milice in Limoges using the name "Deschamps" and began a reign of terror in the Limousin. Most notably on 10 June 1944 he led Waffen-SS troops into the village of Oradour-sur-Glane where, in reprisal for Resistance activities that had claimed German lives the previous day, 642 inhabitants were massacred including 205 children and 247 women who had been rounded up and locked into a church that was then destroyed by an incendiary device. The horror proved to be too much even for his fellow militiamen, and Filliol was transferred to Clermont-Ferrand where he operated under the name "Chef Denis."[74]

On 5 August 1944 Pétain finally denounced the Milice, now hated throughout France. It was too little, too late. The final meeting of the Council of Ministers of Vichy took place on 12 July and on 16 August the Germans evacuated Vichy, taking Laval, Pétain, and the remnants of the Vichy government with them and depositing them at the German castle of Sigmaringen. Filliol and Darnand joined the new SS Charlemagne, a brigade of 1500 French ultra-collaborationist militiamen who fought alongside the Germans in the desperate battles to defend Germany from the Allies.[75] By then, the Germans had also deported Gabriel Jeantet, whom the Milice arrested on 27 July for his Resistance activities. He was interned in a concentration camp in Eisenberg, Germany, to wait out the end of the war. Ironically, he was denounced by a former MSR operative and it was his fellow Cagoulard Darnand who ordered his arrest.[76]

THE "FEAST" OF THE MSR

On 23 January 1946 soon after the war's end, Lucien Fromes, who had dined with Eugène Deloncle the night of Tonia Masse's murder, gave a deposition to Edmond Bascou, of the French judicial police. Bascou was working on the Dormoy case, reopened after the Liberation of France in 1944. Fromes, who had been condemned to death in November of 1945 by a military tribunal in Lyon, had worked from 1940 forward as an interpreter for the German SD. Fromes told Bascou that "for his job" he "saw Deloncle at least once a week" throughout the war. Fromes was also Deloncle's link with the Gestapo since Fromes worked with Herbert Keller, a Benedictine monk who reported to Karl Oberg, head of the Gestapo in Paris.[77] Early in 1943, shortly after the Germans had released Annie Mourraille, Moynier, and Guichard from prison, Fromes was at a party in Deloncle's apartment on the rue Lesueur in Paris. Deloncle asked Fromes, "Would you like me to introduce you to Mourraille, the woman who was part of the assassination team that killed Dormoy?" Fromes accepted the offer and was conducted into a room next to Deloncle's office, where Deloncle introduced Fromes to the now married Annie Mourraille and Yves Moynier.[78]

Deloncle declared to Fromes, "Thanks to you, we have freed the assassins of Dormoy."[79] Fromes explained that by "you," Deloncle meant the German authorities. On several occasions, Fromes added, Deloncle boasted that "[i]t was us, the Cagoule, who organized this blow," because of Dormoy's "activities as Minister of the Interior during the investigation of the Cagoule." Moreover, Fromes avowed, "Captain" Méténier, another Cagoule veteran, told him the same thing on several occasions. Fromes also learned that in Paris Annie Mourraille went to work for German intelligence services.

By the end of 1943 everyone in France knew that Germany was losing the war. That meant that both the Germans and the collaborationists needed financial "nest eggs" upon which they could draw and safe harbors for themselves in neutral countries, which in Europe meant either Portugal, Switzerland, or Spain. It was to this task that the Dormoy assassins and their German mentor, Hans Sommer, who had assumed the name "Herbert Senner" and had a new job heading the Gestapo in Marseille, turned their energies. Senner assembled a team of French operatives, many of them collaborationists previously linked to the MSR and/or the Cagoule, to amass as much money as possible. The source of their money was contraband trade. Senner and his operatives stole merchandise, contraband radios, German war supplies, and valuables that French refugees, especially Jews, had hidden in the Vichy Zone. These they transported to Switzerland and exchanged for Swiss gold, often in the form of watches, that would then be brought back into France and either sold there or sent on to Spain. Senner also used his French employees to investigate whether the Swiss would allow Senner and his operatives to retreat to Switzerland once the Third Reich had collapsed.[80]

Roger Mouraille went to work for Senner. He persuaded Senner to allow him to hire Moynier, Annie Mourraille, and Guichard as part of Senner's network of spies (and thieves). Moynier, always difficult, soon fell out with Senner, and after a couple of trips to Switzerland, he and Annie Mourraille returned to Paris, where in 1943 the couple worked for German intelligence. Annie Mourraille worked with a Yugoslavian spy for the Germans, Draga Jevremovitch, who had lived in Paris since before the war and was fluent in French and German. She and Moynier were still living with her pre-war roommate, Anatole Soungouroff. This time, however, they were sharing an apartment in the 16th arrondissement supplied by the Germans. Guichard also worked for the Gestapo tracking down Resistance operatives in Paris who were in contact with the Marseille and Grenoble Resistance networks. Guichard's job also included finding and denouncing Jews.[81]

According to Commissaire Roux of the Police mobile of Marseille, on 14 January 1944 the Marseille police arrested two of Roger Mouraille's operatives in the city. Infuriated, Mouraille showed up at the police station in the company of another man. Both were heavily armed. Mouraille informed the officers on duty that he was "German police" and ordered them to "stand down." The station head told Mouraille that before he could free Mouraille's men he would first have to discuss the matter with the police chief. Mouraille and his companion were brought to M. Cabanne, *Comissaire de la Section des Affaires politiques*. Mouraille announced to Cabanne that he was "one of the assassins" of Marx Dormoy. Unmoved, Cabanne refused to let Mouraille talk to his men until Cabanne had conferred with the Marseille intendant of police, whom Cabanne immediately telephoned. The intendant told Cabanne that he "did not see any reason" why Mouraille should be allowed to talk to his men in police custody. Enraged, Mouraille shouted that if Cabanne attempted to arrest him, Mouraille would "take him down along with a dozen policemen." At that point Mouraille pulled from his right pocket an automatic pistol and aimed it at Cabanne, who stood his ground and told Mouraille that his "attitude was incorrect and out of place," and that Mouraille should "think again" given that there were several armed police officers in the room with him. Mouraille backed down and stormed out of the station. He subsequently paid a visit to the intendant, who threw him out.[82]

During the final year of the war, Moynier and Guichard were back in the south and once again in cahoots with Roger Mouraille. The trio was growing increasingly brazen – or desperate. In July 1944 Mouraille left Marseille. The Germans told the Marseille police that they had sent Mouraille on a mission to Hungary but in reality he, Moynier, and Guichard were on a "mission" of a very different sort, to find Jews still residing in what had been the Vichy Zone and terrorize them into allowing him to loot whatever valuables they had hidden, in return for not turning them over for deportation to Germany. Some of their victims, perhaps sensing how far the tide had already turned in the war, were bold enough to file formal complaints with the French police at the time of the robbery, whereas others sought to press charges after the war. Via these police reports, one can track Mouraille's progress around southern France. For example, soon after the end of the war, Dr. Maurice Machtou of Cannes gave an affidavit alleging that on 9 December 1943 Mouraille, Moynier, and an "unknown woman," robbed his daughter of "possessions" worth about a million francs (1946 value).[83] The evening before they robbed Machtou, Mouraille and his gang extorted 400,000 francs from a M. Stora, also a Jew, by threatening him with arrest.[84]

Roger Mouraille was still at it in late July 1944, when he again passed himself off as a German police officer and robbed another Jew, this time in Pau. The victim, a M. Haenel, was in hiding, and had a lodger, a M. Teule, who was occupying Haenel's home and guarding Haenel's things. Mouraille and his men searched the premises and took money, jewelry, furs, and shortwave radio equipment. The next day another man, also dressed as a German police officer, returned to Haenel's home, in the company of a "foreign merchant" to whom Mouraille likely intended to sell Haenel's belongings in order to raise cash quickly. Mouraille declared to everyone at the scene, and to the police who evidently were also called but were powerless to stop the theft, that he was a member of the Gestapo who was carrying out an "operation" in Pau before leaving for Spain. The whole affair came before the Appeals Court of Pau on 26 July 1945, when the policeman on the scene, Claude Bonimond, testified that Mouraille turned the radio over to him and told him that Mouraille would have liked to come back again, search for other Jews in Pau and take whatever was left, but that Mouraille had to "be on his way."[85] Guichard, who like Mouraille also had business connections in Spain dating from the 1930s, was already "on his way," as he left Marseille for Barcelona on 6 April, armed with a visa that the Vichy interior ministry had granted him.[86]

JEANTET AND DELONCLE – TWO PATHS

As was the case in the summer and autumn of 1940, the events of November and December 1942 obliged the former members of the Cagoule again to make pivotal choices. The ways in which Jeantet and Deloncle spent the period from November 1942 through August 1944 exemplify those different paths.

Only a handful of Cagoulards, most notably Maurice Duclos and Georges Loustaunau-Lacau, joined de Gaulle in London and the Resistance prior to the German invasion of the Vichy Zone. Once the dream of Vichy sovereignty had collapsed, however, some, like Jeantet, opted for the Resistance. Jeantet, like Chenevier, was reputed to be an "early" supporter of the Resistance, although the support he afforded resisters such as Paul Dungler, with whom Jeantet shared a hostility to de Gaulle, consisted mostly of passing on information to resisters, who in turn forwarded it to London. The problem for Vichysto-Résistants such as Chenevier and Jeantet, whether they formally joined a Resistance group before or after 1943, was figuring out what it meant to be a loyal, patriotic Frenchman. Who was the real "traitor" to France, de Gaulle, who left in order to fight on, or Pétain, who stayed in order, so he claimed at least, to defend France? For Chenevier, the presence in Pétain's government of former Cagoulards whom Chenevier considered criminals, was damning. But like Jeantet, Chenevier also believed that the "better part of valor" consisted in staying in France, upholding the law, and defending French sovereignty against the occupiers as best he could. Jeantet remained convinced during and after the war that Pétain had France's best interests at heart even when the old man was unable to control Laval or make much headway with the Germans. When it became obvious the Vichy regime was essentially moribund, Jeantet began working with Colonel Gaillard, a regional chief of the French Forces of the Interior, as well as with Dungler, and anti-Nazi Germans. Even so, he retained the hope that Pétain, rather than de Gaulle, could ultimately negotiate France's role in the new European order once the country was liberated. Jeantet paid a high price for his decision to resist the Germans, as he spent almost a year, from July 1944 until May 1945, in a German prison camp. When he returned to France, his health was broken.[87]

With little left to lose in 1943, Deloncle also made overtures to the Resistance. Filliol had ejected him from the MSR, Darlan, his protector at Vichy, was dead, and his enemy, Laval, was in control of the tottering Vichy regime. Other enemies, Déat and Doriot, were running the remaining collaborationist organizations and even Deloncle's German supporters in Paris had dropped him. Only a few close friends from his days in the Cagoule, such as Jacques Corrèze, remained by Deloncle's side, but even that loyalty was suspect given Corrèze's relationship with Deloncle's wife. Right around the time that Darlan was going over to the Allies, in November 1942, Deloncle's old friend from the Gestapo, Helmut Knochen, interrogated Deloncle, not surprising given Darlan's change of course. A year later, at the end of 1943, Deloncle seems to have contacted General Giraud, hoping, as had Darlan, to help negotiate a separate peace between the US and Germany that would end the Occupation of France and shut de Gaulle and the Communists out of the post-war French government.[88] But it was too late. Like Pierre Pucheu, who went to Casablanca at Giraud's invitation in May 1943 and instead of being welcomed was charged with treason and shot the following March, Deloncle had burned too many bridges. Once the Germans realized that he had turned on them too, they began to track him and, on 7 January 1944, Gestapo agents invaded his home and killed him in front of his wife and children.[89]

CHAPTER TEN

26 August 1944: Liberation

On 16 August 1944 the Germans retreated from Vichy, taking the remaining officials of the collapsing Vichy regime, now essentially hostages, with them. The same day, Annie Mourraille and Yves Moynier fled Paris for asylum in Spain.[1] Ten days later the German garrison in Paris surrendered, having been overwhelmed by the French 2nd Armored Division and the US 4th Infantry Division. Charles de Gaulle entered the city and established his headquarters on the rue Saint Dominique as well as the myth that Paris had been liberated by her citizens. On 26 August 1944 de Gaulle led a triumphant march down the Champs Élysées.

On 22 January 1945 Félix Gouin was also in Paris.[2] He had attended the trial at Riom from 19 February until 21 May 1942. When the trial ended without a verdict, and it was apparent that Philippe Pétain had no intention of releasing Léon Blum, Gouin, with Blum's blessing, left France to join de Gaulle in London.[3] Gouin was one of the legislators, along with Blum and Dormoy, who had voted against giving Pétain full powers in 1940, and he was well aware that Pétain or the Germans might arrest him given his Gaullist sympathies and close relationship with Blum. He likely escaped arrest in 1940 only because he had not played a prominent role in Blum's government prior to the war. Even so, his wife covered his disappearance in 1942 by proclaiming that Gouin had run off with a mistress, which bought him the time to get to London before the police realized where he had gone.[4] At the Liberation, Gouin followed de Gaulle to Paris and during 1945 Gouin led the Constituent Assembly, tasked with forming France's new government. When de Gaulle later resigned as prime minister in January 1946, Gouin took the helm of an interim administration that lasted six months.[5] Hence during the years immediately after the war, Gouin was a prominent political figure with more than enough clout to settle some scores for old friends.

On 22 January 1945, Gouin wrote a letter to the justice minister requesting that the Dormoy case be reopened. He pointed out that prior to their liberation by the Germans the suspects had confessed to the crime, even boasted about it, and that the police had ample evidence against them. Nevertheless, while Gouin was abroad, and under "poorly defined circumstances," the suspects were transferred to Largentière, from which they fled "with the active assistance of the Gestapo."[6] Since that time the case had languished, with no effort to track down and arrest the suspects. This outcome, Gouin asserted, could be easily understood given the "complicity of certain people of Vichy in this lamentable affair." In the "name of Melle. Jeanne Dormoy," Gouin asked the justice minister, at that time François de Menthon, to reopen the case. He knew Menthon well given that Menthon had been justice minister in de Gaulle's provisional government based in London as well. Gouin realized that locating the files and witnesses would be a tall order. Still he asked Menthon to "unmask, arrest and have judged all of those who, from near or far, participated in the assassination of my regretted colleague and friend Marx Dormoy." Gouin recommended that Menthon have the case transferred to a court in Paris and designate a new judge. He promised that Menthon would have "all of my support to cast some light over this drama which has been willfully obscured by the traitors and usurpers of Vichy." Gouin asked Menthon to keep him updated on the progress of the investigation and assured Menthon that he would intervene whenever necessary to help bring the affair to trial. Thus began the third and final phase of the investigation into the murder of Marx Dormoy.

Menthon chose Robert Lévy, a judge of the *Parquet de la Seine* in Paris, to reopen the Marx Dormoy case. Although deported to Buchenwald and, later, Dachau, Blum survived the war and returned to France. He agreed to help move the Dormoy inquiry forward and to testify if the case ever came to trial. Lévy's initial focus was to gather in Paris all the police files on the assassination that were mostly in Montélimar, Nîmes, and Marseille, as well as to locate as many of the surviving witnesses as possible. He went to work uncovering the details of how the suspects escaped from Largentière and where they had gone when the war ended. Lévy ascertained that the Germans, with the firm support of Laval and decidedly less enthusiastic consent of Joseph-Barthélemy, had liberated the assassins. He also learned that Yves Moynier, Annie Mourraille, and Ludovic Guichard were out of his reach by early 1945.

It must have been painful for Lévy, Gouin, and Jeanne Dormoy to realize that until the end of 1944 it might still have been possible to have detained at least some of the suspects in France. Georges Le Duc, who had been imprisoned for black-market activities in Valence at the same time as the suspects, stated on 1 December 1944 that shortly after the Liberation he "ran into" Guichard, who was in hiding in Paris under the name "Duverney." Guichard told Le Duc that Roger Mouraille had purchased property at Annonay, not far from Valence – evidently Mouraille had not gotten enough of the region while in prison. Annie Mourraille and Yves Moynier had gotten married, but Guichard did not know where the couple had gone.[7] The authorities issued arrest warrants and sentenced them in absentia since the police had not been able to track them down. On 10 January 1945 Guichard was condemned to a year in prison for taking part in their autumn 1942 escape attempt. He was also condemned to death for endangering the security of the state. In February 1945 the Cour d'Appel de Nîmes condemned Annie Mourraille to a year in prison for the attempted escape from Largentière and in addition issued a warrant for her arrest for intelligence with the enemy.[8]

Meanwhile, Lévy tasked Superintendent Christian Leluc with reconstructing the pre-war investigation of the Dormoy case.[9] Lévy ordered the wartime case files transported from the former Vichy Zone to Paris. Some witnesses, such as Joseph-Barthélemy, who had left the Vichy government in March of 1943, were available to be interviewed. Arrested in October 1944 and eager to exculpate himself for his participation in Pétain's regime, he gave a lengthy statement to the police from his hospital bed in Paris on 21 February 1945 before dying a month later. In both that statement and his posthumously published memoirs, he offered a detailed account of his handling of the Dormoy case and – naturally – assigned the blame for the suspects' liberation in 1943 to Pierre Laval.[10]

Other witnesses would be more difficult to interview, however. Investigating Magistrate Jean Marion survived the war, the final years of which he had spent in Papeete, Tahiti. Evidently Marion returned to Montélimar; issued a warrant for the arrest of Moynier, Guichard, and Annie Mourraille; and asked the Sûreté nationale to track down Roger Mouraille and Antoine Marchi. Since the case had been transferred to Paris, however, Marion played little role in the post-war investigation. Christian Leluc interviewed other witnesses, among them Guichard's cellmate at Valence, Henri Eracol, who later went to work for

Roger Mouraille after the latter's release in 1942. He also questioned witnesses of Jacques Doriot's threat against Marx Dormoy at Vichy in 1940, and Annie Mourraille's former roommate, Anatole Soungouroff.[11] Soungouroff told the authorities that the Germans had held him as a prisoner of war until April of 1943. After his release he resided with Annie Mourraille and Moynier until about eight days before the Liberation of Paris, when the pair fled before the Germans surrendered the city to the Allies. Soungouroff stated that Annie Mourraille had affirmed that the Dormoy assassination was "a political affair arranged by Vichy and the Maréchal Pétain," more or less the same story that she had told Charles Chenevier and which she was convinced exonerated her. According to Soungouroff, Pétain wanted the suspects to "disappear" after the crime, but Roger Mouraille managed to get them out of prison before that could happen thanks to his close relationship with the Germans. This may well have been the case given that Roger Mouraille went to work for Gestapo officer Herbert Senner in 1943, an agent previously known as Hans Sommer who was linked to Deloncle and the synagogue bombings in 1941. Mouraille may have been working with the Germans throughout the war.[12] The French authorities did their best during the spring of 1945 to trace the Dormoy assassins' movements but doubted that they would be able to apprehend them since most had fled France.[13]

In June 1945 the police did track down Marchi, whom they incarcerated in the Santé in Paris, along with Gabriel Jeantet in July.[14] But Jeantet, who had returned to Paris in May, had spent much of the previous year in the Eisenberg camp and was hospitalized upon his repatriation. Jeantet was too ill to leave the hospital during the summer, and it was not until 22 September that the police deposed him. His testimony differed little from what he had told Chenevier in 1942. He denied any role in Dormoy's assassination and although he admitted being "acquainted" with Marchi, he argued he did not know the other suspects. The police knew this was a lie. Along with Annie's testimony and other leads, they were aware that shortly before the Germans liberated Guichard from Largentière, his wife wrote him that she had contacted "Gabriel" for assistance.[15] But absent more solid evidence, they would have a difficult time connecting Jeantet to the crime.

One of the most serious obstacles to rebuilding the case against the Dormoy assassins in 1945 was that neither Chenevier nor Georges Kubler could be of much help. They had visited the crime scene, interrogated all the suspects in 1941 and 1942, and heard Annie Mourraille's testimony regarding the complicity of Jeantet and Pétain. But in 1945 Kubler was dead and Chenevier was still ill from his stint in a German concentration camp. Worse, even before he returned to France, the *Commission d'épuration*, charged with purging French society, including the ranks of the police and the government bureaucracy, of collaborators, opened a file on Chenevier. His enemies in the new French government accused him of having been a Gestapo agent who turned over to the Germans the names of young Communist resisters who were subsequently arrested as part of the inquiry into the assassination of Feldkommandant Hotz in Nantes in October 1941. There was ample evidence that Chenevier had been a legitimate member of the Resistance. But because he had also worked for the Vichy police his case was ambiguous; he was suspended from the Sûreté and then forced into retirement, albeit with a pension, in February 1946. In August Chenevier's supporters managed to ensure that he was decorated with the Croix de Guerre for his Resistance activities. Lévy and the Socialist and Communist politicians dominating the provisional government in 1945 nevertheless remained suspicious of him despite the testimony of prominent Resistance figures who knew about the risks he had taken while working on their behalf. It took him two years to clear his name, but finally in January of 1948 he was exonerated in court. In the meantime, Chenevier was sidelined from the renewed Dormoy investigation, which meant that even though the police interviewed him, he could not participate.[16]

In his statement to Lévy in 1946 Chenevier explained the case, which for him began with the tip he had received from an informer in late June 1941 that a serious crime was going to be committed against a Third Republic politician "between Lyon and Marseille."[17] He then related how he had traced the footprint of the crime from Montélimar to Vichy, and reiterated the testimony Annie Mourraille had given him avowing that a "close collaborator of Pétain and a member of the Maréchal's civil cabinet at Vichy" had wanted Dormoy killed. When asked the name of this "close collaborator," Chenevier responded "Estèbe." He was referring to Paul Estèbe, adjunct director of Pétain's cabinet at the same time as Jeantet was working on propaganda for Vichy.[18] Pétain awarded both Jeantet and Estèbe his medal of honor, the Francisque, and although Jeantet avowed a "certain tension" between himself and Estèbe, the two men shared similar political views, including an ardent determination to protect the reputation of the elderly Maréchal at all costs, and both had joined the Resistance late in the war and were deported for their pains.[19] Before mentioning Estèbe, Annie Mourraille told Chenevier "when you have Gabriel Jeantet he won't be able to do anything other than to accept his responsibility as we ourselves have done, and that will take you to Estèbe."[20] Chenevier added that Annie Mourraille assured him that Jeantet was the "liaison agent between Estèbe and Marchi," and that Marchi in turn was the leader of the team that carried out the assassination. It was Jeantet who gave the orders and disbursed the funds, and the likely source of the money was Estèbe.

Chenevier did not offer any motive for why Jeantet and Estèbe wanted Dormoy out of the way. Still, there were the persistent rumors, before, during and after the war, of Pétain's involvement in the Cagoule.[21] Dormoy was summoned in 1941 to testify at the trial at Riom. As interior minister in 1937, Dormoy had overseen the investigation of the Cagoule, to which Jeantet had belonged.[22] If there was any truth to the rumors and Pétain had supported the Cagoulards, even if the Maréchal never officially joined the organization but merely hoped to benefit from the political disruption it would bring about, both Dormoy and Jeantet would have known this. Given their utter devotion to Pétain, neither Jeantet nor Estèbe would have wanted to risk any testimony from Dormoy that might have sullied the Maréchal's reputation.[23] Dormoy was the official from Blum's government who knew the most about the Cagoule, and Jeantet was an ex-Cagoulard. That Dormoy would likely defend Blum and the legacy of the Popular Front during the Riom trial by declaring that Pétain (and other Vichy officials) had undermined the French Republic in the 1930s must have seemed an intolerable risk. Had Dormoy testified that Pétain himself had been a secret Cagoulard or, worse, produced documents to that effect, Pétain's standing in France and abroad could have been seriously jeopardized.[24]

Chenevier's testimony of 3 January 1946 led Lévy to question Jeantet again in the infirmary of the prison at the Santé on 5 January and to take another statement from Jeantet two days later. Jeantet insisted that he had nothing to add to his previous testimony. Lévy also questioned Jeantet's brother Claude, who unsurprisingly attempted to pin Dormoy's death entirely on the conveniently deceased Eugène Deloncle. Both Claude Jeantet and Lucien Fromes claimed to have heard Deloncle boast about being the author of the crime late in 1942. Claude Jeantet averred that he had only recently heard that the police suspected his brother had participated in the Dormoy assassination and suggested that it was Pucheu who had first spread the rumor at Vichy that Gabriel Jeantet had participated in the crime. Pucheu was executed in March 1944 and thus unable to refute Claude's assertion.[25]

On 7 January 1946 the police questioned Marchi, who had already sent Lévy a letter the preceding October in which he asserted his complete innocence in the Dormoy murder and demanded that his case be handled separately from those of the other suspects. Marchi claimed that he always had been extremely anti-German and had fought in the Resistance in 1943 and 1944 under Commanders Grimaldo and Cuttoli, and then fought on the barricades in Paris at the moment of the Liberation, where he was wounded.[26] Given that Marchi had joined Deloncle's LVF forces, the police were skeptical of Marchi's story.

In January of 1946 the police also took a statement regarding the Dormoy case from Bernard Ménétrel, Pétain's physician and confidant. Ménétrel and Gabriel Jeantet were around the same age and had been close friends and collaborators in Vichy. Ménétrel had sponsored Jeantet for the positions the latter held in the regime, both general secretary of the Amicale de France and inspector general of propaganda in the General Secretariat of Information under the vice-president of the Council of Vichy. Ménétrel claimed that when he informed Pétain that Dormoy had been assassinated, Pétain was revolted. Like Claude Jeantet, Ménétrel asserted that it was Pucheu who first bruited it about that officials in Pétain's cabinet were behind the crime. Ménétrel asserted that Jeantet had no official position in the cabinet, although he admitted that Jeantet worked "in liaison with us."[27] This was technically true, but as inspector general of propaganda it is clear that Jeantet was in a position to meet regularly with cabinet members such as Ménétrel and Estèbe, especially as a central part of Jeantet's job was to assure the liaison between the civil cabinet and the Ministry of Information from September of 1941 until January of 1942.[28] Just sixteen days after Dormoy's murder, Darlan ordered the dissolution of the Amicale, and Pétain signed the papers on 11 August 1941, most likely because he and others in his cabinet knew that Jeantet, probably with the support of Estèbe, had engineered the assassination, although Jeantet later claimed it was the anti-German stance of the Amicale that had determined its fate.[29] The Amicale had regrouped former Cagoulards who had reprised their pre-war agenda and terrorist tactics and fomented destabilizing plots to purge France of opponents of the National Revolution. But even though Jeantet may have been briefly exiled from Pétain's side, obliged to cease propaganda work for the Ministry of Information in August of 1941, by September he was back and appears even to have been given a promotion. The idea, therefore, that Jeantet was somehow in a separate anti-German circle at Vichy or acting as a "free agent" was a convenient fiction designed, as always, to protect the Maréchal.[30] According to Ménétrel, despite, or perhaps because of, his friendship with Jeantet, when rumors began to circulate in August 1941, rumors spread by Pucheu and Joseph-Barthélemy, Ménétrel confronted Jeantet and asked him "frankly" if Jeantet was involved in the Dormoy affair. Jeantet gave Ménétrel his "word of honour" that he was not involved and Ménétrel left it at that.[31]

On 29 January 1946 Lévy deposed Estèbe.[32] Estèbe was acquainted with the suspects in the assassination, including Deloncle and Fromes, and Lévy knew that Deloncle may have met with Estèbe in June of 1941.[33] Estèbe explained how he came to work in Pétain's civil cabinet thanks to his secretary Henri du Moulin de Labarthète, and then was forced out by January of 1942 as a result of his clashes with Pucheu and François Darlan – clashes that may have resulted from accusations that he too was enmeshed in the Dormoy affair. He then served in another ministry overseeing food supplies in Vichy until May of 1943, when he was arrested by the Gestapo for his resistance activities and deported to Germany. He claimed to know Jeantet but to have not had much contact with him. In a second statement on 12 February 1946 Estèbe again admitted conversations with Deloncle about the assassination but refuted Fromes' testimony that Deloncle had told Estèbe in Fromes' presence that Deloncle had engineered the Dormoy assassination. Lévy had no solid evidence against Estèbe beyond the testimony of Annie Mourraille, who was in flight, and that of Fromes, who was condemned to death for collaboration. Given Estèbe's clean record before the war – he had not joined the Cagoule – and his work for the Resistance, Lévy did not bring charges against him in the Dormoy affair.[34] Lévy did indict Jeantet on 6 February (see Figure 10.1), however, for his Cagoulard activities. Jeantet continued to insist on his innocence in subsequent statements.[35]

DÉNOUEMENT

It must have been galling to Lévy and Jeanne Dormoy to see the case meticulously reconstructed, despite the difficulties inherent in performing a thorough police investigation in post-war France, only to have the suspects again slip through the net. Annie Mourraille, Yves Moynier, Ludovic Guichard, and Roger Mouraille, as well as their Gestapo employer Herbert Senner, had planned well in 1943 and 1944 for the German defeat they realized was inevitable. Annie and Yves fled Paris shortly before the Liberation and appear to have made their way to Barcelona, and from there to Madrid by August 1946.[36] Guichard had worked for the Gestapo in Marseille after getting out of Largentière and thus knew his life was forfeit should he remain in France. He and his wife also headed for Spain where they, like the other Dormoy suspects, had business, familial, and political connections that dated at least to the Spanish Civil War. Lévy sent formal requests via the French ambassador asking Francisco Franco to extradite the suspects, but these were denied. According to the Spanish Foreign Ministry, in a letter dated 17 April 1947, the Spanish government could not authorize the extradition of

Figure 10.1. Gabriel Jeantet (standing) at the Cagoule trial in 1948. On his right is François Méténier, also on trial. Getty Images: Wikipedia: https://commons.wikimedia.org/wiki/File:Gabriel_Jeantet_1948.jpg. Accessed 12 December 2019.

Guichard, Moynier, or Annie Mourraille because the crimes of which they were accused were committed in the context of the "political struggles that took place in France at the time of the last world war."[37] The three had finally gotten in Spain the status of political prisoners for which they had fruitlessly petitioned the French government since their arrest in 1941. Franco, while ostensibly neutral during the war, was largely pro-Axis and not at all pleased with the prominent role of the Socialists and Communists in the post-war French government. He was disinclined, therefore, to help the French extradite collaborationists who had taken refuge in Spain.

Roger Mouraille was especially badly wanted in France, but because he had fought for Franco in the 1930s, he had a strong claim on Franco's sympathy. Mouraille still ran a business in Barcelona in 1944 and thus headed directly to that city from the Vichy Zone during the chaos of the German retreat. Even so, Roger Mouraille also posed a complicated dilemma for the Spanish because he and Jean Filliol had both worked closely with the Gestapo during the war and were wanted for serious war crimes. The pressure on Franco to turn them over to the Allies was immense.

Unlike Roger Mouraille, Jean Filliol and André Hérard followed the retreating Nazi army into Germany. Only after the German surrender, when the danger of arrest grew each day they remained within reach of the American military, did they join Roger Mouraille in Spain, from which neither of them was ever extradited. Filliol and Hérard were condemned in absentia – Filliol had already been condemned to death at least once prior to the war and was subsequently condemned for his 1944 atrocities in the Milice and his role in the massacre at Oradour-sur-Glane. Hérard received ten years of forced labor for intelligence with the enemy, a sentence he never served although his property in France was confiscated. His post-war life eventually took him to Caracas where many other former Cagoulard/MSR operatives also resided.[38]

Whereas the Spanish government would not budge on extraditing the other suspects, they did expel Roger Mouraille and sent him to Germany and into the waiting arms of the American forces. The Americans had detained Herbert Senner and used him to establish an anti-Communist Cold War spy network run out of London. It is possible the Americans hoped to recruit Mouraille. Senner may even have recommended Mouraille, who was one of his best operatives during the war. In any case, in early April 1945 Spanish police arrested Mouraille in Barcelona. In June they sent him by train to Baden-Baden, Germany, where the Americans took custody of him. On the way, he tried to leap out of the train near Bilbao and broke his right leg in the process. He was captured, however, and brought to Germany, where the Americans placed him in an internment camp in Aspberg near Ludwigsburg. Mouraille claimed that he had leaped from the train in order to commit suicide or at least to "delay my departure for France."[39] Mouraille had good reason to fear the French authorities, as on 25 July 1946 he was condemned to death in absentia for his collaboration with the Gestapo. Perhaps because Mouraille refused to work with them, the Americans handed him over to two French police officers carrying an arrest warrant from Lévy. By September he was in Paris, where Lévy interrogated him.[40]

The French police, meanwhile, continued to take statements from victims of Roger Mouraille's and Senner's extortion schemes in the Vichy Zone. By 1947 there were no less than four criminal warrants filed against Mouraille by judges in Pau, Marseille, and Montélimar.[41] And yet when it came to the Dormoy murder, it was entirely unclear whether he could be implicated in that crime. On 14 August 1947 the police prepared a lengthy summary of their renewed investigation and recommended that Annie Mourraille, Moynier, Roger Mouraille, and Guichard, as well as Marchi, be indicted for assassinating Dormoy. Just as was the situation prior to 1943, the police believed they had their strongest case against these five.[42] But in November Lévy and the public prosecutor were still unsure if the evidence was strong enough to try Roger Mouraille for Dormoy's assassination. Prior to the war's end, he had been released before the other suspects precisely because although there was solid evidence that he had aided a criminal (Moynier) after the fact, it was unclear whether he had helped organize or carry out the murder, given that most of the evidence against him was circumstantial. But it had come to Lévy's attention that after Mouraille was released in October 1942, he boasted on more than one occasion that he was an accomplice of the Dormoy assassins. Lévy was now arranging to track down and interrogate witnesses to these boasts, in hopes of bolstering the case against Mouraille.[43] All this suggests that whereas the French authorities knew they had Roger Mouraille dead to rights on the crimes he committed while in Senner's employ in 1943 and 1944, they were unsure about the evidence linking him to Dormoy's murder.

By August of 1947, therefore, the French police had concluded that neither Jeantet nor Estèbe, nor "anyone else" beyond the five suspects Chenevier had arrested in 1941, would be tried for Marx Dormoy's murder. Absent sufficient evidence (or will) to follow the trail of the murder beyond Marchi and his band of assassins, the assassination ultimately was deemed simply one of the many crimes of the Cagoule, a group the right-wing press consistently ridiculed and dismissed as amateurs before the war. Thus, when in 1948 the French government rebooted the Cagoule trial that had been suspended shortly before the outbreak of war, they attached the Dormoy case to it.[44] When he published in 1995 a book about Chenevier's career, Jean-Émile Néaumet entitled the chapter on the Dormoy assassination, "Comment la Cagoule s'est vengée de Marx Dormoy."[45] Popular French author Philippe Bourdrel, in *Les Cagoulards dans la guerre* (2009) similarly entitled the section on Dormoy: "Marx Dormoy: les temps de la vengeance."[46] Both authors, in other words, interpreted Dormoy's murder as Cagoulard vengeance.

Léon Blum was among the witnesses who testified in 1948 and André Blumel, now representing Jeanne Dormoy, focused especially on Marchi, whom Blum argued in court should be "punished severely" for his role in the Dormoy murder.[47] Jeantet was tried for his pre-war activities as a member of the Cagoule and sentenced to four years of hard labor in prison and *indignité nationale*, essentially, loss of civil and political rights as a French citizen. His indictment for participation in the Dormoy murder, however, was dropped. Moreover, Jeantet did not serve his prison sentence because he benefitted from an amnesty law passed on 16 August 1947, one of a series of such laws that began to rein in the scope of judicial reprisals against collaborators with Vichy and, over time, with the Germans.[48] Although Jeantet was unable to follow the political career he had dreamed of before the war, he had a successful career in journalism and publishing. He joined the editorial board of the publishing company *Éditions de la Table Ronde* and in 1966 he published *Pétain contre Hitler*, a justification of the wartime career of the Maréchal, whom Jeantet still revered.[49] In 1972 Jeantet joined the advisory council of Jean-Marie Le Pen's *Front national*, demonstrating that he remained faithful to his extreme-right political beliefs until his death in 1978. Despite parting ways with Deloncle in 1940, Jeantet remained loyal to the Cagoule leader, whom Jeantet described in 1974 as a brilliant strategist, on a par with Napoleon.[50]

Marchi was tried for his role in the Dormoy case but acquitted. He returned to his extensive properties in Corsica. Roger Mouraille was tried, but only as an accomplice after the fact, and received a sentence of three years in prison and indignité nationale. Within a few years he had relocated to Barcelona, where he lived for the remainder of his life. Although the court condemned Annie Mourraille, Moynier, and Guichard in absentia – yet again! – none of them were successfully extradited from either Spain or Venezuela, to which the trio emigrated a few years after arriving in Spain. Although Mourraille and Moynier had little contact with relatives in France, Annie's family believes that she and Yves remained in South America for the rest of their lives and had at least one child. The last known attempt to extradite them was in February 1950, when Blumel informed Jeanne Dormoy that Guichard had been arrested in Venezuela. Despite the best efforts of the French embassy in Caracas, however, Blumel had to admit that he held out little hope that the Venezuelans would allow Guichard to be extradited, and there is no evidence that he ever returned to France.[51]

The result of the trial was a terrible blow for Jeanne Dormoy, Blum, and Blumel, but the legal process seemed to have run its course. Once it became evident by 1950 that none of the suspected perpetrators could be extradited or arrested except Marchi and Jeantet, both of whom had Resistance credentials, it became apparent to Lévy, Gouin, and Blumel that Dormoy's killers would never be punished for his death. Most of her brother's papers were turned over to Jeanne Dormoy in 1950, along with copies of the police files related to the case, including Annie Mourraille's prison diary. Jeanne thus became the keeper of her brother's memory and began a struggle that endured until the end of her life to make sure that her brother was not forgotten. At this point, however, Jeanne had to fight alone because Léon Blum, Marx Dormoy's loyal friend and other great defender, died in March of 1950. Except for Jeanne, France had turned the page on Marx Dormoy.

FRENCH RECONCILIATION

The French Fourth Republic (1946–58) was not a propitious period to follow up on the murder of a Socialist politician of the Popular Front that took place early in the war. Too much blood had been shed and too much suffering had taken place since July 1941 to make Dormoy's murder a priority to French authorities trying to create a stable government and promote post-war reconciliation in France. French politics remained in turmoil during the Fourth Republic, with struggles between right and left and the advent of post-colonial movements in Algeria and elsewhere that threatened to tear the country apart – again. France had no fewer than twenty prime ministers between January of 1947 and the return of de Gaulle in 1958. During this period French leaders confronted the immediate necessity of putting the country on a sound financial and economic footing even while wars of emancipation engulfed their colonial empire.[52]

The dilemma that faced Robert Lévy and the French judicial system between 1945 and 1950 was much the same that the judges at Riom faced trying to hold Léon Blum and the other defendants culpable in 1942 for their actions as ministers of the French government prior to the war. When the state, or most of its ministers rather than merely one or two, is complicit in a crime, how are they all indicted without, in essence, indicting the state itself? And if the state is indicted, is not the political continuity of the nation-state destroyed, and its institutions and structures delegitimized in the process? Such a step is drastic and requires an almost complete rebuilding of the institutions of the judiciary and government, even as it obviates the possibility of national reconciliation between the supporters and opponents of the repudiated regime. The judges at Riom and Pétain himself had to concede that they could not find the Third Republic ministers guilty because, among other things, they, Pétain, and many of the people in the Vichy regime, had also been Third Republic ministers or officials. And for a regime that was attempting to assert its essential continuity with the past, delegitimizing part of that past opened the door for others to reject the legitimacy of other parts that Pétain and his ministers wanted to preserve. Just as the judges at Riom found it impossible to parse the past and at the same time hold the État français together, so too did de Gaulle and the new French government after the war find it impossible to revive and rebuild France and promote reconciliation among the French, while simultaneously insisting on the remembering and retribution that they also believed the crimes of World War II and the Occupation merited.

As the late Tony Judt, who was Erich Maria Remarque Professor of European Studies at New York University, pointed out:

> The contrast between Norway, Belgium, the Netherlands (and Denmark), where the legitimate government fled into exile, and France, where for many people the Vichy regime *was* the legitimate government, is suggestive ... In France, where wartime collaboration was widespread, it was for just that reason punished rather lightly. Since the state itself was the chief collaborator, it seemed harsh and more than a little divisive to charge lowly citizens with the same crime – the more so since three out of four of the judges at the trials of collaborators in France had themselves been employed by the collaborationist state.[53]

In a France in desperate need of reconciliation to achieve the Gaullist vision of a united nation that would never again be dominated by anyone, Germany, the United States, or Russia included, the deep internal division, the "French civil war" that had percolated in France, breaking out in sporadic violence without ever erupting into a full-scale war, had to be healed. Likewise, the trauma of the Occupation, much of it the result of "homegrown" violence French people inflicted on those whom they perceived as their ideological opponents among their fellow citizens rather than perpetrated by the Germans, had to be surmounted.[54] Dormoy was a victim not of the German Occupation but of the internal struggles tied to Vichy, and his murder was just one of many atrocities that occurred during the wartime civil conflict in France, including the 135,000 persons imprisoned, the 76,000 Jews deported, and the 650,000 laborers sent to Germany to work.[55] The needs of the future – reconciliation, unity, revival, and progress – clashed with the demands of the past for justice. The future won out, and the Dormoy case, emblematic as it was of the old civil conflicts, was closed, and that meant that Marx Dormoy's memory, like the memory of so many other Vichy atrocities, had to be allowed to fade.

CONCLUSION
Today: The Legacy of Marx Dormoy

While Jeanne Dormoy and her friends and allies proved unable to force the post-war judicial system to bring Marx Dormoy's killers to justice, they did manage to spearhead an initiative that enshrined his memory in stone in what they hoped would be a permanent marker commemorating his life and death. Unveiled on 26 July 1948, a statue was placed in a public garden in the center of Montluçon at the head of the newly named Avenue Marx Dormoy, a symbolic victory since during the war the same avenue was named for Maréchal Philippe Pétain. As the self-appointed guardian of her brother's memory, Jeanne Dormoy wanted to remind people not only of her brother's contribution to local and national politics but also of his violent death (see Figure 11.1). She hoped to focus public consciousness on the crime so that people would not forget why he died, by shaping the cultural landscape of Montluçon around the events tied to her brother's murder. The statue, however, brought Jeanne Dormoy even more frustrations because economic interests and local politics eventually led to its transfer to a less prominent location in the city center, subsuming the statue in post-war amnesia of the crime thus making the victim's memory easier to forget. It was moved again twice after her death, mirroring in many ways the shifts in post-war memory of the Vichy regime. Exploration of the fundamental issues tied to the statue's movement helps to explain in part why Marx Dormoy remains today a neglected figure in the history of France during World War II.

The day of the statue's dedication must have been a time of both sorrow and exaltation for Jeanne Dormoy, a painful acknowledgment of her brother's death

Figure 11.1. Jeanne Dormoy. AD Allier, 64/J/136, "Fonds Marx Dormoy: Photographies et autres documents figures."

and yet a fitting glorification of his life and accomplishments (see Figure 11.2). In 1947 her brother had been posthumously inducted into the "Order of the Nation," in recognition of his exceptional devotion to France. Later that year he was awarded the Resistance Medal for his extraordinary acts of courage during the war. The French state thus recognized Dormoy as a resister before the Resistance. At the statue's unveiling in 1948 on the anniversary of his assassination, the whole day was devoted to the glorification of the memory of Marx Dormoy, beginning with a ceremony at his gravesite followed by a reception at the Hôtel de Ville in his former office where the current mayor, Lucien Menut, gave his eulogy. Dignitaries from Paris were in attendance along

Figure 11.2. Statue of Marx Dormoy in its original 1948 placement. "Photos *La Montagne.*"

with his closest friends, including Léon Blum, who reminded the crowds that it was Dormoy who had saved the nation by uncovering the Cagoulard plot to overthrow France in 1937. Blum stated, "To protect itself, the Republic does not need weapons or laws. She is guarded by the people."[1] For Blum, Marx Dormoy represented the ideal patriotic guardian of the legacy of the French Revolution, the man who understood the threat of authoritarian government and faced down the collaborationists who sold France out to the Nazis. He had paid the highest price for standing up for the Republic and workers.

For some people in post-war Montluçon, however, the statue of Dormoy was troubling. In 1946 a monument committee charged with choosing the design had been formed, and the next year Mayor Menut and his municipal council voted to commission a statue paid for with communal contributions.[2] Léon Blum and Jeanne Dormoy took command of the statue's creation, and their choice puzzled many, including members of the monument committee and potentially even the artist who sculpted it.[3] Blum and Dormoy selected Hubert Yencesse to create the monument. The son of Ovide Yencesse, a well-known sculptor, Hubert had already received the "Prix Blumental" for his work in 1934. In 1950 he secured a professorial post at the École des Beaux Arts in Paris, a position he held until 1970.[4] Blum and Dormoy dictated to Yencesse their vision of the statue, a *gisant* or recumbent figure lying on his side covered in a sheet, with one hand over his breast and the other raised and pointing skyward.[5] Blum later articulated that he wanted to capture the moment where Dormoy went from sleeping to consciousness to death just as he was launched from his bed by the bomb that killed him.[6] The sheet hides Dormoy's nakedness, so visible and humiliating in the crime scene photos, and also functions as a shroud, articulating grief. For Jeanne Dormoy the gisant was conceived as a perpetual reminder of the assassination of her brother that the inhabitants of Montluçon would pass on a daily basis. The uplifted hand was to be a visual reminder that his killers had not been brought to justice.[7] The finished statue did not entirely fulfill this vision, however, as Dormoy's right hand rested on his side rather than pointing upward, detracting from the didactic meaning that Jeanne and Blum had intended. Once the trial of the Cagoule fizzled out in 1948 with no convictions for Dormoy's murder, Jeanne may well have feared that the monument in the center of Montluçon was the only thing preventing the memory of his murder from descending into obscurity.

Right from the start, however, the statue caused controversy as many were puzzled by the less than dignified portrayal of Dormoy in his bed. Other observers questioned why the gisant was in the middle of an avenue given that recumbent sculptures usually operate as tomb effigies with backdrops. While this kind of sculpture may have been appropriate to emphasize the history of the fallen martyr, its placement in the center of town left the largely blank back side of the sculpture exposed. It also suggested that in some way the whole town was a mortuary monument for Marx Dormoy. In fact, as one descended the train station and looked up the avenue to the city's chateau, the prominent sight clearly in view was the obverse of the sculpture that revealed the strange sight of rumpled sheets on a concrete block. In 1960 M. Jourdain of the Monument Committee explained that even Yencesse had been embarrassed by the site chosen for the sculpture, but he had felt his hands were tied given the directives of Blum and Jeanne Dormoy.[8]

By the 1960s Montluçon was enjoying a post-war building boom that eventually led to the construction of a medical pavilion, a technology institute, the city's first shopping center, and numerous high-rise apartment structures including ones in the renovated section of town where Marx Dormoy had grown up, the "Ville Gozet." Envisioned in this municipal redesign was also the extension of the Avenue Marx Dormoy to the base of the Chateau des Ducs de Bourbon, the central historic monument in the town. In order to increase tourism, the city magistrates also wanted to destroy some older buildings that obscured the vista of the chateau from the train station. To help finance the improvements, the city negotiated a contract with Standard Oil in which the company agreed to pay for the demolition of the buildings and the moving and cleaning of the Dormoy statue in order to lease the site where the statue originally stood at the head of the avenue and construct a service station and car wash in its place. The Dormoy gisant was to be moved to a site only about a hundred meters away where the reverse of the sculpture would back up to the wall of the chateau.[9] On 7 January 1963 the mayor of Montluçon, Jean Nègre, and the municipal council voted almost unanimously to transfer Dormoy's statue to the base of the chateau and proceed with the Standard Oil project.[10]

Predictably Jeanne Dormoy was incensed, and between 1961 and 1968 she attempted to thwart the action by launching a series of lawsuits against the town of Montluçon that she largely fought alone since Léon Blum had died. She insisted that the statue's movement would result in "irreparable damage" and was appalled that Jean Nègre, a Socialist mayor, was privileging capitalism by negotiating with Standard Oil, an action she was convinced Marx would have despised, and one that proved Nègre had forgotten the common workers he claimed to represent.[11] At the Administrative Tribunal of Clermont-Ferrand, she requested a stay of execution against the municipal deliberations of 7 January 1963, and argued that the original 1948 resolution had included the statement that Dormoy's statue would stay in place "definitively and perpetually."

The municipal leaders had nevertheless taken the movement of the statue very seriously. After Standard Oil approached the city in 1960 with the tempting offer, Nègre asked Pierre Pradel, the chief conservator of sculpture at the Louvre Museum to give his assessment. Pradel's evaluation was important not only as an expert but also as a friend of the late victim. The conservator applauded the move and contended that the view of the statue would be more aesthetically pleasing in the welcoming atmosphere of the chateau's façade, which provided a needed backdrop of greenery and rough stone for the gisant. Pradel also indicated Yencesse's own frustration with the original site and declared that he believed the sculptor himself would have preferred the more tranquil locale of the projected spot as opposed to the original one closer to a busy street with all its traffic.[12] The municipality also referred the matter in 1963 to the commission overseeing historic sites in the department of the Allier. The commission acknowledged that in the present location, the reverse of the statue was exposed, a problem that placing it against the chateau would solve. "This new arrangement will thus enhance the work of the sculptor," the commission concluded.[13] In the first court case in 1963 the city officials emphasized that the current location of the statue in the public garden had always been viewed as temporary until the extension of the public walkway to the base of the chateau was complete precisely because they realized that the exposed back of the statue was unappealing.[14]

Jeanne Dormoy's attempt to block the movement of the statue in 1963 and her subsequent legal pursuits to have it returned to the original site in 1968 were both decided against her, and she was forced to pay all court costs, a blow that must have made her feel the city had turned against Marx. Standard Oil did erect its filling station catering to the post-war economy and the steep rise in automobile ownership. The court's decisions indicated that Jeanne Dormoy's argument that the original site of the gisant was meant to be "definitive and perpetual" was unfounded and never a request of the original Monument Committee in 1947. In addition, the court found in 1963 that no municipality ever has the right to cede public land in perpetuity, and thus the case had no merit. The lawyers defending Montluçon argued that Jeanne Dormoy failed to show any "irreparable consequences" of moving the statute, especially given that the transfer location was only 100 meters away from the original site, and the statue's value was symbolic and thus not damaged by the move. The statue was transferred to the base of the chateau in 1964. Jeanne Dormoy's boycott of its rededication ceremony expressed both her fury and defeat.[15]

It was Marx Dormoy's memory, after all, and especially the remembrance of his terrible demise, that Jeanne fought to protect in the court filings, and she viewed his statue's displacement as a moral disregard of the sacrifice her brother had made for France and a murder of his memory.[16] Replacing his statue with a gas station represented an additional insult. No longer the central figure of the grand avenue, Dormoy's statue now blended into the background of the chateau and was easier to overlook. Moreover, the new placement associated his memory in the minds of tourists with the Renaissance history of the city instead of with his role as a key political figure in the pre-war and wartime periods. The transference thus reflected a larger ideological discussion about how France's role in World War II would be remembered and how the aftermath of war privileged some narratives over others. Dormoy's statue was displaced during the very period in French post-war history in which Charles de Gaulle favored a collective memory that portrayed France as a nation of resisters. Dormoy's murder by right-wing extremists devoted to Pétain and Nazi collaboration was at odds with a national memory that minimized French devotion to Vichy and assimilated Resistance into the nation as a whole. The "irreparable damages" that Jeanne Dormoy alleged resulted not just from the neglect of her brother's individual victimhood but also from the failure of the nation to acknowledge its amorality and wartime crimes during World War II, a self-imposed "amnesia." Her lawsuits revealed that she rejected the idea of a common identity for France, especially one that elided the memory of her brother and the reasons he was assassinated. Jeanne Dormoy died in 1975 but without doubt she would have been equally troubled in 1994 when the statue was shifted again further down the alley along the chateau's base to make room for a public stairwell leading up to the edifice, a transfer that hid the monument even more and imposed an effective erasure by making it quasi-invisible, a site of forgotten memory or even non-memory.[17] Largely obscured from public view, it became fair game for vandals who delighted in breaking off Dormoy's fingers, hands or feet, adding replacement costs to the city's budget. Oddly, each new hand was positioned differently from its predecessor.[18]

Marx Dormoy was not totally forgotten in the post-war period. The traffic circle in front of the Relais de l'Empereur in Montélimar where he was assassinated was named the Place Marx Dormoy and a stele was positioned in front of the now-shuttered hotel (see Figure 11.3). The Relais closed in 2011 and then became a haven for squatters. On 24 July 2017 a fire swept through the abandoned building destroying the room where Dormoy was assassinated as well as the roof. Although a local citizens group has established a petition to save the historic hotel, the Relais may soon succumb to the wrecking ball, leaving the future of the stele precarious as well. In addition to Montélimar, towns throughout the Allier also honored Dormoy in the post-war period with street names, including Montluçon, Bellerive-sur-Allier, Cérilly, Commentry, Doulins, Domérat, Montmarault, Néris-les-Bains, Saint-Gérand-le-Puy, and Vallon-en-Sully. Dormoy's name was rendered prominently on the Parisian urban landscape via the metro stop named in his honor and located in an immigrant neighborhood in the 18th arrondissement of Paris near the northern outskirts of the city. In 1984 the French postal system also issued a stamp featuring Dormoy's image.[19] Thus his memory lingers, but given how little has been published about Dormoy it is questionable whether many who use the metro stop bearing his name know who he was or why he died.

Moreover, in the post-war period what has been most remembered about Marx Dormoy is his terrible death, although even that is often told in incomplete or fantastic accounts (and many people incorrectly assume his name was "Max" rather than "Marx"). On the stele in front of the Relais, "trois hommes" are noted as his murderers with no reference to Annie Mourraille. Historian Philippe Bourdrel's

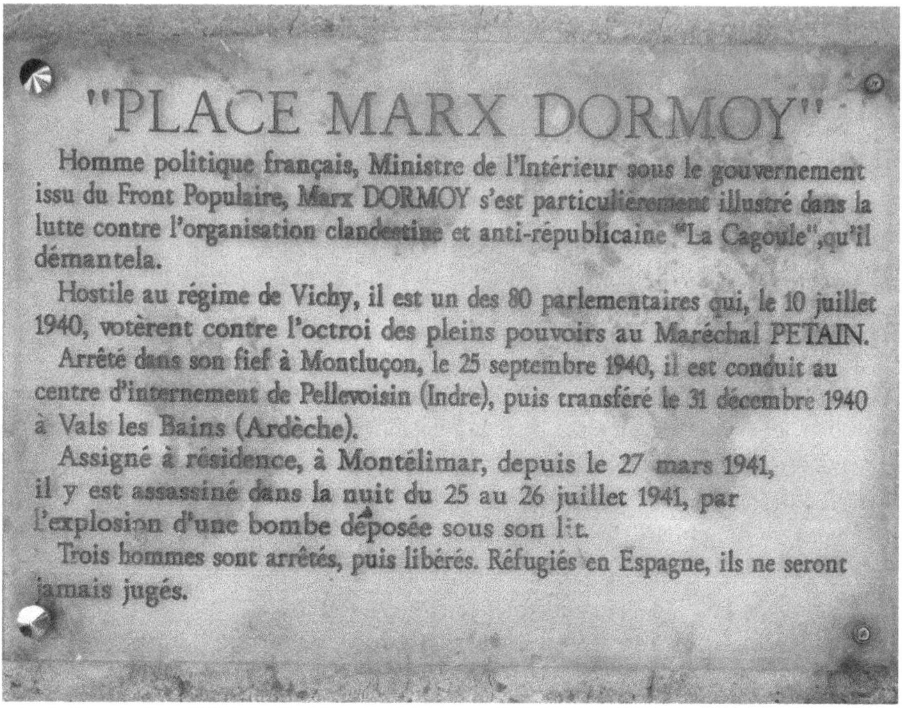

> **"PLACE MARX DORMOY"**
> Homme politique français, Ministre de l'Intérieur sous le gouvernement issu du Front Populaire, Marx DORMOY s'est particulièrement illustré dans la lutte contre l'organisation clandestine et anti-républicaine "La Cagoule",qu'il démantela.
> Hostile au régime de Vichy, il est un des 80 parlementaires qui, le 10 juillet 1940, votèrent contre l'octroi des pleins pouvoirs au Maréchal PETAIN.
> Arrêté dans son fief à Montluçon, le 25 septembre 1940, il est conduit au centre d'internement de Pellevoisin (Indre), puis transféré le 31 décembre 1940 à Vals les Bains (Ardèche).
> Assigné à résidence, à Montélimar, depuis le 27 mars 1941, il y est assassiné dans la nuit du 25 au 26 juillet 1941, par l'explosion d'une bombe déposée sous son lit.
> Trois hommes sont arrêtés, puis libérés. Réfugiés en Espagne, ils ne seront jamais jugés.

Figure 11.3. Stele commemorating Marx Dormoy, Place Marx Dormoy, Montélimar. Photograph by authors.

account of Dormoy's murder portrays Annie as a seductress who successfully lured Dormoy into her own bed before planting the bomb in his. Jeanne Dormoy took issue with Bourdrel's scenario and demanded a retraction. She found the story to be both scandalous and based on a pure fantasy on Mourraille's part that Bourdrel seemed to have swallowed with relish. Jeanne was residing at the hotel when her brother was assassinated and fully aware that he was suspicious of the woman he considered a dangerous threat; he certainly was not sleeping with her. Moreover, Bourdrel's version also makes Dormoy appear either foolish or extremely reckless given the dangerous position he was in at the Relais in 1941. Despite Jeanne's vehement objections, Bourdrel refused to change his version, and Dormoy's reputation has been tarnished as a result. Bourdrel's account is probably the best known to date and represents not so much a forgetting of Dormoy as a redirection of memory, one focused on titillating sexual fantasy as opposed to a courageous fight against fascism. Dormoy's sacrifice is diminished in the process, and Jeanne wrote and told Bourdrel as much.[20]

Marx Dormoy's death traumatized Jeanne Dormoy, especially as she was physically so close to him, just down the hall in the Relais when the bomb went off, making her a witness of sorts. Writing to a friend just after the assassination, Léon Blum mentioned how Dormoy's murder had wounded him, but had nearly destroyed Jeanne. He wrote, "She only had him in the world; she lived only for him. All that remains are her work and her house, the house where they resided together."[21] For Jeanne, the trauma of her brother's death became the obsession of her post-war life as she fought for the survival of her brother's memory and to remind people what had happened. Jeanne saw far too clearly that her brother's legacy was fading, and moving the statue away from the central boulevard was just one more way of forgetting not only him but the cause for which he had fought.[22] Dormoy was a first resister, a martyr for the French Republic who rejected Pétain in 1940, but few remembered him that way; few remember him at all. In the end, even Jeanne vanished, choosing to be buried in her brother's grave with no marker indicating her presence there, opting for anonymity in deference to her brother just as she had done while he was alive. She died in 1975, worn out from fighting for his memory and bitter that it had been dismissed.

History and memory are mutually dependent, however, and the statue's peregrinations were not yet at an end in 1994. If Dormoy's memory had become largely absent, the political narrative of the 1990s forced it back into public discourse. Acknowledgment of the conflicted nature of France's devotion to Vichy and Pétain along with the crimes associated with that regime grew after the publication in 1972 of Robert O. Paxton's *Vichy France: Old Guard and New Order, 1940–1944*. The trials of Vichy henchmen Maurice Papon in 1989 and Paul Touvier in 1998 focused even more attention on French collaboration with the Nazis and participation in the persecution of Jews.[23] Jacques Chirac's public admission in 1995 that the État français under Pétain had collaborated with the Germans in the Holocaust also opened narrative pathways to grapple with other Vichy crimes. By the early 2000s the time was right to honor the "*quatre-vingts*," those 80 legislators out of 569 who voted against giving Pétain dictatorial powers in 1940, among them Marx Dormoy. In 2001 a center-right candidate won the election for mayor in Montluçon, Daniel Dugléry. In an attempt to solidify an alliance with the Socialists in opposition to the Communists, Dugléry decided to reactivate the memory of Marx Dormoy by moving his statue back to the central plaza where it had originally been placed in 1948. The completed transfer was celebrated on 14 July 2005, Bastille Day, the national holiday when France fetes its Revolution. Every 26 July, the anniversary of his assassination, Dormoy is honored in Montluçon with a public commemoration of his life.[24] Dugléry contends that the meaning behind the memory of the man and the statue is just as important today as it was in 1948 because of the growing power of the extreme right in France, led at present by Marine Le Pen.[25] Marx Dormoy's statue thus still serves a political purpose, warning us about ignoring the danger of the resurgence of the extreme right so apparent today in France and in the world.

WHO DID IT, AND WHY?

The story of Marx Dormoy's assassination is at the same time straightforward and complex. On one level those who investigated the crime – Charles Chenevier, Georges Kubler, Jean Marion, Robert Lévy, Georges Richier, all acting in their official capacity for the French government during or after the war, as well as historians such as Georges Rougeron and Philippe Bourdrel, not to mention most journalists – were correct in their assertion that a reconstituted Cagoule ensconced in Vichy was responsible for Dormoy's death. There were rumors that Jacques Doriot and his PPF were behind the crime, but Chenevier and those who investigated the murder never substantiated that version and dismissed it.[26] Thus on 11 December 1945, the headline of the Socialist newspaper, *Le Populaire*, stated, "Transfer of the ashes of Marx Dormoy Socialist and resister assassinated by the Cagoule with the complicity of Vichy."[27] A 27 July 1941 article in *The New York Times* had contended much the same thing, and one witness interviewed in the article stated that Dormoy had predicted that Vichy would have him murdered and stated that "if any accident happens to me [Dormoy], you will know who is responsible."[28]

Most of the assassins were officially members of the Cagoule in the 1930s; they circulated in the milieu of the extreme right in Marseille and they all joined the militant organizations that in 1940 evolved from the Cagoule. The two men who most likely organized and financed the Dormoy affair, Gabriel Jeantet and Eugène Deloncle, created and led the Cagoule before the war. Although the one was a member of Pétain's entourage in Vichy whereas the other was a collaborationist ensconced in Paris, and the Line of Demarcation, personal animosities, and old and new rivalries stood between them, they could and did use intermediaries such as Antoine Marchi and André Hérard to bridge that gap sufficiently to orchestrate the murder. We know that Marchi was tied to Jeantet and recruited the assassins and that Jeantet may have been linked to Estèbe. Hérard worked for both Deloncle and Filliol and had strong ties to Marseille. Witnesses placed both Marchi and Hérard at the scene of the crime in Montélimar in the company of the assassins. Jeantet's and Deloncle's motivation dated back to the Cagoule. The evidence strongly suggests to us, as it did to Chenevier, that Jeantet and Deloncle plotted Dormoy's murder. Their desire to avenge themselves against the man who had exposed their organization in 1937 played a central role in their determination to eliminate Dormoy. For Jeantet and Deloncle, the French civil war of the 1930s was still raging in 1941 and old scores needed to be settled.

But assassinating a former interior minister of France, one who was interned under the protection of Pétain himself, and carrying out the murder in such a brutal and public fashion was an extremely dangerous operation. Deloncle was a risk-taker, but Jeantet was by all accounts a bold but very careful and calculating man. Jeantet paid a high political price for Dormoy's murder, which due to its spectacular and scandalous nature received unwelcome publicity in the European and American press. Immediately after Dormoy's murder Pétain was aware that members of his cabinet suspected Jeantet was involved. Thus, he dissolved the Amicale and forced Jeantet into a lower-profile position. Deloncle too, while less vulnerable than Jeantet, must have known that his German patrons, who fully expected to see the Third Republic and its ministers condemned in the upcoming trial at Riom, would not have approved of an unauthorized murder of such a prominent person as Dormoy, let alone the string of ensuing assassinations that Dormoy's killers maintained had been part of the recompense they expected for arranging his demise. It is likely that the erosion of Deloncle's reputation in the eyes of the Germans in 1941 began with Dormoy's murder, in which they must have known that he was involved. Why then take such a risk? Can vengeance against their pre-war opponent alone explain Jeantet's and Deloncle's actions here? Or is it possible that much more was at stake?

Annie Mourraille repeatedly asserted, not only in testimony to Chenevier but also in at least one private missive to her mother, that one of the things she and her friends hoped to achieve by eliminating Dormoy was to bring about a "change of government" that would force Pétain to replace François Darlan with Pierre Laval as his chief minister, which Pétain did do, albeit not immediately, so great was his dislike of Laval. And Dormoy had hidden many of the papers he had taken from Paris in June of 1940 and sent to the Allier with his chauffeur. These papers, many of them related to the Clichy affair and his investigation of the Cagoule, eventually ended up in the Archives Nationales, where at least some of them remain today, as Jeanne Dormoy informed a researcher in 1973.[29] The most compromising documents, about a hundred of them, he kept with him all the way to Montélimar where, as we have seen, the police confiscated them after his death. Although they were unsealed in 1942, they were resealed and when Dormoy's papers were finally turned over to Jeanne in 1950, these compromising documents had disappeared, never to resurface.

But whom did they compromise? It is well known that Pétain sympathized with the Cagoule and met with Deloncle's representatives on more than one occasion in 1936–37 even though he does not appear to have formally joined the organization as did the less cautious General Édouard Duseigneur and certain other military officers.[30] Still in 1937 and 1938 Dormoy publicly denounced both Pétain and General Maxime Weygand for their ties to the Cagoule.[31] Even today in the Archives de Paris, the documents related to the investigation of the Cagoule and of Dormoy's murder are mixed in with many documents deriving from the investigation and trial of Pétain. After the war, investigators working for de Gaulle's government, such as Georges Richier and many people among the general public, simply assumed that Pétain had been linked to the Cagoule. The Maréchal certainly drew upon a significant number of ex-Cagoulards to staff his cabinet and government at Vichy after the Armistice, including Jeantet, Raphaël Alibert, Xavier Vallat, François Méténier, and Colonel Georges Groussard, among others. It is also likely that Jeantet and possibly Paul Estèbe, devoted as they were to the ideals of the État français and the person of the Maréchal, feared that Dormoy, if called upon to testify at Riom, would expose the close ties between the Cagoule and the Maréchal and many in his government. But was Pétain the only person with something to fear from Dormoy and the history of the Cagoule?

A draft letter Marx Dormoy wrote while he was still imprisoned at Pellevoisin, most likely during the winter of 1940–1, although the draft is undated, suggests that Laval also needed to be worried, possibly very worried, about what Dormoy might say at the Riom trial. In the letter Dormoy reminded Laval that as interior minister and during a delicate and dangerous investigation Dormoy had directed prior to the war, he had obliged Laval by not making public compromising information about Laval's involvement in the affair. He reproached Laval for the latter's ingratitude, reminding Laval that "despite their divergences" in political views had he been in Laval's place, he "would never have acted against you as you have done toward me." In particular he would have warned Laval had he known that "an arrest was imminent."[32] It is important to remember that Laval was for a time a Socialist, the two men had known each other for many years and, Dormoy was suggesting, they had enjoyed a cordial relationship even as their political views diverged during the 1930s. As he pointed out in his letter, Dormoy was well aware that Laval nursed a grudge against the Popular Front and the Socialists for evincing him from power in 1936. But he also noted that when a Senate inquiry had been opened regarding Laval's actions, without demanding any "explanations" from Laval, Dormoy quashed the Senate's probe and ensured that Laval was not implicated in the investigation Dormoy was carrying out at the same time. As interior minister, Dormoy oversaw numerous investigations, but his letter does not indicate to which he was referring. Given that Laval's politics by 1936 had drifted further to the right, and that during the war Laval was tied politically to former Cagoulards such as Deloncle, as well as to the Germans, in addition to which it had been rumored prior to and during the war that Laval had also been a supporter of the Cagoule, it is possible that Laval had at least as much to fear from Dormoy's testimony at Riom as Pétain.

It is also important to recall that it was Laval, not Pétain, who ultimately intervened with the Germans to obtain the release of the assassins. Thus it is possible and perhaps even likely that Deloncle was acting on behalf of Laval when he helped fund and organize Dormoy's murder, especially because in the summer of 1941 Deloncle was still part of the RNP that Laval had created and may have been hoping that if Laval returned to power in Vichy, Deloncle would finally obtain the cabinet post that he had coveted but never received from Pétain in 1940. By August the "bloom was off the rose," perhaps because Deloncle had realized that Dormoy's murder in July would not suffice to bring Laval to power immediately, and that Laval was working with his rivals Déat and Doriot to squeeze Deloncle out of the RNP while stealing his MSR recruits. Hence Deloncle organized Paul Collette's assassination attempt that put Laval in the hospital and poisoned any remaining entente between them. That fall Laval returned to the Vichy Zone and began courting Pétain again, and Deloncle during the same period saw his credit with the Germans and within the MSR steadily erode, no doubt in part due to Laval. But it is quite likely that in July of 1941, both Deloncle and Laval had good reason to want Dormoy silenced forever.

THE LEGACY OF MARX DORMOY

If Marx Dormoy died before he could defend the French Republic in the courtroom at Riom, what then was the significance of his life, and of his death? On 12 January 1938 the leaders of the Socialist Party meeting at their Congress in

Marseille saluted Dormoy, one of their "most devoted and active members," for his courageous work as interior minister in opposing the infiltration of France by fascist ideology and agents of Mussolini and Hitler. In particular they applauded him for "unmasking instigators of civil war, conspiracies and violent attacks" against democracy and France.[33] Despite the ridicule that the conservative press and politicians heaped upon Dormoy in 1938 regarding the "phantasm" of the Cagoule and the danger it posed to the Third Republic, neither Dormoy nor Blum was ever in any doubt regarding the determination of agents of fascism and Nazism outside France or proto-fascists within the country to incite civil war, overturn the democratic order, and replace it with an authoritarian government. Dormoy knew what was at stake in France, and Europe, in the fraught years leading up to the outbreak of World War II and reminded his fellow Socialists of this in speeches and in the press.

Historians, moreover, have noted that after 1937 violence in France declined until the outbreak of World War II. These scholars offer multiple explanations for the reduction in street violence, chief among them the dissolution of the right-wing leagues in 1936.[34] None have recognized that the relative quiet was also the result of Dormoy's clampdown on the Cagoule in 1937 after their failed coup attempt in November. Dormoy arrested numerous Cagoulard leaders, including Deloncle, and forced others into exile in Italy and Spain. By 1938 there were simply fewer free Cagoulards in France to act as terrorists, murderers, and *provocateurs*. Perhaps even more important, and possibly Dormoy's greatest contribution to French political stability, was that the arrests of the Cagoulards permitted the police to confiscate the huge arsenals the Cagoule had hidden in all the major cities of France, including one in every arrondissement of Paris. To foment further violence the Cagoulards would have had to rebuild their weapons depots, which would have taken time and money. It is true that they had large stockpiles of arms hidden just across the border, in Spain, but whereas Franco was willing to offer sanctuary to the fugitive Cagoulards and their weapons alike, he was not willing to permit them to repatriate the arms. For more than a year, while Aristide Corre, Gabriel Jeantet, Jean Filliol, and other Cagoulards cooled their heels in Spain, and despite their best efforts to persuade their Spanish minders otherwise, the arms stayed put. There are two likely reasons for Franco's reticence. First, in 1938 Franco was bringing to a successful close the war that brought him to power and, after his victory in April 1939, attempting to stabilize Spain and mop up the resistance to his rule. It was not in his interest to become embroiled in additional friction with the French government. Second, Franco and Pétain had been on good terms since the 1920s, and in 1939 Pétain was appointed French ambassador to Spain. His star was ascending in France, and with the Popular Front no longer in power, Pétain too had little incentive to allow the Cagoule to create instability or disrupt France's preparations for war with Germany. Given the persistent rumors linking him to the Cagoule, Pétain could not afford to let the Cagoulards off their leash in a period when France was frantically trying to build national unity.

Eugene Deloncle also had a vision of the stakes for France and the world of the struggle against Communism and socialism in which his Cagoulard and MSR operatives were enmeshed before and during World War II. On 1 July 1937 precisely one year to the day after the founding of the Cagoule, and during its general meeting at the Chateau of Nandy, Deloncle ordered that the "N" of the organization's official acronym (OSARN – *Organisation secrète d'action révolutionnaire nationale*) be removed. As Deloncle proclaimed before calling for a champagne toast, "Our vocation from this point forward will be international."[35] Deloncle knew that the struggle between the right and the left in Europe had begun long before the outbreak of World War II. By 1943 he also expected that the battle against international Communism he had waged for much of his adult life would go on long after the war's end. He also knew that the United States and Britain, although battling the Nazis, were also deeply anti-Communist. Deloncle's overtures to the Americans in 1943 that cost him his life resulted from his understanding that once the Nazis were defeated, the "Anglo-Saxons" would resume their pre-war struggle against the left everywhere in the world. Neither the MSR nor the post-war trajectory of its surviving members can be understood without taking into account their self-perception as participants in a worldwide struggle. After the war most of those who participated in Dormoy's assassination ended up in South America under the protection of Franco and the firmly anti-Communist dictator of Venezuela, General Marcos Perez Jimenez. Some of them – Roger Mouraille, Raymond Hérard (M. André), Ludovic Guichard – joined Cold War spy networks run by the United States, Britain, or France. In this respect, and despite their deeply opposing ideologies, Dormoy and Deloncle shared an understanding of the meaning and potential consequences of the political conflict wracking France in the 1930s. And one reason Dormoy had to be eliminated was precisely his determined opposition to the rightist authoritarianism that the anti-Communists like Deloncle seemed to believe was the only viable antidote to the spread of Communism.

In the twenty-first century, in an era that is witnessing the resurgence of anti-democratic political movements in Europe, the United States, and elsewhere in the world, some of which have managed to gain political power – Russia, Turkey, Poland, Hungary, Venezuela, Brazil, and even Italy – it is important to remember Dormoy and his battle against the Cagoule. Journalists in the 1930s and 1940s and post-war scholars have often belittled the Cagoule because it remained a small organization, primarily underground, often fractious, and at times amateurish in the "direct actions" it carried out. In recent years scholars such as Joel Blatt, D.L.L. Parry, and Chris Millington have challenged the narrative of the weak and insignificant Cagoule, and our own research has been at the forefront of this reassessment of the organization and its MSR incarnation. Millington argues that the construction of this simplistic image reflects the Cagoulards' status as "home grown" terrorists and not foreign threats. He states, "In the public understanding of terrorism established during the 1930s, terrorism as the foreign 'Other' could not be committed by Frenchmen in the name of French values."[36] As such, the Cagoule/MSR were dismissed as "play actors" or the "gang that couldn't shoot straight."[37] Moreover, Eugène Deloncle failed to achieve the political power he so avidly sought, and the Third Republic tottered on until 1940, when the rump French parliament voted to eliminate it and grant power to Pétain's autocratic regime. In the eyes of many, then and now, the Cagoulards had failed to achieve their goals. This discourse allowed authorities to deny the existence of "domestic" French terrorists even as it became increasingly apparent in the final years of the decade that French citizens sharing an extreme right ideology were indeed plotting and carrying out violence on French soil.

But Dormoy realized that the Cagoule/MSR did not have to achieve a coup d'état to alter the political discourse in France or infiltrate the armed forces already staffed by conspirators. Extremists do not have to win elections or bring down governments to shift the political center to the right or the left, undermine faith in the integrity of the political process, and destabilize the government even in a venerable democracy like France. Terrorists are effective simply by communicating with the public via their violent, destructive acts that invariably sway political decisions and political agendas.[38] Fragile democracies, such as those of Spain in the 1930s or Poland today, are only that much more vulnerable to the pressure proto-fascist groups can exert. In the 1930s Dormoy understood that in a France struggling to recover from the Great Depression, seeking political unity in a badly and ideologically divided nation, and preparing for the coming war that all but the most convinced pacifists knew was inevitable, the Cagoule could achieve at least part of its goals simply by inhibiting the government from carrying out its mandate to govern.

Once Pétain was in power, it was the reconstituted Cagoule/MSR around him that vigorously promoted the National Revolution. In the post-war period many recognized the direct links that connected Pétain and the Cagoule. In 1946 Charles Serre authored an official report to the National Assembly on the causes of France's defeat in 1940. He concluded that "in France, some wanted to prevent the normal functioning of democracy in our country ... These men who had stood against the Republic gathered around Pétain to realize their antiparliamentarian projects at the defeat."[39] Dormoy perhaps summed up the Cagoule best himself when he stated in 1938, "To the many qualities already enumerated of the Cagoule and their proteges in the right wing press we can add high treason." In the end the Cagoulards and their supporters solicited the aid of foreign powers hostile to France in order to overthrow their own legally elected government. As Dormoy baldly stated, that constituted treason.[40]

Dormoy was largely forgotten by 1950 because France needed to recover from the trauma of the war and construct a consensus about French identity that required a selective amnesia about the troubled 1930s and the war years. The very existence of a French "civil war" needed to be evinced from historical memory in order to avoid the same conflicts that rent France before the war from breaking out again once peace in Europe had been restored. Most historians in the post-war period downplayed the impact of the far-right in the 1930s and 1940s and blithely interpreted the Cagoule/MSR as clumsy amateurs.[41] Yet those "amateurs" in Paris and around Pétain in Vichy succeeded in assassinating a prominent and heroic French politician and getting away with it. The Cold War likewise required a similar amnesia regarding the sins of the right as Western governments focused obsessively on those of the left for several decades after 1945. The price of that amnesia, however, was steep, because in 2020 a resurgence of the same extreme right discourses is underway – nationalist, anti-democratic, antisemitic, anti-immigrant, nativist, glorifying violent patriotism – that characterized proto-fascist, fascist, and Nazi discourse prior to the war.[42]

Former Popular Front minister Pierre Cot, when eulogizing Dormoy in *The Nation* on 9 August 1941, stated that Dormoy "was murdered not for vengeance alone; he was murdered because fascists feared him."[43] Other friends of Dormoy asserted much the same thing.[44] What Dormoy's enemies feared about him was less the power he wielded as interior minister to arrest them – many Cagoulards escaped the police in 1937, and by 1940 most of those Dormoy put behind bars were out of prison anyway – but that he *saw* them for what they were and, in exposing them, forced France to see the danger as well. With an Allied victory, had Dormoy survived the war, he would have pursued the Cagoulards just as relentlessly as he had in 1937, and they were well aware of this.

On 11 November 2018 *The New York Times Magazine* published an article entitled "State of Denial: How the Federal Government, Intelligence Agencies and Law Enforcement Have Systematically Failed to Recognize the Threat of White Nationalism."[45] The author, journalist Janet Reitman, contends that even though "white supremacists and other far-right extremists have killed far more people since Sept. 11, 2001, than any other category of domestic extremist," law enforcement agencies in the United States have largely ignored the extreme right even as they have focused on the extreme left.[46] Dormoy's legacy is that he did not look away, from the threat of the extreme right in France and from the rise of fascism and Nazism abroad, and the danger both posed to democracy in France. Both the Cagoule and the MSR were home-grown French organizations committed to using terror to enact an authoritarian "National Revolution" in France and they were also deeply embedded in a network of international right-wing terrorism that commenced years before World War II. As this study has shown, the founders of the Cagoule and the MSR received logistical and financial support from Franco, Mussolini, and Hitler. Cagoulard and MSR terrorists purchased their arms with Italian money from arms dealers based in Belgium, Germany, and Italy, and hid many of these weapons in Spain, with Franco's approval. Despite the ultra-nationalistic rhetoric of the Cagoule, in reality they were entrenched in an international network in which states sponsored terror abroad to undermine liberal democracies from within. As a defender of democracy, Dormoy set an example that twenty-first-century people would do well to follow in confronting the resurgence of right-wing terrorism that constitutes a renewed cultural swerve toward autocracy in our era. For Dormoy was assassinated by more than just the Cagoule/MSR, the far-right terrorists who planted the bomb that took his life. In 1941, he was murdered by the whole collaborationist establishment, Pétain included, who in that moment turned toward Hitler as opposed to de Gaulle (see Figure 11.4).

Why is Jean Moulin, France's greatest Resistance leader, buried in the Panthéon in Paris, while Marx Dormoy, both a first resister and a martyr of World War II, is interred in an obscure graveyard on the outskirts of a provincial town in central France? The fact that Moulin died in the hands of the Gestapo while Dormoy was murdered while in the custody of his fellow Frenchmen in Vichy, most likely with the complicity of a French state most citizens in France

Figure 11.4. Grave of Marx and Jeanne Dormoy in Cemetery-West, Montluçon. Photograph by authors.

during the war recognized as legitimate, will suffice to explain Dormoy's absence in most histories of World War II. Remembering Marx Dormoy means confronting the difficult history of France and the war, for it evokes memory of the political turbulence and latent civil war of the 1930s, the incompetence of the French army and its infiltration by the extreme right, the shame of the Armistice, and the national betrayal of the French legislators who gave Pétain dictatorial power. Dormoy opposed right-wing extremism, as was evident in his exposure of the Cagoule in 1937. He understood the causes of the defeat of 1940 and the failure of leadership in France all too well, and he rejected Pétain and collaboration. And yet even after his heroic deeds, he has been largely dismissed from French history. Why? The simple explanation is that to recognize Marx Dormoy means confronting not the glory of the French Resistance but rather the humiliation of the "strange defeat"; few countries are capable of owning such intensity of national repentance and remorse.

Admitting to French culpability in the Shoah, even to collaboration with the Nazis, took decades to achieve in France. The assassination of a man devoted to the French Republic, whom his fellow French citizens blew to pieces, is the kind of uneasy knowledge that is hard to position in the national narrative of World War II France. Even more difficult to digest is that those who instigated the crime acted to preserve the reputation of a World War I hero turned collaborator with the Germans. The still-troubling explanation for Marx Dormoy's murder lies at the intersection of France's failure of judgment leading to the Armistice and the country's collective wartime moral decline.[47] Moreover, Marx Dormoy today stands as a moral reproach to leaders around the world unwilling to confront the resurging autocratic tendencies within their own societies. His memory thus remains unpalatable in France even nearly eighty years after his death, and yet remembering his heroism is perhaps more important today to all who believe in democracy than ever before.

Glossary of Names

Otto ABETZ (1903–58). German diplomat in France during World War II stationed in Paris where he advised the German military and the Gestapo.

JOSEPH-BARTHÉLEMY (1874–1945). Justice minister under Vichy (27 January 1941–26 March 1943).

Léon BLUM (1872–1950). French Socialist politician and three-time prime minister of France (and the first Jew to hold this office). A close friend of Marx and Jeanne Dormoy, Blum was arrested in 1940 and put on trial in 1942. He survived the war.

Charles CHENEVIER (1901–83). Commissioner, judicial police at Vichy, principal investigating officer of Marx Dormoy's assassination. A member of the Resistance, Chenevier was deported to Neuengamme but survived and resumed his police career after the war.

François DARLAN, Admiral (1881–1942). Chief of staff of the French Navy in 1939 before joining the Council of Ministers of the Vichy regime in 1940. In 1942, Darlan defected to the Allies.

Joseph DARNAND (1897–1945). World War I war hero who joined the AF and later headed the Cagoule in Nice. During World War II, he was a collaborationist and supporter of fascism, and from 1943 he headed the Milice française.

Marcel DÉAT (1894–1955). Originally a Socialist academic and politician who briefly participated in the Popular Front government in 1936. During the war he adopted a fully collaborationist stance and helped found the *Rassemblement national populaire* (RNP).

Charles DE GAULLE, General (1890–1970). French general who, upon the collapse of the French government in June of 1940, fled to London, where he headed a government in exile and a branch of the Resistance. He helped to liberate France in 1944 and chaired the Provisional Government from 1944 to 1946. After the ratification of the constitution of the French Fifth Republic in 1958 he was elected president of France, a position he held until 1969.

Eugène DELONCLE (1890–1944). Founder of the Cagoule prior to the war and of the MSR in 1940, Deloncle was a naval engineer and banker who collaborated with the Germans during the war. He helped to organize and finance Dormoy's murder. Murdered in Paris in 1944, most likely by his former Gestapo patrons.

Jacques DORIOT (1898–1945). Founded the ultra-nationalist political party Parti populaire français (PPF) in 1936. The PPF was the largest collaborationist party in World War II.

Jeanne DORMOY (1886–1975). Devoted older sister of Marx Dormoy, she ran an orphanage in Montluçon. She valiantly defended her brother's legacy after his death.

Marx DORMOY (1888–1941). Interior minister of France during the Popular Front government of Léon Blum, 1936–1938. A Socialist politician who unmasked the Cagoule in 1937, he voted against dismantling the Third Republic in 1940. Dormoy was assassinated in Montélimar on 26 July 1941.

Paul ESTÈBE (1904–91). Member of Maréchal Philippe Pétain's cabinet. Annie Mourraille claimed that Estèbe conspired with Jeantet and Marchi to plan the murder of Dormoy.

Jean FILLIOL (b. 1909). French extreme-right militant, founding member of both the Cagoule and the MSR. Filliol was responsible for some of the most violent crimes of both organizations.

Félix GOUIN (1884–1977). A lawyer and politician from Bouches-du-Rhône, Gouin refused to vote full powers to Pétain in 1940. Gouin was a close friend of Jeanne and Marx Dormoy and represented Jeanne during the war in her civil suit related to her brother's assassination. Joined de Gaulle in London in 1942 and played a leading role in the formation of a new French government after the war.

Ludovic Joseph GUICHARD (b. 30 June 1914). A right-wing militant from Marseille and a co-conspirator in Marx Dormoy's assassination. Guichard fled to South America in 1945.

Lucien GUYON, pseudonym, Simon. Co-conspirator in the Dormoy assassination, killed in Nice, 14 August 1941, preparing to bomb a synagogue at Marseille.

Raymond HÉRARD, pseudonym, André (b. 15 August 1905). Deloncle's secretary in the MSR and a collaborator who worked for the Gestapo in Paris. Hérard was the go-between linking the Dormoy assassins and the MSR.

Gabriel JEANTET (1906–78). A founding member of the Cagoule who specialized in smuggling arms, Jeantet joined the cabinet of Maréchal Pétain in 1940 as inspector general of propaganda and head of the Amicale de France. Annie Mourraille insisted, and Inspector Chenevier agreed, that Jeantet helped organize Marx Dormoy's assassination in 1941.

Georges KUBLER (1913–45). Commissaire of the judicial police of the 10e Mobile Brigade in Lyon.

Pierre LAVAL (1883–1945). Socialist politician who chose collaborationism during the war. Laval was vice-president of the council of ministers in Pétain's government until December of 1940, when the two fell out over collaboration with Germany. Arrested at the end of the war, Laval was tried for treason and executed in October of 1945.

Maurice Joseph Marius MARBACH (1912–41). Co-conspirator in the Marx Dormoy assassination. Killed in an explosion with Horace Vaillant and Lucien Guyon in the Albert-1er garden at Nice the night of 14 August 1941.

Antoine François MARCHI (b. 13 July 1907 at Vescovato in Corsica). In 1941, he was affiliated with Jacques Doriot and Eugène Deloncle and organized the team of assassins who murdered Marx Dormoy.

Jean MARION. Instructing magistrate in the Dormoy case, at Montélimar and Nyons.

Annie Félicie MOURRAILLE, aka Annie Morène and Florence Gérodias (b. 1913 or 1915). An actress and one of the assassins of Marx Dormoy, she married fellow assassin Yves Moynier in 1943.

Roger Albert Marius MOURAILLE (b. 10 June 1913). A member of multiple extreme-right groups prior to and during the war, including the Cagoule and the MSR, Mouraille (no relation to Annie Mourraille) fought for General Franco during the Spanish Civil War. An accomplice in Dormoy's assassination.

Yves Alexandre Léon Marie MOYNIER (b. 22 March 1914). Member of the AF of Marseille, the Parti populaire français, and in 1940 joined the Amicale de France. Moynier was the self-proclaimed leader of the team of assassins who killed Marx Dormoy. He and Annie Mourraille married in 1943 and escaped France together at the end of the war.

Philippe PÉTAIN, Maréchal (1856–1951). Pétain presided over the dissolution of the Third Republic, became the president of the État français in 1940, based in Vichy. Pétain headed the Vichy regime until August 1944. Tried after the war, he was sentenced to life in prison.

Horace Marius Alexandre VAILLANT (1909–41). Taxi driver in Marseille. Killed in an explosion in the Albert-1er garden of Nice along with Marbach and Guyon the night of 14 August 1941. Vaillant was a principal conspirator in the Dormoy assassination.

Organizations

ACTION FRANÇAISE (AF). An anti-republican, ultra-nationalist, and pro-monarchical political movement founded at the end of the 19th century by Charles Maurras as a reaction to the Dreyfus affair.

AMICALE DE FRANCE. A pro-Pétain propaganda and police organization based at Vichy and under the leadership of Gabriel Jeantet.

CENTRE D'INFORMATION ET D'ÉTUDES (CIE). Intelligence branch of the Groupes de protection.

COMITÉ SECRET D'ACTION RÉVOLUTIONNAIRE (CSAR, nicknamed the "Cagoule" – "the Hood" – and also known as the *Organisation secrète d'action révolutionnaire nationale* or OSARN). Founded by Eugène Deloncle in 1936, the CSAR became the political party called Mouvement social révolutionnaire (MSR) in 1940.

FRONT RÉVOLUTIONNAIRE NATIONALE (FRN). A coalition of collaborationists created by Pierre Laval and Marcel Déat in February 1943.

GROUPES DE PROTECTION (GP). Founded and led by General Georges Groussard in 1940 to protect the National Revolution. The GP and the CIE were both disbanded at the behest of the Germans in December of 1940. Most of the assassins of Marx Dormoy had worked for the GP and/or the CIE.

LÉGION DE VOLONTAIRES FRANÇAIS CONTRE LE BOLSHEVISME (LVF). An anti-Bolshevik legion formed in 1941 to recruit French volunteers to fight on the Russian front.

LÉGION NATIONALE POPULAIRE (LNP). Militia force of the Rassemblement National Populaire (RNP).

MILICE FRANÇAISE. A paramilitary organization the Vichy regime founded in January 1943 to combat the French Resistance. Its leader was Joseph Darnand.

MOUVEMENT SOCIAL RÉVOLUTIONNAIRE (MSR). Eugène Deloncle founded the collaborationist political party MSR, essentially a revived Cagoule, in September of 1940, and turned it into one of the smaller but most violent of the collaborationist parties operating in France during the war. Headquartered in Paris, the MSR helped to fund Marx Dormoy's assassination.

PARTI POPULAIRE FRANÇAIS (PPF). Former Communist politician Jacques Doriot formed the PPF in June 1936. During the war Doriot led the PPF to a collaborationist stance.

PARTI SOCIAL FRANÇAIS (PSF). Ultra-conservative political party founded in July 1936 by Colonel François de La Rocque after the dissolution of his veterans league, the Croix de Feu. Dissolved in 1941.

POPULAR FRONT. The Popular Front was a political movement comprised primarily of Radicals and Socialists who, with the contingent support of the Communists, won the elections of May 1936. Under the leadership of Léon Blum, the Popular Front governed France from 1936 until 1938.

RASSEMBLEMENT NATIONAL POPULAIRE (RNP). Political group created in 1941 at the behest of Pierre Laval, with the goal of uniting all of Paris' collaborationist parties, including the MSR.

SECTION FRANÇAISE DE L'INTERNATIONALE OUVRIÈRE (SFIO). The French Section of the Workers' International, in which Marx Dormoy was a lifelong member and leading figure, was the French Socialist Party founded by Jules Guesde in 1905. It was replaced in 1969 by the Parti socialiste.

SERVICE D'ORDRE LÉGIONNAIRE (SOL). Collaborationist militia created by Joseph Darnand in 1943.

SERVICE DU TRAVAIL OBLIGATOIRE (STO). A compulsory labor service Laval was forced to introduce in February of 1943 to meet the escalating German demand for French labor.

SICHERHEITSDIENST (SD). Security Service of the Reichsführer-SS.

SICHERHEITSPOLIZEI (SiPo). German Security Police comprised of the Gestapo (Secret State Police) and the KRIMINALPOLIZEI (criminal police; Kripo).

Timeline

1939

3 September – France and Great Britain formally enter war with Germany.

1940

22 March – Paul Reynaud becomes head of the French government.

10 May – German invasion of France begins.

28 May – Belgium surrenders to the Nazis.

5 June – German offensive in the Somme begins. The Germans break through the French lines the following day.

10 June – Italy formally declares war on France.

17 June – After the collapse of Paul Reynaud's government, Maréchal Pétain forms a new government and, using Spain as an intermediary, requests an armistice with Germany.

18 June – De Gaulle makes a speech from London calling on French people to resist the Germans.

24 June – The Armistice with Germany takes effect and Germany withdraws beyond the Line of Demarcation.

1 July – The French government with Pétain at its head and Pierre Laval as vice-president of the governing council installs itself at Vichy.

9 July – Dormoy takes the floor in the debate in the Grand Casino over the fate of the Third Republic and asks for a resolution in support of the Republic. Laval violently opposes him.

10 July – Dormoy and Blum are among 80 legislators who vote against dissolving the Third Republic (569 votes in favor, 12 abstentions) and granting Pétain full powers to create a new constitution for France.

2 August – Charles de Gaulle is condemned to death in absentia.

8 August – The Battle of Britain begins.

16 September – Léon Blum is arrested and interned.

25 September – Marx Dormoy is arrested and interned.

24 October – Hitler and Pétain have their first face-to-face encounter at Montoire and shake hands.

30 October – Pétain makes a speech announcing an official policy of collaboration between Vichy and the Germans.

10 November – Creation of the Amicale de France, with Gabriel Jeantet at its head.

13 December – Laval is expelled from Pétain's cabinet.

22 December – The Germans oblige Pétain to dissolve the Groupes de Protection.

31 December – Marx Dormoy and the other detainees at Pellevoisin are sent to Vals-les-Bains in the Ardèche.

1941

13 January – Dormoy and fourteen other detainees are installed in the Grand Hôtel at Vals-les-Bains, converted into a prison.

1 February – Foundation of the Rassemblement national populaire at Laval's instigation and with Marcel Déat as its head.

9 February – Admiral Darlan becomes the head of Pétain's cabinet.

17 March – Vichy orders Marx Dormoy placed under forced residence in Montélimar.

19 March – Marx Dormoy arrives at the Relais de l'Empereur in Montélimar.

22 June – Germany invades the Soviet Union.

18 July – Creation of the LVF.

25/26 July – Dormoy is killed during the night.

10 August – German Siege of Leningrad begins.

12 August – Pétain gives his famous "Vent Mauvais" speech in which he decries the beginnings of French resistance to Vichy's policy of collaboration with the Germans.

27 August – Paul Collette attempts to assassinate Laval and Déat at an RNP rally in Versailles.

24 September – Charles de Gaulle creates a shadow French government in exile, the Comité national français.

2–3 October – During the night Eugène Deloncle and his MSR blow up seven synagogues in Paris with the help of explosives supplied by the Gestapo.

19 October – German siege of Moscow begins.

7 December – The Pearl Harbour attack brings the United States formally into the war.

1942

1–2 January – During the night Jean Moulin parachutes into France to coordinate the Resistance networks with London.

19 February – Opening of the trial at Riom in which Léon Blum is among the defendants.

5 April – Gestapo is installed in the Vichy Zone with Hugo Geissler in charge.

15 April – The Riom trial is suspended without a verdict.

18 April – Pierre Laval returns to power as the head of Pétain's cabinet.

29 May – Jews are required to wear the yellow star in the Occupied Zone.

16 June – Beginning of the "Relève," in which for every three French persons who agreed to work in Germany one French prisoner of war would be freed.

22 June – Laval states that he "hopes for a German victory" in the war.

16–17 July – Raids on Jews throughout Paris, who are interned at the Vélodrôme d'Hiver before being deported to concentration camps.

26–28 August – Raids and arrests of Jews in the Vichy Zone.

4 October – The Battle of Stalingrad begins.

7–8 November – "Operation Torch," the Allied invasion of North Africa, begins.

11 November – The Germans invade the Vichy Zone, ending any remaining pretense of sovereignty of Pétain's regime.

22 November – Admiral Darlan reaches an agreement with Allied General Clark to rally the French Navy in North Africa to the Allies.

24 December – Assassination of Admiral Darlan in Algeria.

1943

22 January – Generals Giraud and de Gaulle meet at Anfa and agree to combine forces.

30 January – Creation of the Milice.

8 September – Italy surrenders and the Germans assume control of the former Italian occupied zones in France.

1944

17 January – Assassination of Deloncle in his Paris apartment, probably by the Gestapo.

6 June – D-Day.

10 June – Massacre at Oradour-sur-Glane.

12 July – Final meeting of the Vichy Conseil des ministers. Germans deport Chenevier to Neuengamme.

20 July – Failed assassination attempt against Hitler.

6 August – Pétain finally disavows the increasingly violent Milice.

16 August – The Germans retreat from Vichy, taking the remnants of the Vichy regime, including Pétain and Laval, to Sigmaringen Castle in Germany.

19 August – Paris revolts against the Germans.

25 August – General Dietrich von Choltitz surrenders Paris to the Allies. Charles de Gaulle enters the liberated city and establishes his headquarters on the rue Saint-Dominique.

Notes

Introduction

1 Most of the documents related to the police investigation of the assassination of Marx Dormoy are housed in the Archives de Paris (hereafter AP), in the series PEROTIN 212/79/3, cartons 47–51, "Cour d'assises de Paris, affaire du CSAR—Comité secret d'action révolutionnaire et autres mouvements nationalistes de droit." Boxes 49–51, "Affaire Dormoy," are directly related to the Dormoy case. For the most part, the documents are organized in dossiers and enumerated, and where possible, the dossier titles and document numbers are given for each source. Please note that the compilers of PEROTIN were inconsistent in where they placed and how they entitled and enumerated certain folders and sub-folders. We attempted to offer maximum information to help other researchers track down our sources within PEROTIN. During the time that we were producing the book, the Archives de Paris was reclassifying the PEROTIN documents under new codes, but this process was not complete by the time we finished the book and we did not have access to the new codes, with the exception of the crime-scene photos. When the archivist reclassified and reorganized PEROTIN, they also removed many, but not all, of the sub-folder headings in the dossiers.
2 AP PEROTIN 212/79/3/50, "Instruction à Montélimar," Pièce #8, Statement of Louis Pinard, night clerk at the Hotel du Relais de L'Empereur.
3 This and the following paragraphs are based on: AP PEROTIN 212/79/3/50, "Instruction à Montélimar," Pièce #1, Procès-verbal de Marc Fra, commissaire de police à Montélimar, 26 July 1941, Pièce #4, Georges Bonnet, juge d'instruction [substitute—the actual juge d'instruction for Montélimar was out of town on vacation], Procès-verbal de Transport judiciaire, 26 July 1941, at 3:00 a.m.; Pièce #5, interview with Mme. Louise Vilnat, 26 July 1941; Pièce #15, Second statement from Mme. Louise Vilnat, 26 July 1941; Pièce #37, Report from le commissaire

principal, chef de la 10e Brigade de la police mobile à Lyon, to M. l'inspecteur général chargé des services de Police judiciaire à Vichy, 28 July 1941.
4 AP PEROTIN 212/79/3/50, "Instruction à Montélimar," Pièce #5, First statement from Mme. Louise Vilnat, 26 July 1941.
5 AP PEROTIN 212/79/3/50, "Instruction à Montélimar," Pièce #8, Statement of Louis Pinard, night clerk at the Hotel du Relais de l'Empereur, 26 July 1941.
6 AP PEROTIN 212/79/3/50, "Instruction à Montélimar," Pièce #1, Procès-verbal, 26 July 1941, Marc Fra, commissaire de police à Montélimar.
7 Archives Départementales de l'Allier (AD Allier), 64/J/78, "Arrêté d'internement administratif à Pellevoisin du 24 septembre 1940."
8 For one analysis of these divisions, see Guilluy, *Twilight of the Elites*.
9 Gordon, *Historical Dictionary of World War II France*, 257–8; Millington, *A History of Fascism*, 94–101.
10 Corre (pseud. Dagore), *Les carnets secrets*, 445.
11 Eugène Deloncle, *Les Idées et L'Action* (Paris: Mouvement Social Révolutionnaire, 1941), 7.
12 For the historiography of the Cagoule see, Brunelle and Finley-Croswhite, *Murder in the Métro*, 201–9. For general references on terrorism see Hoffman, *Inside Terrorism* and Lynn, *Another Kind of War*.
13 Touret, *Marx Dormoy (1888–1941)*, 231.
14 AD Allier, 26J/465, "Hommage de 1948," Marx Dormoy, transcription of Gouin's speech, 6.
15 Quoted by Daniel Mayer in Noguères, Degliame-Fouché, and Vigier, *Histoire de la Resistance*, 1:74.
16 Rousso, *The Vichy Syndrome*, 7.
17 Wieviorka, *Orphans of the Republic*, 82–108. In France politicians can hold local, regional, and national offices simultaneously.
18 Colton, *Léon Blum*, 129–97, 200–2, 205, 207; see also Olivier Dard, *Les Années 30: Le choix impossible*, 110–211; Martin, *France in 1938*, 47–86.
19 Rougeron, *Marx Dormoy*.
20 Fogg, *The Politics of Everyday Life in Vichy France*.
21 Kennedy, *Reconciling France against Democracy*; Samuel Kalman, *The Extreme Right*; Millington, *Fighting for France*.
22 Rougeron, *Marx Dormoy*.
23 Dugléry, *Marx Dormoy*, 174; Touret, *Marx Dormoy*, 7, 44.
24 Rousso, *The Vichy Syndrome*; Jackson, *France: The Dark Years*, 65–80; Paxton, *Vichy France*; Kelly, "War and Culture," 91–100.
25 Berstein, "L'affrontement simulé des années 1930," 39–54; Berstein, "Consensus politique et violences civiles," 51–60; Burrin, "Poings levés et bras tendus," 5–20.
26 Millington, *Fighting for France*, xii–xiii.
27 This paragraph and the next are drawn from the following sources: Jackson, *France: The Dark Years*, 65–80; Millington, *Fighting for France*, xxii–xxxv; Millington, "Street-fighting Men," 607–13; Atkin, *The French at War*, 15–39; Millington and Passmore, eds., *Political Violence and Democracy*.

28 Machefer, *Ligues et fascismes en France*; Olivier Dard, *Les Années 30: Le choix impossible*; Soucy, *French Fascism: The Second Wave*; Jenkins, ed., *France in the Era of Fascism*; Kennedy, *Reconciling France against Democracy*, 2007.
29 Millington, *Fighting for France*, xxvi.
30 Parry, "Counter Revolution by Conspiracy," in *The Right in France*, ed. Atkin and Tallett, 67–92.
31 Jackson, *France: The Dark Years*, 65.
32 Millington, "February 6, 1934," 545–72.
33 Transcriptions of these eulogies can be found in the AD Allier, 26J/465, "Homage de 1948."
34 Cot, "My Friend Marx Dormoy," 113–14.
35 Rougeron, *Marx Dormoy*, 14. Rougeron called Dormoy a "martyr," 15.

1. 1888–1941: Marx Dormoy and the Fall of France

1 Rougeron, *Marx Dormoy*, 1.
2 Rougeron, *Marx Dormoy*, 1; Touret, *Marx Dormoy*, 7–15.
3 "Pages d'histoire Marx Dormoy: Deux universitaires américaines se penchant sur son assassinat," *Vu du Bourbonnais: Actualité, lettres, histoire, arts & culture*, 20 April 2017, https://vudubourbonnais.wordpress.com/2017/04/20/deux-universitaires-americaines-se-penchent-sur-lassassinat-de-marx-dormoy/.
4 Touret, *Marx Dormoy*, 21–33.
5 AD Allier, 64/J/78, Fonds Marx Dormoy, Henri Ribière, "Mon ami, Marx Dormoy," funeral oration for Marx Dormoy.
6 AD Allier, 64/J/78, Fonds Marx Dormoy, Henri Ribière, "Mon ami, Marx Dormoy," funeral oration for Marx Dormoy.
7 Touret, *Marx Dormoy*, 27–8.
8 AD Allier, 64/J/78, Fonds Marx Dormoy, Henri Ribière, "Mon ami, Marx Dormoy," funeral oration for Marx Dormoy. See also the article "Marx Dormoy" in *Le Populaire*, Special edition, 6 June 1936.
9 Rougeron, *Marx Dormoy*, 2.
10 "Marx Dormoy," *Le Populaire*, 6 June 1936.
11 Ligou, *Histoire du socialisme*, 179ff.
12 Graham, *Choice and Democratic Order*, 8–10; Ligou, *Histoire du socialism*, 238ff.
13 Touret, *Marx Dormoy*, 34–43; Rougeron, *Marx Dormoy*, 2.
14 Ligou, *Histoire du socialisme*, 237.
15 Quoted in Colton, *Léon Blum*, 396; see Léon Blum, *L'Oeuvre de Léon Blum*, 5:179–80.
16 AD Allier, 64/J/79, Fonds Marx Dormoy: Notes durant la détention de Marx Dormoy, 1940–41, "Photographies de Marx Dormoy et sa famille."
17 In January of 1941, while Dormoy was in prison at Pellevoisin, he received a letter from the leader of the French Senate at Vichy regarding a law requiring anyone in France who exercised a public function to declare whether or not they were Jewish, and to resign their office if they were. Dormoy replied that he was not Jewish, although by then he had been forcibly removed from the elected

offices he had held in 1940, making the issue moot. AD Allier, 64/J/78, Fonds Marx Dormoy, "Lettre du 20 janvier 1941 du président du Sénat à Marx Dormoy sur l'application de la loi sur l'accès et l'exercice des fonctions publiques et mandats interdits aux juifs."

18 For more about Blum and the Popular Front, see Jackson, *The Popular Front in France*; Lacouture, *Leon Blum*; and Rémond and Renouvin, *Léon Blum*.

19 Jacques Nobécourt, in his biography of Colonel de La Rocque, contends that the Clichy meeting was an innocent fundraiser organized by the Clichy branch of the PSF: Nobécourt, *Le colonel de La Rocque*, 509–14; 543–6.

20 AD Allier, 64/J/78, Fonds Marx Dormoy; Léon Blum, "Le Crime," funeral oration for Marx Dormoy.

21 "Une odieuse agression contre Marx Dormoy," *Le Populaire*, 6 July 1938.

22 Touret, *Marx Dormoy*, 163–7; Jackson, *The Popular Front in France*, 104ff; Blatt, "The Cagoule Plot, 1936–37," 87. This note covers the following paragraph as well.

23 Blatt, "The Cagoule Plot," 147–9.

24 Graham, *Choice and Democratic Order*, 15–17; Ligou, *Histoire du socialisme*, 413–40.

25 Copy of an anonymous letter dated 27 September 1937 addressed to Dormoy, minister of the interior.

26 Martin, *France in 1938*, 85.

27 Graham, *Choice and Democratic Order*, 200.

28 Parti Socialiste (SFIO), 35e Congrès national, Royan, 4–7 juin 1938, *Compte rendu sténographique*, 389–90; AD Allier, 64/J/58, "Émeute de Clichy le 16 mars 1937."

29 For more on the Spanish Civil War and its impact on France, see Wingeate Pike, *France Divided*.

30 "Discourse of Marx Dormoy," published in *Le Populaire*, 6 March 1939. See also Berdah, "The Devil in France," 301–18.

31 Touret, *Marx Dormoy*, 167–70. For the history of Doriot's PPF, see Soucy, *French Fascism*, 204ff.

32 Freigneaux, "Histoire d'un movement terroriste," 336–8, Marx Dormoy communiqué to the press corps, 23 November 1937, reprinted in Freigneaux; Marx Dormoy, "AGENTS de l'ETRANGER, les TERRORISTES ASSASSINS du C.S.A.R. SONT DEMASQUES," *Le Combat social*, 16 January 1938; Brunelle and Finley-Croswhite, *Murder in the Métro*, 154–6.

33 AN BB/18/3061/2, "Etat approximative des armes, munitions, explosifs découverts dans les depots de l'OSARN." This paragraph and the succeeding ones are also based on Blatt, "The Cagoule Plot," 86–104; Brunelle and Finley-Croswhite, *Murder in the Métro,* 154–6; Finley-Croswhite and Brunelle, "Lighting the Fuse," 148. See also Soucy, *French Fascism: The Second Wave, 1933–1939*, 46–53, and Tournoux, *L'Histoire secrete*, 11ff.

34 Brunelle and Finley-Croswhite, *Murder in the Métro*, 105–10.

35 See Deloncle interview in *Le Gerbe*, printed in Péan, *V, enquête sur l'affaire des "avions renifleurs,"* 36.

36 The Radical government of Édouard Daladier that came to power upon the fall of the Popular Front was eager to exculpate the military from any involvement in the Cagoule affair and likely suppressed evidence that might have implicated senior active military officers, including Pétain. Even so, there remains a good deal of evidence that the Cagoule recruited, and received support from, both officers and the military rank and file, and that Pétain was, at the very least, in touch with the Cagoule and sympathetic toward its aims. In a self-published study Michel Rateau synthesizes much of this evidence: Rateau, *Les faces cachées*, 77–136. See also Lacroix-Riz, *Le choix de la défaite*, 270–2; Monier, *Le complot dans la république*, 310–17.
37 See Brunelle and Finley-Croswhite, *Murder in the Métro*, 126–32, 149–54.
38 AD Allier, 64/J/57, Marx Dormoy au gouvernement, copy of article by Marx Dormoy entitled "Agents de l'Etranger, les TERRORISTS ASSASSINS du C.S.A.R sont Démasques," *Le Combat social*, 16 January 1938.
39 Freigneaux, "Histoire d'un mouvement terroriste," 336–8.
40 *L'Écho de Paris*, 25 November 1937.
41 "L'Affaire des Cagoulards," *L'Action française*, 30 November 1937. The 1 December 1938 edition of the Socialist newspaper *Le Populaire* contained a number of articles about the CSAR and congratulated Dormoy on moving against the clandestine organization that posed a real danger to French security. It also contained an interesting article whose author, A.-M. Desrousseaux, recognized that the conservative newspapers were doing everything possible to deny the reality of the plot and heap ridicule on Dormoy: A.-M. Desrousseaux, "La Press de droite est désemparée," *Le Populaire*, 1 December 1938.
42 Corre (pseud. Dagore), *Les carnets secrets*, 319.
43 Rateau, "Extrait des dessins humoristiques d'André-René Charlet."
44 Finley-Croswhite and Brunelle, "Lighting the Fuse."
45 "*Bande de salauds! Et d'abord, un juif vaut bien un Breton.*" This incident is well discussed in Birnbaum, *Un Mythe politique*, 153–6; Joly, "Antisémites et antisémitismes à la Chambre des *députés*," 85–6.
46 Birnbaum, *Un Mythe politique*, 155.
47 Legrand, *Paroles vivantes*, 196–8.
48 *Le Nouveau Cri* cited in Birnbaum, *Un Mythe politique*, 155.
49 Martin, *Years of Plenty, Years of Want*, 175–82.
50 Speech of Marx Dormoy, in *Le Populaire*, 6 March 1939. Quotes in this paragraph come from this source.
51 Touret, *Marx Dormoy (1888–1941)*, 193.
52 Tooze, *The Wages of Destruction*, xxii.
53 Jackson, *France: The Dark Years*, 112–36. This paragraph and the next five paragraphs are largely based on Jackson's account of the "debacle." For other works on the period see Burrin, *France Under the Germans*; Rossi-Landi, *La Drôle de Guerre*; Gates, *The Collapse of the Anglo-French Alliance*; Jean-Louis Crémieux, *La Guerre oui ou non?*; Noguères, *Vichy, Juillet 40*.
54 Alexander, *The Republic in Danger*.

55 Diamond, *Fleeing Hitler, France 1940*, 1–52.
56 Vinen, *France, 1934–1970*, 25–69; Mendès-France, *Liberté, liberté, chérie*, 15–21; Wieviorka, *Orphans of the Republic*, 16–81. Wieviorka contends that France's political leaders, including Blum, could have mobilized more effectively to block Pétain's rise, but were more interested in preserving their own party structures than in uniting against Laval and Pétain.
57 Jackson, *France: The Dark Years*, 126–7.
58 Jackson, *France: The Dark Years*, 151.
59 Paxton's book, though dated, remains the best English-language book on Vichy: Paxton, *Vichy France*. See also Remond, *Le Gouvernement de Vichy*; Aron, *Histoire de Vichy*; Burrin, *France Under the Germans*.
60 Jackson, *De Gaulle*, 120.
61 Jackson, *De Gaulle*, 125–50.
62 Bloch, *L'Étrange Défaite*.
63 Delpla, *Qui a Tué Georges Mandel?* 105.
64 Jackson, *France: The Dark Years*, 85–96.
65 Blum, *L'Oeuvre de Léon Blum*, 5:23.
66 Blum, *L'Oeuvre de Léon Blum*, 5:30; Graham, *Choice and Democratic Order*, 242–53; Graham follows Blum's memoirs in recounting this harrowing time in his life. Shirer, *The Collapse of the Third Republic*, 795–815; Colton, *Léon Blum*, 368–84.
67 Graham, *Choice and Democratic Order*, 244. This paragraph and the next five are largely based on Blum's account in his *L'Oeuvre de Léon Blum* and Graham's assessment in *Choice and Democratic Order*.
68 Conversation quoted in Blum, *L'Oeuvre de Léon Blum*, 5:30. The rest of the dialogue in this exchange comes from this source.
69 Blum, *L'Oeuvre de Léon Blum*, 5:30.
70 Blum, *L'Oeuvre de Léon Blum*, 5:30–2.
71 AD Allier, 64/J/117, Fonds Jeanne Dormoy, Letter dated 5 February 1973 from Jeanne Dormoy to Renée Blum with reference to Dormoy's flight from Paris and his papers.
72 Colton, *Léon Blum*, 368–84; Jean Lacouture, *Leon Blum*, 412–18.
73 AP PEROTIN 212/79/3, Carton 50, "Second Dossier, Instruction à Montélimar, Pièce #256," Testimony of Jules Moch.
74 For more on Laval, see J.-P. Cointet, *Pierre Laval*; Jackson, *The Dark Years*, 132–3; F. Broche and J.-F. Muracciole, *Histoire de la Collaboration*, 77.
75 Sagnes, "Le refus républicain," 555–89.
76 Blum, *L'Oeuvre de Léon Blum*, 5:83.
77 Colton, *Léon Blum*, 365.
78 *Informations générales*, publication of the Ministère de l'intérieur, Bureau d'études juridiques et de documentation générale, no. 5, 1 Octobre 1940. The issue covered the news for the week of 23–9 September 1940. See also the internment order, dated 24 September 1940, issued by the préfet de l'Allier, in accord with the instructions he had received from the Vichy Ministry of the Interior. See copies of these documents in the AD Allier, 64/J/79, Fonds Marx Dormoy.

79 AD Allier, 64/J/79, Fonds Marx Dormoy, document entitled "Arrestation du 26 Septembre."
80 Both notes can be found in AD Allier, 64/J/79, Fonds Marx Dormoy, but are undated in both the handwritten drafts and the typed copies that the prison authorities kept of all prisoner correspondence. The documents in the Fonds Dormoy have no individual call numbers.
81 M. Cointet, *Nouvelle histoire de Vichy*, 367–400.
82 During the Third Republic France had a parliamentary government with a president, whose office was largely ceremonial, and a premier who filled the role that the prime minister holds in Great Britain. In the État français Pétain disbanded the French parliamentary system and replaced it with a Council of Ministers which Pétain headed. The ministers in this Council changed frequently, and under Pierre Laval's second term in the Vichy government the structure of the regime changed again.
83 Delpla, *Qui a Tué Georges Mandel?* 144.
84 Delpla, *Qui a Tué Georges Mandel?* 143–4.
85 Touret, *Marx Dormoy*, 211–15.

2. 1941: A Long, Hot Summer

1 AP PEROTIN 212/79/3/50, "'Dossier de la Détention,' Letter from Félix Gouin, lawyer from Marseille representing Jeanne Dormoy, to Pétain, Marseille, August 19, 1941"; AP PEROTIN 212/79/3/50, "'Instruction à Montélimar,' Vichy order to place Marx Dormoy under house arrest in Montélimar," Pièces #185, 186; AD Allier, 64/J/78, Fonds Marx Dormoy, undated note from Marx Dormoy to Vichy requesting that he be interned in his own region.
2 AD Allier, 64/J/80–81, Fonds Marx Dormoy, Marx Dormoy's correspondence while in prison.
3 Touret, *Marx Dormoy*, 172–9.
4 AP PEROTIN 212/79/3/50, "Instruction à Montélimar," Pièce #256, testimony of Jules Moch, on 17 March 1945.
5 The literature on Occupied France is vast. See Azéma and Bédarida, *La France des années noires*, 2 vols.; Burrin, *France Under the Germans*; M. Cointet, *Nouvelle histoire de Vichy*; Gildea, *Marianne in Chains*; Glass, *Americans in Paris*; Jackson, *France: The Dark Years*; Mitchell, *Nazi Paris*; Ousby, *Occupation: The Ordeal of France*; Vinen, *The Unfree French*.
6 M. Cointet, *Nouvelle histoire de Vichy*, 131–4; Delpla, *Qui à tué Georges Mandel*, 95–112; Sherwood, *Georges Mandel and the Third Republic*, 262–77; Joseph-Barthélemy, *Ministre de la Justice*, 211–37.
7 For more on Dr. Martin see Péan, *Le mystérieux Docteur Martin*, and for his activities during the war, see especially 206ff.
8 AP PEROTIN 212/79/3/51, Ministère de l'intérieur, Diréction générale de la Sûreté nationale, Diréction des services de police judiciaire, extrait du scellé no. 2, Côte 17; see also Procès-verbal, no. 1, with a copy of the note in question; Péan, *Le mystérieux Docteur Martin*, 256.

9 Eugène Deloncle's ideology and psychology can best be grasped through reading his 23-page self-published 1941 manifesto, *Les idées et l'action*. The best synthesis of Deloncle's wartime career and history of the MSR can be found in Gordon, "The Condottieri of the Collaboration," 261–82. See also Brunelle and Finley-Croswhite, *Murder in the Métro*, 159–67; Jackson, *France: The Dark Years*, 192–3; Tournoux, *L'Histoire secrete*, 127ff.
10 As quoted in Tournoux, 127–8.
11 Williams, *Pétain*, 172–83.
12 Gordon, *Collaborationism in France*, 63–7.
13 Deloncle used these words to describe Pétain even as he was maneuvering to become head of a political party that, he hoped, would vault him to leadership of France under German patronage. See Deloncle, *Les idées et l'action*, 17.
14 Gordon, *Collaborationism in France*, 59–62.
15 Gordon, "The Condottieri of the Collaboration," 264. Jacques Doriot's PPF was also a collaborationist movement, but it predated the war.
16 See Deloncle's *Les idées et l'action*, which spells out his ideology.
17 Bourdrel, *Les Cagoulards dans la guerre*, 90–107; Davey, "The Origins of the Légion des Volontaires Français," 29–45; Gordon, *Collaborationism in France*, 244–66; Paxton, *Vichy France*, 51–101, 249–59.
18 Chenevier authored two sets of memoirs and his grandson-in-law, Jean-Émile Néaumet, also published a biography of Chenevier. The material in this and the following paragraphs are based on those works: Chenevier, *De La Combe au fées à Lurs*; Chenevier, *La grande maison*; Néaumet, *Les grandes enquêtes du Commissaire Chenevier*.
19 It is unclear exactly when Chenevier joined the resistance network "Jacques OSS," but by July of 1941 he was already providing intelligence to the Resistance, which complicated his pursuit of Marx Dormoy's assassins: Néaumet, *Les grandes enquêtes du Commissaire Chenevier*, 163.
20 Chenevier, *De La Combe au fées à Lurs*, 6–7; Néaumet, *Les grandes enquêtes du Commissaire Chenevier*, 25–30.
21 Jean Belin published his memoirs, which were translated into English as *Secrets of the Sûreté: The Memoirs of Commissioner Jean Belin, Master Detective of France*. For the career of Pierre Mondanel, see Berlière and Chabrun, *Les policiers français sous l'Occupation*, 98–105. See also Chenevier, *De La Combe au fées à Lurs*, 11; Néaumet, *Les grandes enquêtes du Commissaire Chenevier*, 41.
22 Néaumet, *Les grandes enquêtes du Commissaire Chenevier*, 65ff.
23 AP PEROTIN 212/79/3/43, "Dossiers relatifs au C.S.A.R, Agents d'exécution," Paris, 13 June 1937, Note from Chenevier to Mondanel, relative to the Cagoule assassination of the Rosselli brothers; Corre (pseud. Dagore), *Les carnets secrets*, 391.
24 Belin, *Secrets of the Sûreté*, 127–30, 214–19, 225–6; Chenevier, *De La Combe au fées à Lurs*, 20–3, 28.
25 AP PEROTIN 212/79/3/51, Pièce #32, "Deposition before Judge Robert Lévy, 3 January 1946, of Charles Chenevier, aged 44, commissaire principal à la Sûreté nationale, at present on convalescence leave, residing at 14 Bd. St. Michel, Paris."

26 AP PEROTIN 212/79/3/50, "Instruction à Montélimar," Pièce #37, Report from le commissaire principal, chef de la 10e Brigade de la police mobile à Lyon to M. l'inspecteur général chargé des services de police judiciaire à Vichy.

3. 26–30 July 1941: Anatomy of a Crime Scene

1 Ploscowe, "The Investigating Magistrate (Juge d'Instruction)," 1010–36. See also Van Ruymbeke, *Le juge d'instruction*.
2 AP PEROTIN 212/79/3/50, "Instruction à Montélimar," Pièce #4, Georges Bonnet, Procès-verbal de Transport judiciaire, 26 July 1941, 3:00 a.m.
3 AP PEROTIN 212/79/3/50, "Instruction à Montélimar," Pièce #4, Georges Bonnet, Procès-verbal de Transport judiciaire, 26 July 1941, 3:00 a.m. The sketch is drawn in pencil on the back page of the report. The size of the room can be found in AP PEROTIN 212/79/3/50, "Instruction à Montélimar," Pièce #37, Report from le commissaire principal, chef de la 10e Brigade de la police mobile à Lyon to M. l'inspecteur général chargé des Services de Police Judiciaire à Vichy.
4 AP PEROTIN 212/79/3/50, "Instruction à Montélimar," Pièce #37.
5 AP PEROTIN 212/79/3/50, "Instruction à Montélimar," Pièce #6, Statement of Dr. Chapuis.
6 AP PEROTIN 212/79/3/50, "Instruction à Montélimar," Pièce #1, Procès-verbal, Marc Fra, 26 July 1941.
7 Joseph-Barthélemy, *Ministre de la Justice*, 237; Delpla, *Qui à tué Georges Mandel*, 290.
8 Bretty, *La Comédie-Française à l'envers*. See also Jeanney, *Georges Mandel*, 175–6 and Sherwood, *Georges Mandel and the Third Republic*, 186, 253–4, 256, 279, 283–8.
9 AP PEROTIN 212/79/3/50, "Instruction à Montélimar," Pièce #4, Georges Bonnet, Procès-verbal de Transport judiciaire, 26 July 1941. See also AP PEROTIN 212/79/3/50, "Instruction à Montélimar," Pièce #5, Mme. Louise Vilnat's first official statement to the police.
10 AP PEROTIN 212/79/3/50, "Instruction à Montélimar," Pièce #4.
11 AP PEROTIN 212/79/3/50, "Instruction à Montélimar," Pièce #15, Second statement from Mme. Louise Vilnat, 26 July 1941.
12 AP PEROTIN 212/79/3/50, "Instruction à Montélimar," Pièce #5, Interview with Mme. Louise Vilnat, 26 July 1941; Pièce #8, Statement of Louis Pinard; and Pièce #15, Second statement from Mme. Louise Vilnat, 26 July 1941. The quotes in this paragraph derive from this source.
13 AP PEROTIN 212/79/3/50, "Instruction à Montélimar," Pièce #64, Report from Kubler to the commissaire divisionnaire at Lyon, 9 August 1941.
14 AP PEROTIN 212/79/3/50, "Instruction à Montélimar," Pièce #5, Interview with Mme. Louise Vilnat, 16 July 1941.
15 For more about Dormoy's life and career, see chapter 1.
16 AP PEROTIN 212/79/3/50, "Instruction à Montélimar," Pièce #15, Second statement from Mme. Louise Vilnat, 26 July 1941.

17 AP PEROTIN 212/79/3/50, "Instruction à Montélimar," Pièce #15, Second statement from Mme. Louise Vilnat, 26 July 1941. The quotes that follow are also from this source.
18 AP PEROTIN 212/79/3/50, "Instruction à Montélimar," Pièce #7, Statement of Mme. Béatrice dite Bretty Veuve Dangel, née Bolchesi, 26 July 1941; see also AP PEROTIN 212/79/3/50, "Instruction à Montélimar," Pièce #21, Bretty Dangel's second statement, given later in the morning of 26 July, to the Lyonnais police.
19 AP PEROTIN 212/79/3/50, "Instruction à Montélimar," Pièce #37, Report dated 28 July 1941, from le commissaire principal, chef de la 10e Brigade de la police mobile à Lyon, to M. l'inspecteur général chargé des Services de police judiciaire à Vichy.
20 AP PEROTIN 212/79/3/50, "Instruction à Montélimar," Pièce #9, Statement of Barba Dialo, 26 July 1941. Dialo's actual name was Baba Diallo.
21 AP PEROTIN 212/79/3/50, "Instruction à Montélimar," Pièce #21, Statement from Mme. Béatrice dite Bretty Veuve Dangel, née Bolchesi, 26 July 1941.
22 AP PEROTIN 212/79/3/50, "Instruction à Montélimar," Pièce #37.
23 AP PEROTIN 212/79/3/50, "Instruction à Montélimar," Pièce #19, Statement from M. Louis Chevet, barman at the Hotel Relais de L'Empereur, 26 July 1941. All quotes in this paragraph are from this source.
24 AP PEROTIN 212/79/3/50, "Instruction à Montélimar," Pièce #15, Second statement from Mme. Louise Vilnat, 26 July 1941, and Pièce #19, Statement from Louis Chevet, 26 July 1941. All quotes in this paragraph are from these sources.
25 AP PEROTIN 212/79/3/50, "Instruction à Montélimar," Pièce #19, Statement from Louis Chevet, 26 July 1941. All quotes in this paragraph are from this source.
26 AP PEROTIN 212/79/3/50, "Instruction à Montélimar," Pièce #19, Statement from Louis Chevet, 26 July 1941. All quotes in this paragraph are from this source.
27 AP PEROTIN 212/79/3/50, "Instruction à Montélimar," Pièce #15, Second statement from Mme. Louise Vilnat, 26 July 1941.
28 AP PEROTIN 212/79/3/50, "Instruction à Montélimar," Pièce #22, Statement from Mlle. Jeanne Dormoy, 26 July 1941. All quotes in this paragraph derive from this source.
29 AP PEROTIN 212/79/3/50, "Instruction à Montélimar," Pièce #22, Statement from Mlle. Jeanne Dormoy, 26 July 1941. All quotes in this paragraph derive from this source.
30 AP PEROTIN 212/79/3/50, "Instruction à Montélimar," Pièce #21, Statement of Mme. Béatrice dite Bretty Veuve Dangel, née Bolchesi, 26 July 1941.
31 There are photos of all these objects still extant, AP PEROTIN 212/79/3/50, "Instruction à Montélimar," Pièce #13, "Second Dossier, Instruction à Montélimar." See also #42–9, and photos of tracings of footsteps in the room, Pièces #50–3, and another schematic drawing of the room, including the placement of the corpse, as well as the hallways leading to and from the room, and of the staircase and landing on the third floor, Pièce #54.
32 AP PEROTIN 212/79/3/50, "Instruction à Montélimar," Pièce #12; Pièce #13, Statement from Maximin Dubois, Inspecteur photographe de police mobile à la 10e Brigade de police mobile, Lyon, 26 July 1941; Pièce #37, Report from le

commissaire principal, chef de la 10e Brigade de la police mobile à Lyon to M. l'inspecteur général chargé des Services de police judiciaire à Vichy.
33 AP PEROTIN 212/79/3/50, "Instruction à Montélimar," Pièce #37, Report from le commissaire principal, chef de la 10e Brigade de la police mobile à Lyon to M. l'inspecteur général chargé des Services de police judiciaire à Vichy.
34 Néaumet, *Les grandes enquêtes du Commissaire*, 178. Prior to the reform the Vichy regime instituted in April 1941, France had not one police force, but in fact at least five: the *police municipale*, or local police forces; the Parisian *Préfecture de police* that answered to the interior minister as a separate jurisdiction controlling all policing in Paris and the surrounding Department of the Seine; the *Gendarmerie*, a branch of the military responsible for maintaining order on public thoroughfares, which had become a de facto shadow police force in many small towns that could not afford their own local police force; the *Deuxième bureau*, France's external military intelligence branch that often became involved in cases within France where espionage played a role; and the *Sûreté nationale*. It was to this branch that Chenevier and Kubler belonged, and Kubler was assigned specifically to the 9th Division, based in Lyon, of the *Brigades mobiles de police judiciaire*. The closest analogy to the Sûreté in the United States would be the Federal Bureau of Investigation. Berlière, *Le Monde des polices*, 19ff, 36–7, 166–7.
35 AP PEROTIN 212/79/3/50, "Instruction à Montélimar," Pièce #14, Statement of Georges Kubler, commissaire de la Police mobile, Lyon, and Pièce #37, Report from le commissaire principal, chef de la 10e Brigade de la police mobile à Lyon to M. l'inspecteur général chargé des Services de police judiciaire à Vichy.
36 AP PEROTIN 212/79/3/50, "Instruction à Montélimar," Pièce #14, Statement of Georges Kubler, commissaire de la Police mobile, Lyon, and Pièce #37, Report from le commissaire principal, chef de la 10e Brigade de la police mobile à Lyon to M. l'inspecteur général chargé des Services de police judiciaire à Vichy, 28 July 1941.
37 Front page, *Le Petit Parisien*, 27 July 1941.
38 AP PEROTIN 212/79/3/50, "Instruction à Montélimar," Pièce #37, Report from le commissaire principal, chef de la 10e Brigade de la police mobile à Lyon to M. l'inspecteur général chargé des Services de police judiciaire à Vichy; Touret, *Marx Dormoy*, 219.
39 AP PEROTIN 212/79/3/50, "Instruction à Montélimar," Pièce #29, Statement from Georges Kubler, commissaire de Police mobile, Lyon, 27 July 1941, and Pièce #37, Report from le commissaire principal, chef de la 10e Brigade de la police mobile à Lyon to M. l'inspecteur général chargé des Services de police judiciaire à Vichy.
40 AP PEROTIN 212/79/3/50, "Instruction à Montélimar," Pièce #15, Second statement of Mme. Louise Vilnat, 26 July 1941.
41 AP PEROTIN 212/79/3/50, "Instruction à Montélimar," Pièce #18, Statement from Mme. Marie Behuret, née Gropetti, 26 July 1941.
42 AP PEROTIN 212/79/3/50, "Instruction à Montélimar," Pièce #18. All quotes that follow are from this source.
43 AP PEROTIN 212/79/3/50, "Instruction à Montélimar," Pièce #15.

44 AP PEROTIN 212/79/3/50, "Instruction à Montélimar," Pièce #17, Statement of Louis Pinard, aged 26, night watchman at the Relais de l'Empereur, 27 July 1941.
45 AP PEROTIN 212/79/3/50, "Instruction à Montélimar," Pièce #19, Statement of Louis Chevet, 26 July 1941.
46 AP PEROTIN 212/79/3/50, "Instruction à Montélimar," Pièce #20, Statement of Ernest Ceccheto, 41 years old, porter de chambre at the Relais de l'Empereur, 27 July 1941.
47 AP PEROTIN 212/79/3/50, "Instruction à Montélimar," Pièce #20, Statement of Ernest Ceccheto, 41 years old, porter de chambre at the Relais de l'Empereur, 27 July 1941; Pièce #9, Statement of Louis Pinard, 26 July 1941.
48 AP PEROTIN 212/79/3/50, "Instruction à Montélimar," Pièce #20.
49 AP PEROTIN 212/79/3/50, "Instruction à Montélimar," Pièce #23, Statement of Marie Salgon, aged 51, florist, 26 July 1941.
50 AP PEROTIN 212/79/3/50, "Instruction à Montélimar," Pièce #23, Statement of Marie Salgon, aged 51, florist, 26 July 1941.
51 AP PEROTIN 212/79/3/50, "Instruction à Montélimar," Pièce #24, Statement of Camille Humber, aged 58, truck driver, residing at rue Curaterie; Pièce #29, Montélimar, 26 July 1941; Pièce #36, Statement of Mme. Augustine Sauvan, née Rivier, aged 43, employed, residing at rue Curaterie, 28 July 1941.
52 See Louis Pinard's description of the man, AP PEROTIN 212/79/3/50, "Instruction à Montélimar," Pièce #27.
53 Their testimony can be found in AP PEROTIN 212/79/3/50, "Instruction à Montélimar," Pièce #28, Statement of Mme. Marie Rose Mouzon, épouse Lurol, hôtelière, rue Aristide Briand, Montélimar, 27 July 1941; Pièce #33, Statement from Mlle. Raymonde Fracou, aged 14, residing at the Hôtel de la Place d'Armes, Montélimar, 28 July 1941. Much of the testimony is also summarized in Pièce #37, Report from le commissaire principal, chef de la 10e Brigade de la police mobile à Lyon to M. l'inspecteur général chargé des Services de police judiciaire à Vichy.
54 AP PEROTIN 212/79/3/50, "Instruction à Montélimar," Pièces #28 and 33.
55 AP PEROTIN 212/79/3/50, "Instruction à Montélimar," Pièce #33.
56 AP PEROTIN 212/79/3/50, "Instruction à Montélimar," Pièce #29, Statement from Georges Kubler, commissaire de police mobile, Lyon, 27 July 1941.
57 AP PEROTIN 212/79/3/50, "Instruction à Montélimar," Pièce #34, Statement of Mme. Marthe Barnier, aged 55, laundress, residing at 84 Grand Rue, Montélimar, 28 July 1941.
58 AP PEROTIN 212/79/3/50, "Instruction à Montélimar," Pièce #34.
59 AP PEROTIN 212/79/3/50, "Instruction à Montélimar," Pièce #28.
60 AP PEROTIN 212/79/3/50, "Instruction à Montélimar," Pièce #37.
61 AP PEROTIN 212/79/3/50, "Instruction à Montélimar," Pièce #56, Statement from Mme. Lucienne Ceyte, née Petrenille, aged 32, owner of a hotel, Boulevard Marre-Desmarais, Montélimar, 30 July 1941.
62 AP PEROTIN 212/79/3/50, "Instruction à Montélimar," Pièce #56. The quotes in this paragraph derive from this source.

63 AP PEROTIN 212/79/3/50, "Instruction à Montélimar," Pièce #57, Statement from Mlle. Lucie Bisazza, aged 30, waitress, residing at rue Puitseigneur #7, Montélimar, 30 July 1941.
64 AP PEROTIN 212/79/3/50, "Instruction à Montélimar," Pièce #57.
65 AP PEROTIN 212/79/3/50, "Instruction à Montélimar," Pièce #57.
66 AP PEROTIN 212/79/3/50, "Instruction à Montélimar," Pièce #57. The quotes in this paragraph derive from this source.
67 AP PEROTIN 212/79/3/50, "Instruction à Montélimar," Pièces #56, 57.
68 AP PEROTIN 212/79/3/50, "Instruction à Montélimar," Pièces #31, 32, 62, 63, 65.
69 AP PEROTIN 212/79/3/50, "Instruction à Montélimar," Pièce #25, Statement of Jean Porterte, aged 30, clerk at the SNCF [the French national train company], 26 July 1941; AP PEROTIN 212/79/3/50, "Instruction à Montélimar," Pièce #26, Statement of Jolima Nal, aged 42, employee of the SNCF at Montélimar, 26 July 1941.
70 AP PEROTIN 212/79/3/50, "Instruction à Montélimar," Pièce #60, Report from Lyon, dated 2 August 1941, from the commissaire de police mobile, J. Dargaud, to M. le commissaire divisionnaire, chef de la 10e Brigade régionale de police mobile, Lyon; Pièce #61, Statement from Ludovic Guichard, aged 27, salesman, residing rue Pastoret, Marseille, 2 August 1941.

4. 14 August 1941: A Bombing in Nice

1 AP PEROTIN 212/79/3/50, "Dossier Montélimar, Renseignements en forme de détention, dossier de la détention," Pièce #10; AD Allier, 64/J/104, Fonds Jeanne Dormoy, 64/J/104, "Enquête et préparation du procès d'assises de 1948," Note on the letterhead of the Relais de l'Empereur, dated 4 August 1944.
2 Van Ruymbeke, *Le juge d'instruction*, 17–20.
3 AD Allier, 64/J/104, Fonds Jeanne Dormoy, "Enquête et préparation du procès d'assises de 1948," handwritten note from Jeanne Dormoy, dated 29 December 1941 in which she responds to communications and his bill for expenses.
4 Delpla, *Qui a tué Georges Mandel?* 201–15.
5 AP PEROTIN 212/79/3/50, "Instruction à Montélimar," Pièce #63.
6 AP PEROTIN 212/79/3/50, "Dossier Montélimar, Renseignements en forme de détention, dossier de la détention," Pièce #4, Copy of a report, marked "Urgent," to the inspecteur général chargé des Services de police judiciaire à Vichy from M. le commissaire divisionnaire chef de la 10e Brigade régionale de police mobile, Paris, 28 July 1941; AP PEROTIN 212/79/3/50, "Instruction à Montélimar," Pièce #32, 4 August 1941.
7 AP PEROTIN 212/79/3/50, "Dossier Montélimar, Renseignements en forme de détention, dossier de la détention," Pièce #14, Statement from Inspector Marc, 3 August 1941; AP PEROTIN 212/79/3/50, "Instruction à Montélimar," Pièce #60, Report from Lyon, 2 August 1941, stating that the Lyonnais police had issued

arrest warrants for all five suspects and that all trains were being searched as well.
8 AP PEROTIN 212/79/3/50, "Dossier Montélimar, Renseignements en forme de détention, dossier de la détention," Pièce #13, Bill from Dr. Edmond Locard, directeur du laboratoire de police technique, for 1,000 francs; Pièce #16.
9 AP PEROTIN 212/79/3/50, "Dossier Montélimar, Renseignements en forme de détention, dossier de la détention," Pièce #17, Report from Dr. Charles Sannie, chef du Service de l'identité judiciaire, 13 August 1941.
10 AP PEROTIN 212/79/3/50, "Dossier Montélimar, Renseignements en forme de détention, dossier de la détention," Pièce #14, Statement from Inspector Marc, dated 3 August 1941, with a note from Mme. Vilnat to the juge d'instruction attached.
11 AP PEROTIN 212/79/3/50, "Instruction à Montélimar," Pièce #72, Report from George Kubler to M. le commissaire divisionnaire chef de la 10e Brigade de police mobile, Lyon; AP PEROTIN 212/79/3/50, "Instruction à Montélimar," Pièce #95, Report, Marseille, 21 August 1941, from le commissaire principal de Police mobile, Étienne Mercuri, to M. le commissaire divisionnaire, chef de la 9e Brigade régionale.
12 The materials to manufacture cheddite – chlorates mixed with nitroaromatics mixed with a small amount of paraffin or castor oil – were common and the production process was relatively easy. This made cheddite a popular and common "homemade" explosive used by resistance groups in World War II, although it was also used in manufacturing explosives. Cheddite today is used primarily as a primer in shotgun cartridges.
13 AP PEROTIN 212/79/3/51, Pièce 14, Report from Nice dated 16 August 1941.
14 AP PEROTIN 212/79/3/50, "Instruction à Montélimar," Pièce #95, Report from Marseille, dated 21 August 1941, from le commissaire principal de Police mobile, Étienne Mercuri, to M. le commissaire divisionnaire, chef de la 9e Brigade régionale, Marseille.
15 AP PEROTIN 212/79/3/50, "Instruction à Montélimar," Pièces #66, 67, 68, 69, 70, statements given on 16 and 17 August 1941, from Ceyte, Bisazza, and Burgaud.
16 AP PEROTIN 212/79/3/50, "Instruction à Montélimar," Pièce #95, Report from Marseille, dated 21 August 1941, from le commissaire principal de Police mobile, Étienne Mercuri, to M. le commissaire divisionnaire, chef de la 9e Brigade régionale, Marseille.
17 AP PEROTIN 212/79/3/51, ministère de l'Intérieur, diréction générale de la Sûreté nationale, direction des Services de police judiciaire, extrait du scellé no. 2, Côte 14, Report dated Nice, 16 August 1941.
18 AP PEROTIN 212/79/3/50, "Instruction à Montélimar," Pièce #72, Report from George Kubler to M. le commissaire divisionnaire chef de la 10e Brigade de police mobile, Lyon.

19 AP PEROTIN 212/79/3/50, "Instruction à Montélimar," Pièce #72.
20 AP PEROTIN 212/79/3/50, "Instruction à Montélimar," Pièce #73, Second Statement from Ludovic Guichard, 17 August 1941 and Pièce #74, Report of George Kubler to M. le commissaire divisionnaire chef de la 10e Brigade de police mobile, Lyon, undated.
21 AP PEROTIN 212/79/3/50, "Instruction à Montélimar," Pièce #73, Second statement from Ludovic Guichard, 17 August 1941.
22 AP PEROTIN 212/79/3/50, "Instruction à Montélimar," Pièce #74, Report of George Kubler to M. le commissaire divisionnaire chef de la 10e Brigade de police mobile, Lyon, undated.
23 AP PEROTIN 212/79/3/50, "Instruction à Montélimar," Pièce #76, Statement from Elie Tudesq at Marseille, dated 18 August 1941, relating the results of the search of Guichard's home in the company of Georges Kubler.
24 AP PEROTIN 212/79/3/50, "Instruction à Montélimar," Pièce #76. A copy of this note and of Guichard's statements can be found at the Archives Départementales des Bouches-du-Rhône (AD Bouches-du-Rhône), Marseille, 1269/W/77, Dossiers d'enquêtes de police judiciaire concernant des dossiers d'affaires particulières: assassinat de Marx Dormoy (1941). This file contains the reports of commissaire principal de Police mobile, Étienne Mercuri, who was based in Marseille. Mercuri and his men did most of the interviews and police leg work in Marseille. This file also contains the police photos of the assassins.
25 AP PEROTIN 212/79/3/50, Renseignements en forme de détention, sous-dossier "Dossier de renseignement," Pièce #47, Undated letter, probably 1942, from Ludovic Guichard's mother to Judge Marion.
26 See Charles Chenevier's description of Guichard in Néaumet, *Les grandes enquêtes du Commissaire Chenevier*, 178.
27 AP PEROTIN 212/79/3/50, Renseignements en forme de détention, sous-dossier "Dossier de renseignement," Pièce #43, Notice individuelle, Guichard, Pièce #44, on Guichard's military service, and Pièce #45, Report of inspecteur principal Marc Mandin to M. le commissaire divisionnaire, chef de la 9e Brigade régionale de police judiciaire à Marseille, 31 October 1941.
28 AP PEROTIN 212/79/3/50, Renseignements en forme de détention, sous-dossier "Dossier de renseignement," Pièce #47, Statement from Mme. Leschi, professor at the Institut Leschi, Marseille, 23 October 1941. All quotes in this paragraph are from this source.
29 AP PEROTIN 212/79/3/50, Renseignements en forme de détention, sous-dossier "Dossier de renseignement," Pièce #34, Statement from Ludovic Guichard dated 4 October 1941.
30 AP PEROTIN 212/79/3/50, Renseignements en forme de détention, sous-dossier "Dossier de renseignement," Pièce #59, Report on the mental state of Ludovic Guichard, November 1941.
31 Néaumet, *Les grandes enquêtes du Commissaire Chenevier*, 178.

32 AP PEROTIN 212/79/3/50, Renseignements en forme de détention, sous-dossier "Dossier de renseignement," Pièce #45, Report of Inspecteur Principal Marc Mandin to M. le commissaire divisionnaire, chef de la 9e Brigade régionale de police judiciaire à Marseille, 31 October 1941.

33 AP PEROTIN 212/79/3/50, Renseignements en forme de détention, sous-dossier "Dossier de renseignement," Pièce #34, Statement from Ludovic Guichard dated 4 October 1941.

34 AP PEROTIN 212/79/3/50, "Instruction à Montélimar," Pièce #61, First statement from Ludovic Guichard, 2 August 1941.

35 AP PEROTIN 212/79/3/50, "Instruction à Montélimar," Pièce #61.

36 AP PEROTIN 212/79/3/50, "Instruction à Montélimar," Pièce #256, Testimony of Jules Moch, 17 March 1945.

37 AP PEROTIN 212/79/3/50, Renseignements en forme de détention, sous-dossier "Dossier de renseignement," Pièce #45, Report of Inspecteur Principal Marc Mandin to M. le commissaire divisionnaire, chef de la 9e Brigade régionale de police judiciaire à Marseille, 31 October 1941; AP PEROTIN 212/79/3/50, "Instruction à Montélimar," Pièce #73, Second statement from Ludovic Guichard, 17 August 1941. See also Groussard, *Service Secret 1940–1945*, 53–137; Lambert and Le Marec, *Vichy 1940–1944*, 23–7.

38 AP PEROTIN 212/79/3/50, "Instruction à Montélimar," Pièce #74, Report from Kubler to le commissaire divisionnaire chef de la 10e Brigade de police mobile, Lyon.

39 AP PEROTIN 212/79/3/50, "Instruction à Montélimar," Pièce #75, Statement given to Elie Tudesq, commissaire de police mobile, 9e Brigade, Marseille, 18 August 1941, from Émile Roux.

40 AP PEROTIN 212/79/3/50, "Instruction à Montélimar," Pièce #81, Statement from Mme. Zöe Hosch, aged 35, waitress, residing in Marseille, dated 19 August 1941.

41 AP PEROTIN 212/79/3/50, "Instruction à Montélimar," Pièce #73, Second statement from Ludovic Guichard, 17 August 1941.

42 AP PEROTIN 212/79/3/50, "Instruction à Montélimar," Pièce #73.

43 AP PEROTIN 212/79/3/50, "Dossier de la détention," Pièce #58. By 19 August Marion already knew about the likely involvement of both the MSR and Jeantet, via Chenevier. See also AP PEROTIN 212/79/3/50, Second dossier, "Instruction à Montélimar," Pièce #88, and Néaumet, *Les Grandes enquêtes du Commissaire Chenevier*, 177; AP PEROTIN 212/79/3/51, Pièce #32, Deposition of Charles Chenevier, 3 January 1946.

44 AP PEROTIN 212/79/3/49, "Dossier Derville, Mouraille, Roger," Pièce #483, "Réquisitoire définitif, Tribunal de première instance du Département de la Seine, séant à Paris." The document on Mouraille can be found on pages 40–1.

45 Keene, *Fighting for Franco*, 135–74.

46 AP PEROTIN 212/79/3/50, Second dossier, "Instruction à Montélimar," Pièce #16, Statement of Henri Durand.

47 AP PEROTIN 212/79/3/50, Second dossier, "Instruction à Montélimar," Pièce #119; Corre (pseud. Dagore), *Les carnets secrets*, 509, 522–3, 530–1, 534–5, 573.
48 AP PEROTIN 212/79/3/50, Second dossier, "Instruction à Montélimar," Pièces #78, 80.
49 AP PEROTIN 212/79/3/50, Second dossier, "Instruction à Montélimar," Pièces #33–41.
50 For the interrogation of Moynier of 19 August, and two handwritten notes from Moynier to the police, see AP PEROTIN 212/79/3/50, Second dossier, "Instruction à Montélimar," Pièces #79 and 80.
51 AP PEROTIN 212/79/3/50, Second dossier, "Instruction à Montélimar," Pièce #95.
52 AP PEROTIN 212/79/3/50, Second dossier, "Instruction à Montélimar," Pièce #79.
53 AP PEROTIN 212/79/3/50, Second dossier, "Instruction à Montélimar," Pièces #34, 80, 98.
54 AP PEROTIN 212/79/3/50, Second dossier, "Instruction à Montélimar," Pièce #85, Roger Mouraille's first statement to the police, 19 August 1941.
55 AP PEROTIN 212/79/3/50, Second dossier, "Instruction à Montélimar," Pièce #85.
56 AP PEROTIN 212/79/3/50, Second dossier, "Instruction à Montélimar," Pièce #80, Statement of Yves Moynier, 19 August 1941.
57 Alary, *La ligne de démarcation*, 124–32.
58 AP PEROTIN 212/79/3/50, Second dossier, "Instruction à Montélimar," Pièces #80, 84, 132, 190.
59 AP PEROTIN 212/79/3/50, Second dossier, "Instruction à Montélimar," Pièces #80, 85.
60 AP PEROTIN 212/79/3/50, Second dossier, "Instruction à Montélimar," Pièce #85.
61 AN Pierrefitte, Z/6/121, "Dossier #1740, Raymond Hérard."
62 APP B/A 1914, "Mouvement social révolutionnaire (1939–1944)," Pièce dated 22 June 1942 from police investigation noting Hérard passed as an official agent of the 'services secrets allemands'"; AN F/7/14958, "Mouvement social révolutionnaire."
63 AP PEROTIN 212/79/3/50, Second dossier, "Instruction à Montélimar," Pièces #85, 95, Mercuri's report dated 21 August 1941.
64 AP PEROTIN 212/79/3/50, Second dossier, "Instruction à Montélimar," Pièce #88.

5. Summer 1941: Recruiting the Assassins

1 Tumblety, "Revenge of the Fascist Knights," 11–20, 11.
2 Chenevier, *De la Combe aux fées à Lurs*, 79–81; Néaumet, *Les grandes enquêtes du Commissaire Chenevier*, 188–91. Since both works were published decades after the investigation, and decades apart, there are some differences between them.
3 Mouraille's grand-niece, Michèle Halligan, née Pruniéras, researched Annie's life, and is currently translating a journal Annie Mouraille's mother, Auguste

Claire Mathilde Fehr, née Lamouroux, wrote from 1908 until 1926. See as well Février, *Le royaume de Pipétides*.

4 See the playbill for *Les Chevaliers de la Table Ronde*, 1937, on the website of the Association de la Régie Théâtrale, http://www.regietheatrale.com/index /index/programmes/programmes.php?recordID=23&Les%20Chevaliers %20de%20la%20Table%20ronde-COCTEAU-1937 (accessed 25 January 2019).

5 What makes the issue of the family name more confusing is that even though the family's descendants today still spell the name "Mourraille," in Gattières, where Léon Mourraille, Annie's father, was mayor and owned a home, the name is usually spelled "Mouraille," and sometimes "Muraille." See Google Maps of the city of Gattières, https://plus.google.com/113539908015554360773 /about?gl=us&hl=en (accessed 25 January 2019) and the website of the school itself, at Annuaire Mairie Gattières, http://www.annuaire-mairie.fr/education -ecole-maternelle-publique-mouraille.html (accessed 25 January 2019).

6 AP PEROTIN 212/79/3/50, "Second dossier, Instruction à Montélimar," Pièce #105, Statement from Victor Chauvin, commissaire divisionnaire de Police mobile, Sûreté de Vichy.

7 Chenevier, *De la Combe aux fées à Lurs*, 80.

8 Chenevier, *De la Combe aux fées à Lurs*, 80.

9 AP PEROTIN 212/79/3/50, "Second dossier, Instruction à Montélimar," Pièce #100, Report from Louis Moulard, inspecteur principal à Marseille.

10 AP PEROTIN 212/79/3/50, "Second dossier, Instruction à Montélimar," Pièce #102. Both the quote from the letter and that from Carretier come from this police report, again by Louis Moulard.

11 AP PEROTIN 212/79/3/50, "Second dossier, Instruction à Montélimar," Pièce #102. Carretier used the term "genre Tarzan" to describe the tall and athletic Moynier.

12 AP PEROTIN 212/79/3/50, "Premier dossier, Renseignements en forme détention," Pièce #10.

13 AP PEROTIN 212/79/3/50, "Premier dossier, Renseignements en forme détention," Pièce #10.

14 AP PEROTIN 212/79/3/50, "Premier dossier, Renseignements en forme détention," Pièce #10. Quotes in this paragraph come from this source.

15 AP PEROTIN 212/79/3/50, "Second dossier, Instruction à Montélimar," Pièce #104, and AP PEROTIN 212/79/3/50, "Renseignements en forme détention," Pièces #2–10.

16 The 1913 date is from Hillard's report, "Renseignements en forme détention," Pièce #10. Henri Dumas, inspecteur sous-chef de la Sûreté de la police d'État de Nice, stated that Mourraille was born in 1915. "Renseignements en forme détention," Pièce #4. Since she claimed to be 27 years old in August of 1941, the 1913 birthdate is probably correct.

17 Léon Mourraille was mayor of Gattières from 1904 until 1944.

18 Manuscript copy of Mathilde Lamouroux's journal, translated by Michèle Halligan, n.p., 3.

19 Lamouroux journal, 36.

20 Lamouroux journal, 36.
21 Chadwick and Latimer, "Becoming Modern: Gender and Sexual Identity," 3–19, and especially 3–7.
22 AP PEROTIN 212/79/3/50, "Premier dossier, Renseignements en forme détention," Pièce #10.
23 AP PEROTIN 212/79/3/50, "Premier dossier, Renseignements en forme détention," Pièce #10.
24 AP PEROTIN 212/79/3/50, "Premier dossier, Renseignements en forme de détention," Pièce #10.
25 Dubuis, *Émergence de l'homosexualité*, 227.
26 AP PEROTIN 212/79/3/50, "Premier dossier, Renseignements en forme de détention," Pièce #10.
27 AP PEROTIN 212/79/3/50, "Premier dossier, Renseignements en forme de détention," Pièce #10.
28 AP PEROTIN 212/79/3/50, "Second dossier, Instruction à Montélimar," Pièce #108.
29 AP PEROTIN 212/79/3/50, "Second dossier, Instruction à Montélimar," Pièce #104.
30 De Renzis, "Andromaque au Volant," article from *Le Petit Provençal-Marseilles*. Information regarding Annie Mourraille's military service can be found AP PEROTIN 212/79/3/50, "Dossier des Renseignements, Notice individuelle pour Annie Mourailles [sic]," Pièces #17 and 18.
31 Pollard, *Reign of Virtue*, 5, 6–41. The literature on gender and fascism is extensive; see Capdevila, "The Quest for Masculinity," 423–45; Campbell, *Political Belief in France, 1927–1945*, 178–202; Campbell, "Women and Men in French Authoritarianism," 3–5, 18–19, 210; Gottlieb, *Feminine Fascism*; Green, "Gender, Fascism and the Croix de Feu," 229–39; Koos, "Fascism, Fatherhood, and the Family in Interwar France," 317–29; Millington, *Fighting for France*, 24–6, 92, 99, 111, 177–8; Muel-Dreyfus, *Vichy and the Eternal Feminine*.
32 Capdevila, "The Quest for Masculinity in a Defeated France," 435. Gottlieb in *Feminine Fascism* contends that there were "gangs of militant British fascist women" who offered "a striking contrast to the prevalent notions of women's history during the inter-war period as a return to ideals of female domesticity," 3, 29–30. See also Sarnoff, "In the Cervix of the French Nation," 44–6; Lower, *Hitler's Furies*. Chris Millington has documented the participation of women on the left and the right in street violence in France during the 1930s: Millington, "Street-fighting Men," 606–38, especially 628.
33 Chadwick and Latimer, "Becoming Modern: Gender and Sexual Identity," 3–7.
34 AP PEROTIN 212/79/3/50, "Second dossier, Instruction à Montélimar," Pièce #80.
35 AP PEROTIN 212/79/3/50, "Second dossier, Instruction à Montélimar," Pièce #104.
36 AP PEROTIN 212/79/3/50, "Second dossier, Instruction à Montélimar," Pièce #104.

37 AP PEROTIN 212/79/3/50, "Second dossier, Instruction à Montélimar," Pièce #104.
38 The literature on masculinity in interwar French and European culture is extensive. See Campbell, *Political Belief in France*; Capdevila, "The Quest for Masculinity in a Defeated France"; Heurtaud-Wright, "*Les Hommes nouveaux*," 215–26; Kalman, "*Faisceau* Visions of Physical and Moral Transformation," 343–66; Koos, "Fascism, Fatherhood, and the Family in Interwar France," 317–29; Millington, "Fighting for France"; Millington, "Street-fighting Men," 606–38; Passmore, "Boy Scouting for Grown-Ups?" 527–57; Read, "*Des hommes et des citoyens*," 88–111; Read, "He Is Depending on You," 261–91; Joan Tumblety, *Remaking the Male Body*; Tumblety, "Revenge of the Fascist Knights," 11–20.
39 Childers, *Fathers, Families, and the State in France*, 3. See also Koos, "Fascism, Fatherhood, and the Family in Interwar France," 318.
40 Campbell, "Women and Men in French Authoritarianism," 42; Passmore, "Boy Scouting for Grown Ups?" 529.
41 Campbell, "Women and Men in French Authoritarianism," 25. For more on the history of the CF and the PSF, see Kennedy, "Pitfalls of Paramilitarism," 64–79; Machefer, *Ligues et fascismes en France*, 21–6; Passmore, *The Right in France*, 291ff; Read, "He Is Depending on You," 261–91. For a thorough but sympathetic biography of the founder of the *Croix de Feu*, see Nobécourt, *Le Colonel de La Rocque*.
42 Childers, *Fathers, Families and the State in France*, 5.
43 For a discussion of this "new man," see Read, *The Republic of Men*, 10–11, 54–6.
44 AP PEROTIN 212/79/3/50, "Second dossier, Instruction à Montélimar," Pièces #79, 80.
45 Childers, *Fathers, Families, and the State in France*, 43; Read, *The Republic of Men*, 33.
46 Hertaud-Wright, "*Les Hommes nouveaux*," 216–17.
47 Hertaud-Wright, "*Les Hommes nouveaux*," 423.
48 The best description of France between the wars remains Weber, *The Hollow Years*. For French pacifism in this era, see 19–25. See also Ingram, "'Nous allons vers les monastères,'" 132–51.
49 Millington, *Fighting for France*, 26–30, 90–1, 95, 100; Tumblety, *Remaking the Male Body*, 1.
50 Kalman, "*Faisceau* Visions of Physical and Moral Transformation," 344.
51 Read, *The Republic of Men*, 55.
52 Tumblety, *Remaking the Male Body*, 95.
53 Millington, "Street-Fighting Men," 624–5.
54 Yagil, "*L'Homme Nouveau*," 11, 20.
55 AP PEROTIN 212/79/3/50, "Second dossier, Instruction à Montélimar," Pièce #87.
56 Read, *The Republic of Men*, 72–89.
57 Yagil, "*L'Homme Nouveau*," 17–20, 29, 35–8.
58 Read, "He Is Depending on You," 278.

59 Capdevila, "The Quest for Masculinity in a Defeated France," 428–30.
60 AP PEROTIN 212/79/3/50, "Second dossier, Instruction à Montélimar," Pièce #80.
61 Millington, "Political Violence in Interwar France," 246–59; Millington, "Street-fighting Men," 606–16.
62 Most of what follows comes from Moynier's confession, AP PEROTIN 212/79/3/50, "Second dossier, Instruction à Montélimar," Pièce #80, and that of Annie Mourraille, AP PEROTIN 212/79/3/50, "Second dossier, Instruction à Montélimar," Pièce #104. Much of the evidence and witness testimony is also included in a 28 July 1941 police report, AP PEROTIN 212/79/3/50, "Second dossier, Instruction à Montélimar," Pièce #37.
63 AP PEROTIN 212/79/3/50, "Second dossier, Instruction à Montélimar," Pièce #80.
64 AP PEROTIN 212/79/3/50, "Second dossier, Instruction à Montélimar," Pièce #80.
65 AP PEROTIN 212/79/3/50, "Second dossier, Instruction à Montélimar," Pièce #104.
66 AP PEROTIN 212/79/3/50, "Second dossier, Instruction à Montélimar," Pièce #80.
67 AP 1320W/119, "Conclusions de M. Le Procureur de la République," 21 August 1946, Cabinet de M. Robert Lévy, juge d'instruction, 2.
68 AP PEROTIN 212/79/3/50, "Second dossier, Instruction à Montélimar," Pièce #104.
69 AP PEROTIN 212/79/3/50, "Second dossier, Instruction à Montélimar," Pièce #80.
70 AP PEROTIN 212/79/3/50, "Second dossier, Instruction à Montélimar," Pièces #5, 7, 9.
71 AP PEROTIN 212/79/3/50, "Second dossier, Instruction à Montélimar," Pièce #19.
72 AP PEROTIN 212/79/3/50, "Second dossier, Instruction à Montélimar," Pièce #80.
73 AP PEROTIN 212/79/3/50, "Second dossier, Instruction à Montélimar," Pièce #104.
74 AP PEROTIN 212/79/3/50, "Second dossier, Instruction à Montélimar," Pièce #104.

6. August–October 1941: The Net Widens

1 AP PEROTIN 212/79/3/51, Côte 14, Nice, 16 August 1941.
2 On 16 September 1937, officers of the Sûreté searched Corre's Parisian apartment and discovered a list of the most important members of the Cagoule, which helped Dormoy track and arrest many of them later that year. Brunelle and Finley-Croswhite, *Murder in the Métro*, 100–1; Corre (pseud. Dagore), *Les carnets secrets*.
3 According to one witness, Deloncle boasted about his acquaintance with Annie Mourraille and Yves Moynier, and his involvement in the plot. AP PEROTIN

212/79/3/61, Statement of Lucien Fromes, 23 January 1946; see also, AP PEROTIN 212/79/3/51, "Exposé," 19, 24.
4 M. Cointet, *Nouvelle histoire de Vichy*, 367–76; Jackson, *France: The Dark Years*, 172–4, 276.
5 AP PEROTIN 212/79/3/61, Statement of Lucien Fromes, 23 January 1946; Bourdrel, *Les Cagoulards dans la guerre*, 164–9.
6 *L'Étudiant français: Organe mensuel de la Fédération nationale des étudiants d'Action française*, 25 June 1926, 6e année, no. 13, 4; *L'Étudiant français*, 10 December 1927, 8e année, no. 2, 2. For Jeantet's relationship with Mitterrand, see Péan, *Une jeunesse française*, 12, 127, 177, 185, 225, 234, 268–70, 288–92, 424, 558, 561.
7 *Le Petit Parisien*, Sunday, 23 December 1928, 53e année, no. 18926, 2.
8 Péan, *Une jeunesse française*, 424.
9 AN Z/6/689/A, "Cour de justice du département de la Seine, dossiers d'affaires jugées (1944–1951), dossier, 5348, Michel Harispe et autres," Dossier 5348 Harispe, Procès-verbal, Michel Harispe, 26 September 1945, 2.
10 Lacroix-Riz, *Le choix de la défaite*, 278–81.
11 For more on Claude Jeantet, who, unlike his brother Gabriel, was an open collaborator with the Germans, see Lacroix-Riz, *Le choix de la défaite*, 269, 270, 271, 274, 279, 288, 323–4; Pascal Ory, *Les collaborateurs*, 23, 27, 62, 73, 111, 117–18, 122.
12 AP PEROTIN 212/79/3/50, "Ordonnance de dessaisisement," 15 November 1945.
13 Quoted in Bourdrel, *La Cagoule: Histoire d'une société secrète*, 276.
14 Finley-Croswhite and Brunelle, "Creating a Holocaust Landscape on the Streets of Paris"; Bourdrel, *Les Cagoulards dans la guerre*, 38–9; Lacroix-Riz, *Le choix de la défaite*, 42–3.
15 Péan, *Une jeunesse française*, 185.
16 Bourdrel, *Les Cagoulards dans la guerre*, 89–96.
17 Lambert and Le Marec, *Vichy 1940–1944*, 301–14; Ory, *Les collaborateurs*, 98–100, 102, 241–2, 244, 246, 248, 249; Valode, *Les hommes de Pétain*, 367–8.
18 Amouroux, *La grande histoire des Français*, 3:358–72.
19 Calvi and Masurovsky, *Le festin du Reich*, 265–8.
20 Archives de la Préfecture de Paris (APP), 21.704/77W/1476, "Renseignement sur le Mouvement social révolutionnaire et ses principaux dirigeants," "Rapports," 9 April 1941 and 4 June 1941. See also Bourdrel, *Les Cagoulards dans la guerre*, 155–9.
21 "Le caractère 'NEO-CAGOULARD' de l'Amicale de France apparait dans le regroupement de ces gens qui, au lendemain de l'Armistice ont fondés à Marseille une organisation dont les dirigeants 'Gabriel JEANTET, VAUDREMER, DAUSSIN, BAGARRY, BARON, BERTHIER, DERCHEU, DUNGLER, etc.' étaient tous royalistes notoires ou figuraient sur la liste 'CORRE,'" AP PEROTIN 212/79/3/47, 5 June 1946, Direction des Services de police judiciaire, P.J./R.Rch.N. ministère de l'Intérieur, Direction générale de la Sûreté nationale,

Direction des Services de police judiciaire, "Note sur l'Amicale de France, Reconstitution de la Cagoule," 2e enquête, 2.
22 AP PEROTIN 212/79/3/47, 5 June 1946, Direction des Services de police judiciaire, P.J./R.Rch.N. ministère de l'Intérieur, Direction générale de la Sûreté nationale, Direction des Services de police judiciaire, "Note sur l'Amicale de France, Reconstitution de la Cagoule," 2e enquête. The author of this report, Georges Richier, was quoting here material from the archives of Dr. Martin that the police confiscated during the war. Les Archives du Docteur MARTIN, au sujet de "L'AMICALE DE FRANCE" (scellé no. 4), 19–25.
23 AP PEROTIN 212/79/3/47, "Note sur l'Amicale de France, Reconstitution de la Cagoule," 2e enquête.
24 Péan, *Une jeunesse française*, 225.
25 AP PEROTIN 212/79/3/51, Declaration of Gabriel Jeantet to M. Perez, juge d'instruction, 22 September 1945.
26 AN Z/6/689/A, Dossier 5348 Harispe, Procès-verbal, Michel Harispe, 26 September 1945, 7–8.
27 Deacon, *The Extreme Right in the French Resistance*, 163.
28 AN Z/6/689/A, Dossier 5348 Harispe, Procès-verbal, Michel Harispe, 26 September 1945, 8; AN Z/6/689/A, Dossier 5348 Harispe, folder 95, containing miscellaneous papers of Dr. Martin.
29 AN Z/6/689/A, Dossier 5348 Harispe, Procès-verbal, Michel Harispe, 26 September 1945, 9.
30 AP PEROTIN 212/79/3/50, Statement of Eugène Deloncle, December 1941.
31 AP PEROTIN 212/79/3/47, "Declaration of Michel Harispe to M. Perez, juge d'instruction," no date, but probably also September 1945; AP PEROTIN 212/79/3/51, 19 April 1945.
32 AN Pierrefitte, Z/6/689/A, Dossier 5348 Harispe, "Le Mouvement social révolutionnaire: Première note d'enquête générale," 24.
33 AN Z/6/689/A, Dossier 5348 Harispe, "Le Mouvement social révolutionnaire: Première note d'enquête générale," 24.
34 AN Z/6/689/A, Dossier 5348 Harispe, folder 95, containing miscellaneous papers of Dr. Martin; Transcript of Deloncle's speech delivered on Radio-Paris at 5:45 p.m. on 14 February 1941, 3.
35 Bourdrel, *La Cagoule*, 94–95; Brunelle and Finley-Croswhite, *Murder in the Métro*, 113, 129; Monier, *Le complot dans la république*, 308.
36 AN Z/6/689/A, Dossier 5348 Harispe, folder 95, containing miscellaneous papers of Dr. Martin; Transcript of Deloncle's speech delivered on Radio-Paris at 5:45 p.m. on 14 February 1941, 3.
37 AN Z/6/689/A, Dossier 5348 Harispe, "Le Mouvement social révolutionnaire: Première note d'enquête générale," 16; AP PEROTIN 212/79/3/47, "Rapport d'ensemble sur le 'Mouvement social révolutionnaire,'" 2e enquête, Paris, 15 January 1947, 15.
38 AN Z/6/689/A, Dossier 5348 Harispe, folder 95, containing miscellaneous papers of Dr. Martin; Memo dated Marseille, 17 June 1941, memo dated

28 October 1941, and memo dated 20 November 1941; and a police report dated 2 February 1941 that states "I have been informed just now of the attachment, stronger than ever, between Jeantet and Deloncle."
39 AN Z/6/689/A, Dossier 5348 Harispe, folder 95, containing miscellaneous papers of Dr. Martin; Memos dated 2 August 1941, 21 August 1941, 22 August 1941, and 14 October 1941.
40 AN Z/6/689/A, Dossier 5348 Harispe, Procès-verbal, Michel Harispe, 26 September 1945, 10–11, 25.
41 AN Z/6/689/A, Dossier 5348 Harispe, folder 95, containing miscellaneous papers of Dr. Martin.
42 Brunelle and Finley-Croswhite, *Murder in the Métro*, 155; Corre (pseud. Dagore), *Les carnets secrets*, 220.
43 Brunelle and Finley-Croswhite, *Murder in the Métro*, 103, 121, 147, 160; M. Cointet, *Nouvelle histoire de Vichy*, 109; Delpla, *Qui a tué Georges Mandel?* 219; Péan, *Une jeunesse française*, 12, 273.
44 AN Z/6/121, Dossier 1740 Raymond Hérard, "Procès-verbal de M. Eugène Pillière de Tanouarn."
45 Joly, *Vichy dans la "solution finale,"* 295, 320, 446–7; AN Z/6/121, "Dossier 1740, Raymond Hérard," "Procès-verbal, Procédure Hérard, Raymond, 20 September 1945, Statement of Jehan Castellane"; AN BB/18/3353, "L'attentat commis contre la synagogue de Marseille," 9 January 1942, Parquet de la Cour d'Appel; *Centre de documentation juive contemporaine*, Paris (CDJC), CCCLXX-110-125, "Document précisant les adresses d'immeubles juifs occupés par le Rassemblement nationale populaire suivi d'une lettre du chef du Mouvement social révolutionnaire."
46 AN Pierrefitte, Z/6/689/A, Dossier 5348 Harispe, "Le Mouvement social révolutionnaire: Première note d'enquête générale," 137–55, 234–8.
47 AP PEROTIN 212/79/3/50, "Second dossier, Instruction à Montélimar," Pièces #50, 114; AP PEROTIN 212/79/3/50, Renseignements en forme de détention, sous-dossier "Dossier de renseignement," 58 bis.
48 AP PEROTIN 212/79/3/50, "Second dossier, Instruction à Montélimar," Pièces #92, 145.
49 AP PEROTIN 212/79/3/50, "Second dossier, Instruction à Montélimar."
50 Chenevier, *De la Combe aux fées à Lurs*, 80.
51 AP PEROTIN 212/79/3/50, "Dossier de la détention," Pièce #58.
52 Millington, "Immigrants and Undesirables," 40–59, 44.
53 AP PEROTIN 212/79/3/50, "Second dossier, Instruction à Montélimar," Pièce #110.
54 AP PEROTIN 212/79/3/50, "Instruction à Montélimar," Pièce #74, Report from Kubler to the commissaire divisionnaire chef de la 10e Brigade de police mobile, Lyon.
55 AP PEROTIN 212/79/3/50, "Dossier de la détention," Pièce #58, Hérard file.
56 AP PEROTIN 212/79/3/50, "Second dossier, Instruction à Montélimar," Pièces #68, 73, 88.

57 AP PEROTIN 212/79/3/50, "Second dossier, Instruction à Montélimar," Pièce #133.
58 All quotes in this and the following paragraph come from AP PEROTIN 212/79/3/50, "Second dossier, Instruction à Montélimar," Pièce #104.
59 Azéma, "Le régime de Vichy," 1:159–90; Curtis, *Verdict on Vichy*, 70–4; Paxton, *Vichy France*, 33–8; Sweets, *Choices in Vichy France*, 165–6.
60 M. Cointet, *Nouvelle histoire de Vichy*, 624–7; Jackson, *France: The Dark Years*, 272–81, 480–1.
61 Azéma and Wieviorka, *Vichy, 1940–1944*, 65–7, 74–7; M. Cointet, *Nouvelle histoire de Vichy*, 154–61.
62 Amouroux, *La grande histoire des Français*, 3: 153–5; M. Cointet, *Nouvelle histoire de Vichy*, 394, 507–8, 512; Jackson, *France: The Dark Years*, 145–6, 174–6.
63 Jackson, *France: The Dark Years*, 175, 178–81.
64 Lambert and Le Marec, *Vichy 1940–1944*, 272, 303.
65 AP PEROTIN 212/79/3/50, "Second dossier, Instruction à Montélimar," Pièce #190.
66 AP PEROTIN 212/79/3/50, "Second dossier, Instruction à Montélimar," Pièce #114.
67 AP PEROTIN 212/79/3/50, "Second dossier, Instruction à Montélimar," Pièces #115, 116.
68 AP PEROTIN 212/79/3/50, "Diréction générale de la Sûreté nationale: scellé no. 2, direction des Services de police judiciaire"; AP PEROTIN 212/79/3/50, "Exposé," 12; AP PEROTIN 212/79/3/50, "Second dossier, Instruction à Montélimar," Pièce #82.
69 AP PEROTIN 212/79/3/50, "Second dossier, Instruction à Montélimar," Pièce #135.
70 AD Allier, 64/J/104, "Suites judiciaires de l'assassinat de Marx Dormoy, Archives de Jeanne Dormoy, Période de Guerre, suite Période 1945–1963." Excerpts from the diary of Annie Mourraille, 23.
71 AP PEROTIN 212/79/3/50, "Second dossier, Instruction à Montélimar," Pièce #134.
72 AP PEROTIN 212/79/3/50, "Second dossier, Instruction à Montélimar," Pièce #135.
73 AD Allier, 64/J/104, "Suites judiciaires de l'assassinat de Marx Dormoy, Archives de Jeanne Dormoy, Période de Guerre, suite Période 1945–1963." Excerpts from the diary of Annie Mourraille, 23–4.
74 AP PEROTIN 212/79/3/50, "Second dossier, Instruction à Montélimar," Pièce #135.
75 AP PEROTIN 212/79/3/50, "Second dossier, Instruction à Montélimar," Pièce #135.
76 Colton, *Léon Blum*, 405–27; Jackson, *France: The Dark Years*, 185, 419; Lacouture, *Léon Blum*, 428–40.

77 AP PEROTIN 212/79/3/50, "Second dossier, Instruction à Montélimar," Pièce #138.
78 AP PEROTIN 212/79/3/50, "Dossier de la détention," Pièce #74.
79 AP PEROTIN 212/79/3/50, "Exposé," 29 and AP PEROTIN, 212/79/3/50, Affaire Dormoy, "Affaire Dormoy, dossier Montélimar, Renseignements en forme de détention," Pièces #22–34.
80 *Paris-Soir*, 17 August 1940, front page.
81 AP PEROTIN 212/79/3/50, "Affaire Dormoy, dossier Montélimar, Renseignements en forme de détention," Pièce #22.
82 AP PEROTIN 212/79/3/50, "Affaire Dormoy, dossier Montélimar, Renseignements en forme de détention," Pièce #24.
83 AP PEROTIN 212/79/3/50, "Exposé," 29.
84 AP PEROTIN 212/79/3/50, "Second dossier, Instruction à Montélimar," Pièces #139, 140, 141, 142 and AP PEROTIN 212/79/3/50, "Dossier de la détention, Sous-dossier Marchi, Pièce #13.
85 This and the rest of the quotes in this paragraph come from AP PEROTIN 212/79/3/50, "Second dossier, Instruction à Montélimar," Pièce #139.
86 AP PEROTIN 212/79/3/50, "Second dossier, Instruction à Montélimar," Pièce #141.
87 AP PEROTIN 212/79/3/50, "Second dossier, Instruction à Montélimar," Pièce #104.
88 Brunelle and Finley-Croswhite, *Murder in the Métro*, 155; Joly, *Vichy dans la "solution finale,"* 236–8, 248.
89 AP PEROTIN 212/79/3/50, "Dossier de la détention, Sous-dossier Marchi, Pièce #13.
90 AP PEROTIN 212/79/3/50, "Second dossier, Instruction à Montélimar," Pièce #140.
91 AP PEROTIN 212/79/3/50, "Second dossier, Instruction à Montélimar," Pièce #141.
92 AP PEROTIN 212/79/3/50, "Second dossier, Instruction à Montélimar," Pièce #141.
93 AP PEROTIN 212/79/3/50, "Dossier de la détention, Sous-dossier Marchi, Pièce #13.

7. October 1941–March 1942: The Waiting Game

1 AP PEROTIN 212/79/3/50, "Dossier de détention," Pièces #90, 90 bis and "Instruction à Montélimar," Pièces #231 and 234.
2 AP PEROTIN 212/79/3/50, "Dossier de détention," Pièces #52, 90, 90 bis.
3 AP PEROTIN 212/79/3/50, "Dossier de détention," Pièces #52, 90, 90 bis.
4 AP PEROTIN 212/79/3/50, "Second dossier: Instruction à Montélimar," Pièce #247.
5 Vinen, *The Politics of French Business*, 119–21; Vinen, *The Unfree French*, 219–23.
6 Burrin, *France Under the Germans*, 96–7; M. Cointet, *Nouvelle histoire de Vichy*, 465–8; Paxton, *Vichy France*, 80–1.

7   Laub, *After the Fall*, 135–67.
8   Burrin, *France Under the Germans*, 195.
9   M. Cointet, *Nouvelle histoire de Vichy*, 466–87; for the earliest stages of resistance, see Jackson, *France: The Dark Years*, 278–82 and 402–10; Sweets, *The Politics of Resistance in France*, 7–10; and Veillon, "Les réseaux de Résistance," 1:407–39.
10 Joseph-Barthélémy described these events and the establishment of the *Tribunal d'État*, whose creation he ascribed to Pucheu, in his memoirs. Joseph-Barthélemy, *Ministre de la justice*, 244–50.
11 M. Cointet, *Nouvelle histoire de Vichy*, 466–7, 472.
12 M. Cointet, *Nouvelle histoire de Vichy*, 473.
13 Burrin, *France Under the Germans*, 190–3; Jackson, *France: The Dark Years*, 239.
14 Sweets, "Hold That Pendulum!" 731–58, 754.
15 Paxton, *Vichy France*, 239.
16 Jackson, *France: The Dark Years*, 430–6. See also Sweets, *The Politics of Resistance*, which focuses on the *Mouvements Unis de la Résistance*; Jackson, *De Gaulle*, 125–200.
17 Burrin, *France Under the Germans*, 148–9.
18 Jackson, *France: The Dark Years*, 234–5; Mitchell, *Nazi*, 64–8; Vinen, *The Unfree French*, 219–46; Calvi and Masurovsky, *Le festin du Reich*. The authors discuss thoroughly ways in which the Germans extracted enormous wealth from the French economy during the war.
19 Jackson, *France: The Dark Years*, 234–5; Mitchell, *Nazi Paris*, 69–72; Vinen, *The Unfree French*, 247–79.
20 AD Allier, extracts from Annie Mourraille's diary, in 64/J/104, Fonds Jeanne Dormoy. Mourraille had "code names" for each of the individuals she mentioned in her diary. Among those for Yves Moynier was "Booby." The cat-and-mouse game Mourraille plays becomes apparent in reading the diary.
21 AP PEROTIN 212/79/3/50, "Second dossier: Instruction à Montélimar," Pièce #257.
22 AP PEROTIN 212/79/3/50, "Dossier de la détention," "Sous-dossier Marchi," Pièce #13.
23 This material comes from a supplemental dossier in AP PEROTIN 212/79/3/50, "Instruction à Montélimar," that has no number and appears to be material redacted from the main dossier by the police in 1945.
24 AP PEROTIN 212/79/3/50, "Second dossier, Instruction à Montélimar," Pièce #134.
25 Finley-Croswhite and Brunelle, "Creating a Holocaust Landscape on the Streets of Paris," 60–89; *Centre de documentation juive contemporaine*, Musée de la Shoah, Paris (CDJC), I-19, "Rapport daté du 3/10/1941du délégué au chef de la SiPo-SD pour la Belgique et la France." See published version in Poliakov, "A Conflict between the German Army and the Secret Police," 253–66; CDJC, CCCLXIV-7_31-37 "Retranscription des minutes du

procès Oberg-Knochen ayant eu lieu au tribunal militaire permanent de Paris, 24 Septembre 1956."

26 Archives de la Prefecture de Police, Paris (APP), B/A 1817, "Attentats contre les Synagogues de Paris, Octobre 1941–Juillet 1942"; Archives du Consistoire Central, Paris [ACC], Dossier C.C-33-c, "Synagogues et organisations, 1941–1942."

27 Bourdrel, *Les Cagoulards dans la guerre*, 149–55; Finley-Croswhite and Brunelle, "Creating a Holocaust Landscape on the Streets of Paris," 60–89.

28 Vincent Giraudier argues that the synagogue bombings and the Dormoy assassination were engineered by the same cabal of Deloncle, Jeantet, and their German supporters: Giraudier, *Les Bastilles de Vichy*, 121–2.

29 AP PEROTIN 212/79/3/47, Report, "Le Mouvement social révolutionnaire, Première note d'enquête générale," 30 April 1946, 21; AP PEROTIN 212/79/3/47, Rapport d'ensemble sur le "Mouvement social révolutionnaire," 2e enquête, 15 January 1947, 15; AP PEROTIN 212/79/3/47, ministère de l'Intérieur, Direction générale de la Police nationale, N. 283; Procès-verbal, Guy Delioux, 10 July 1945.

30 AN Z/6/689/A, Dossier 5348, Procès-verbal, Michel Harsipe, 26 September 1945, 9. See MSR material quoted in Péan, *V, enquête sur l'affaire des "avions renifleurs,"* 39–40.

31 AP PEROTIN 212/79/3/47, Report, "Le Mouvement social révolutionnaire, Première note d'enquête générale," 30 April 1946, 25. The full transcript of Deloncle's 14 February 1941 radio address to France can be found in the appendix to the report. The antisemitic statement is on page 3 of the transcript.

32 AP PEROTIN 212/79/3/47, Report, "Le Mouvement social révolutionnaire, Première note d'enquête générale," 30 April 1946, 30–6.

33 After the war one German source indicated that Deloncle and the MSR were receiving subsidies of at least 200,000 to 300,000 francs per month from German Ambassador Otto Abetz. AP PEROTIN 212/79/3/47, Dossier #3, "Supplement d'information 1945 (M. Robert Levy)," Memo dated Paris, 6 February 1946, containing extracts of the interrogation of Rudolph Schleier, deputy to German Ambassador Otto Abetz in Paris.

34 Gordon, "The Condottieri of the Collaboration," 261–82.

35 AP PEROTIN 212/79/3/50, "Second dossier, Instruction à Montélimar," Pièce #173.

36 AP PEROTIN 212/79/3/50, "Second dossier, Instruction à Montélimar," Pièce #174. Copies of the letters are also preserved in the AD Allier, 64/J/104, Fonds Dormoy, "Enquête et préparation du procès d'assises de 1948," and "Arrestation des assassins et suites du procès d'assises, 1950-s.d."

37 AP PEROTIN 212/79/3/50, "Second dossier, Instruction à Montélimar," Pièce #174.

38 AP PEROTIN 212/79/3/50, "Second dossier, Instruction à Montélimar," Pièces #190, 191, 193.

39 AN BB/18/3353. See a handwritten letter, dated 14 May 1945, from Paule Trivine of Nice regarding Faraut's activities before and during the war.

40 AP PEROTIN 212/79/3/50, Report from inspecteur principal de la Police judiciare de Paris dated 8 May 1945.
41 AD Allier, 64/J/104, Fonds Jeanne Dormoy, "Enquête et préparation du procès d'assises de 1948"; Extract from Mourraille's diary, 25.
42 AP PEROTIN 212/79/3/50, "Dossier Montélimar, Renseignements en forme de détention," Pièce #58 bis.
43 AP PEROTIN 212/79/3/50, "Dossier Montélimar, Renseignements en forme de détention," Pièce #58 bis, 25.
44 AP PEROTIN 212/79/3/50, "Dossier Montélimar, Renseignements en forme de détention," Pièce #58 bis, 65.
45 AP PEROTIN 212/79/3/50, "Dossier Montélimar, Renseignements en forme de détention," Pièce #58 bis, 69, 85, 90; AD Allier, 64/J/104, Fonds Jeanne Dormoy, "Enquête et préparation du procès d'assises de 1948"; Extract from Mourraille's diary, 109.
46 AD Allier, 64/J/104, Fonds Jeanne Dormoy, "Enquête et préparation du procès d'assises de 1948"; Extracts from Mourraille's diary, 126, 127, 128, 136, 138.
47 AD Allier, 64/J/104, Fonds Jeanne Dormoy, "Enquête et préparation du procès d'assises de 1948"; Extract from Mourraille's diary, 140, 142; and AP PEROTIN 212/79/3/50, "Second dossier, Instruction à Montélimar," Pièces #169, 170, 171. See also AD Allier, 64/J/104, Fonds Jeanne Dormoy, "Enquête et préparation du procès d'assises de 1948"; Extracts from Mourraille's diary, 144, 146.
48 AP PEROTIN 212/79/3/50, "Second dossier, Instruction à Montélimar," Pièce #181; AP PEROTIN 212/79/3/50, "Dossier de la détention," "Sous-dossier Marchi," Pièce #13.
49 AD Allier, 64/J/104, Fonds Jeanne Dormoy, "Enquête et préparation du procès d'assises de 1948; Extract from Mourraille's diary, 149.
50 AP PEROTIN 212/79/3/50, "Dossier de la détention," "Sous-dossier Marchi," Pièce #20.
51 AP PEROTIN 212/79/3/50, "Dossier de la détention," "Sous-dossier Marchi," Pièce #13.
52 AD Allier, 64/J/104, Fonds Jeanne Dormoy, "Enquête et préparation du procès d'assises de 1948; Extract from Mourraille's diary, 129.
53 AP PEROTIN 212/79/3/50, "Second dossier, Instruction à Montélimar," Pièce #190.
54 AP PEROTIN 212/79/3/50, "Dossier Montélimar, Renseignements en forme de détention," Pièce #58 bis.
55 AP PEROTIN 212/79/3/50, "Dossier de la détention," Pièce #74.
56 AP PEROTIN 212/79/3/50, "Second dossier, Instruction à Montélimar," Pièce #143.
57 AP PEROTIN 212/79/3/50, "Second dossier, Instruction à Montélimar," Pièce #154.
58 AP PEROTIN 212/79/3/50, "Second dossier, Instruction à Montélimar," Pièce #154.

59 AP PEROTIN 212/79/3/50, "Dossier de la détention," Pièce #74.
60 AP PEROTIN 212/79/3/50, "Second dossier, Instruction à Montélimar," Pièce #190.
61 AP PEROTIN 212/79/3/50, "Dossier de la détention," Pièces #55, 57.
62 AP PEROTIN 212/79/3/50, "Second dossier, Instruction à Montélimar," Pièce #198.
63 AD Allier, 64/J/104, Fonds Jeanne Dormoy, "Enquête et préparation du procès d'assises de 1948"; Extract from Mourraille's diary, 235–6, 241.
64 AP PEROTIN 212/79/3/50, "Dossier de la détention," Pièce #74, Note from Judge Marion to the procureur at Montélimar dated 15 April 1942.
65 AP PEROTIN 212/79/3/51, "Exposé," 15.
66 AP PEROTIN 212/79/3/50, "Second dossier, Instruction à Montélimar," Pièce #202.
67 AP PEROTIN 212/79/3/50, "Second dossier, Instruction à Montélimar," Pièce #204.
68 AP PEROTIN 212/79/3/50, "Second dossier, Instruction à Montélimar," Pièce #201.
69 AP PEROTIN 212/79/3/50, "Second dossier, Instruction à Montélimar," Pièce #201.
70 AP PEROTIN 212/79/3/50, "Dossier de la détention," Pièce #59.
71 AP PEROTIN 212/79/3/50, "Second dossier, Instruction à Montélimar," Pièce #198.
72 AP PEROTIN 212/79/3/50, "Second dossier, Instruction à Montélimar," Pièce #200.
73 AD Allier, 64/J/104, Fonds Jeanne Dormoy, "Enquête et préparation du procès d'assises de 1948"; Extract from Mourraille's diary, 185.
74 AP PEROTIN 212/79/3/50, "Second dossier, Instruction à Montélimar," Pièce #205.
75 AN BB/18/3353, Tribunaux de première instance de Montélimar et de Nyons, Parquet du procureur de la République, No. 1337, Montélimar, 28 July 1942.
76 AP PEROTIN 212/79/3/50, "Second dossier, Instruction à Montélimar," Pièce #214.
77 AP PEROTIN 212/79/3/50, "Second dossier, Instruction à Montélimar," Pièce #214.
78 AP PEROTIN 212/79/3/50, "Second dossier, Instruction à Montélimar," Pièce #217.
79 AP PEROTIN 212/79/3/50, "Second dossier, Instruction à Montélimar," Pièce #214.
80 This and the subsequent quotes come from AP PEROTIN 212/79/3/50, "Second dossier, Instruction à Montélimar," Pièce #217.
81 AP PEROTIN 212/79/3/50, Exposé, Pièce #35.
82 AP PEROTIN 212/79/3/50, "Dossier Montélimar, Renseignements en forme de détention," Dossier de renseignement, Pièce #40.

8. 18 April 1942: The Return of Pierre Laval

1. M. Cointet, *Nouvelle histoire de Vichy*, 523–35.
2. AP PEROTIN 212/79/3/50, "Second dossier: Instruction à Montélimar," Pièce #234.
3. Burrin, *France Under the Germans*, 496–513; Frank, "Pétain, Laval, Darlan," 307–8, 318–19; Paxton, *Vichy France*, 249–58.
4. For more about the trial at Riom, see Béteille and Rimbaud, *Le Procès de Riom*; Michel, *Le Procès de Riom*; and Ribet, *Le Procès de Riom*.
5. Colton, *Léon Blum*, 385.
6. M. Cointet, *Nouvelle histoire de Vichy*, 496–7; Colton, *Léon Blum*, 386–7.
7. M. Cointet, *Nouvelle histoire de Vichy*, 496–8; Colton, *Léon Blum*, 400–1, 424.
8. M. Cointet, *Nouvelle histoire de Vichy*, 500.
9. Colton, *Léon Blum*, 406–7.
10. Jean-Pierre Azéma, "Le choc armé et les débandades," 105–37, 110–17; Azéma and Wieviorka, *Vichy, 1940–1944*, 22–3; M. Cointet, *Nouvelle histoire de Vichy*, 499; Colton, *Léon Blum*, 387.
11. Colton, *Léon Blum*, 386, 397–401.
12. M. Cointet, *Nouvelle histoire de Vichy*, 500–2; Colton, *Léon Blum*, 410–27; Lacouture, *Leon Blum*, 428–40; Monier, *Léon Blum*, 189–201. For a transcript of the proceedings, see Bracher, *Riom 1942: Le procès*. See also Daladier, *Journal de captivité*.
13. M. Cointet, *Nouvelle histoire de Vichy*, 502; Colton, *Léon Blum*, 424–47.
14. J.-P. Cointet, *Pierre Laval*, 363–74; M. Cointet, *Nouvelle histoire de Vichy*, 405–506; Frank, "Pétain, Laval, Darlan," 338–41.
15. Burrin, *France Under the Germans*, 150–1; M. Cointet, *Nouvelle histoire de Vichy*, 507–13, 517; Jackson, *France: The Dark Years*, 213–15.
16. J.-P. Cointet, *Pierre Laval*, 380–4; M. Cointet, *Nouvelle histoire de Vichy*, 543. "Je souhaite la victoire de l'Allemagne, parce que, sans elle, le bolchevisme demain s'installerait partout."
17. Burrin, *France Under the Germans*, 185–90; M. Cointet, *Nouvelle histoire de Vichy*, 518–19; Frank, "Pétain, Laval, Darlan," 342–8; Paxton, "La collaboration d'État," 349–83.
18. Jackson, *France: The Dark Years*, 354–60.
19. Bédarida and Bédarida, "La persecution des Juifs," 149–82; J.-P. Cointet, *Pierre Laval*, 378–92; Curtis, *Verdict on Vichy*, 112–14, 123–55; Fogg, *The Politics of Everyday Life*, 113–19; Jackson, *France: The Dark Years*, 360; Laub, *After the Fall*, 168–93; Marrus and Paxton, *Vichy et les Juifs*, 140–68, 196–205, 313–18, 321, 339; Rayski, *The Choice of the Jews under Vichy*, 12–14; Zuccotti, *The Holocaust and the French Jews*, 56–7, 81–102.
20. M. Cointet, *Nouvelle histoire de Vichy*, 538–53; Curtis, *Verdict on Vichy*, 180–8; Jackson, *France: The Dark Years*, 358–9; Marrus and Paxton, *Vichy et les Juifs*, 306–9, 321–9.

21 Bédarida and Bédarida, "La persécution des Juifs," 169, 268–72; Valode, *Les hommes de Pétain*, 346–9.
22 J.-P. Cointet, *Pierre Laval*, 393–403; M. Cointet, *Nouvelle histoire de Vichy*, 553–66; Jackson, *France: The Dark Years*, 360–2, 374–81; Kedward, *Occupied France*, 62–3; Kitson, *Police and Politics in Marseille*, 69; Marrus and Paxton, *Vichy et les Juifs*, 351–69; Mitchell, *Nazi Paris*, 81–90; Sweets, *Choices in Vichy France*, 133–6; Zuccotti, *The Holocaust and the French Jews*, 103–17; Lévy and Tillard, *Le Grande Rafle du Vel d'Hiv*.
23 Jackson, *France: The Dark Years*, 217; Kitson, *Police and Politics in Marseille*, 152, 163–4; Lacroix-Riz, *Les élites françaises entre 1940 et 1944*, 209–12.
24 Kitson, *Police and Politics in Marseille*, 116–17.
25 For these reforms, see Kitson, *Police and Politics in Marseille*, 80–2.
26 AP PEROTIN 212/79/3/50, "Second dossier, Instruction à Montélimar," Pièce #234.
27 APP, Rapports, 21.704/77W/466, "Renseignements sur le Mouvement social révolutionnaire et ses principaux dirigeants," 13 May 1942, Hérard.
28 AN Z/6/121, "Dossier 1740, Raymond Hérard, Procès-verbal de Jehan Castellane, 27 August 1945."
29 AP PEROTIN 212/79/3/50, "Second dossier, Instruction à Montélimar," Pièce #235.
30 AP PEROTIN 212/79/3/50, "Second dossier, Instruction à Montélimar," Pièce #235.
31 AP PEROTIN 212/79/3/50, "Second dossier, Instruction à Montélimar," Pièce #85.
32 AP PEROTIN 212/79/3/50, "Second dossier, Instruction à Montélimar," Pièce #235.
33 Dr. Farout's name is also often spelled "Faroud" in the documents.
34 AP PEROTIN 212/79/3/50, "Second dossier, Instruction à Montélimar," Pièce #236.
35 AP PEROTIN 212/79/3/50, "Second dossier, Instruction à Montélimar," Pièce #236.
36 AP PEROTIN 212/79/3/50, "Second dossier, Instruction à Montélimar," Pièce #239, a folder containing copies of both letters.
37 AP PEROTIN 212/79/3/50, "Second dossier, Instruction à Montélimar," Pièce #239.
38 AP PEROTIN 212/79/3/50, "Affaire Dormoy, Dossier Montélimar, Renseignements en forme de détention," Pièce #74.
39 AP PEROTIN 212/79/3/50, "Affaire Dormoy, Dossier Montélimar, Renseignements en forme de détention," Pièces #81: 20 May 1942, #84: 2 June 1942, #87: 28 May 1942, #95: 15 July 1942.
40 AP PEROTIN 212/79/3/50, "Second dossier, Instruction à Montélimar," Pièce #239.
41 Archives Nationales (AN), BB/18/3353, ministère de la Justice, Note sur l'affaire Dormoy, 21 July 1942.

42 AN BB/18/3353, ministère de la Justice, Note sur l'affaire Dormoy, 21 July 1942, 3.
43 AN BB/18/3353, tribunaux de première instance de Montélimar et de Nyons, parquet du procureur de la République, no. 1337, Montélimar, 28 July 1942.
44 AN BB/18/3353, ministère de la Justice, Note sur l'affaire Dormoy, 21 July 1942, 3.
45 AN BB/18/3353, tribunaux de première instance de Montélimar et de Nyons, parquet du procureur de la République, no. 1337, Montélimar, 28 July 1942.
46 AN BB/18/3353, ministère de la Justice, Note sur l'affaire Dormoy, 21 July 1942, 4.
47 AN BB/18/3353, ministère de la Justice, Letters dated 27 March 1942, 24 April 1942, 5 May 1942, 10, 12, and 16 November 1942.
48 AN BB/18/3353, ministère de la Justice, Note sur l'affaire Dormoy, 21 July 1942, 5.
49 AP PEROTIN 212/79/3/50, "Affaire Dormoy, Dossier Montélimar, Renseignements en forme de détention," Pièce #99.
50 Joseph-Barthélemy, *Ministre de la Justice*, 369. Copies of dozens of these letters and petitions can be found in AN BB/18/3353.
51 AD Allier, 64/J/104, Fonds Jeanne Dormoy, Prison Journal of Annie Mourraille, excerpts, 325.
52 AD Allier, 64/J/104, Fonds Jeanne Dormoy, "Enquête et préparation d'assisses de 1948," sub-folder "Arrestation des assassins et suites du procès d'assises—1950-s.d."
53 AP PEROTIN 212/79/3/50, First dossier, "Dossier de Détention," Pièce #100.
54 AN BB/18/3353, ministère de la Justice, Sub-folder with documents related to the escape attempt, report dated Nîmes le 26 octobre 1942.
55 AP PEROTIN 212/79/3/50, First dossier, "Dossier de Détention," Pièces #101, 101 bis.

9. 23 January 1943: German Intervention

1 APP B/A/M5, "Dossier Antoinette Masse." See also Bourdrel, *Les Cagoulards dans la guerre*, 164–9. Bourdrel's source here is the police report "Résumé de la Procédure. Meurtre de Mme. Masse," Sûreté nationale, Inspection générale des services de police criminelle, 22 October 1941.
2 Bourdrel, *Les Cagoulards dans la guerre*, 166.
3 Bourdrel, *Les Cagoulards dans la guerre*, 177; see also APP, 21/704/77W/1476, "Renseignement sur le Mouvement social révolutionnaire et ses principaux dirigéants," "Rapports," 13 May 1942 and AN Z/6/689/A, Police judiciaire, Rapport, 28 November 1945, Jacques Fauran.
4 Bourdrel, *Les Cagoulards dans la guerre*, 167.
5 APP 21/704/77W/1476, "Rapports," "Renseignement sur le Mouvement social révolutionnaire et ses principaux dirigéants," 13 May 1942.

6 AP PEROTIN 212/79/3/47, Supplément d'Information, 1945, Judge Lévy, Pièce #66, Procès-verbal, Moreau de la Meuse, s.d.
7 AP PEROTIN 212/79/3/47, Supplément d'Information, 1945, Judge Lévy, Pièce #66, Procès-verbal, Moreau de la Meuse, s.d.
8 APP, 21/704/77W/1476, "Rapports," Report dated 11 May 1942. The police also had a file on one Pierre Jouanny. Pierre Jouanny was a war veteran who joined Doriot's PPF and later the LVF and ended up as a guard at the LVF headquarters in Paris. AN Z/6/53, "Dossier 886, Pierre Jouanny."
9 APP, 21/704/77W/1476, "Renseignement sur le Mouvement social révolutionnaire et ses principaux dirigeants," "Rapports," 13 May 1942; Bourdrel, *Les Cagoulards dans la guerre*, 168–9.
10 APP, 21/704/77W/1476, "Rapports," Notes dated 9 April and 4 June 1941.
11 Bourdrel, *Les Cagoulards dans la guerre*, 170–1.
12 AN Z/6/689/A, Papers of Dr. Martin, Pièce #35, Report dated 9 August 1941.
13 APP, 21/704/77W/1476, "Filliol."
14 APP, 21/704/77W/1476, "Filliol," Note dated Vichy, 25 March 1941.
15 Burrin, *France Under the Germans*, 391–7; Kingston, "The Ideologists: Vichy France," 47–71, 55–9.
16 AN Z/6/689/A, Papers of Dr. Martin, Pièce #70, Note dated 12 February 1941, Pièce #11, transcript of Deloncle's speech, given on 14 February 1941.
17 APP, 21/704/77W/1476, "Filliol," 6 April 1941.
18 APP, 21/704/77W/1476, "Filliol," Reports dated 29 July and 31 July 1941. Berlière, *Polices des temps noirs*, 655–8.
19 AN Z/6/689/A, Papers of Dr. Martin, Pièce #16, 26 May 1941.
20 M. Cointet, *Nouvelle histoire de Vichy*, 605.
21 AN Z/6/689/A, ministère de l'Intérieur, "Le Mouvement social révolutionnaire: Première note d'enquête générale," Paris, 30 April 1946, 38.
22 AP PEROTIN 212/79/3/50, "Second dossier, Instruction à Montélimar," Pièce #104.
23 AN Z/6/689/A, Papers of Dr. Martin, Pièce #45, Note dated 10 November 1941.
24 AP PEROTIN 212/79/3/47, Supplément d'information, 1945, Judge Lévy, ministère de l'Intérieur, direction générale de la Police nationale, N. 283, Procès-verbal, Guy Delioux, 10 July 1945; AP PEROTIN 212/79/3/47, Supplément d'information, 1945, Judge Lévy, Pièce #63, Procès-verbal, Lucien Fromes, 24 January 1946; AP PEROTIN 212/79/3/47, Supplément d'information, 1945, Judge Lévy, Pièce #66, Procès-verbal, 27 February 1946, Louis Lemaigre-Dubreuil; AP PEROTIN 212/79/3/47, Supplément d'information, 1945, Judge Lévy, Pièce #68, Procès-verbal, Eugène Schueller, 28 February 1946; AN Z/6/689/A, ministère de l'Intérieur, "Le Mouvement social révolutionnaire: Première note d'enquête générale," Paris, 30 April 1946, 15, 20–3, 27, 31, 35, 41, 42, 44, 45; AN Z/6/689/A, Papers of Dr. Martin, Pièce #29, Notes dated 14 June 1941, 21 July 1941, and 17 October 1941; APP, 21/704/77W/1476, "Rapports," Report dated 25 October 1941 and marked "Archives confidentielles,

pièce unique n. 2139," and in the same collection, "Renseignement sur le Mouvement social révolutionnaire et ses principaux dirigeants," 13 May 1942.
25 APP, 21/704/77W/1476, "Filliol," Note dated 1942.
26 AN Z/6/689/A, ministère de l'Intérieur, "Le Mouvement social révolutionnaire: Première note d'enquête générale," Paris, 30 April 1946, 26.
27 CDJC, Xia,b,c, "Institut d'études des question juives," also available at the United States Holocaust Memorial Museum (USHMM) 1998.A.0098, RG-43.139M, Reels 2–4.
28 For example, Lehrer, *Wartime Sites in Paris*, 150, 220–1.
29 APP, 21/704/77W/1476, "Filliol," Note dated 4 June 1941.
30 AN Z/6/689/A, ministère de l'Intérieur, "Le Mouvement social révolutionnaire: Première note d'enquête générale," Paris, 30 April 1946, 45.
31 AN Z/6/689/A, Papers of Dr. Martin, Pièces #28, 32, Notes dated 10 July 1941 and 10 September 1941.
32 AN Z/6/689/A, Procès-verbal, Michel Harispe, 26 September 1945.
33 In June of 1941 François Lehideux alone supposedly had given the MSR two million francs; APP, 21/704/77W/1476, "Rapports," Reports dated 14 June 1941, 21 July 1941, and 17 October 1941.
34 AN Z/6/689/A, Papers of Dr. Martin, Pièce #27, Note dated 18 July 1941.
35 AN Z/6/689/A, Ministère de l'intérieur, "Le Mouvement social révolutionnaire: Première note d'enquête générale," Paris, 30 April 1946, 13–14.
36 AN Z/6/689/A, Ministère de l'intérieur, "Le Mouvement social révolutionnaire: Première note d'enquête générale," Paris, 30 April 1946, 13–14.
37 AN Z/6/689/A, Papers of Dr. Martin, Pièce #33, Note dated 18 August 1941.
38 AN Z/6/689/A, Papers of Dr. Martin, Pièce #91, page 3 of a note dated 19 December 1941.
39 AN Z/6/689/A, Papers of Dr. Martin, Pièce #75, Note dated 5 December 1941.
40 AN Z/6/689/A, Papers of Dr. Martin, Pièce #46, Note dated 11 November 1941.
41 AN Z/6/689/A, Papers of Dr. Martin, Pièce #74: 9 October 1941; Pièce #83: 30 October 1941; Pièce #84: October 30, 1941; Pièce #78: 11 November 1941, Pièce #65: 2 December 1941.
42 APP, 21/704/77W/1476, "Rapports," Pièce #38, Report on the MSR, no date.
43 APP, 21/704/77W/1476, "Rapports," Police report dated 21 November 1942.
44 APP, 21/704/77W/1476, "Filliol," Note dated 13 May 1942. It was common knowledge that Corrèze and Mercédés Deloncle were having an affair that began prior to the war. They married after Deloncle's death. Corre (pseud. Dagore), *Les carnets secrets*, 319, 359, 362.
45 APP, 21/704/77W/1476, "Filliol," undated tract, probably May or early June 1942.
46 APP, 21/704/77W/1476, "Filliol," Notes dated 13 and 14 May 1942.
47 APP, 21/704/77W/1476, "Filliol," Note dated 21 May 1942.
48 APP, 21/704/77W/1476, "Filliol," Prefecture de Police, Ville de Paris, Procès-verbal, 28 November 1942; Letter from Filliol to Laval, 28 November 1942; Letter from Filliol to the MSR, 29 November 1942.

49 Parrotin, "Victimes du tortionnaire," 1–4, 1, note 4.
50 AN BB/18/3353, Nîmes, 26 October 1942 and 24 November 1941.
51 Chenevier, *De la Combe aux fées à Lurs*, 81.
52 Joseph-Barthélemy, *Ministre de la Justice*, 369.
53 Joseph-Barthélemy, *Ministre de la Justice*, 369, 370. See also AD Allier, 64/J/104, Fonds Jeanne Dormoy, "Correspondances entre André Blumel et Jeanne Dormoy pour le procès de 1948," "Extrait de l'interrogatoire de Barthélemy du 21 février 1945."
54 AN BB/18/3353, Cour d'Appel de Nîmes, 12 December 1942.
55 Burrin, *France Under the Germans*, 165–71; M. Cointet, *Nouvelle Histoire de Vichy*, 573–602; Jackson, *France: The Dark Years*, 221–6.
56 Jackson, *France: The Dark Years*, 226.
57 M. Cointet, *Nouvelle Histoire de Vichy*, 573–602; Mitchell, *Nazi Paris*, 93–4.
58 Johanna Barasz, "De Vichy à la Résistance," 27–50. Vichysto-Résistants is a term created by historians in the late 1980s to denote faithful followers of Pétain who were loyal to Vichy, partisans of the National Revolution and anti-German, but later became resisters. During the early part of the war they might have viewed themselves as "Giraudistes," to denote General Giraud's anti-German stance. After the German invasion of southern France on 11 November 1942, many of these "Vichystes" or "Giraudistes" metamorphosed into "résistants": Vergez-Chaignon, *Les vichysto-résistantes*, 12.
59 AN BB/18/3353, Nîmes, "Le procureur général près la Cour d'appel de Nîmes à M. le garde des Sceaux, ministre de la Justice," 9 January 1943.
60 AN BB/18/3353, Nîmes, "Le procureur général près la Cour d'appel de Nîmes à M. le garde des Sceaux, ministre de la Justice," 9 January 1943, Letter from Moynier, 7 January 1943.
61 AP PEROTIN 212/79/3/51, Pièce #301, Deposition of Roger Mouraille, given to the commanding officer of the internment center at Asperg near Ludwigsburg (Stuttgart), where Mouraille was in custody, on 8 July 1946, and forwarded to Edmond Bascou, commissaire de la Police judiciaire, Paris.
62 AN BB/18/3353, Nîmes, Note, date illegible, but stamped "Seen by M. le garde de Sceaux," thus evidently informing Joseph-Barthélemy of the events of 23 January. The note also states that Laval read the report as well. Michel Harispe, a friend of Gabriel Jeantet and Deloncle, member of the MSR and, by 1943, Gestapo informer, also confirmed that Geissler and Deloncle knew each other, and that Geissler "intervened" to free the suspects in January of 1943. AN Z/6/689/A, "Dossier Harispe." See also Chenevier, *De La Combe aux fées à Lurs*, 81.
63 The material in this and the following paragraph comes from AN BB/18/3353, parquet de Largentière, Affaire Guichard, Moynier, Mourraille, Report from le procureur de la République to M. le procureur de la République, Montélimar, 23 January 1943. AP PEROTIN 212/79/3/50, "Dossier de la détention," Pièce #106 and "Second dossier, Instruction à Montélimar," Pièce #255.
64 Joseph-Barthélemy, *Ministre de la Justice*, 485.

65 Joseph-Barthélemy, *Ministre de la Justice*, 370, 484.
66 Meyssonnier, "Le Réseau Gallia, 1943–1944," 86–7.
67 Chenevier, *La Grande maison*, 89–94; Chenevier, *De La Combe aux fées à Lurs*, 33–48.
68 Néaumet, *Les grandes enquêtes du Commissaire Chenevier*, 163.
69 Berlière, *Polices des temps noirs*, 245; Berlière and Chabrun, *Les policiers français sous l'Occupation*, 124; Deacon, *The Extreme Right in the French Resistance*, 146–55. See also "Amis de la Fondation pour la Mémoire de la Déportation de l'Allier," http://www.afmd-allier.com/PBCPPlayer.asp?ID=776564 (accessed 12 November 2018).
70 M. Cointet, *Nouvelle histoire de Vichy*, 618; Kershaw, *Avenue of Spies*, 120.
71 M. Cointet, *Nouvelle histoire de Vichy*, 607–60; Jackson, *France: The Dark Years*, 226–30.
72 Bourdrel, *L'épuration sauvage*, 7–57.
73 Valode, *Les hommes de Pétain*, 360–1; Jackson, *The Fall of France*, 106–11.
74 Burrin, *France Under the Germans*, 444–53; Jackson, *France: The Dark Years*, 533–6.
75 M. Cointet, *Nouvelle histoire de Vichy*, 676–701.
76 AP PEROTIN 212/79/3/47, Pièce #169.
77 AN Z/6/689/A, Dossier 5348, Harispe, Procès-verbal de Michel Harispe, alias Henri Mercier, 11, 15.
78 AP PEROTIN 212/79/3/51, "Sous-dossier, Attentat contre Marx Dormoy, Enquête," Pièce #61, Deposition, 23 January 1946, Lucien Fromes.
79 AP PEROTIN 212/79/3/51, "Sous-dossier, Attentat contre Marx Dormoy, Enquête," Pièce #61, Deposition, 23 January 1946, Lucien Fromes.
80 AN Z/6/689/A, Dossier 5348, Harispe, Procès-verbal de Michel Harispe, alias Henri Mercier, 16–20. This dossier also contains the Procès-verbal de Guy Delioux, given on 3 July 1946 to a juge d'instruction of Lambourg, as Delioux was imprisoned at Fresnes. Delioux, like Harispe, worked for Senner and was a member of the Cagoule and the MSR. For more on Senner, see Levendel, *Hunting Down the Jews*.
81 AN Z/6/689/A, Dossier 5348, Harispe, Procès-verbal de Michel Harispe, alias Henri Mercier, 18–20; AP PEROTIN 212/79/3/51, "Sous-dossier, Attentat contre Marx Dormoy, Enquête," Pièce #61, Deposition, 23 January 1946, Lucien Fromes.
82 AP PEROTIN 212/79/3/51, "Sous-dossier, Attentat contre Marx Dormoy, Enquête," Pièce #240, 4, Extract from a report to commissaire Roux, Police mobile de Marseille, dated 31 January 1944.
83 AP PEROTIN 212/79/3/51, "Sous-dossier, Attentat contre Marx Dormoy, Enquête," Pièce #238.
84 AP PEROTIN 212/79/3/51, "Sous-dossier, Attentat contre Marx Dormoy, Enquête," Pièce #240.
85 AP PEROTIN 212/79/3/51, "Sous-dossier, Attentat contre Marx Dormoy, Enquête," Pièce #240.

86 AP PEROTIN 212/79/3/50, "Second dossier, Instruction à Montélimar," Pièce #255; AD Bouches-du-Rhône, 1269/W/77, "Assassinat de M. Marx Dormoy, Dossier d'Affaire."
87 Bourdrel, *La Cagoule*, 314–20; Brunelle and Finley-Croswhite, *Murder in the Métro*, 167–9; Deacon, *The Extreme Right in the French Resistance*, 161–6.
88 AP PEROTIN 212/79/3/47, Ministère de l'intérieur, Direction général de la Police nationale, No. 283, Procès-verbal, Guy Delioux, 10 July 1945, 22. See also Bourdrel, *La Cagoule*, 312–13.
89 AP PEROTIN 212/79/3/47, "Supplément d'information pour M. Robert Levy," No. 10, Procès-verbal, Mme. Claude Servant née Deloncle, 18 December 1948; AP PEROTIN 212/79/3/47, "Supplément d'information pour M. Robert Levy," No. 11, Procès-verbal, Mme. Mércedès Deloncle née Cachier, 17 December 1948; AP PEROTIN, 212/79/3/47, Ministère de l'intérieur, Direction général de la Police nationale, No. 283, Procès-verbal, Guy Delioux, 10 July 1945, 22; see also Bourdrel, *La Cagoule*, 313–14 and Bourget, *Paris Année 44*, 134.

10. 26 August 1944: Liberation

1 AP PEROTIN 212/79/3/51, Pièce #169; 212/79/3/50, "Second dossier, Instruction à Montélimar," Pièce #259.
2 AD Allier 64/J/104, Fonds Jeanne Dormoy, "Enquête du procès d'Assises de 1945"; Archives Nationales (AN), BB/18/3353, Assemblée consultative provisoire, Letter from Félix Gouin to M. le garde des Sceaux, Paris, 22 January 1945.
3 Wieviorka, *Orphans of the Republic*, 242.
4 *Life Magazine* interview with Félix Gouin: "French President: A Political Unknown Takes Over after de Gaulle's Resignation," *Life Magazine*, 25 March 1946, 48–9.
5 "Felix Gouin, Who Served as French Premier in '46," *The New York Times*, 26 October 1977.
6 AN BB/18/3353, Assemblée consultative provisoire, Letter from Félix Gouin to M. le garde des Sceaux, Paris, 22 January 1945. All subsequent quotes in this paragraph come from this document.
7 AP PEROTIN 212/79/3/50, "Second dossier, Instruction à Montélimar," Pièce #257.
8 AP PEROTIN 212/79/3/51, Pièce #32, Exposé.
9 AP PEROTIN 212/79/3/50, "Second dossier, Instruction à Montélimar," Pièce #255.
10 AD Allier, 64/J/104, Fonds Jeanne Dormoy, "Enquête du procès d'Assises de 1945," sous-dossier "Correspondances entre André Blumel et Jeanne Dormoy pour le procès de 1948." See also Joseph-Barthélemy, *Ministre de la Justice*, 248–9 and 367–70.
11 AP PEROTIN 212/79/3/50, "Second dossier, Instruction à Montélimar," Pièces #256, 257, and 259.
12 AP PEROTIN 212/79/3/50, "Affaire Dormoy Dossier Montélimar," Renseignement Pièce #10.

13 AP PEROTIN 212/79/3/50, "Second dossier, Instruction à Montélimar," Pièces #258, 260, and 263; Finley-Croswhite and Brunelle, "Creating a Holocaust Landscape on the Streets of Paris."
14 AP PEROTIN 212/79/3/51, Sous-dossier "Attentat contre Marx Dormoy," Pièce #169.
15 AP PEROTIN 212/79/3/51, Sous-dossier "Attentat contre Marx Dormoy," Pièce #35; AD Allier, 64/J/104, Fonds Jeanne Dormoy, Dossier, "Enquête du procès d'Assises de 1945," Letter dated "Marseille, le 5 janvier 1943."
16 Berlière, *Les policiers français sous l'Occupation*, 123–31; AP PEROTIN 212/79/3/51, Exposé, Pièce #32; AP PEROTIN 212/79/3/51, Sous-dossier "Attentat contre Marx Dormoy," Pièce #32.
17 AP PEROTIN 212/79/3/51, Pièce #32, Exposé; AP PEROTIN 212/79/3/51, Sous-dossier "Attentat contre Marx Dormoy," Pièce #32.
18 See the brief biography of Estèbe that can be found at the website of the French National Assembly, "Assemblée Nationale," http://www2.assemblee-nationale.fr/sycomore/fiche/(num_dept)/2852 (accessed 25 January 2019).
19 Bourdrel, *La Cagoule*, 378–9; M. Cointet, *Nouvelle histoire de Vichy*, 121; Lacroix-Riz, *Le choix de la défaite*, 35.
20 AP PEROTIN 212/79/3/51, Exposé, Pièce #32; AP PEROTIN 212/79/3/51, Sous-dossier "Attentat contre Marx Dormoy," Pièce #32.
21 Kupferman, *Le Procès de Vichy*, 77; Lacroix-Riz, *Le choix de la défaite*, 551; M. Cointet, *Nouvelle histoire de Vichy*, 708; Atkin and Tallett, *The Right in France*, 167.
22 AD Allier, 64/J/104, Fonds Jeanne Dormoy, "Suites judiciaires de l'assassinat de Marx Dormoy, Archives de Jeanne Dormoy, Période de Guerre, suite Période 1945–1963," "Enquête et préparation du procès d'assises de 1948," "Note, M. Marx Dormoy est invité à se rendre le lundi 3 février 1941 à la Cour supérieur de justice à Riom."
23 Bourdrel, *La Cagoule*, 276.
24 Even after the war, Chenevier was circumspect in the motivations he ascribed to the killers for eliminating Dormoy. Néaumet, *Les Grandes Enquêtes du Commissaire Chenevier*, 167.
25 AP PEROTIN 212/79/3/51, Exposé, Pièce #35; AP PEROTIN 212/79/3/51, Sous-dossier "Attentat contre Marx Dormoy," Pièces #38 and 39.
26 AP PEROTIN 212/79/3/50, "Second dossier, Instruction à Montélimar," Pièce #267; 212/79/3/51, Sous-dossier "Attentat contre Marx Dormoy," Pièce #36.
27 AP PEROTIN 212/79/3/51, Sous-dossier "Attentat contre Marx Dormoy," Pièce #38, Statement from Bernard Ménétrel; see also AN BB/18/3353, 4205 A 41.4, 12 février 1946, dossier "G. Jeantet, 1946."
28 AN BB/18/3353, 4205 A 41.4, 12 February 1946, dossier "Gabriel Jeantet, 1946."
29 Deacon, *The Extreme Right*, 162–3.
30 AP PEROTIN 212/79/3/50, "Ordonnance de dessaisissement," 15 November 1945.

31 AP PEROTIN 212/79/3/51, Sous-dossier "Attentat contre Marx Dormoy," Pièces #38 and 39.
32 AP PEROTIN 212/79/3/51, Sous-dossier "Attentat contre Marx Dormoy," Pièce #59.
33 AN Z/808/5672, "Dossier 349.894, Archives centrales du ministre de l'interieur, concernant le nommé Van Ormelingen," 2–3.
34 AP PEROTIN 212/79/3/51, Sous-dossier "Attentat contre Marx Dormoy," Pièce #70.
35 AP PEROTIN 212/79/3/51, Sous-dossier "Attentat contre Marx Dormoy," Pièce #169.
36 AP 1320W/119, Arrest warrant for Annie Mourraille issued by Judge Robert Lévy, 21 August 1946.
37 AD Allier, Dossier 64/J/104, Fonds Jeanne Dormoy, "Suites judiciaires de l'assassinat de Marx Dormoy, Archives de Jeanne Dormoy, Période de Guerre, suite Période 1945–1963," "Enquête du procès d'Assises de 1945," sous-dossier "Correspondances entre André Blumel et Jeanne Dormoy pour le procès de 1948," Note verbale, traduction, ministère des Affaires extérieures," C.4, N. 189, Madrid, 17 April 1947; United States National Archives and Records Administration, College Park, Maryland, Washington Registry Intelligence Files – ACC 174, RG 226/109/36, Records of the Office of Strategic Services, A1 Entry 109/Box 36, Interrogation of Guy DeLioux by Major Benjamin Wells, 13 July 1945.
38 AN BB/18/3061/9, "Dossier Filliol," 15 June 1949; Farmer, *Martyred Village*; AN Z/6/121, "Dossier 1740, Raymond Hérard."
39 AP PEROTIN 212/79/3/51, Sous-dossier "Attentat contre Marx Dormoy," Pièce #301.
40 AN BB/18/3353, Parquet du tribunal de première instance du Département de la Seine, Note from the procureur de la République dated Paris, 1 December 1946; AP PEROTIN 212/79/3/51, Sous-dossier "Attentat contre Marx Dormoy," Pièce #301; AP PEROTIN 212/79/3/51, Exposé; AP PEROTIN 212/79/3/49, "Dossier Derville, Mouraille, Roger," Pièce #483.
41 AP PEROTIN 212/79/3/51, "Direction générale de la Sûreté nationale, scellé no. 2, Diréction des Services de police judiciaire."
42 AP PEROTIN 212/79/3/51, Pièce #32, Exposé.
43 AN BB/18/3353, Parquet du tribunal de première instance du Département de la Seine, Note from the procureur de la République dated Paris, Paris, 14 November 1946.
44 Bourdrel, *La Cagoule*, 323–33; Touret, *Marx Dormoy*, 224–5.
45 Néaumet, *Les grandes enquêtes du Commissaire Chenevier*, 167.
46 Bourdrel, *Les Cagoulards dans la guerre*, 107.
47 AD Allier, 64/J/104, Fonds Jeanne Dormoy, "Equête du procès d'Assises de 1945," sous-dossier "Correspondances entre André Blumel et Jeanne Dormoy pour le procès de 1948," Letters from Blumel to Jeanne Dormoy, 13 May 1948 and 16 November 1948.

48 AP PEROTIN 212/79/3/51, "Direction générale de la Sûreté nationale, scellé no. 2, Diréction des Services de police judiciaire"; Brunelle and Finley-Croswhite, *Murder in the Métro*, 169.
49 Jeantet, *Pétain contre Hitler*.
50 Bertram Gordon, Interview with Gabriel Jeantet, Paris, France, 27 June 1974.
51 AD Allier, 64/J/104, Fonds Jeanne Dormoy, "Enquête et préparation du procès d'assises de 1948," sous-dossier "Arrestation des assassins et suites du procès d'assises – 1950."
52 Mendes-France, "The Crisis of France, 1945–1959," 285–94; Kirchmeimer, "France from the Fourth to the Fifth Republic," 379–414; Fenby, *France: A Modern History*, 315–42.
53 Judt, *Postwar: A History of Europe since 1945*, 46.
54 Rousso, *The Vichy Syndrome*, 9.
55 Rousso, *The Vichy Syndrome*, 7.

Conclusion

1 As cited by Touret, *Marx Dormoy*, 244, reprinted from Léon Blum's speech printed in *Le Centre Républicain*, 26 July 1948.
2 Archives Municipales, Montluçon (AMM), 1D1/36, Registre des délibérations du Conseil municipal, 15 March 1947 to 24 September 1948, deliberation of 19 September 1948.
3 AMM 1/M/37/6, Monument de Marx Dormoy, "Commission départementale des sites, 1963."
4 "Hubert Yencesse," Galerie Gabrielle Laroche (website), http://www.gabrielle-laroche.com/artistes-contemporains/hubert-yencesse (accessed 25 January 2018).
5 AMM 1/M/37/3, Monument de Marx Dormoy, "Procès-verbal du 7 Octobre 1960 des délibérations des membres du Comité d'érection du monument Marx Dormoy," Statement of M. Villatte.
6 Touret, *Marx Dormoy*, 242.
7 Dugléry, *Marx Dormoy*, 205.
8 AMM, 1/M/37/3, Monument de Marx Dormoy, "Procès-verbal du 7 Octobre 1960 de la délibérations des membres du Comité d'érection du monument Marx Dormoy," Statement of M. Jourdain.
9 See file AMM 1/M/37/9, Monument de Marx Dormoy, "Transfert du monument, procédure engagé par Melle Dormoy, 1961–1968"; Touret, *Montluçon après la tourmente*, 247–56.
10 AMM 1/M/37/1–9, Monument de Marx Dormoy, "Station Service Avenue Marx Dormoy, Mobile Oil Française," Dossier d'exécution, Transfert Monument 1963; "Déclassement du jardin public de l'Avenue Marx Dormoy," Transfert de Monument, 1962–3; AMM 1010/283/11, "Prolongement Avenue Marx Dormoy; Installation d'une station service Mobil Oil, 1960–67, démolie le 17.2.1999."
11 Dugléry, *Marx Dormoy*, 212.

12 AMM 1/M/37/6, Monument de Marx Dormoy, "Transfert du monument, Procédure engagé par Melle Dormoy, 1961–1968"; "Lettre de M. Pradel," dated 22 May 1961.
13 AMM 1/M/37/6, Monument de Marx Dormoy, "Transfert du monument, Procédure engagé par Melle Dormoy, 1961–1968"; "Commission départementales des sites perspectives et paysages, Séance du 25 mars 1963."
14 AMM 1/M/37/6, Monument de Marx Dormoy, "Procès-verbal du 7 Octobre 1960 de la délibérations des membres du Comité d'érection du monument Marx Dormoy."
15 AMM 1/M/37/6, Monument de Marx Dormoy, "Transfert du monument, Procédure engagé par Melle Dormoy, 1961–1968"; "Ville de Montluçon—Déplacement monument Marx Dormoy, Requête de Melle Dormoy-Sursis à l'exécution, mémoire en réponse"; "Tribunal administratif de Clermont-Ferrand," Notification d'un jugement.
16 Dugléry, *Marx Dormoy*, 212. For further studies on monuments, see Johnson, "Cast in stone," 51–65; Forest and Juliet, "Confederate monuments," 127–31; Forest and Johnson, "Monumental Politics," 269–88; Leib, "Separate Times, Shared Spaces," 286–312.
17 Hirszowicz and Neyman, "The Social Framing of Non-memory," 74–88.
18 Rousso, *The Vichy Syndrome*; Conan and Rousso, *Vichy: An Ever-Present Past*.
19 Malleret, *Pour voir Montluçon d'une autre façon*, 288.
20 Bourdrel, *La Cagoule*, 251; Bourdrel repeated the story, only slightly toned down and still relying entirely on Annie Mourraille, in Bourdrel, *Les Cagoulards dans la guerre*, 124. As Dormoy's biographers Georges Rougeron and André Touret demonstrated, other testimony, including that offered by Yves Moynier, strongly suggests that Mourraille was lying. See Touret, *Marx Dormoy*, 217–18.
21 Blum, *L'Oeuvre de Léon Blum*, 5:182.
22 Edkins, *Missing Persons and Politics*, 4–5.
23 Paxton, *Vichy France*; Goslan, *Memory, the Holocaust and French Justice*; Goslan, *The Papon Affair*.
24 Dugléry, *Marx Dormoy*, 215–18.
25 Dugléry, discussion with the authors, Montluçon, 2 December 2016.
26 Delpla, *Qui a Tué Georges Mandel?* 201–3. Delpla mentions the Doriot connection with regard to a document penned by Robert Courrier, but for our purposes we followed the men who investigated the crime and who determined that it was members of the Cagoule who were behind the murder. For more on Doriot's PPF see Millington, *A History of Fascism*, 91–4.
27 *Le Populaire*, 11 December 1945, front page.
28 *The New York Times*, 27 July 1951, "Socialist Leader Killed in France," 22.
29 AD Allier, 64/J/117, Fonds Jeanne Dormoy, Letter from Jeanne Dormoy dated 5 February 1973.
30 Michel Rateau contends that Pétain did indeed belong to the Cagoule. Most scholars are more reserved regarding Pétain's membership in the Cagoule, but they do agree that he had close contacts with members of the Cagoule: Rateau,

Les faces cachées de la Cagoule, 33–8, 40–3, 96–8, 247–9, 259–61. François Broche and Jean-François Muracciole argue that Pétain was a "républicain légaliste" who disdained the Third Republic but was unwilling to associate himself with any effort to enact a coup d'état: Brioche and Muracciole, *Histoire de la collaboration*, 35.
31 *The New York Times*, 27 July 1951, "Socialist Leader Killed in France," 22.
32 AD Allier, 64/J/78, Fonds Marx Dormoy, dossier "Projets de lettres à Pierre Laval et à l'amiral Darlan," undated.
33 *Le Populaire*, "La vie du Parti: supplément du 'Populaire,'" no. 77, Thursday, 10 March 1938, 312.
34 Millington, *Fighting for France*, 183–94.
35 Corre (pseud. Dagore), *Les carnets secrets*, 16.
36 Millington, "Immigrants and Undesirables," 54.
37 Benamou, *Jeune homme*, 167–8; Blatt, "The Cagoule Plot," 104, n. 101; Parry, "Counter Revolution by Conspiracy," 67–91: Brunelle and Finley-Croswhite, *Murder in the Métro*, 197–9.
38 For more on terrorism as a means of communication see Finley-Croswhite and Brunelle, "Lighting the Fuse."
39 Serre, *Rapport fait au nom de la commission*, 12, 14; Finley-Croswhite and Brunelle, "Lighting the Fuse, 154–5.
40 AD Allier, 64/J/57, Extrait du journal "Le Combat Social," 6 Feb. 1938.
41 For the historiography of the Cagoule see Brunelle and Finley-Croswhite, *Murder in the Métro*, 201–9; Millington, "Immigrants and Undesirables."
42 Since the election of Donald Trump as president of the United States, a plethora of works about his particular blend of populist, nativist, and authoritarian politics have been published: Albright, *Fascism: A Warning*; Goldberg, *Suicide of the West*; Levitsky and Ziblatt, *How Democracies Die*; Stanley, *How Fascism Works*.
43 Cot, "My Friend Marx Dormoy," 113–14.
44 *The New York Times*, 27 July 1951, "Socialist Leader Killed in France," 22.
45 Reitman, "State of Denial," 38–49, 66–71.
46 Reitman, "State of Denial," 41.
47 Judt, *Reappraisals*, 181–95; Lehrer, Milton, and Patterson, *Curating Difficult Knowledge*, 1–19.

Suggested Reading in English for Students and General Readers

The volume of works published on France during World War II is vast, even though little has been written on Marx Dormoy. Works in English for student readers also abound. Those interested in modern French history more broadly should begin with Jonathan Fenby, *France: A Modern History from the Revolution to the War with Terror* (London: St. Martin's Press, 2016); Charles Sowerwine, *France since 1789: Culture, Politics and Society*, Third Edition (London: Springer Nature Limited, 2019); and Jeremy D. Popkin, *A History of Modern France,* Fifth Edition (New York and London: Routledge, 2020). For a classic volume see Stanley Hoffmann, *Decline or Renewal? France since the 1930s* (New York: Viking Press, 1974). Readers will find that the following two works offer insight into the social, economic, and political crises besetting France between World Wars I and II: Benjamin F. Martin, *Years of Plenty, Years of Want: France and the Legacy of the Great War* (Dekalb, Illinois: Northern Illinois University Press, 2013) and Eugen Weber, *The Hollow Years: France in the 1930s* (New York: W.W. Norton, 1996). To explore the history of the Third Republic, 1870–1940, and also the Popular Front, 1936–8, readers should consult Paul Bernard and Henri Dubief, *The Decline of the Third Republic, 1914–1938* (Cambridge: Cambridge University Press, 1990), Frederick Brown, *The Embrace of Unreason: France, 1914–1940* (New York: Random House, 2015), and Julian Jackson, *The Popular Front in France, 1934–1938: Defending Democracy* (Cambridge: Cambridge University Press, 1988). A very short summary of the Third Republic is found in Nicholas Atkin, *The French at War, 1934–1944* (London: Longman, 2001), pp. 13–28.

Examination of the violence wracking France during the interwar period and leading to the fall of France in 1940 is found in Chris Millington, *Fighting for France: Violence in Interwar French Politics* (Oxford: Oxford University Press, 2018). The extent to which fascism took root in France is a highly controversial topic in French history, but for a thorough overview see Chris Millington, *A History of Fascism in France: From the First World War to the National Front* (New York: Bloomsbury, 2020). Histories of the French right include Kevin Passmore, *The Right in France from the Third Republic to Vichy* (Oxford: Oxford University Press, 2013) and Brian Jenkins, ed., *France in the Era of Fascism: Essays on the French Authoritarian Right* (New York: Berghahn Books, 2007). The latter introduces historiographical debates about the French right, as does Samuel Kalman and Sean Kennedy, eds., *The French Right between the Wars: Political and Intellectual Movements from Conservatism to Fascism* (New York: Berghahn Books, 2014). An excellent overview of genocide, revolution, and terrorism during the period is found in Donald Bloxham and Robert Gerwarth, *Political Violence in Twentieth-Century Europe* (Cambridge: Cambridge University Press, 2011). Right-wing violence and terrorism in France is explored in several of the essays in Chris Millington and Kevin Passmore, eds., *Political Violence and Democracy in Western Europe, 1918–1940* (New York: Palgrave Macmillan, 2015).

There are few works in English on the Cagoule but broad overviews include Joel Blatt, "The Cagoule Plot, 1936–1937," in *Crisis and Renewal in France, 1918–1963,* ed. Kenneth Mouré and Martin S. Alexander (New York: Berghahn Books, 2002), pp. 86–104, and D.L.L. Parry, "Articulating the Third Republic by Conspiracy Theory," *European History Quarterly* 2, no. 2 (1998): 163–88. Chapter 5, "Bombs, Bullets and Bloody Murder: The Cagoule," in Millington's *A History of Fascism in France*, pp. 93–104 (cited above) is the most up-to-date short summary. Our book is the only full-length work on the Cagoule, although the Cagoule is not the sole focus of the monograph: Gayle K. Brunelle and Annette Finley-Croswhite, *Murder in the Métro: Laetitia Toureaux and the Cagoule in 1930s France* (Baton Rouge: Louisiana State University Press, 2010). An exploration of the wartime evolution of the Cagoule into the Mouvement social révolutionnaire is found in Bertram M. Gordon, *Collaborationism in France during the Second World War* (Ithaca, New York: Cornell University Press, 1980). The Cagoule's wartime ties to the French Resistance, complicating the image of the Resistance, are examined in Valerie Deacon, *The Extreme Right in the French Resistance: Members of the Cagoule and Corvignolles in the Second World War* (Baton Rouge: Louisiana State University Press, 2016).

The best comprehensive English-language history of France during World War II remains Julian Jackson, *France: The Dark Years, 1940–1944* (Oxford: Oxford University Press, 2001). Another standard edition from a major French historian is Jean-Pierre Azéma, *From Munich to the Liberation, 1938–1944*, trans. Janet Lloyd (New York: Cambridge University Press, 1984). For a concise approach see Thomas Christofferson and Michael Christofferson, *France during World War II: From Defeat to Liberation* (New York: Fordham University Press, 2006). Chris Millington's *France in the Second World War: Collaboration, Resistance, Holocaust, Empire* (London: Bloomsbury, 2020) synthesizes many of the main themes and debates surrounding the French experience during the war. Robert Gildea, *Marianne in Chains: Daily Life in the Heart of France during the German Occupation* (New York: Picador, 2002), Ian Ousby, *Occupation: The Ordeal of France 1940–1944* (London: Thistle Publishing, 2017), and Roland C. Rosbotto, *When Paris Went Dark: The City of Light under German Occupation, 1940–1944* (New York: Back Bay Books, 2015) all offer an intimate look at the struggles of French people trying to survive the Occupation. To explore the lives of populations targeted for abuse during the war see Shannon L. Fogg, *The Politics of Everyday Life in Vichy France: Foreigners, Undesirables and Strangers* (Cambridge: Cambridge University Press, 2009). The trials and tribulations the war brought on are also explored in Hanna Diamond, *Fleeing Hitler: France 1940* (Oxford: Oxford University Press, 2007), Allan Mitchell, *Nazi Paris: The History of an Occupation, 1940–1944* (New York: Berghahn Books, 2008), and Julian Jackson, *The Fall of France: The Nazi Invasion of 1940* (Oxford: Oxford University Press, 2003).

The classic work on France during the Vichy period is Robert O. Paxton, *Vichy France: Old Guard and New Order, 1940–1944* (New York: Columbia University Press, 2001). Michael Curtis, *Verdict on Vichy: Power and Prejudice in the Vichy France Regime* (New York: Arcade, 2002) is a very accessible history of the Vichy regime. The best biographies of Maréchal Pétain are in French, but Charles William, *Petain: How the Hero of France Became a Convicted Traitor and Changed the Course of History* (London: Palgrave Macmillan, 2005) is a solid assessment. For an award-winning and comprehensive biography of General Charles de Gaulle see Julian Jackson, *De Gaulle* (Cambridge, MA: The Belknap Press of Harvard University Press, 2018). An excellent biography of Léon Blum is Pierre Birnbaum, *Léon Blum: Prime Minister, Socialist, Zionist*, trans. Arthur Goldhammer (New Haven and London: Yale University Press, 2015). The literature on the French Resistance during the Vichy period is also extensive. A good place to start is with H.R. Kedward, *Resistance in Vichy France: A Study of Ideas and Motivations in the Southern Zone, 1940–42* (New York: Oxford University Press, 1978). A gripping microhistory and must-read is Caroline Moorehead, *Village of Secrets: Defying the Nazis in Vichy France* (New York: Harper Perennial, 2015). Another excellent local study is H.R. Kedward, *In Search of the Maquis: Rural Resistance in Southern France* (New York: Oxford University Press, 1993), and for a work on women see Margaret Collin Weitz, *Sisters in the Resistance: How Women Fought to Free France* (New York: John Wiley & Sons, 1995). For a military history of the liberation of France see Peter Caddick-Adams, *Sand & Steel: The D-Day Invasion and the Liberation of France* (New York: Oxford University Press, 2019). A brisk narrative about the liberation of Paris is found in Jean Edward Smith, *The Liberation of Paris: How Eisenhower, De Gaulle and Von Choltitz Saved the City of Light* (New York: Simon and Schuster, 2019).

Among the more focused themes that arise in this book are gender, antisemitism, and memory. For a good introduction to gender studies during wartime France begin with Hannah Diamond, *Women and the Second World War in France, 1939–1948: Choices and Constraints* (London: Routledge, 1999) and Geoff Read, *The Republic of Men: Gender and the Political Parties in Interwar France* (Baton Rouge: Louisiana State University Press, 2014). For more on gender in the right-wing context see Caroline Campbell, *Political Belief in France, 1927–1945: Gender, Empire, and Fascism in the Croix de feu and Parti social français* (Baton Rouge: Louisiana State University Press, 2015). For works tied to antisemitism and the Shoah, the best place to start is Michel R. Marrus and Robert O. Paxton, *Vichy France and the Jews*, 2nd edition (Stanford, California: Stanford University Press, 2019), a re-edition of their essential 1981 work. A general overview is found in Susan Zuccotti, *The Holocaust, the French and the Jews* (New York: Basic Books, 1993). For a new work focused on Jewish survival during the war and one that has caused much debate see Jacques Semelin, *The Survival of Jews in France, 1940–44*, trans. Cynthia Schoch and Natasha Lehrer (New York: Oxford University Press, 2018). For another view see Renée Roznanski, *Jews in France during World War II*, trans. Nathan Brucher (Hanover and London: University Press of New England, 2001). The ramifications of antisemitism are explored in Shannon L. Fogg, *Stealing Home: Looting, Restitution and Reconstructing Jewish Lives in France, 1942–1947* (Oxford: Oxford University Press, 2017). The history of the memory of Vichy is quite complex. Students should begin with Henry

Rousso, *The Vichy Syndrome: France since 1944*, trans. Arthur Goldhammer (Cambridge, MA: Harvard University Press, 1994), Eric Conan and Henry Rousso, *Vichy: An Ever-present Past*, trans. Nathan Bracher (London: University Press of New England, 1998), and Richard Goslan, *Vichy's Afterlife: History and Counterhistory in Postwar France* (Lincoln, NE: University of Nebraska Press, 2000). To explore Holocaust and memory see Rebecca Clifford, *Commemorating the Holocaust: The Dilemmas of Remembrance in France and Italy* (Oxford: Oxford University Press, 2013). The themes of film, Vichy, and Holocaust are examined in Ferzina Banaji, *France, Film, and the Holocaust: From génocide to shoah* (New York: Palgrave Macmillian, 2012). Finally, for an excellent book on the reflections of scholars who have spent their careers working on France and the World War II period, see Manuel Bragança and Fransiska Louwagie, *Ego-histories of France and the Second World War: Writing Vichy (The Holocaust and Its Contexts)* (New York: Palgrave Macmillan, 2018).

For more information on authors Gayle K. Brunelle and Annette Finley-Croswhite and to access resources linked to this book see: http://www.historys-crucible.com.

Bibliography

Archival Sources

Newspapers and Magazines

L'Action française
Le Combat social
L'Écho de Paris
L'Étudiant français
L'Émancipation nationale
Je suis partout
Life Magazine
The New York Times
Le Nouveau Cri
Paris-Soir
Le Petit Provençal-Marseilles
Le Populaire
Time Magazine

Archives du Consistoire Central, Paris (ACC)

C.C-33-c   "Synagogues et organisations, 1941–1942."

Archives des Cartes Postales: Marc Combier

Fonds Combier, Musée Niépce, Chalon-sur Saône.

Archives Départementales de l'Allier (AD Allier)

26/J/465   "Hommage de 1948," Marx Dormoy.
47/J/117   "Brouillons de lettres de Jeanne Dormoy, 1973."

64/J/57	"Marx Dormoy au gouvernement: Lutte contre les opposants au front populaire."
64/J/58	"Marx Dormoy au gouvernement: Émeute de Clichy le 16 mars 1937."
64/J/78	"Fonds Marx Dormoy: Internement de Marx Dormoy à Pellevoisin, Aubenas et Vals-les-Bains puis mise en résidence à Montélimar; Papiers administratifs et correspondance sur la détention de Marx Dormoy, 1940–41."
64/J/79	"Fonds Marx Dormoy: Notes durant la détention de Marx Dormoy, 1940–41."
64/J/80	"Fonds Marx Dormoy: Correspondances adressées à Marx Dormoy, 1940–41."
64/J/81	"Fonds Marx Dormoy: Correspondance de Marx Dormoy, 1940–41."
64/J/82	"Fonds Marx Dormoy: Correspondances de Marx Dormoy à sa sœur Jeanne, 1940–41."
64/J/99	"Fonds Jeanne Dormoy: L'assassinat de Marx Dormoy, Archives de Jeanne Dormoy, 1940–41."
64/J/100	"Fonds Jeanne Dormoy: Diffusion de l'information de l'assassinat de Marx Dormoy, Archives de Jeanne Dormoy, 1940–41."
64/J/101	"Fonds Jeanne Dormoy: Condoléances adressées de Jeanne Dormoy à la mort de Marx Dormoy, Archives de Jeanne Dormoy, 1940–41."
64/J/102	"Fonds Jeanne Dormoy: Documents envoyés à Jeanne Dormoy en 1959, Archives de Jeanne Dormoy, 1941–1959."
64/J/103	"Fonds Jeanne Dormoy: Obsèques de Marx Dormoy du 9 décembre 1945 à Montluçon, Archives Jeanne Dormoy, 1945."
64/J/104	"Fonds Jeanne Dormoy: Suites judiciaires de l'assassinat de Marx Dormoy, Archives de Jeanne Dormoy, Période de Guerre, suite Période 1945–1963."
64/J/112	"Fonds Jeanne Dormoy: Interventions de Jeanne Dormoy pour préserver la mémoire de son frère. Archives de Jeanne Dormoy, 1953."
64/J/117	"Fonds Jeanne Dormoy: Archives de Marx Dormoy."
64/J/136–138	"Fonds Marx Dormoy: Photographies et autres documents figures."

Archives Départementales du Bouches-du-Rhône (AD Bouches-du-Rhône)

1269/W/77   Dossiers d'enquêtes de police judiciaire concernant des dossiers d'affaires particulières: Assassinat de Marx Dormoy (1941).

Archives Municipales de Montluçon (AMM)

1D1/36   "Registre des délibérations du Conseil municipal, March 15, 1947–September 24, 1948."
1/M/37/1–9   "Monument de Marx Dormoy," Marx Dormoy, Notices bibliographiques, Comité d'érection d'un monument à la mémoire de Marx Dormoy; Déplacement des monuments aux morts et Marx Dormoy; La statue de Marx Dormoy."
1010/283/11   "Prolongement Avenue Marx Dormoy: Installation d'une station service Mobile Oil, 1960–67, démolie le 17.2.1999."

Archives Nationales, Paris (AN)

BB/18/3061/2 to 3061/9   "Affaire de la Cagoule, 1947–1951."
BB/18/3353   "Direction des affaires criminelles et des grâces du ministère de la justice. Dossiers classés chronologiquement. Série A."
F/7/14815   "CSAR Dossiers personnels dont chefs, 1937–40."
F/7/14958   "Mouvement social révolutionnaire."

Archives Nationales, Pierrefitte (AN)

Z/6/53   "Dossier 886, Pierre Jouanny."
Z/6/121   "Dossier 1740, Raymond Hérard."
Z/6/689/A   "Cour de justice du département de la Seine, dossiers d'affaires jugées (1944–1951), dossier, 5348, Michel Harispe et autres."
Z/6/808   Dossier 5672, "Dossier Jean-Louis Van Ormelinguen, dit Vanor."

Archives de Paris (AP)

PEROTIN, 212/79/3/47–51   "Cour d'assises de Paris, affaire du CSAR – Comité secret d'action révolutionnaire et autres mouvements nationalistes de droit." Cartons 49–51, "Affaire Dormoy."

134W/130	Dossier Marx Dormoy.
1320W/119	"Dossier du service central du Parquet général de la cour d'appel de la Seine sur le complot de la Cagoule,' 1945–48."

Archives de la Préfecture de Police, Paris (APP)

B/A 1817	"Attentats contre les Synagogues de Paris, Octobre 1941–Juillet 1942."
B/A 1914	"Mouvement social révolutionnaire (1939–1944)."
B/A/M5	"Dossier Antoinette Masse."
21.704/77W/1476	"Renseignement sur le Mouvement social révolutionnaire et ses principaux dirigeants."

Archives of the United States Holocaust Memorial Museum (USHMM)

RG-43.069M, Reel 5	"Selected Records from the Consistoire Central, 1933–1948."
RG43.139M/1998.A.0098	"Records, Commissariat générale aux questions juives."

Centre de Documentation Juive Contemporaine, Paris (CDJC)

CCCLXIV	"Retranscription des minutes du procès Oberg-Knochen ayant eu lieu au tribunal militaire permanent de Paris en Septembre 1954."
CCCLXX	"Document précisant les adresses d'immeubles juifs occupés par le Rassemblement nationale populaire suivi d'une lettre du chef du Mouvement social révolutionnaire." XIa,b,c "Institute d'études des questions juives."

United States National Archives and Records Administration, College Park, Maryland

174, RG 226/109/36	"Washington Registry Intelligence Files, Records of the Office of Strategic Services."

Primary Sources

Barthélemy, Joseph. *Ministre de la Justice, Vichy 1941–1943: Mémoires*. Paris: Éditions Pygmalion/Gérard Watelet, 1989.

Belin, Jean. *Secrets of the Sûreté: The Memoires of Commissioner Jean Belin, Master Detective of France*. New York: G.P. Putnam's Sons, 1950.

Blum, Léon. *L'Oeuvre de Léon Blum*. 7 vols. Paris: Albin Michel, 1954–64.

Chenevier, Charles. *De La Combe au fées à Lurs: Souvenirs et révélations*. Paris: Flammarion, 1962.

———. *La Grande maison*. Paris: Presses de la Cité, 1976.
Corre, Aristide (pseud. Dagore). *Les carnets secrets de la Cagoule*. Edited by Christian Bernadac. Paris: Éditions France-Empire, 1977.
Cot, Pierre. "My Friend Marx Dormoy." *The Nation*, 9 August 1941, 113–14.
Deloncle, Eugène. *Les idées et l'action*. Paris: Mouvement social révolutionnaire, 1941.
Groussard, Georges A. *Service secret, 1940–1945*. Paris: La Table Ronde, 1964.
Mourraille, Auguste Claire Mathilde. *Lamoureux Journal*. Translated by Michele Halligan. n.p., 2016.

Secondary Sources

Alary, Eric. *La ligne de démarcation, 1940–1944*. Que sais-je? Paris: Presses Universitaires de France, 1995.
Albright, Madeleine. *Fascism: A Warning*. New York: Harper Books, 2018.
Alexander, Martin. *The Republic in Danger: General Maurice Gamelin and the Politics of French Defence, 1933–1940*. New York: Cambridge University Press, 1992.
Amouroux, Henri. *La grande histoire des Français sous l'occupation*. Vol. 3, *Les beaux jours des collabos, juin 1941–juin 1942*. Paris: Éditions Robert Laffont, 1978.
Aron, Robert. *Histoire de Vichy, 1940–44*. Paris: Fayard, 1954.
Atkin, Nicholas. *The French at War, 1934–1944*. Edinburgh: Pearson Educational, 2001.
——— and Frank Tallett, *The Right in France: From Revolution to Le Pen*. London: I.B. Tauris, 2003.
Azéma, Jean-Pierre. "Le choc armé et les débandades." In *La France des années noires*, 2nd ed., vol. 1, *De la défaite à Vichy*, edited by Jean-Pierre Azéma and François Bédarida, 105–37. Paris: Éditions du Seuil, 2000.
———. "Le régime de Vichy." In *La France des années noires*, 2nd ed., vol. 1, *De la défaite à Vichy*, edited by Jean-Pierre Azéma and François Bédarida, 159–90. Paris: Éditions du Seuil, 2000.
——— and François Bédarida, eds. *La France des années noires*. 1st and 2nd eds. 2 vols. Paris: Éditions du Seuil, 1993, 2000.
——— and Olivier Wieviorka. *Vichy, 1940–1944*. Paris: Éditions Perrin, 2004.
Barasz, Johanna. "De Vichy à la Résistance: Les vichysto-résistants 1940–1944." *Guerres mondiales et conflits contemporains* 242 (February 2011): 27–50.
Bédarida, François, and Renée Bédarida. "La persecution des Juifs." In *La France des années noires*, 2nd ed., vol. 2, *De l'Occupation à Liberation*, edited by Jean-Pierre Azéma and François Bédarida, 149–82. Paris: Éditions du Seuil, 2000.
Benamou, Georges-Marc. *Jeune homme, vous ne savez pas de quoi vous parlez*. Paris: Plon, 2001.
Berdah, Jean-François. "The Devil in France. The Tragedy of Spanish Republicans and French Policy after the Civil War (1936–1945)." In *CLIOHRES:*

Discrimination and Tolerance in Historical Perspective, edited by Guðmundur Hàlfdanarson, Transversal 3:301–18. Pisa: Edizioni Plus, Pisa University Press, 2008. https://hal.archives-ouvertes.fr/hal-00374318/document.

Berlière, Jean-Marc. *Le monde des polices en France XIXe–XXe siècles*. Bruxelles: Éditions Complexe, 1996.

———. *Polices des temps noirs: France 1939–1945*. Paris: Perrin, 2018.

——— and Laurent Chabrun. *Les policiers français sous l'Occupation, d'après les archives inédites de l'épuration*. Paris: Perrin, 2001.

Berstein, Serge. "L'affrontement simulé des années 1930." *Vingtième Siècle: Revue d'histoire* 5 (January–March 1985): 39–54.

———. "Consensus politique et violences civiles dans la France du 20e siècle." *Vingtième Siècle: Revue d'histoire* 69 (January–March 2001): 51–60.

Béteille, Pierre, and Christiane Rimbaud. *Le Procès de Riom*. Paris: Plon, 1973.

Birnbaum, Pierre. *Un mythe politique: La "République Juive" de Léon Blum à Pierre Mendès-France*. Paris: Fayard, 1988.

Blatt, Joel. "The Cagoule Plot, 1936–1937." In *Crisis and Renewal in France, 1918–1962*, edited by Kenneth Mouré and Martin S. Alexander, 86–104. London: Berghahn Books, 2002.

Bloch, Marc. *L'Étrange Défaite: Témoignage écrit en 1940*. Paris: Franc-Tireur, 1946.

Bourdrel, Philippe. *La Cagoule: Histoire d'une société secrète du Front populaire à la Ve République*. Paris: Albin Michel, 2000.

———. *L'épuration sauvage*. Paris: Éditions Perrin, 2008.

———. *Les Cagoulards dans la guerre*. Paris: Éditions Albin Michel, 2009.

Bourget, Pierre. *Paris Année 44: Occupation—Libération—Épuration*. Paris: Plon, 1984.

Bracher, Julia, ed. *Riom 1942: Le procès*. Paris: Omnibus, 2012.

Bretty, Béatrice. *La Comédie-Française à l'envers*. Paris: Fayard, 1957.

Broche, François, and Jean-François Muracciole. *Histoire de la Collaboration 1940–1945*. Paris: Éditions Tallandier, 2019.

Brunelle, Gayle K., and Annette Finley-Croswhite. *Murder in the Métro: Laetitia Toureaux and the Cagoule in 1930s France*. Baton Rouge: Louisiana State University Press, 2010.

Burrin, Philippe. *France Under the Germans: Collaboration and Compromise*. Translated by Janet Lloyd. New York: The New Press, 1996.

———. "Poings levés et bras tendus: La contagion des symboles au temps du Front populaire." *Vingtième Siècle: Revue d'histoire* no. 11 (July–September 1986): 5–20.

Calvi, Fabrizio, and Marc J. Masurovsky. *Le festin du Reich: Le pillage de la France occupée 1940–1945*. Paris: Fayard, 2006.

Campbell, Caroline Jane. *Political Belief in France, 1927–1945: Gender, Empire, and Fascism in the Croix de feu and Parti social français*. Baton Rouge: Louisiana State University Press, 2015.

———. "Women and Men in French Authoritarianism: Gender in the *Croix de Feu* and *Parti Social Français*, 1927–1945." PhD diss., University of Iowa, 2009.

Capdevila, Luc. "The Quest for Masculinity in a Defeated France, 1940–1945." *Contemporary European History* 10, no. 3 (2001): 423–45.

Chadwick, Whitney, and Tirza True Latimer, "Becoming Modern: Gender and Sexual Identity after World War I." In *The Modern Woman Revisited: Paris between the Wars*, edited by Whitney Chadwick and Tirza True Latimer, 3–19. New Brunswick: Rutgers University Press, 2003.

Childers, Kristin Stromberg. *Fathers, Families, and the State in France 1914–1945*. Ithaca: Cornell University Press, 2003.

Cointet, Jean-Paul. *Pierre Laval*. Paris: Fayard, 1993.

Cointet, Michèle. *Nouvelle histoire de Vichy (1940–1945)*. Paris: Fayard, 2011.

Colton, Joel. *Léon Blum: Humanist in Politics*. Durham: Duke University Press, 1987.

Conan, Eric, and Henry Rousso. *Vichy: An Ever-Present Past*. Hanover: University Press of New England, 1998.

Crémieux, Jean-Louis. *La Guerre oui ou non?* Paris: Gallimard, 1980.

Curtis, Michael. *Verdict on Vichy: Power and Prejudice in the Vichy France Regime*. New York: Arcade, 2002.

Daladier, Édouard. *Journal de captivité, 1940–1945*. Paris: Calmann-Lévy, 1991.

Dard, Olivier. *Les annnées 30: Le choix impossible*. Paris: Le Livre de Poche, 1999.

Davey, Anthony Owen. "The Origins of the Légion des Volontaires Français Contre le Bolchevisme." *Journal of Contemporary History* 6, no. 6 (October 1971): 29–45.

Deacon, Valerie. *The Extreme Right in the French Resistance: Members of the Cagoule and Corvignolles in the Second World War*. Baton Rouge: Louisiana State University Press, 2016.

Delpla, François. *Qui a Tué Georges Mandel?* Montreal: L'Archipel, 2008.

Diamond, Hanna. *Fleeing Hitler, France 1940*. Oxford: Oxford University Press, 2007.

Dubuis, Patrick. *Émergence de l'homosexualité dans la littérature française: d'André Gide à Jean Genet*. Paris: Harmattan, 2011.

Dugléry, Daniel. *Marx Dormoy: La force des racines*. Montluçon: PHR Éditions, 2013.

Edkins, Jenny. *Missing Persons and Politics*. Ithaca: Cornell University Press, 2011.

Farmer, Sarah. *Martyred Village: Commemorating the 1944 Massacre at Oradour-sur-Glane*. Berkeley: University of California Press, 1999.

Fenby, Jonathan. *France: A Modern History from the Revolution to the War with Terror*. New York: St. Martin's Press, 2016.

Février, Lucien. *Le royaume des Pipétides*. Paris: Éditions de "La Caravelle." 1930.

Finley-Croswhite, Annette and Gayle K. Brunelle. "Creating a Holocaust Landscape on the Streets of Paris: French Agency and the Synagogue Bombings of October 3, 1941." *Holocaust and Genocide Studies* 33, no. 1 (Spring 2019): 60–89.

———. "Lighting the Fuse: Terrorism as Violent Political Discourse in Interwar France." In *Political Violence and Democracy in Western Europe, 1914–1940*, edited by Christopher Millington and Kevin Passmore, 144–59. London: Palgrave, 2015.

Fogg, Shannon L. *The Politics of Everyday Life in Vichy France: Foreigners, Undesirables, and Strangers*. Cambridge: Cambridge University Press, 2009.

Forest, Benjamin, and Juliet Johnson. "Confederate Monuments and the Problem of Forgetting." *Cultural Geographies* 26, no.1 (2019): 127–31.

———. "Monumental Politics: Regime Type and Public Memoir in Post-Communist States." *Post-Soviet Affairs* 27, no. 3 (2011): 269–88.
Frank, Robert. "Pétain, Laval, Darlan." In *La France des années noires*, 1st ed., vol. 1, *De la défaite à Vichy*, edited by Jean-Pierre Azéma and François Bédarida, 307–48. Paris: Éditions du Seuil, 2000.
Freigneaux, Frédéric. "Histoire d'un Mouvement Terroriste de l'Entre-Deux Guerres: "La Cagoule." MA Thesis, University of Toulouse, Mirail, 1991.
Gates, Eleanor. *The Collapse of the Anglo-French Alliance, 1939–1940*. Berkeley: University of California Press, 1981.
Gildea, Robert. *Marianne in Chains: Everyday Life in the French Heartland under the German Occupation*. New York: Metropolitan Books, 2002.
Giraudier, Vincent. *Les bastilles de Vichy: Répression politique et internement administrative, 1940–1944*. Paris: Éditions Tallandier, 2009.
Glass, Charles. *Americans in Paris: Life and Death under Nazi Occupation*. New York: Penguin, 2010.
Goldberg, Jonah. *Suicide of the West: How the Rebirth of Tribalism, Populism, Nationalism, and Identity Politics Is Destroying American Democracy*. New York: Crown, 2018.
Gordon, Bertram M. *Collaborationism in France during the Second World War*. Ithaca: Cornell University Press, 1980.
———. "The Condottieri of the Collaboration: *Mouvement Social Révolutionnaire*." *Journal of Contemporary History* 10, no. 2 (April 1975): 261–82.
———. *Historical Dictionary of World War II France: The Occupation, Vichy, and the Resistance, 1938–1946*. Westport, CT: Greenwood Press, 1998.
Goslan, Richard. *Memory, the Holocaust and French Justice: The Bousquet and Touvier Affairs*. Hanover: University Press of New England, 1996.
Goslan, Richard, ed. *The Papon Affair: Memory and Justice on Trial*. London: Routledge, 2000.
Gottlieb, Julie V. *Feminine Fascism: Women in Britain's Fascist Movement, 1923–1945*. London: I.B. Tauris, 2000.
Graham, Bruce Desmond. *Choice and Democratic Order: The French Socialist Party, 1937–1950*. Cambridge: Cambridge University Press, 1994.
Green, Mary Jane. "Gender, Fascism and the *Croix de Feu*: The 'Women's Pages' of *Le Flambeau*." *French Cultural Studies* 8, no. 23 (1997): 229–39.
Guilluy, Christophe. *Twilight of the Elites: Prosperity, the Periphery, and the Future of France*. Translated by Malcolm DeBevoise. New Haven, CT: Yale University Press, 2019.
Heurtaud-Wright, Marie-Hélène. "*Les Hommes nouveaux* (Marcel l'Herbier, 1936): Nostalgia, Masculinity and the French Colonial Film of the 1930s." *Modern and Contemporary France* 8, no. 2 (2000): 215–26.
Hirschfeld, Gerhard and Patrick March, eds. *Collaboration in France: Politics and Culture during the Nazi Occupation, 1940–1944*. Oxford: Berg, 1989.
Hirszowicz, Maria, and Elżbieta Neyman. "The Social Framing of Non-memory." *International Journal of Sociology* 37, no. 1 (Spring 2007): 74–88.

Hoffman, Bruce. *Inside Terrorism*. New York: Columbia University Press, 2006.
Ingram, Norman. "'*Nous allons vers les monastères*': French Pacifism and the Crisis of the Second World War." In *Crisis and Renewal in France*, edited by Kenneth Mouré and Martin S. Alexander, 132–51. New York: Berghahn Books, 2002.
Jackson, Julian. *De Gaulle*. Cambridge, MA: The Belknap Press of Harvard University Press, 2018.
———. *The Fall of France: The Nazi Invasion of 1940*. Oxford: Oxford University Press, 2003.
———. *France: The Dark Years, 1940–1944*. Oxford: Oxford University Press, 2001.
———. *The Popular Front in France: Defending Democracy, 1934–38*. Cambridge: Cambridge University Press, 1985.
Jeanney, Jean-Noël. *Georges Mandel: L'homme qu'on attendait*. Paris: Éditions Tallendier, 2009. First published 2001.
Jeantet, Gabriel. *Année 40: Londres, de Gaulle, Vichy*. Paris. La Table Ronde, 1965.
———. *Pétain contre Hitler*. Paris: La Table Ronde, 1966.
Jenkins, Brian, ed. *France in the Era of Fascism: Essays on the French Authoritarian Right*. New York: Berghahn Books, 2005.
Johnson, Nuala. "Cast in Stone: Monuments, Geography, and Nationalism." *Environment and Planning Society and Spaces* 13 (1995): 51–65.
Joly, Laurent. "Antisémites et antisémitismes à la Chambre des *députés* sous la IIIe République." *Revue d'histoire moderne et contemporaine* 54, no. 3 (July–September 2007): 63–90.
———. *Vichy dans la "solution finale": Histoire du Commissariat général aux questions juives 1941–1944*. Paris: Bernard Grasset, 2006.
Judt, Tony. *Postwar: A History of Europe since 1945*. New York: Penguin Books, 2005.
———. *Reappraisals: Reflections on the Forgotten Twentieth Century*. New York: Penguin Press, 2008.
Kalman, Samuel. *The Extreme Right in Interwar France: The Faisceau and the Croix de Feu*. Aldershot, UK: Ashgate Publishing Limited, 2008.
———. "*Faisceau* Visions of Physical and Moral Transformation and the Cult of Youth in Inter-war France." *European History Quarterly* 33, no. 3 (2003): 343–66.
Kedward, Harry Roderick. *Occupied France: Collaboration and Resistance, 1940–1944*. London: Basil Blackwell, 1985.
Keene, Judith. *Fighting for Franco: International Volunteers in Nationalist Spain during the Spanish Civil War*. London: Hambledon Continuum, 2001.
Kelly, Michael. "War and Culture: The Lessons of Post-war France." *Synergies Royaume-Uni et Irlande* no. 1 (2008): 91–100. http://gerflint.fr/Base/RU-Irlande/kelly.pdf.
Kennedy, Sean. "Pitfalls of Paramilitarism: The *Croix de Feu*, the *Parti Social Français*, and the French State, 1934–39." *The Journal of Conflict Studies* 27, no. 2 (2007): 64–79.
———. *Reconciling France against Democracy: The Croix de Feu and the Parti Social Français, 1927–1945*. Montreal: McGill-Queen's University Press, 2007.
Kershaw, Alex. *Avenue of Spies: A True Story of Terror, Espionage, and One American Family's Heroic Resistance in Nazi-Occupied Paris*. New York: Broadway Books, 2015.

Kingston, Paul J. "The Ideologists: Vichy France, 1940–1944." In *Collaboration in France: Politics and Culture during the Nazi Occupation, 1940–1944*, edited by Gerhard Hirschfeld and Patrick March. Oxford: Berg, 1989.

Kirchmeimer, Otto. "France from the Fourth to the Fifth Republic." *Social Research* 25, no. 4 (Winter 1958): 379–414.

Kitson, Simon. *Police and Politics in Marseille, 1936–1945*. Leiden: Brill, 2014.

Koos, Cheryl A. "Fascism, Fatherhood, and the Family in Interwar France: The Case of Antoine Rédier and the Légion." *Journal of Family History* 24, no. 3 (1999): 317–29.

Kupferman, Fred. *Le procès de Vichy: Pucheu, Pétain, Laval*. Bruxelles: Éditions Complexe, 1980.

Lacouture, Jean. *Leon Blum*. Translated by George Holoch. New York: Holmes and Meier, 1982.

Lacroix-Riz, Annie. *Le choix de la défaite: Les élites françaises dans les années 1930*. Paris: Armand Colin, 2008.

———. *Les élites françaises entre 1940 et 1944: De la collaboration avec l'Allemagne à l'alliance américaine*. Paris: Armand Colin, 2016.

Lambert, Pierre-Philippe, and Gérard Le Marec. *Vichy 1940–1944: Organisations et mouvements*. Paris: Éditions Grancher, 2009.

Laub, Thomas J. *After the Fall: German Policy in Occupied France, 1940–1944*. Oxford and New York: Oxford University Press, 2009.

Legrand, Jean-Charles. *Paroles vivantes*. Paris: Éditions Baudinière, 1942.

Lehrer, Erica, Cynthia E. Milton, and Monica Eileen Patterson. *Curating Difficult Knowledge: Violent Pasts in Public Places*. New York: Palgrave Macmillan, 2011.

Lehrer, Steven. *Wartime Sites in Paris, 1939–1945*. New York: SF Tafel Publishers, 2013.

Leib, Jonathan. "Separate Times, Shared Spaces: Arthur Ash, Monument Avenue and the Politics of Richmond, Virginia's Symbolic Landscapes." *Cultural Geographies* 9, no. 3 (2002): 286–312.

Levendel, Isaac. *Hunting Down the Jews: Vichy, the Nazis and Mafia Collaborators in Provence, 1942–1944*. New York: Enigma Books, 2011.

Levitsky, Steven, and Daniel Ziblatt. *How Democracies Die*. New York: Crown, 2018.

Lévy, Claude, and Paul Tillard. *Le Grand Rafle du Vel d'Hiv*. Paris: Éditions Robert Laffont, 1967.

Ligou, Daniel. *Histoire du socialisme en France, 1871–1961*. Paris: Presses Universitaires de France, 1962.

Lower, Wendy. *Hitler's Furies: German Women in the Nazi Killing Fields*. New York: Houghton Mifflin Harcourt, 2013.

Lynn, John A. II. *Another Kind of War: The Nature and History of Terrorism*. New Haven: Yale University Press, 2019.

Machefer, Phillipe. *Ligues et fascismes en France (1919–1939)*. Paris: Presses Universitaires de France, 1974.

Malleret, Maurice. *Pour voir Montluçon d'une autre façon: L'histoire, les monuments, les hommes célèbres, les artistes à travers les noms des rues*. Charroux, France: Éditions des Cahiers Bourbonnais, 1989.

Marrus, Michaël R., and Robert O. Paxton. *Vichy et les Juifs*. Paris: Calmann-Lévy, 1981.
Martin, Benjamin F. *France in 1938*. Baton Rouge: Louisiana State University Press, 2005.
———. *Years of Plenty, Years of Want: France and the Legacy of the Great War*. Dekalb: Northern Illinois University Press, 2013.
Mendès-France, Pierre. "The Crisis of France, 1945–1959." *International Affairs (Royal Institute of International Affairs)* 35, no. 3 (July 1959): 285–94.
———. *Liberté, liberté, chérie: 1940–1942*. Paris: Fayard, 1977.
Meyssonnier, Jean-Philippe. "Le Réseau Gallia, 1943–1944." Memoire presented at the DEA d'Histoire du XXe siècle, Institut d'Études Politiques de Paris, 1994.
Michel, Henri. *Le Procès de Riom*. Paris: Albin Michel, 1979.
Millington, Chris. "February 6, 1934: The Veteran's Riot." *French Historical Studies* 33, no. 4 (2010): 545–72.
———. *Fighting for France: Violence in Interwar French Politics*. London: The British Academy, 2018.
———. *A History of Fascism in France: From the First World War to the National Front*. London: Bloomsbury, 2019.
———. "Immigrants and Undesirables: 'Terrorism' and the 'Terrorist' in 1930s France." *Critical Studies on Terrorism* 12, no. 1 (2019): 40–59. https://doi.org/10.1080/17539153.2018.1489210.
———. "Political Violence in Interwar France." *History Compass* 10, no. 3 (2012): 246–59.
———. "Street-fighting Men: Political Violence in Inter-war France." *English Historical Review* 129, no. 538 (June 2014): 607–13.
——— and Kevin Passmore, eds. *Political Violence and Democracy in Western Europe, 1918–1940*. New York: Palgrave Macmillan, 2015.
Mitchell, Allan. *Nazi Paris: The History of an Occupation, 1940–1944*. New York: Berghahn Books, 2010.
Monier, Frédéric. *Le complot dans la république: Stratégies du secret de Boulanger à la Cagoule*. Paris: Éditions La Découverte, 1998.
———. *Léon Blum: La morale et le pouvoir*. Paris: Armand Colin, 2016.
Mouré, Kenneth, and Martin S. Alexander, eds. *Crisis and Renewal in France, 1918–63*. New York: Berghahn Books, 2002.
Muel-Dreyfus, Francine. *Vichy and the Eternal Feminine: A Contribution to a Political Sociology of Gender*. Translated by Kathleen A. Johnson. Durham: Duke University Press, 2001. First published as *Vichy et l'éternel féminine*, 1996.
Néaumet, Jean-Émile. *Les grandes enquêtes du Commissaire Chenevier: De la Cagoule à l'Affaire Dominici*. Paris: Éditions Albin Michel, 1995.
Nobécourt, Jacques. *Le colonel de La Rocque (1885–1946) ou les pièges du nationalisme chrétien*. Paris: Fayard, 1996.
Noguères, Henri, Marcel Degliame-Fouché, and Jean-Louis Vigier. *Histoire de la Resistance en France, 1940 à 1945*. Paris: R. Laffont, 1967.
Noguères, Louis. *Vichy, Juillet 40*. Paris: Fayard, 2000.
Ory, Pascal. *Les collaborateurs, 1940–1945*. Paris: Éditions du Seuil, 1976.

Ousby, Ian. *Occupation: The Ordeal of France, 1940–1944*. New York: St. Martin's Press, 1997.

Parrotin, Marc. "Victimes du tortionnaire et assassin Filliol en Limousin (May–Juin 1944)." *Bulletin de la Société Historique et Archéologique du Périgord* no. 3 (2005): 1–4.

Parry, D.L.L. "Counter Revolution by Conspiracy, 1935–37." In *The Right in France, 1789–1997*, edited by Nicholas Atkin and Frank Tallett, 67–92. London: I.B. Tauris, 1998.

Passmore, Kevin. "Boy Scouting for Grown-Ups? Paramilitarism in the Croix de Feu and the Parti Social Français." *French Historical Studies* 19, no. 2 (Autumn 1995): 527–57.

———. *The Right in France from the Third Republic to Vichy*. Oxford: Oxford University Press, 2013.

Paxton, Robert O. "La collaboration d'État." In *La France des années noires*, 2nd ed., vol. 1, *De la défaite à Vichy*, edited by Jean-Pierre Azéma and François Bédarida, 349–83. Paris: Éditions du Seuil, 2000.

———. *Vichy France: Old Guard and New Order*. New York: Columbia University Press, 1972.

Péan, Pierre. *Le mystérieux Docteur Martin 1895–1969*. Paris: Fayard, 1993.

———. *Une jeunesse française: François Mitterrand, 1934–1947*. Paris: Fayard, 1994.

———. *V, enquête sur l'affaire des "avions renifleurs" et ses ramifications proches ou lointaines*. Paris: Fayard, 1984.

Ploscowe, Morris. "The Investigating Magistrate (Juge d'Instruction) in European Criminal Procedure." *Michigan Law Review* 33, no. 7 (May 1935): 1010–36.

Poliakov, Leon. "A Conflict between the German Army and the Secret Police over the Bombings of the Paris Synagogues." *Jewish Social Studies* 16, no. 3 (1954): 253–66.

Pollard, Miranda. *Reign of Virtue: Mobilizing Gender in Vichy France*. Chicago: University of Chicago Press, 1998.

Rateau, Michel. "Extrait des dessins humoristiques d'André-René Charlet parus dans l'Émancipation Nationale du 24 septembre 1937 (coll. M. Rateau), le journal du PPF de Jacques Doriot." Facebook, 12 April 2017. https://www.facebook.com/lecomplotdelacagoule/photos/a.1032548336877984.1073741827.1032506453548839/1032548190211332/?type=1&theater.

———. *Les faces cachées de la Cagoule*. Amiens: Michel Rateau, 2016.

Rayski, Adam. *The Choice of the Jews under Vichy: Between Submission and Resistance*. Translated by Will Sayers. Notre Dame, IN: University of Notre Dame Press, 2005.

Read, Geoff. "*Des hommes et des citoyens*: Paternalism and Masculinity on the Republican Right in Interwar France, 1919–1939." *Historical Reflections* 34, no. 2 (Summer 2008): 88–111.

———. "He Is Depending on You: Militarism, Martyrdom, and the Appeal to Manliness in the Case of France's 'Croix de Feu,' 1931–1940." *Journal of the Canadian Historical Association* New Series, 16, no. 1 (2005): 261–91.

———. *The Republic of Men: Gender and Political Parties in Interwar France*. Baton Rouge: Louisiana State University Press, 2014.
Reitman, Janet. "State of Denial: How the Federal Government, Intelligence Agencies and Law Enforcement Have Systematically Failed to Recognize the Threat of White Nationalism." *The New York Times Magazine*, 11 November 2018. https://www.nytimes.com/2018/11/03/magazine/FBI-charlottesville-white-nationalism-far-right.html.
Rémond, René, ed. *Le gouvernement de Vichy, 1940–1942*. Paris: Armand Colin, 1972.
——— and Pierre Renouvin, eds. *Léon Blum: Chef du gouvernement 1936–1937*. Paris: Presses de la Fondation Nationale des Sciences Politiques, 1967.
Ribet, Maurice. *Le procès de Riom*. Paris: Flammarion, 1945.
Rossi-Landi, Guy. *La Drôle de Guerre: La vie politique en France, 2 Septembre 1939–10 mai 1940*. Paris: Colin, 1971.
Rougeron, Georges. *Marx Dormoy 1888–1941*. Paris: Éditions du Parti socialiste SFIO, 1956.
Rousso, Henry. *The Vichy Syndrome: History and Memory in France since 1914*. Translated by Arthur Goldhammer. Cambridge, MA: Harvard University Press, 1991.
Sagnes, Jean. "Le refus républicain: Les quatre-vingts parlementaires qui dirent 'non' à Vichy le 10 juillet 1940." *Revue d'histoire moderne et contemporaine* 38, no. 4 (October–December 1991): 555–89.
Sarnoff, Daniella. "In the Cervix of the French Nation: Women in French Fascism, 1919–1939." PhD diss., Boston College, 2001.
Serre, Charles. *Rapport fait au nom de la commission chargée d'enquêter sur les événements survenus en France de 1933 à 1945*. Première Partie, *Les événements du 7 mars 1936*. Paris: Assemblée Nationale, 1951.
Sherwood, John M. *Georges Mandel and the Third Republic*. Stanford, CA: Stanford University Press, 1970.
Shirer, William L. *The Collapse of the Third Republic: An Inquiry into the Fall of France in 1940*. New York: Simon and Schuster, 1969.
Soucy, Robert. *French Fascism: The Second Wave, 1933–1939*. New Haven: Yale University Press, 1995.
Stanley, Jason. *How Fascism Works: The Politics of Us and Them*. New York: Random House, 2018.
Stromberg Childers, Kristine. *Fathers, Families, and the State in France 1914–1945*. Ithaca and London: Cornell University Press, 2003.
Sweets, John F. *Choices in Vichy France: The French under Nazi Occupation*. Oxford and New York: Oxford University Press, 1994.
———. "Hold that Pendulum! Redefining Fascism, Collaborationism and Resistance in France." *French Historical Studies* 15, no. 4 (Fall 1988): 731–58.
———. *The Politics of Resistance in France, 1940–1944: A History of the Mouvements Unis de la Résistance*. DeKalb: Northern Illinois University Press, 1976.
Tooze, Adam. *The Wages of Destruction: The Making and Breaking of the Nazi Economy*. New York: Penguin Books, 2006.

Touret, André. *Marx Dormoy (1888–1941): Maire de Montluçon, Ministre du Front Populaire*. Nonette, France: Éditions CRÉER, 1998.

———. *Montluçon après la tourmente*. Nonette, France: Créer, 2003.

Tournoux, Jean Raymond. *L'Histoire secrete: La Cagoule, le Front Populaire, Vichy, Londres, Deuxième bureau, l'Algérie française, l'OA.S*. Paris: Plon, 1962.

Tumblety, Joan. *Remaking the Male Body: Masculinity and the Uses of Physical Culture in Interwar and Vichy France*. Oxford: Oxford University Press, 2012.

———. "Revenge of the Fascist Knights: Masculine Identities in *Je suis partout*, 1940–1944." *Modern and Contemporary France* 7, no. 1 (1999): 11–20.

Valode, Philippe. *Les hommes de Pétain*. Paris: Nouveau Monde Éditions, 2011.

Van Ruymbeke, Renaud. *Le juge d'instruction*. Que sais-je? Paris: Presses Universitaires de France, 1988.

Veillon, Dominique. "Les réseaux de Résistance." In *La France des années noires*, 2nd ed., vol. 1, *De la défaite à Vichy*, edited by Jean-Pierre Azéma and François Bédarida, 407–39. Paris: Éditions du Seuil, 2000.

Vergez-Chaignon, Bénédicte. *Les vishysto-résistants*. Paris: Éditions Perrin, 2008.

Vinen, Richard. *France, 1934–1970*. New York: St. Martin's Press, 1996.

———. *The Politics of French Business, 1936–1945*. Cambridge: Cambridge University Press, 2009.

———. *The Unfree French: Life under the Occupation*. New Haven: Yale University Press, 2006.

Vu du Bourbonnais: Actualité, Lettres, Histoire, Arts & Culture. "Pages d'histoire Marx Dormoy: Deux Universitaires Américaines se penchent sur son assassinat." Last accessed 5 January 2019. https://vudubourbonnais.wordpress.com/2017/04/20/deux-universitaires-americaines-se-penchent-sur-lassassinat-de-marx-dormoy/.

Weber, Eugen. *The Hollow Years: France in the 1930s*. 2nd ed. New York: W.W. Norton, 1996.

Wieviorka, Olivier. *Orphans of the Republic: The Nation's Legislators in Vichy France*. Translated by George Holoch. Cambridge, MA: Harvard University Press, 2009.

Williams, Charles. *Pétain: How the Hero of France Became a Convicted Traitor and Changed the Course of History*. New York: Palgrave Macmillan, 2005.

Wingeate Pike, David. *France Divided: The French and the Civil War in Spain*. Eastbourne, UK: Sussex Academic Press, 2011.

Yagil, Limore. *"L'Homme Nouveau" et la Révolution Nationale de Vichy (1940–1944)*. Paris: Presses Universitaires du Septentrion, 1997.

Zuccotti, Susan. *The Holocaust and the French Jews*. New York: Basic Books, 1993.

Index

Abetz, Otto, 42, 70, 76, 115, 154–5, 223.
Action française (AF), 77, 110, 227
 (see also *L'Action française*
 [royalist newspaper])
 right-wing organization 11–12, 75,
  79, 157, 223, 225
 youth organization, 85
Africa, 29, 132, 182
 Allied invasion of, 176–8, 231
 French empire in, 44, 77, 133
Algeria, 176, 201, 231
Alibert, Raphaël, 45, 214
Allied powers, 133, 152, 220, 231
 Army, 28
 Axis versus, 114, 183, 187, 192,
  198, 232
 French versus, 27, 132–3, 176–8,
  182, 223
 Operation Torch, 176–7, 181, 231
Amicale de France, 119, 227, 230
 dissolution of, 111, 195, 213
 National Revolution propaganda, 77,
  86, 107, 148
 recruitment, 79, 81, 115, 125–7,
  225–6
 right-wing extremism, 108, 111,
  113, 134

anarchists, 132
André, M., 49, 57–60, 107, 117, 142,
 157, 160, 217, 225. See also
 Hérard, Raymond (André)
antisemitism, 10
 in French society, 18, 30, 114–15,
  126, 182, 219
 in the press, 26–7, 172
 right-wing, 23, 71, 81–2, 90, 96, 111,
  126, 156, 170
Appeals Courts, 132, 186
 Grenoble, 140, 144, 162–3
 Nîmes, 179, 191
Archives Nationales, 213
Archives de Paris, 214, 233n1
Armistice, 45, 75, 102
 Army, 177
 opposition to, 7–8, 31, 34, 43, 221
 post-, 78, 93, 95, 100, 149, 214
 signing of, 27, 29, 31, 111, 229
 terms of, 31, 36–7, 44, 47, 131
 "waiting game," 130–4, 177
assassination, Dormoy's, 1–3, 48–9,
 79, 228
 bomb construction, 58–63, 79, 103–6,
  210, 220
 documentation for, 87, 108, 212–15

investigation, 3, 48–52, 59–72, 115–22, 190–3, 223 (*see also* crime scene investigation)
   justice for, 17, 48, 69–70, 189–90, 199, 203–12
   larger scheme of, 37–40, 95–8, 106–7, 192, 213, 217–20
   lawyer involvement , 19–21, 116, 128, 200–1, 208
   as political, 3–7, 43–6, 142–4, 161–3, 191, 202, 212, 221
   surveillance, right-wing, 103–4, 114, 125, 136
   suspects in, 53, 76–89, 97, 103–4, 108–18, 126–9, 134–42, 184, 194–9, 224–6
   Vichy regime and, 13, 107–16, 121, 126–8, 139, 144–53, 159–62
attentisme, 130–4, 177
Auriol, Vincent, 5, 35, 43
authoritarianism,
   acquiescence to, 9
   democracy versus, 41, 219–20
   government, 3–11, 35, 216
   struggle against, 18, 205, 217
autocracy, 6–7, 13, 23, 43–4, 163, 218–21
Axis powers. *See* Allied powers, Axis versus

Bagarry, Pierre, 111, 127
Barnier, Marthe, 65–6
Barthélémy, Joseph, 150, 195
   as justice minister, 131–2, 167, 179, 223
   pressure on, 161–3, 165, 176, 180, 190–1
Bascou, Edmond, 183–4, 268n61
Batissier, Joany (Jany) Georges, 179
Béguin, Antoinette. *See* Masse, Antoinette
Behuret, Émilien, 2, 61
Belgium, 28, 100, 168, 202, 229
Belin, Jean, 47–8
Berstein, Serge, 10
Bisazza, Lucie, 66, 71
Bloch, Marc, 32

Blum, Léon, 12, 152, 206–7
   attempted assassination, 23
   correspondence with Dormoy, 39, 145
   friendship with Dormoy, 8, 12, 18, 32–5, 146, 194, 205, 211
   imprisonment, 36, 39–42, 123, 150–2, 189, 230–1
   opposition to, 24, 26–7, 151, 190, 200–1
   political leadership, 5–8, 18–22, 32–3, 153–4, 228, 230
   Riom trials, 150–4, 189, 194, 200–1, 223
Blumel, André, 5, 19–21, 200–1
Boemelburg, Karl, 181
Bolshevism, 39
   fear of, 11, 18, 23, 155
   organizing against, 24–5, 32, 100, 227
bombings, 78
   businesses, French, 22, 133
   Dormoy's (*see* assassination, Dormoy's)
   planned, 71–2, 76, 106
   synagogues, 71–2, 82, 111, 114–15, 135–6, 171, 192, 225
Bonnet, Georges, 50–3, 58
Bordeaux, France, 23
   government reassembling, 29, 33–4
bouquet, gift of, 61–4, 79, 105–6
Bourdrel, Philippe, 199, 209–10, 212
Bousquet, René, 156–7
Brasserie des Danaïdes, 83–4
Brasserie Delhoste, 66–7, 71, 76, 107
"Brexit," 3
Briand, Aristide, 151
   rue, 64
Britain, 11, 34, 50, 239n82
   Battle of, 44, 230
   French alliance with, 21, 28, 32, 229
   Nazis versus, 44, 176–7, 217
   social division in, 3
Brittany, France, 26
Bucard, Marcel, 11, 141
Burrin, Philippe, 133

Cabanne, M., 185
Cagoule, the (Comité secret d'action révolutionnaire), 3
  affiliation with, 39, 70–1, 129, 137–8, 146, 200, 213–17
  agents provocateurs, 20, 216
  characterization of, 4, 22–3, 62, 73–85, 93–103, 112, 193
  discourse around, 4, 25–6, 73, 199–200, 218–19
  founding of, 12, 22–3, 157, 227
  funding of, 23–5, 76, 157, 172
  investigation of, 48–9, 58, 70–7, 108, 181, 197–8, 205–6, 221
  intelligence gathering, 43–4, 75–6, 78, 184–5, 198, 227
  members of, 8, 43–5, 75–9, 108–18, 126, 171, 182, 194, 223–5
  militias, 23, 112–13, 182, 228
  organization of, 23, 77, 157–8, 184, 212, 220, 228
  political polarization, 9, 23, 120, 123, 196
  strongholds, 23, 39, 77–8
  terrorism, 10–11, 22–3, 26, 48, 55, 111, 195, 199, 216–20
  weapons of, 22–3, 25, 71, 181, 216
Cannes, France, 23, 89, 186
Caous, Pierre, 153–4
capitalism,
  critique of, 14, 45, 135
  privileging of, 207–8
capitulation, French, 27, 31
Carretier, Antony, 89–90, 94, 105
Casablanca, Morocco, 176, 188
Catholicism, 26
  right wing and, 4, 11, 78, 110
  traditional values and, 29–30, 100, 102, 182
Ceccheto, Ernest, 53, 62–3
Centre d'information et d'études (CIE), 75–9, 113, 118, 125, 227
Ceyte, Lucienne, 66–7, 71

Chambre des députés, 26, 33
Chapuis, Dr., 2, 50, 52
Charlet, André-René, 25–6
Chenevier, Charles, 3, 10, 13, 157, 160, 175, 192, 232
  career growth, 46–9, 223
  Dormoy investigation, 59–60, 63, 71, 82, 88–90, 103, 108–17, 138–48
  informant interviewing, 70, 74–80, 85–7, 92–4, 106–7, 118–30, 134, 212–13
  Resistance movement, 180–2, 187, 193–5, 199, 223
Chenevier, Cyril, 47–8
Chevet, Louis, 56–7, 62
Chirac, Jacques, 211
Choltitz, Dietrich von, 232
citizenship, 33, 151
  Jewish community, 26, 156
  paternity, 98, 102
Clark, Mark, 176, 231
Clermont-Ferrand, 38, 153, 179, 183, 207
Clichy, Paris,
  communism in, 19–21, 213, 236n19
  riots, 24–5
Cold War, 219
  spy networks, 198, 217
collaborationism, Nazi-focused, 9, 154, 211–12
  covert, 36, 181
  danger of, 46, 145, 156–7
  deportation and, 30–1, 156
  journal publishing, 157
  promotion of, 44, 111–15, 120, 155, 223–5, 230
  MSR and, 45, 112–13, 171, 174, 228
  parties, 163, 170–4, 182, 187, 220, 224, 227–8
  punishment for, 196–8, 200, 202
  rejection of, 109, 120, 180–1, 205, 208, 221
  ultra-, 183–4, 193, 228
Collette, Paul, 149, 171, 215, 231

Comité national française, 133, 231
Comité secret d'action révolutionnaire (CSAR). *See* Cagoule, the (Comité secret d'action révolutionnaire)
Commissariat général aux questions juives (CGQJ), 115
Commission d'épuration, 193
Communauté française, La, 172
Communism, 113
  conservatives versus, 4, 19–20, 23–5, 188, 217
  fear of, 9, 25, 28, 135, 198
  masculinity, 99
  National Revolution versus, 11, 100–2
  Popular Front, 12–13, 19, 102–3, 228
  Resistance movement and, 120, 182, 193
Communist Party, 4, 22, 127, 130–2, 197, 228
  versus socialists, 12–13, 18–21, 35, 182, 211
concentration camps, 115, 182, 187, 231
  Auschwitz-Birkenau, 156
  Buchenwald, 190
  Dachau, 190
  Eisenberg, 183, 192
  Neuengamme, 181, 193, 223, 232
conservatives (*see also* National Revolution)
  alliances with, 18–19
  beliefs of, 4, 7, 44, 75, 95
  Dormoy versus, 12, 21, 38–9, 41, 83
  gym socializing, 99–100
  media portrayals, 25–6, 95, 216, 237n41
  in policing, 47
  politicians, 8, 12, 31, 47, 228
Constans, Paul, 17–18
Constituent Assembly, 5, 189
Constitution (French), 224 (*see also* Third Republic)
  reform of, 34–5, 43, 230
Constitutional Acts, 151, 153, 155
Corre, Aristide, 4, 25, 78, 108, 114, 216

Corrèze, Jacques, 45, 111, 113, 169, 187, 267n44
  Eugène Deloncle versus, 172–5
Cot, Pierre, 12, 21, 151, 153, 219
Coty, François, 11
coup d'état, 218
  planning of, 25, 43, 107, 170, 274n30
  prevention of, 4, 12, 25, 216
courts, French. *See* judiciary, French
crime, organized, 47
crime scene investigation, 70 (*see also* Gérodias, Florence)
  autopsy, 52, 60
  bomb, planting of, 58–63, 79, 103–6, 210, 220
  connections, political, 77–82, 213
  forensic evidence, 58–60, 70, 103
  interviewing, 52–8, 60–8, 79–82, 146–8, 212
  room description, 1–3, 49–52, 206
  system of, 50, 192
Croix-de-feu (CF), 11, 100, 228
currency devaluation, 11, 172

Daladier, Édouard, 8, 12, 27, 42, 151–4, 237n36
Dangel, Béatrice "Bretty," 41–2, 53, 55–6, 58, 61, 106
Darlan, François, 36, 121, 145, 182, 187–8, 195–6, 223, 230–1
  ousting of, 149, 154–5, 167, 176–9, 213
Darnand, Joseph, 23, 111, 114, 182–3, 223, 228
Daussin, André, 111, 115, 126
Deacon, Valerie, 112
Déat, Marcel, 32, 111, 149, 215, 230–1
  collaborationism, 45, 120, 170–4, 182, 187, 223, 227
de Brinon, Ferdinand, 115
defendants, criminal case, "confrontations," 50
  Riom trial, 123, 150, 152–4, 162, 201, 231

de Gaulle, Charles, 9, 45, 110, 120,
    181, 201–2, 224, 229–32
  hostility to, 31–2, 90, 132–3, 177,
    182, 187–8, 220
  sympathies, 189–90, 202
Deloncle, Claude, 169, 173–4
Deloncle, Eugène, 192–6, 231–2
  Cagoule leadership, 8, 22–4, 70,
    108–11, 200, 212–17, 227
  deposition of, 160–2, 167–75, 183–8
  downfall, 134–43, 149, 155–9, 170
  financial expenditures, 168–75
  Les idées et l'action, 43, 83
  MSR leadership, 112–22, 126–8,
    170–4, 217, 228
  political organizing, 44–6, 49, 84–5,
    218, 224–5
  punitive expeditions, 43
  RNP contributions, 120, 171–3, 215
Deloncle, Henri, 111
Deloncle, Louis, 174
democracy, 154
  defense of, 25, 216–21
  extreme right versus, 12–13, 29, 41
  liberal, 7
Department of the Allier, 5, 7–8, 17–18,
    207–9, 213
deportation,
  collaborationists and, 30–1, 155
  French officials', 180–3, 190, 193,
    196, 223, 232
  Jews, 30–1, 155–6, 162, 186, 202,
    231
depression, economic, 9, 97. *See also*
    Great Depression
Dercheu, Pierre, 111, 113
detainees, political, 3, 42, 116, 129,
    166, 230
Diallo, Baba, 41, 53, 56
dictatorship, French, 9
  advocacy of, 23–4, 35, 211, 217, 221
  opposition to, 7, 221
Didelot, Chief Warden, 179
domesticity, 91, 95, 101, 251n32

Doriot, Jacques, 21–6, 39, 111, 120,
    192, 215, 224–5
  political collaborationism, 158–9,
    170, 182 187
  PPF leadership, 8, 12, 34, 44–5, 68,
    75, 125, 212, 228
Dormoy, Jean, 14–17
Dormoy, Jeanne, 2–3, 221
  civil suit, 69–70, 121, 140, 203–11,
    214, 224
  crime scene investigation, 41–2, 55,
    58–61, 106, 196
  Marx, bond with, 14, 16–17, 36–8,
    200–1, 224
  political involvement, 18, 146,
    190–1, 223
Dormoy, Marx, 2–3
  assassination (*see* assassination,
    Dormoy's)
  awards, 204–5
  biographies, 10
  Bolshevism, conflation with, 11, 18,
    25, 39, 100
  burial, 5–6, 9, 60, 220
  Cagoule versus, 5–9, 20–6, 108, 114,
    146, 194–6, 205–6, 212–25, 228
  career, 6–8, 16–20, 25–7, 32, 55,
    146, 194, 203, 218–20
  childhood, 14–18
  classified papers, 34, 42, 59–63, 123,
    144–6, 201, 213–14
  commemoration of, 203–12, 219–20
  derision of, 19–21, 25–6, 35–9, 102,
    144–5, 209–10, 235–6n17
  imprisonment, 27, 35–41, 55, 103,
    145–6, 209–10, 224, 230
  as interior minister, 3–8, 25–7, 32,
    39, 55, 146, 194, 214–19, 224
  as martyr, 3–5, 12, 60, 206, 211,
    220
  political affiliations, 5–8, 14, 17, 25,
    32–4, 201, 203, 216, 224
  Resistance involvement (*see*
    Resistance, the French, Dormoy in)

right wing versus, 8–12, 21, 38–41,
  83, 106–7, 117–18, 138, 208
symbolism of, 8–9, 100–3, 200–4,
  212, 215–16
Drôme, Assizes Court of, 52, 162–4
Dugléry, Daniel, 10, 211–12
Dungler, Paul, 111, 187
Duseigneur, Édouard, 138, 214

Éditions de l'État nouveau, les, 111
Erard, André. *See* Andre, M.; Hérard,
  Raymond (André)
Estèbe, Paul, 199, 224
  assassination connections, 193–6,
    213–14
État français, 3, 77, 120, 155, 202, 214
  in Vichy, 7, 27, 180, 211, 226, 239n82
  Europe, 27, 44, 70, 184, 213, 219
  masculinity, notions of, 95–7
  Nazis versus, 28, 32, 35, 112, 120,
    151, 156, 187
  right-wing groups, 21–2, 41, 100, 112
  social division in, 3, 11–12, 44, 70,
    216–17
extortion,
  from Jews, 115, 186
  schemes, 199

Faraut, Jean-Louis François, 129–30,
  137–8, 141–2, 160
fascism,
  fear of, 9–10
  feminine, 95
  French politics, 11, 22, 99–100, 182
  paternal authority, 22, 98–100
  proto-, 216, 218
  struggle against, 8, 12–13, 41, 210
  support for, 5, 11, 32, 219, 223
Fauran, Jacques, 111, 168–9, 172, 174
Fédération nationale des étudiants
  d'Action française. *See* Action
  française (AF)
Filliol, Jean, 49, 78, 141, 181–3, 216, 224
  Cagoule involvement, 25, 111, 198, 213
  MSR involvement, 45, 111, 117–18,
    158, 168–75, 187
  fitness, culture of, 91–2
  masculinity, 99–100
Flandin, Pierre-Étienne, 36, 132
Fontenoy, Jean, 111
Fontes, Guy, 71, 103
Fourth Republic, the, 201
Fra, Marc, 2, 50–1, 53
France, 32–5, 44–7, 70–3, 112, 120,
  184, 224, 229
  amnesia, 203, 208–9, 219
  Armistice (*see* Armistice)
  civil war, 10, 12–13, 21, 25, 182,
    202, 213, 219–21
  defeat of, 19, 27–8, 36, 41–4, 95–6,
    120, 135–6, 181, 218–21
  extreme right (*see* right-wing
    extremism)
  fascism in (*see* fascism)
  governance of, 21–3, 47, 101–2, 132,
    176–7, 189, 230
  international relations, 21, 27, 33–4,
    133, 217
  laws of, 50, 69, 116, 150
  military, 23, 27–33, 39, 87, 93,
    97–100, 152–6
  Nazi invasion, 11, 19–20, 27–36, 75,
    90, 102, 175–7, 205, 229
  occupation of (*see* Occupied Zone,
    France)
  social division in, 9–11, 28, 55, 110,
    130, 183, 201–3, 211–16
  values, traditional, 26, 29–30,
    44, 47, 92, 95–8, 100–3, 151,
    182
  wartime roles, 35, 53, 111, 187,
    208–9, 219, 221–2
  worker strikes, 19–20, 102
France-Europe, 157
France, revue l'État nouveau, 111
Franceschi, Jean, 121, 125, 128
  suspect representation, 116, 126,
    144–6, 178

Franco, Francisco, 21–2, 78, 157–8, 196–8, 216–17, 225
Freemasons, 7, 45, 101, 113, 135, 140
French National Assembly, 5, 18, 34–5, 43, 219
French Revolution, 7, 13, 26, 30, 35, 45, 75, 151, 205
French Socialist Party. *See* Section française de l'internationale ouvrière
French Worker's Party. *See* Parti ouvrier français
Frente populaire, 21
Fromes, Lucien, 169, 183–4, 194, 196
Front révolutionnaire nationale (FRN), 45, 227

Gamelin, Maurice, 28, 151–4
gangsters, 61–4, 66, 107
Geissler, Hugo, 157, 179–81, 231
gender roles,
  crisis, 97–9
  flouting, 91–2, 95
  wartime, 96–7
German Supreme Military Command (Militärbefehlshaber in Frankreich, MBF), 131
Germany, Nazi, 153, 177, 230, 168–87
  (*see also* France; Nazis)
  Armistice (*see* Armistice)
  autocratic model, 13, 43, 220
  Britain versus, 44, 176, 217
  collaboration with, 9, 30–1, 44–5, 133, 156, 202, 225, 231
  communism versus, 13, 28, 99–102, 113, 120, 131, 188, 193
  French versus (*see* France)
  invasion of (*see* France, Nazi invasion)
  leadership, 28–31, 42–5, 76, 109–15, 130–3, 152–6, 200, 211, 230
  prisoners of war in, 44, 93–4, 120, 132–3, 180–6, 192, 196
  war, declaration of, 32, 42, 78–9, 152, 217, 229

Gérodias, Florence, 68 (*see also* Mourraille, Anne-Félice)
  identity of, 85–8, 104, 225
  suspicious behavior, 53–63
  visitors, 56–7, 60–1, 64–7, 72, 79
Gestapo, 157, 179, 184–93, 220, 228, 231–2
  French collaboration, 85, 111, 114–17, 135, 141–2, 196, 198, 224
Giraud, Henri, 176–7, 188, 232, 268n58
gisant of Dormoy. *See* statue of Dormoy
Gottlieb, Julie, 95, 251n32
Gouin, Félix, 5–6, 12, 60, 69, 140, 154, 163, 189–90, 201, 224
Goy, Jean, 173
Great Depression, 11, 27, 97, 103, 218
Groupes de protection (GP), 75–9, 83–5, 99–100, 118, 125–7, 144, 147, 227, 230
Groussard, Georges, 45, 75, 77, 100, 214, 227
Guesde, Jules, 14, 17, 228
Guichard, Ludovic, 96, 100, 121, 125, 134, 191–2, 217
  emotional problems, 73–4
  imprisonment, 157, 164–8, 172, 177–80, 184, 199–200
  political affiliations, 68, 70–82, 103–8, 115–17, 141–8, 185–6, 224
Guyon, Lucien, 71–3, 77–85, 96, 100–8, 125, 134, 147, 225–6
gyms, socializing, 82
  politics, 99–100

Haenel, M., 186
Harispe, Michel, 110, 112
Hérard, Raymond (André), 49, 84–5, 115–21, 128, 137–43, 198, 217, 225
  MSR involvement, 84–5, 111, 117, 122, 157–62, 175, 212–13
Hitler, Adolf, 42–4, 100, 112, 177, 200, 216, 232

French negotiation with, 29, 32–6,
120, 183, 220, 230
New European Order, 35, 44, 112,
151, 156, 163
Riom trials, 152–4
hostages, 33, 42
executing, 130–2, 162
German, 31, 131–2, 189
Hôtel de la Place d'Armes, 60, 64–68,
79, 105
Huntziger, Charles, 29, 132

identity cards, 71, 107–11
fake, 53, 59, 64, 67, 104, 118–19, 147
lack of, 85, 122, 126–7, 141
informants, reliance on, 48–9, 70, 77–
85, 107–8, 113–17, 122, 170
internment camps. *See* concentration
camps
interwar period, 7
conflict, 10, 77
French economy, 27
gender identity crisis, 92, 95–102
Italy, 229, 232
anti-fascism, 22
autocratic model, 23, 43, 218
fleeing to, 25, 78, 114, 216
spies, 32, 48

Jackson, Julian, 10, 12, 31, 177
Jacomet, Pierre, 151
Jeantet, Claude, 194–5
Jeantet, Gabriel, 107–38, 141–50, 167,
224, 227, 230
Cagoule involvement, 25, 45, 77,
158–60, 183, 212–16, 225
inspector general of propaganda, 194–6
interrogation of, 187, 192–7, 199
Resistance involvement, 186–7, 200
Jeunesses patriotes, 11
Jeunes socialistes, 17
Jewish community, 19 (*see also*
antisemitism)
defense of, 7, 18, 26

deportation, 45, 113, 156, 202, 231
killing of, 81–2, 113–14, 155–6,
162, 166
persecution of, 30–1, 90, 115, 127,
130–1, 172, 185–6, 211
raids on, 111, 115, 126, 135, 172–3
roundups of (*see* roundups of Jews)
stereotypes of, 26–7, 101, 103, 135,
140
synagogue bombings (*see* bombings,
synagogues)
Jouanny, Auguste, 169, 266n8
judicial police, French, 59, 90, 111,
181, 183, 225
judiciary, French (*see also* Riom trials;
tribunals)
Dormoy case, 127–9, 190, 199
Nazi pressure on, 130–1, 150
processes of, 50, 150–1, 162–3
rebuilding, 201–2
Judt, Tony, 202
July note. *See* Note sur l'affaire Dormoy

Knochen, Helmut, 135, 155, 187
Kubler, Georges, 192, 212, 225
criminal investigation, 49, 54, 59–60,
63–72, 76–82, 108, 117
Resistance involvement, 115, 180–1

labor draft, 133
La Chambre, Guy, 151
L'Action française (royalist
newspaper), 25, 110
Lafargue, Paul, 14, 17
La lutte sociale, 17
Lamouroux, Mathilde, 90–1
Largentière, France, 150, 196
imprisonment in, 153–4, 163–4
Nazi visit, 177–80, 192
prisoner escape, 165–7, 175–6,
190–1
La Rocque, François de, 11, 20–1,
44, 228
Laval, Pierre, 76, 145, 225, 227–32

Dormoy case involvement, 175–6, 213–15
   Nazi affiliation, 107, 120, 130, 133, 136–7, 183–90
   right-wing support, 7, 34–6, 45, 113
   Vichy government and, 149–57, 163–7, 170–6
Lebrun, Albert, 28–9, 34
L'Echo de Paris, 25
Le Combat social, 17, 25
Le Duc, Georges, 191
Légion française des combattants, 182
Légion nationale populaire (LNP), 171, 228
Légion des volontaires français contre le bolchevisme (LVF), 45, 84, 134, 139–41, 147, 160–4, 171, 195, 227
Leluc, Christian, 191–2
L'Émancipation nationale, 25–6
Le Napolitan (restaurant), 158–9
Leningrad, siege of, 130, 230
Le Pen, Marine, 200, 212
Le Populaire, 18, 212
Les Cagoulards dans la guerre (Bourdrel), 199
L'Étudiant français: organe mensuel de la Fédération nationale des étudiants d'Action française, 110
Lévy, Robert, 190–1, 193–4, 196–201, 212
liberal democracy. *See* democracy, liberal
Limoges, France, 36, 175, 183
Line of Demarcation, the, 29–31, 109, 114, 156, 212, 229
   crossing, 47, 58, 61, 83, 176–7, 181
L'Institut d'étude des questions juives (IEQJ), 172
London, England, 45, 198, 231
   de Gaulle in, 31–2, 120, 133, 181, 187–90, 224, 229
L'Oréal. *See* Schueller, Eugène
Loustaunau-Lacau, Georges, 45, 114, 187
Lurol, Marie-Rose, 60, 64, 71, 117

Lurol, Raymonde, 64–6
Lyon, France, 23, 38–40, 49, 68–70, 90, 104–6, 113, 126, 180
   police mobile, 52–4, 58–60, 67, 225

Machtou, Maurice, 186
Maginot Line, 32, 153
magistrate, investigating, 191, 212, 225
   Dormoy investigation, 50–2, 59, 69–70, 110, 121–9, 136–50, 157–66
   risk to, 3, 10, 13, 116–17, 134, 161
Mandel, Georges, 29, 41–3, 53, 123, 153, 178
Marbach, Maurice, 76, 79, 117
   Nice bomb explosion, 103–8, 147, 225
   right-wing militancy, 71–2, 82–5, 96, 119, 122, 125
Marchi, Antoine, 114, 134–48, 172, 191–5, 199–200, 224–5
   right-wing militancy, 75–7, 83–4, 117–30, 158–67, 212–13
Marion, Jean René, 191, 212, 225
   Dormoy investigation, 50–2, 59, 69–70, 110, 121–9, 136–50, 157, 161–6
   risk to, 3, 10, 13, 116–17, 134, 161
Marly-le-Roi, France, 168
Marseille, France, 29, 94, 178, 184–6, 193, 216, 224–6
   Dormoy investigation, 49, 52, 88–90, 99, 122–35, 140, 190, 199
   right-wing organizations, 23, 59, 66–85, 103–18, 147, 157–60, 212–13
   trains through, 40, 52, 54, 62, 165
Martin, Henri, 43, 46, 111, 113, 174
martyrdom,
   Dormoy, 12, 60, 206, 211, 220
   National Revolution, 102
   wartime, 98, 102
Marxism, 14
Marx, Karl, 14, 17
Marx, Laura, 17
masculinity, crisis of, 96–100, 103
   toxic, 99

Masse, Antoinette "Tonia," 168–71, 183
  as German asset, 174
Masse, Jean, 168
Matignon Accords, 19
Maurras, Charles, 11, 75, 227
Mayer, Cletta, 7
Mayer, Daniel, 7
media. *See* press, the
Mediterranean ports, 49, 89
  control of, 29, 176–7
Menard, Paullette. *See* Paullette Pax
Mendès-France, Pierre, 26, 29
Ménétrel, Bernard, 77, 110, 115, 162, 195
Menthon, François de, 190
Menut, Lucien, 205
metal workers, union of, 17
Méténier, François, 45, 77, 184, 197, 214
Milice Française, the, 182–3, 198, 223, 228, 232
militancy, culture of, 7, 97–100, 224
  German, 18
  right-wing, 23, 62, 71, 75, 90, 94, 175, 212
  socialism, 17, 20–1
Militärbefehlshaber in Frankreich (MBF). *See* German Supreme Military Command
military, French, 46, 214, 237n36, 243n34
  court, 128, 173, 183
  experience, 9, 47–8, 83, 92–5, 118, 124
  intervention, 24, 78, 87, 132
  Nazis versus, 27–8, 32, 127, 130–1, 151–4, 223
  para-, 39, 228
  training, 2, 73–4
  weak, 176, 179–80
Millington, Chris, 11–12, 218
Mitterrand, François, 110
Mondanel, Pierre, 47–9, 86–7, 156–7, 170–1
Montélimar, France, 38, 160, 165
  bombing suspects in, 54, 60–73, 82–5, 104–7, 117–24, 213–14

Dormoy in, 1–5, 27, 37–41, 103, 145–6, 209–10, 224, 230
  investigation in, 49, 52, 69–71, 76–7, 88, 136, 225
  police, 2, 47, 59, 142, 162, 190–3, 199
Montluçon, France, 10, 224
  communism, 13, 211–12
  Dormoy's life in, 2, 5–8, 17, 38, 59–60, 146
  lawsuit against, 207
  statue of Dormoy (*see* statue of Dormoy)
  traveling through, 33–5
  post-war building, 206–7
  worker organizing, 14
Montpellier, 74, 113
Morène, Annie. *See* Mourraille, Anne-Félice
Moscow, 18
  attack on, 130, 231
Moulin, Jean, 220, 231
Mouraille, Roger, 135, 141–6, 217, 225
  business partnership, 76–9, 178, 196
  dangerousness, 79–87, 97, 128, 143–4, 150, 198–200
  loyalties, 107–8, 118
  mental breakdown, 161–2, 164
  police investigation, 114–19, 147–8, 170–1, 184–6, 191–2
  right-wing affiliations, 78–9, 107–8, 122–6, 157–66
Mouraille, Anne-Félice, 87, 102–8, 224–6 (*see also* Gérodias, Florence)
  childhood, 90–2
  Dormoy, interactions with, 103–5
  exaltée, 92, 95, 105
  marriage, 92, 176, 184–5, 191
  military service, 94
  murder involvement, 87–9, 96–7, 111–30, 147–50, 159–67
  political activities, 90, 93–4, 115, 136–44, 184–201, 213–14
  Vichy funding, 172–80, 209–10

Mourraille, Léon, 90–1, 94–5
Mouvement social révolutionnaire
 (MSR), 5, 198, 215–20, 227–8
 (*see also* Deloncle, Eugène)
 bookkeeping issues, 167–75
 ideology, 45, 83, 111–12
 involvement with, 84–5, 113–22,
  135–8, 149, 183–7
 German financing of, 172–4
 members of, 49, 108, 126, 168,
  158–61, 224–5
 RNP, merging with, 120, 168–74,
  215, 228
Moynier, Yves, 71, 79–83, 196–200,
  225–6
 identity, fascism and, 97–103
 interrogation, 115–28, 134–50, 161–80
 loyalties, 114–15, 118
 mental breakdown, 161–6
 marriage, 176, 184–6, 191–2
 role in Dormoy murder, 84–9, 95–6,
  103–9, 157–60
*Murder in the Métro: Laetitia Toureaux
 and the Cagoule in 1930s France*,
 3–4
Mussolini, Benito, 23, 216
 "March on Rome," 112, 136

Nation, The, 219
nationalism,
 Bolshevism versus, 10–11, 23
 political movements, 21, 45, 78, 81,
  171, 219, 224, 227
 right-wing militants, 84, 94, 99, 101,
  144, 160
National Police. *See* Sûreté
National Revolution, the, 70, 123, 145,
 163–5, 182, 195, 268n58
 advancing the, 23, 44–7, 100–3,
  112–14, 135–7, 174, 218–19, 227
 ideology, 4, 11, 29–31, 39, 77–82,
  101–2, 127
 masculinity, 75, 98–103
 women in, 94–5, 101–2

Nazis, the, 22, 28, 153, 181, 216, 229
 (*see also* Germany, Nazi; Gestapo)
 allying with, 13, 35, 109–27, 151,
  198, 205–8, 211, 219–21
 communism versus, 28, 127, 217
 invasion of, 11, 19–21, 27–36, 75,
  102, 175–7, 229
 occupation of, 9, 41, 75, 163, 170, 177
 resisting, 32–4, 152, 187
 Vichy Zone, 90, 155–9, 205
Néaumet, Jean-Émile, 181, 199,
  240n18
Nègre, Jean, 206–7
newspapers. *See* press, the
New York Times, 212
 Magazine, 220
Nice, France, 93, 178
 bomb explosion, 71–2, 76–9, 82, 96,
  225–6
 Cagoule organizing, 23, 70–8, 89,
  108, 113–18, 129, 223
 Dormoy investigation, 52, 76–85, 88,
  105–6, 138
Nîmes, France, 176, 190–1
prison system, 166–7, 179
Note sur l'affaire Dormoy (July note),
 162–5

Oberg, Karl, 184
Occupied Zone, France, 142, 231–2
 anger over, 9, 43–4, 75, 187–8
 collaboration in, 44–5, 120, 133,
  156, 202, 225, 231
 costs of, 3, 31, 41, 102, 202
 criminal investigation, 77–8, 84,
  115, 160
 Paris (*see* France, Nazi invasion)
 right-wing militants in, 39, 61,
  111–14, 172–3
 Vichy regime versus, 29, 47, 83–4,
  109, 130–3, 155–7, 177–82
Organisation secrète d'action
 révolutionnaire nationale
 (OSARN), 217, 227

pacifism, 32, 97, 99, 218
Paillole, Pierre, 181
Papon, Maurice, 211
Paris, 67–71, 90–4, 132, 209, 220–5, 228, 231–2
    abandonment of, 28–9, 32–4, 47
    Dormoy investigation, 13, 25, 40–3, 48–61, 77–85, 107–9, 141–50, 189–98, 213–14
    Occupied, 5, 29, 31, 133, 156, 180, 184
    right-wing organizing in, 18–25, 44–6, 96, 111–22, 125–35, 158–75, 212
Parquet de la Seine, 190
Parti franciste, 11
Parti ouvrier français, 14
Parti populaire français (PPF), 8, 81, 224–5, 228
    danger of, 22, 34, 68, 75
    right-wing organizing, 12, 45, 77, 79, 125, 212
Parti social français (PSF), 19–20, 228
paternity,
    authority of, 98
    breadwinner, importance of, 102
patriotism, 4, 47, 110–12, 120, 180–2, 187, 205
    extreme, 23, 96–7, 102, 219
patronage, 18
    Nazi, 44–5, 111, 121, 170, 213
    Vichy regime, 44, 46–7, 121, 224, 240n13
Patton, George, 176
Pau, France, 93, 186, 199
Paullette Pax (Paullette Menard), 92
Paxton, Robert O., 132, 211
Payre, Marie Thérèse, 129–30, 161, 172
Péan, Pierre, 112
Pellevoisin (prison), 35–7, 39, 41, 214, 230
Pétain, Maréchal Philippe, 145, 226
    (*see also* National Revolution)
    autocratic regime, 3–9, 28–39, 75, 107–18, 130–8, 224–5

Germans versus, 176–86, 211–21
    murder involvement, 60, 70, 87–8, 148–50, 162–7, 192–208
    right-wing organizations, 24, 76–7, 111, 124, 127, 146, 181
    wartime credibility, 28–9, 42–7, 97–102, 119–20, 151–7
Pinard, Louis, 2, 53–4, 60, 62
Place, Henri, 115
Poland, 32, 134, 141–2, 152, 160, 218, 223, 225
police, French, 46–8, 70, 114, 214
    burden on, 8–10, 47
    control of, 12, 43, 135, 162, 179, 228
    Dormoy investigation, 1–7, 50–90, 94–108, 144–50, 159–61, 169–75, 190–8
    informants, 74–80, 85–94, 106–7, 115–30, 134, 143, 212–13
    Nazis versus, 109–13, 144, 156–7
    overhaul of, 150, 162
    panicking, 20
    right wing versus, 5, 21–5, 84, 132, 180–90, 199–201, 216, 219, 227
Pons, Warden, 177–8
Popular Front, 5, 152, 217, 219
    conflict within, 21, 41, 223
    discrediting of, 19–23, 27, 32–5, 96, 151, 215
    government of, 7–8, 12, 19, 43, 102, 194, 201, 224, 228
Portugal, 184
postal service, French (PTT), 127, 209
post-colonial movements, 201
post-war era, 165, 198
    economy, 206, 208
    government, 5, 188, 201, 203
    Dormoy investigation, 178, 191, 196–7, 203, 208–11
    political tensions, 13, 205–6, 217–19
    reconciliation, 9, 201–3
Pradel, Pierre, 207–8
press, the, 103, 112, 124, 160
    cartoons, political, 25–6

conservative, 25, 42, 94–5, 110–11, 158, 199, 216
control of, 4, 60, 176, 178
fake news, 25, 174
international, 213
left-wing, 18, 212, 237n41
prisoners of war, 31, 36, 44, 94–5, 178, 192, 231
release of, 120, 132–3
propaganda, 135, 225, 227
antisemitic, 26, 82, 172
centers of, 77, 110, 126, 147
National Revolution, 30, 83, 100–2, 107, 148, 158, 193–5
pro-war, 30, 86, 95, 100–1, 161
PTT. *See* postal service, French
publishing industry, 110–11, 157, 200
Pucheu, Pierre, 131–2, 176, 181–2, 188, 194–6

Radical Party, 12, 19, 42, 228, 237n36
Rassemblement nationale populaire (RNP), 45, 120, 149, 168–74, 215, 223, 228, 230
rationing, 41, 67, 170, 180
rearmament, French, 32, 153
Relais de l'Empereur, Le, 209
criminal investigation, 50–72, 76–9, 85, 88
Dormoy's confinement, 1–3, 37–42, 123, 211, 230
right-wing organizing, 103–6, 119, 141–2, 145
Resistance, the French, 5–9, 120, 177, 183–5 (*see also* Moulin, Jean)
Dormoy in, 6–7, 204, 220–1, 223–4
ideology, 47, 102, 208
opposition to, 228, 230
principal figures in, 31–2, 110, 114–15, 180–2, 187, 193–6, 200, 231
Reynaud, Paul, 28–9, 33–4, 36, 42, 123, 152, 229
Ribière, Henri, 5–6, 17
Ribière, René, 5, 60

Richier, Georges, 111, 212, 214
right-wing extremism, 3–4 (*see also* Cagoule, the (Comité secret d'action révolutionnaire); conservatives; Deloncle, Eugène; militancy, culture of; patriotism; terrorism)
bombers, 58–63, 71–2, 79, 103–6, 210, 220, 225
Dormoy assassination, 8–11, 96, 106–7, 117–18, 138, 208
French Revolution versus, 13, 26, 35, 45, 75, 102, 151, 205
journalists, 25, 75, 110–11, 157, 200, 220
leagues, 4, 11–12, 23, 216, 228
left wing versus, 21, 41, 55, 74, 97, 182–3, 200–1, 217–21
organizations, affiliated, 23, 75–7, 93, 111, 125, 157–8, 184, 212, 228
threats of, 21–5, 34, 44, 82–5, 97, 150, 186, 205, 212
Vichy regime versus, 46, 70, 77–8, 93, 96, 110–15, 129, 134–41, 194
Riom trials, 123, 189, 191, 213–15
charges laid, 39, 152
Council of Political Justice, 153–4
defendants, 36, 145, 150–2, 162–5, 231
focus of, 152, 201–2
kangaroo court, 39, 162–3
Roche, Joel, 138–9
Roosevelt, Franklin, 182
Rougeron, Georges, 10, 212
roundups of Jews, 155
Vel d'Hiv, 156
Rousso, Henry, 10
royalists, 25, 75, 110–11
Russian Revolution, 18

Salgon, Marie, 63–4
Schueller, Eugène, 23, 172
Section française de l'internationale ouvrière (SFIO; French Socialist Party), 8, 17–18, 20, 78, 228

Senner, Herbert, 198–9, 269n80
  suspects in cahoots with, 184–5,
    192, 196
Serre, Charles, 218
Servant, Guy, 174
Service d'ordre légionnaire (SOL), 182,
  228. *See also* Milice Française, the
Service du travail obligatoire (STO),
  133, 177, 182, 228
Sézille, Paul Léopold, 115, 172
Sicherheitspolizei und Sicherheitsdienst
  (Security Police and Security
  Service, SiPo-SD), 135, 179,
  183, 228
Sigmaringen Castle, Germany, 183, 232
Simon, René, 93
smuggling,
  arms, 103, 110, 117, 225
  documents, 145, 213
  letters, 129, 136
  people, 78, 84
socialism, 27, 207, 223, 225
  communists versus, 17–21, 102, 182,
    193, 197, 211
  Dormoy's involvement in, 2–3, 6–8,
    14, 17, 25, 32–4, 201, 216, 224
  fascism versus, 11, 41, 103, 170
  political parties (*see* Socialist Party,
    French)
  Vichy regime versus, 110, 212, 214–15
Socialist Party, French, 5–8, 12–13,
  17–19, 38–9, 44–5, 78, 182, 215,
  228. *See also* Section française de
  l'internationale ouvrière (SFIO)
Socialist Popular Front. *See* Popular
  Front
soldiers, 75, 124
  capture of, 28
  evacuation of, 28–9, 94
  German, 130–1, 178–80
  payment to, 171
  representation of, 97, 99–100, 102
Solidarité française, 11
Sommer, Hans. *See* Senner, Herbert

Soungouroff, Antonin Ivanovitch
  ("Anatole"), 93, 185, 192
South America, 3, 200, 217, 224
Soviet Union, 9, 44, 155, 230
Spain, 10, 82, 200, 217–18, 229
  fleeing to, 3, 25, 114, 184–6, 189,
    196–8, 216
  weapons to, 21–2, 108, 117
Spanish Civil War,
  French presence in, 21, 83, 157–8,
    196, 225
  Nationalists, 78
  spies, 6, 55, 78, 83, 184, 243n34
  international, 32, 48, 113, 174, 181
Standard Oil, 206–8
statue of Dormoy, 203–9, 212
  controversial movement of, 206–9,
    211
street fighting, 11, 23–4, 99, 216
women in, 95
Stülpnagel, Otto von, 131
Supreme Court of France, 146, 151, 153–4
Sûreté (National Police), 42, 180, 193
  (*see also* police, French)
  authority of, 8, 47
  criminal investigation, 49, 191
  intelligence, 43, 48, 171
  overhaul of, 150, 162
  Vichy Zone, 107, 119, 147, 156, 162
Switzerland, 110, 184–5
synagogue bombings, 82, 111, 114–15,
  135–6, 171, 192, 231
  attempted, 71–2, 225

Taittinger, Pierre, 11
terrorism, 130, 183, 185 (*see also*
  Cagoule, the [Comité secret
  d'action révolutionnaire])
  organizations, 3–4, 48, 195
  pre-war, 10
  right-wing, 11, 21–6, 55, 111, 135,
    216–20
Third Reich, 34, 184. *See also*
  Germany, Nazi; Nazis, the

Third Republic, the, 8, 154, 201–2, 213, 218
  conservative conceptions of, 43–4, 75, 81, 100–1
  ending of, 5–6, 23, 43, 110, 145, 216, 226, 229–30
  flaws of, 11, 13
  leadership of, 32, 41–2, 46, 72, 112, 132, 151, 224
  opposition to, 3–4, 29, 34–9, 86, 94, 123, 136, 193
  portrayals of, 99–102, 123, 127
Toulouse, France, 23, 35, 38, 113
Toureaux, Laetitia, 3
Touret, André, 10
Touvier, Paul, 211
trade unions, 22
  organizing, 14, 17, 19
  right wing versus, 11
tribunals, 207 (*see also* judiciary, French)
  military, 131, 183
  State, 132, 162–4
Trump, Donald, 3

unemployment, 26, 45
  masculinity and, 75, 82, 98
United States, 13, 50, 202, 231, 243n34
  masculinity, culture of, 97, 219
  social division in, 3, 217–19
Unoccupied Zone, the (*see also* Occupied Zone, France; Vichy regime)
  German invasion of, 155
  Jews in, 156

Vaillant, Horace Marius Alexandre,
  death of, 79, 83–5, 96, 147, 226
  right-wing involvement, 71, 81, 100–3, 105–8, 125, 134, 142
Valence, France, 121, 143, 191
  imprisonment in, 52, 116, 128–9, 134, 148–50, 161
  travel to, 106

Vallat, Xavier, 126, 156, 214
Vals-les-Bains, France, 37, 39, 230
Veau, Pierre, 126
Védrine, Jean, 110
Vel d'Hiv. *See* roundups of Jews
Venezuela, escape to, 200, 217–18
veterans, war,
  French identity and, 11–12, 22–3, 102
  mystique of, 95, 97–8
  organizing, 11, 28, 182, 228
Vichy France: Old Guard and New Order, 1940–1944 (Paxton), 211
Vichy regime, 34–9, 44, 55, 184–7, 211–15 (*see also* Deloncle, Eugène; Pétain, Maréchal Philippe)
  anxiety in, 41–3, 46, 120, 153–5, 190, 196
  aryanization program, 115, 126, 172–3
  Cagoule affiliations, 45–6, 70, 77–8, 96, 110–15, 129, 134–41, 194
  critiques of, 12, 31, 103, 133, 149, 155–6, 200–3, 220
  Dormoy investigation, 59–60, 80, 107–9, 116–28, 143–8, 164–70, 192
  intelligence gathering, 46–9, 53, 69–70, 192, 228
  National Revolution, 29–31, 95, 98–103, 127, 158
  Nazis versus, 44, 83, 120, 130–1, 152–6, 189, 230–2
  police in, 41–3, 52, 59, 84–90, 109, 156, 162, 182
  Popular Front versus, 7, 110
  regional control, 3–6, 27–9, 37–40, 45–7, 150, 173–9, 229–30
  Resistance versus, 180–2, 187, 195
  Riom trials (*see* Riom trials)
  sovereignty versus Germany, 176–9, 187–8
  travel to, 42, 58, 83–7, 113–14, 124, 158, 170, 184, 215
  vision, political 29–31, 95, 100–1, 132

Vichysto-Résistants, 177, 180, 187, 268n58
Vilnat, Louise, 1–2, 52–64, 141, 142
  hotel repair, 70–1
violence, 169, 182, 216
  civil, 10–11, 95–6, 176, 182, 202–3
  culture of, 4, 12, 82, 90, 97, 102, 110–12
  political, 20, 49, 72, 100, 124–5, 218–19
  right-wing, 4, 12, 39, 45, 82, 118, 140, 150, 224
  state, 12, 24, 109, 170, 228
virility, culture of, 92, 95, 97–9

war, 185 (*see also* Spanish Civil War; World War I; World War II)
  avoiding, 27
  casualties, 26–8, 31, 81, 94, 97, 131, 180, 183, 201
  declaration of, 32, 42, 152, 216, 229, 231
  impact of, 35, 97, 115, 132–3, 172, 206, 219
  losing the, 28, 97–8, 102, 152, 184, 221
  mobilization for, 20, 27, 32, 86, 95, 124, 153–5, 217
  orphans, 81, 97–8, 100
  "Phony," 28
  resistance to (*see* Resistance, the French)
  wartime, 61, 102, 135, 191, 221
    crime, 13, 61, 138, 185–6, 192, 198–202, 209
    propaganda, 30, 95, 86, 100–1, 161, 152
    resistance, 9, 47, 180–2, 187, 193–5, 199, 223
    role of France, 35, 53, 111, 187, 208–9, 219, 221

Weber (police superintendent), 149
Weygand, Maxime, 28, 132, 214
women, 133, 156, 168, 182
  in National Revolution, 99, 101–2, 119
  violence, 4, 183
  wartime, 31, 95, 97
wood shards, clues in, 58, 60
workers, French, 207 (*see also* labor draft)
  German demand for, 133, 155, 177
  National Revolution, 102
  organizing, 14, 17, 205, 228
  right wing versus, 11, 21
  striking, 19
World War I, 8 (*see also* interwar period; post-war era; veterans, war; World War II)
  Armistice (*see* Armistice)
  impact of, 35, 96–7, 152, 180
  principal figures in, 9, 17, 22, 29, 90, 119, 182, 200
  strategy during, 26, 153
World War II, 3, 176 (*see also* Germany, Nazi; Nazis, the; interwar period; post-war era; World War I)
  allegiance during, 6, 32, 66, 107, 110, 153–4, 194, 215
  impact of, 96–7, 115, 120, 172, 183–4, 219
  impoverishment during, 31, 44, 102, 127, 130–3
  political parties, 5, 42, 119, 177, 224, 228
  principal figures in, 13, 26, 42–7, 78–9, 87, 94–5, 110, 138, 197
  strategy during, 152–3

Yencesse, Hubert, 205–6

Lightning Source UK Ltd.
Milton Keynes UK
UKHW022353191120
373390UK00017B/578